Praise for **HARD DRIVE** by James Wallace and Jim Erickson

"A stupendous success story. This is the most informative book yet on Bill Gates and Microsoft."
—*Washington Post*

"Remarkable.…[*Hard Drive*] will almost certainly leave you wistful. No, not wishing that you worked for Microsoft, which sounds like what you might experience if you combined Marine boot camp, a fraternity party, and a trip to the zoo. The book will make you wonder why you didn't buy Microsoft stock when it went public."
—*Wall Street Journal*

"Wallace and Erickson display an admirable sense of journalistic detachment and detail, plumbing the depths of Gates's experience to see what makes him tick. Everyone from Gates on down to his ex-Scoutmaster seems to have chatted with the authors."
—*San Francisco Chronicle*

"This well-written book deserves an audience beyond the computer literate. Packed with anecdotes, *Hard Drive* helps show that from the beginning of his career to today, Gates has always been something more than a 98-pound megalomaniac."
—*Detroit Free Press*

"An engaging, almost classic tale of a boy who finds power in gadgets and then won't let go."
—*Los Angeles Times*

"An exciting tale, told in racy style, with plenty of detail and well researched quotations, all focused on the enigmatic personality of Bill Gates."
—*London Financial Times*

"A biting biography and computer industry exposé."
—*Publishers Weekly*

"Captivating reading, more enthralling than any thriller." —*Nature*

HARD
DRIVE

Bill Gates and the Making of the Microsoft Empire

James Wallace

Jim Erickson

*From one redhead to another
Merry Christmas!
Bryan*

HarperBusiness
A Division of HarperCollinsPublishers

To my mother and father; and to Linda Joyce Buzbee,
because a promise is, after all, a promise.
James

To my mother, father, and to Nancy.
Jim

A hardcover edition of this book was published in 1992 by John Wiley & Sons, Inc. It is here reprinted by arrangement with John Wiley & Sons, Inc.

HarperCollins books may be purchased for educational, business, or sales promotional use. For information please write: Special Markets Department, HarperCollins Publishers, Inc., 10 East 53rd Street, New York, NY 10022.

First HarperBusiness edition published 1993.

Library of Congress Cataloging-in-Publication Data

Wallace, James. 1947–
    Hard drive : Bill Gates and the making of the Microsoft empire / James Wallace, Jim Erickson. — 1st HarperBusiness ed.
        p.   cm.
    Reprint. Originally published: New York : Wiley, 1992.
    Includes index.
    ISBN 0-88730-629-2 (pbk.)
    1. Gates, Bill, 1956– . 2. Microsoft Corporation—History. 3. Businessmen—United States—Biography. 4. Computer software industry—United States—History.
I. Erickson, Jim. II. Title
[HD9696.C62G3378 1993]
338.4′70053′092—dc20   92-54845

96 97 98 ❖/RRD H 10

Acknowledgments

This is not a book about computers or the dazzling technology that sparked one of the world's great revolutions less than two decades ago. Rather, it is a story about people, a remarkable collection of individuals led by one man, Bill Gates, whose drive, genius, vision, and entrepreneurial spirit created one of the great success stories in the history of American business. We wanted to write a book that would appeal as much to those who know nothing about computers as it would to those who regard these machines as the most important thing in their lives. We hope we have done that.

The book grew out of a series of stories on Gates and Microsoft published in the *Seattle Post-Intelligencer* newspaper in May of 1991. The subsequent project, a book-length profile of Gates, took the better part of a year to complete and was undertaken without the help or cooperation of Microsoft. Even so, more than 150 people, many of them past and current employees and executives of Microsoft, were interviewed. We are indebted to everyone who helped us tell this story, regardless of how much of what they told us found its way into the book.

We would like to begin by thanking J.D. Alexander, executive editor of the *Seattle Post-Intelligencer*, who not only allowed us the time to research and write this book but also gave his support and generously allowed some of the paper's photographs of Gates to be reprinted in the book.

Others at the paper we would like to thank are Lytton Smith, who helped with the research, and all the people in systems, who provided technical assistance.

We are deeply grateful to our publisher, John Wiley & Sons, who saw the possibilities of such a book and gave us the opportunity to do it.

No one deserves more credit, or thanks, than our editor, Roger Scholl, whose patience, editorial guidance, hard work, and encouragement were invaluable. Anyone who writes a book should be so fortunate to have such an understanding editor.

This book would not have been possible without the tireless efforts of several others at John Wiley & Sons, including Marcia Samuels, production manager, and Elizabeth Doble, director of production. Our appreciation goes to all those at Impressions in Madison, Wisconsin, who spent many hours copyediting.

Finally, special thanks to many good friends who saw us through the months this project took, and who continuously offered their support—in particular, to Mary Williams, Angelo Bruscas, Ceceilia Dominique, and Dick Clever.

In addition to interviews, our research was based on a number of books, national magazines, newspapers, and trade publications. The books included *Fire in the Valley* by Paul Freiberger and Michael Swaine; *Hackers* by Steven Levy; *Blue Magic* by James Chposky and Ted Leonsis; *The Making of Microsoft* by Daniel Ichbiah and Susan Knepper; and *Programmers at Work* by Susan Lammers. The newspapers upon which we based our research included the *Seattle Post-Intelligencer*, *Seattle Times*, *New York Times*, *Wall Street Journal*, *Washington Post*, *LA Times* and *San Jose Mercury News*. National magazines included *Forbes*, *Fortune*, *Money*, *Time*, *Newsweek*, and *Business Week*, as well as the trade publications *PC Week* and *InfoWorld*.

For those curious about such things, this book was written on a Leading Edge compatible PC with an 8088 chip and XyWrite word processing program.

James Wallace and Jim Erickson
Seattle, February 1992

Contents

Prologue *1*

1
The Early Years *5*

2
"It's Going to Happen" *53*

3
The Microkids *85*

4
Hitching a Ride with Big Blue
139

5
Growing Pains *207*

6
King of the Hill *319*

Index *421*

HARD DRIVE

The Winds
of Fortune

William Gates III, chairman of the largest computer software company on earth, stood nervously at the front of the ballroom of the 308-foot cruise yacht *New Yorker*. He was about to unveil Microsoft's fifth and latest version of the most popular piece of software ever created, a computer operating system known as MS-DOS.

It was to be the biggest launch of a software product in computer industry history. More than 500 people had turned out on a humid Tuesday evening in New York City in the summer of 1991 to board the yacht—playfully dubbed *"DOS Boat"*—to listen to Gates and his corporate sidekick, Microsoft operating systems chief Steve Ballmer, make an impassioned sales pitch for MS-DOS 5.0. Both industry analysts and the press had gathered for the gala event, which promised free food, music by jazz master Dave Brubeck, and a five-hour cruise on the Hudson River and around the New York City harbor. Computer hardware and software executives had flown in from around the country to get a glimpse of Gates and to listen to the industry's *enfant terrible* and biggest star announce where he, and Microsoft, were headed.

At 35, Gates was at the pinnacle of his young career. In 1990 Microsoft, the company he and childhood friend Paul Allen had founded barely sixteen years before, had become the first software company to sell more than a billion dollars worth of products in a single year. Gates was the undisputed mastermind of that success, a brilliant technocrat, ruthless salesman, and manipulative—some said devious—businessman. His company's astounding ascension had just a few years earlier made him the youngest billionaire in the history of America. By 1992 his net worth stood at more than $4 billion, making him the second richest man in the country.

His word had become the closest thing to gospel in the godless computer industry. A month earlier in Atlanta, at an industry trade show known as Comdex where Gates was the keynote speaker, people lined up for two city blocks to hear him speak on the future of the industry. Executives in business suits spilled out into the aisles and sat cross-legged on the floor when the seats were filled. But on this June evening in the Big Apple, as Gates moved stiffly to the microphones at the podium on the *New Yorker*, powerful and opposing forces were gathered across the Hudson, in Armonk, New York, headquarters of International Business Machines.

Gates straightened his 5-foot-11-inch frame and began his pitch, a condensed version of the history of MS-DOS.

"In the last ten years, DOS has become the foundation of the PC industry and has sold more than ten times any other software package," Gates intoned in his oddly high-pitched voice, which cracked occasionally like a nervous teenager's, despite the extensive speech lessons he had taken months before. Microsoft's operating system, he went on, was now installed on more than 60 million personal computers, which represented about 75 percent of all the personal computers in the world. He predicted that another 18 million copies of DOS would be sold with computer systems in 1991. "It's not just that number that's astounding, it's the whole phenomenon behind it."

Gates did not depart from the prepared text or interject words like "cool" or "super," which normally were part of his standard vocabulary.

Make-up, hurriedly applied so his face would not shine into the television cameras that would beam his presentation via satellite to some 300 locations around the United States, hid the acne to which he was still prone. Lights glared off his oversize glasses, blotting out his blue eyes. His mop of dishwater blond hair was, uncharacteristically, neatly combed. But those who looked closely could see the small flakes of dandruff on the shoulders of his black suit. The joke around the industry was that Gates never went anywhere without his dandruff.

A most unlikely captain of industry, he looked as if he could have been 25, or younger. There was an engaging, boyish charm about the former computer hacker whom many in the press had once described as a nerd. No one underestimated Bill Gates, though. Too many people had done that in the past. Most of the guests in the audience already knew Microsoft's history. In 1980 the company had sold the MS-DOS operating system to IBM when it made its irresistible entry into the desktop computing marketplace and established industry standards that have yet to be supplanted. The revenue from that partnership gave Gates a guaranteed income stream and the push he needed to make his vision—Microsoft software on every desktop PC—come true. Not long after he made the deal with IBM, the fiery, competitive Gates had slammed his fist into his palm and vowed to put several of his major software competitors out of business. By 1991, many of those competitors were indeed in full retreat under a barrage of Microsoft products.

But Gates had made a great many enemies along the way. He had stepped on too many toes on his way to the top, and subjected countless colleagues to his abrasive, childish rants and intellectual browbeatings. The Federal Trade Commission, acting on anonymous complaints, had begun investigating Microsoft for possible anti-trust violations. Many competitors wanted to see Microsoft dismantled the way the federal government had carved up Ma Bell into so many Baby Bells. Even Microsoft's enormously profitable and long-running marriage with IBM was threatening to unravel into a messy divorce. In a magazine article about Gates entitled "The Silicon Bully," one unnamed IBM official was quoted as saying he would like to put an icepick in Gates' head.

Retribution was in the wind. While Gates spoke, across the Hudson in Armonk executives from IBM were huddled with the top brass of onetime archrival Apple Computer. The two giants of the computer world, threatened by Microsoft's domination of the software industry, were plotting to form an alliance to create their own operating system, a new standard that would supplant DOS and wrest control of the industry away from Gates.

Outside *"DOS Boat,"* a thunderstorm had gathered in the muggy evening air above the harbor. Gates and Ballmer had finished their monologues and were now fielding questions from the audience. A reporter fired three quick questions designed to put Gates and Ballmer on the spot over the rift with IBM.

Before either could answer, something—a rogue wave from the storm, the passing wake of a freighter—disturbed the *New Yorker.* The huge yacht lurched sickeningly.

"Our boat is rocking here in New York," a startled Ballmer said into the microphone for the benefit of the closed-circuit TV audience.

"IBM has great powers" piped up someone from the audience. The crowd began laughing, then burst into applause.

Gates, a silly grin across his face, seemed to roll with the punch. But it was as if some invisible force had landed a couple of solid body blows to Microsoft's euphoria, auguring darker things to come.

CHAPTER 1

The Early Years

The earth fell away, and the city spread out beneath the sandy-haired, 11-year-old boy, as the elevator hurried higher and higher into the last light of a beautiful fall day. Glass windows on the tallest downtown buildings caught what was left of the sunlight and tossed back hues of crimson and gold. Far below to the west a ferry boat glided across Elliott Bay, with the rugged Olympic Mountains in the distance beyond.

Though there was a strong breeze blowing across the Sound, from this height the cold, dark waters looked like smoked glass, and the only sign that the ferry was moving was the lighter-colored green water left behind in its wake.

The thin, gawky boy squeezed past the elbows and legs of the adults and other kids around him until he could stand unobstructed against the glass side of the elevator for a better view.

"Welcome to the Space Needle," the elevator operator intoned. "You are in the west elevator travelling at ten miles per hour, or 800 feet per minute. The Space Needle was built as part of the 1962 World's Fair, known as the Century 21 Exposition. . . ."

But Bill Gates heard none of this. His thoughts were 3,000 miles away, blasting off from Cape Canaveral in a rocket ship of his imagination, fueled by the stories of Edgar Rice Burroughs and Isaac Asimov and a dozen other science fiction writers who had carried him on so many voyages of fantasy and discovery.

Forty seconds after liftoff, the view and the daydream were over as the elevator slipped into its berth at the Space Needle Restaurant 600 feet above Seattle. The dinner at the Space Needle was part of the Reverend Dale Turner's annual treat for all those who had accepted and met his yearly challenge. And in 1966, none had done it better than Trey, as Bill Gates was called.

The evening marked a tradition going back to Reverend Turner's teaching days at the University of Kansas in Lawrence. At the beginning of each school year, he would challenge his students to memorize chapters 5, 6, and 7 of the Book of Matthew, which are better known as the Sermon on the Mount. Turner had left Lawrence in 1958 and was now pastor of the University Congregational Church in Seattle's University District, across the street from the University of Washington. Founded nine years before the turn of the century, the church is one of the oldest in the city.

The Gates family were regulars in the congregation, and Bill Gates was enrolled in Turner's confirmation class. One Sunday morning, Turner threw down his yearly challenge to the class—he would buy dinner at the Space Needle Restaurant for anyone who memorized the Sermon on the Mount. It was the same challenge he made to the full congregation.

The Sermon on the Mount is a difficult passage to put to memory. The words do not rhyme, the sentence structure is disjointed, and it is very long—the equivalent of nearly four standard newspaper columns of type.

Twenty-five years later Turner can still remember the afternoon he sat down with Gates in the living room of the Gates' home, to hear him recite the passage.

"And seeing the multitudes," the young boy began, "He went up onto a mountain, and when He was set, His disciples came unto Him, and He opened his mouth, and taught them, saying:

"Blessed are the poor . . .

"Blessed are the meek . . .

"Blessed are the merciful . . ."

Listening to Gates, Turner was astounded. No one, in all his years in the ministry, had been able to make it through the entire passage without stumbling over at least a few words or lines. But Gates had recited the passage nonstop from the beginning, never missing a line.

"I needed only to go to his home that day to know that he was something special," Turner later recalled. "I couldn't imagine how an 11-year-old boy could have a mind like that. And my subsequent questioning of him revealed a deep understanding of the passage."

Thirty-one others from the University Congregational Church that year stuttered and stammered their way through the passage, and in the fall Reverend Turner took his 32 disciples to the plush, revolving restaurant on top of the Space Needle.

At dinner that night, "Trey" Gates feasted his eyes on the region where he would later make his mark. To the northeast was the University of Washington and the nearby residential district of Laurelhurst, where the Gates family lived, along the shores of Lake Washington. To the south, the Seattle waterfront jutted into the Sound, with its ships, piers, seafood restaurants, and curiosity shops. To the southeast rose the skyscrapers of the city, with 14,410-foot Mt. Rainier looming like a sentinel in the distance. To the east, against the backdrop of the Cascade Mountain range on the horizon, were the suburbs of Bellevue and Redmond, where 13 years later Gates would build his computer software empire.

That evening, as Gates looked out on the city, the suburbs, the mountains, and the waters of the Sound, he was oblivious to his destiny slowly revolving around him. Although he had memorized the Sermon on the Mount and received his free

Space Needle dinner, the boy would never become a regular in the church. He would soon find himself spending most of his free time immersed in the exciting new world of computers. He and Turner, however, would remain friends in the coming years.

"He loved challenges," Turner said, remembering his bright charge. "Even though a Space Needle meal was enticing back then, a lot of kids, on hearing my challenge, weren't ready to pay the price. Trey was."

As Gates had told the pastor that day in his house, "I can do anything I put my mind to."

If bloodlines are an indication of future success, then Bill Gates was born into a family generous with its gifts.

His great-grandfather on his mother's side of the family, J.W. Maxwell, was a nationally prominent banker. Born on an Iowa farm in the nineteenth century, he decided to seek his fortune behind a bank teller window rather than toil in poverty behind a plowshare. He left home for Lincoln, Nebraska, at age 19—the same age at which his great-grandson would found Microsoft nearly a century later—to begin a career in banking. In Lincoln, he became good friends with William Jennings Bryan, the orator and politician, and John J. Pershing, who would command the nation's armies during World War I.

In 1892, heeding the advice of editor and political leader Horace Greeley, Maxwell headed west with his wife to the town of South Bend in Washington State. There he continued his banking career, was elected mayor, and served in the state legislature. The family moved to Seattle in 1906, where Maxwell founded National City Bank and gained a national reputation in the banking industry.

Maxwell's son, James Willard Maxwell, began his own banking career in 1925 as a messenger in his father's bank after graduating from the University of Washington. At the university he met his future wife, Adelle Thompson, a smart, spirited, athletic woman from Enumclaw, a hamlet nestled in the foothills of the Cascade Mountains southeast of Seattle. She had been a star forward on the women's high school basketball team and class valedictorian.

The younger Maxwells became one of Seattle's most socially prominent families, active in numerous community organizations, including United Good Neighbors, the predecessor of United Way. Willard Maxwell enjoyed both wealth and power in Seattle, eventually becoming vice president of Pacific National Bank (which later became First Interstate, the nation's ninth largest bank). Several decades later they would leave their grandson a million dollar trust fund. Despite their wealth, the Maxwells disdained ostentation, a trait that has been passed down through the family.

Their daughter Mary was born in Seattle in 1929. A vivacious young beauty she grew up among some of the most prominent families in the Northwest. Like her mother before her, Mary Maxwell met her future husband, a tall, athletic, prelaw student by the name of Bill Gates, Jr., while she was a co-ed at the University of Washington. A school cheerleader, Mary was as outgoing and gregarious as Bill was shy and reserved. A mutual friend, Brock Adams, had introduced the couple while Adams was student body president, and Mary was an officer in the student government association. (Adams went on to a career in politics, serving as secretary of transportation under President Jimmy Carter. He is currently one of Washington's U.S. senators and remains a close friend of the Gates family.)

While Bill Gates, Jr., did not have the wealthy and prominent family background of his wife, he did have the same drive and ambition. He was born in Bremerton, Washington, an hour's ferry ride from Seattle, where his father owned a furniture store. Upon graduation from high school in 1943, Gates enlisted in the Army. By the end of World War II two years later, he was enrolled in officers' training school at Fort Benning, Georgia.

Discharged in 1946 as a first lieutenant, he promptly enrolled at the University of Washington, where he became the first member of his family to graduate from college.

After getting a law degree from the university in 1950, Gates returned to Bremerton as assistant city attorney. Mary Maxwell, a couple years behind him in college, graduated in 1952, and they married shortly afterward. But a Navy homeport like Bremerton, with its ubiquitous sailors, fast-food restaurants, and tattoo parlors, was not the place to climb social or legal ladders, so the couple moved to Seattle, where Mary taught school and Gates went into private practice, eventually becoming a partner in the firm of Shidler, McBroom, Gates & Lucas.

In 1954, Mary Gates gave birth to a daughter, Kristi. A year later, she gave birth to their only son.

William Henry Gates III was born on October 28, 1955, shortly after 9:00 P.M. His parents nicknamed him "Trey," reflecting the III after his name. The moniker stuck—no one in the family ever called him anything else. He was born under the sign of Scorpio, and the traits ascribed to his astrological sign would prove eerily correct: aggressive and stimulated by conflict; prone to change moods quickly; a dominating personality with outstanding powers of leadership. Scorpios are known for having the respect, rather than the affection, of others, according to the World Book Encyclopedia. Trey Gates read the encyclopedia, from beginning to end, when he was only seven or eight years old.

Trey was an unusually energetic child, even as a baby. He learned to make the cradle rock on his own and would rock incessantly for hours at a time. When he was old enough, his parents bought him a rocking horse, which was akin to feeding sweets to a hyperactive kid. Even today, his rocking habit is legendary in the computer industry, as much of a signature of the man as Arnold Palmer hitching up his pants as he strolls down the fairway or Michael Jordan sticking out his tongue as he drives for a basket. It has become part of the corporate culture at Microsoft among programmers trying to re-create themselves in the chairman's image. Gates often rocks himself in a chair, elbows on knees, to contain his intensity, especially when the talk is about computers; it's not unusual to walk into a room of Microsoft managers and find most of them rocking in sync with him during an important meeting.

His rocking addiction notwithstanding, Trey Gates had a fairly typical childhood. After her son was born, Mary Gates gave up teaching to raise the family while her husband established his legal practice. As an alternative to teaching, she followed her mother's lead and became a community volunteer. One of her first volunteer jobs, working on behalf of Seattle's Museum of History and Development, involved going to area schools and giving short talks on the region's culture and history. Trey, who was only three or four years old, would accompany his mother and sit on the desk in front of the class while she showed museum items to the students.

A recent book, *The Making of Microsoft* by Daniel Ichbiah and Susan Knepper, gave short shrift to what the authors described as Gates' "uneventful" childhood, other than to leave the impression he was a deeply introspective child who stayed in his room most of the time in intense, reflective thought. Gates was certainly an introspective child, but he hardly grew up like a hermit in his room. For one thing, it is unlikely even Gates could have tolerated being cooped up for long periods of time in his room—it was usually in a state of chaos. His parents couldn't train him to pick up his clothes. Eventually they tried taking his clothes away from him. When even that didn't work, they finally gave up, requesting that he at least keep the door to his room closed so no one else would have to look at the mess.

Mary Gates, in describing her son, has said that he has pretty much done what he wanted since the age of eight. Trey's closest childhood friend was Carl Edmark, whom Gates met in the fourth grade. Edmark said of him "He was very eccentric even back then." The two went to elementary school together, graduated from high school together, and continued to be good friends for years afterward. Their families were also good friends; Edmark's father was a prominent Seattle heart surgeon who had invented a defibrillator that corrected abnormal heart rhythms during surgery.

Even as a child Gates had an obsessive personality and a compulsive need to be the best. "Any school assignment, be it playing a musical instrument or writing papers, whatever, he would do at any or all hours of the day." said Edmark. What seemed like eccentric behavior to fellow fourth graders, however, was likely nothing more than his competitive spirit. One of the first major assignments in his fourth grade class was to write a four or five page report on a particular part of the human body. Gates wrote more than 30 pages. Later, the class was told to write a short story of no more than two pages. Trey's story was five times that length.

"Everything Bill did, he did to the max," said Edmark. "What he did always went well, well beyond everyone else."

Gifted children—those with IQs near or above the genius level—sometimes grow up to be socially inept, due to limited childhood interactions and experiences. Bill and Mary Gates were determined to see that that didn't happen to their son. They tried to expose him to as many opportunities and experiences as possible. When he was old enough, he was encouraged to join Troop 186 of the Boy Scouts. His father had been an Eagle Scout as a youth, and understood the value of Boy Scout activities and camaraderie. The troop met at an elementary school not far from the Gates' neighborhood. Trey stayed with the Scouts not only because he liked the outdoors, but because being a Scout fulfilled a need.

"His father was an attorney and very busy, and Bill needed a lot of companionship, which he got from the other boys," recalled Scoutmaster Don Van Wieringen.

One year during a Boy Scout jamboree—where Scouts from around the state gather to show off knot tying and fire building skills—Gates and a friend rounded up computer equipment and set up a hands-on demonstration of what a computer could do. At that time, few of the boys had even heard of a computer, much less used one. Today, thanks in part to Gates' software systems, computing can earn Scouts a merit badge.

Unlike some Scout troops, which cared more about selling light bulbs and candy at Christmas, Troop 186 made year round efforts to hike and camp in the woods.

On one 50-mile summer hike, Gates demonstrated the persistence and tenacity that was to be his trademark later in life. Gates showed up for the week-long hike in a new pair of hiking boots that were not suited for hiking eight miles a day. By the end of the first day, his heels had been rubbed raw and his toes badly blistered. By the end of the second day, his feet were raw and bleeding openly. One of the adults on the trip, who was a doctor, gave him some codeine for the pain. The next day some of the Scouts carried his equipment, and Trey continued on, limping along until he reached the halfway checkpoint on day four, where hikers could bail out in an emergency. At that point, he could no longer walk. His mother had to be called in Seattle to come get him. One of the adults on the hike recalled that when she arrived, Mary Gates was not a happy camper. "She was busy being a socialite," he said, "and thought Bill was taken care of for the week."

Mary's passion for education fueled a desire to return to teaching, but her career plans changed with the birth of a second daughter, Libby, nine years after Trey. Instead, she continued with her volunteer public service, which led to a seat on the boards of several of the Northwest's largest corporations, including First Interstate Bank and Pacific Northwest Bell. Mary

Gates was a quick study with a strong will, incisive intelligence and good business instincts.

"The driving force in the family has always been Mary Gates," one friend observed. "She seemed to tie everything together with the family. Mary was the smart one, Bill, Jr., was the shy one."

Despite her volunteer activities and community involvement that kept her busy, Mary Gates was a devoted mother. She also loved to socialize, and she and her husband threw frequent parties for their friends, who included many of Seattle's wealthiest and most powerful individuals. A charming, gracious host, warm and outgoing, she could nonetheless be quite assertive, with a steely gaze and a firm handshake.

"She is very much the kind of person who sizes you up, makes quick conversation and moves along, exiting gracefully but forcefully," a business friend said.

As successful as the gregarious Mary Gates was in Seattle's community, the quieter Bill, Jr., also became a respected figure. His legal career was furthered by his relationship through marriage to the Maxwells. He was active in the bar, eventually serving as president of the Washington State Bar Association, and chairing several American Bar Association commissions. In 1966, he became a senior partner in the law firm of Shidler, McBroom, Gates & Lucas, a firm rooted in Republican politics.

"My sense is that Bill, Jr., always wanted to position himself to exert quiet control in the law firm, and Mary was more inclined to pull public strings and press the switches," said one Seattle attorney who knows the family.

Both Mary and Bill, Jr., became active in Republican party circles as well, although they kept in the political shadows and out of the public eye. In 1973, Governor Evans, a family friend, quietly pushed to have Gates nominated to a federal judgeship in Seattle. But the state's two U.S. senators at the time, Henry "Scoop" Jackson and Warren Magnuson, both Democrats, preferred a local attorney with more liberal leanings to fill the vacancy on the federal bench.

In local politics, Bill, Jr., refused to make personal appearances for candidates or do anything that might draw public attention to his political beliefs. Nontheless, his beliefs were rock-solid. When a lawyer seeking re-election as a Democrat to the state legislature called on him to ask him for a campaign endorsement and financial contribution, he replied, "Jesus! I've never given money to a Democrat in my life."

Bill, Jr., set a firm and strong example for his children. "I've always wondered how Trey responded to his father," said another Seattle attorney who has worked with Bill, Jr. "He can be a hard man, difficult and demanding." Not unlike his son.

Although both were strong-willed, Trey and his father got along very well, and their relationship was an important influence on his childhood. The Gateses were a closely knit family. Trey Gates' maternal grandmother, Adelle Maxwell, was also an important influence on him, encouraging him to read as much as possible, pushing him to excel in all that he did, challenging him to use his mind. They played card games together frequently, especially games like Concentration that required mental agility. Gates would remain close to his grandmother until her death in 1987.

"His family has always been a very important part of him," observed Paul Allen, cofounder of Microsoft and one of Bill's best friends. "That has never changed, going back to when we first met as kids." Dinner was always a time for lively discussions. Gates and his sisters used to question their parents about their work at the dinner table when they were growing up. "It was a rich environment in which to learn," Gates said of his childhood.

It was also extraordinarily competitive. His competitive fire was ignited early in life and fanned by childhood games, sports, and the driving ambition of his parents. Whether racing with

his older sister to finish a 300-piece jigsaw puzzle, playing pickleball at the family's annual tournament, or swimming laps with
his friends at the country club pool, Gates loved competing—
and winning. Just as importantly, he hated losing. He thrived
on competition, as long as he was playing or doing something
he was good at, and relished opportunties to prove himself,
physically and mentally.

A friend who knew Gates in his early teens said: "Bill loved
playing pickleball and was fiercely competitive. He loved playing tennis and was fiercely competitive. He loved water skiing
and was fiercely competitive. Everything he did, he did com-
petitively and not simply to relax. He was a very driven
individual."

More than once the family flew down to California for the
Rose Bowl game, a time for Mary and Bill, Jr., to socialize and
visit friends. Trey spent hours at nearby amusement parks playing Demolition Derby in bumper cars. Although he was barely
big enough to see over the steering wheel of the cars, he took
particular delight in slamming into adult drivers.

His favorite competitive arena for boyhood games was summer camp, at a place on Hood Canal known as Cheerio. The
camp consisted of tennis courts and a dozen or so rustic cabins
near the water. Each July the Gates family piled into the car
and made the trip to Cheerio, where they would spend two
weeks with about a dozen other families. It was a successful and
competitive crowd, which included lawyers, business leaders,
and politicians.

Bill, Jr., was always designated as the "mayor." The families
staged "Olympic Games" featuring events such as the egg toss
and relay races. Trey became particularly good at the game
"Capture the Flag," which required skill and cunning, as well
as athletic ability. His team almost always won.

"He was never a nerd or a goof or the kind of kid you didn't
want on your team," recalled another of the Cheerio brethren.
"We all knew Bill was smarter than us. Even back then, when

he was nine or ten years old, he talked like an adult and could express himself in ways none of us understood. When you are a kid, if someone is good at math, that's what sets them apart. We all knew he was very, very good at math."

Trey first learned to water-ski and play tennis at Cheerio, as well. The entire family played tennis—Trey's sister Kristi won many of the Cheerio tennis tournaments for the girls. It was Brock Adams who taught Trey to play tennis at Cheerio, and he soon developed into an exceptional player. (Several years ago, Gates came up with an interesting—some might say eccentric—method to work on his game and not lose valuable work time. He would practice writing nonsense words with his racket hand to improve his fine muscle coordination. Gates would sit in meetings with his Microsoft managers, scribbling meaningless words on a piece of paper, rocking back and forth in his chair.)

Mary Gates helped organize many of the activities at Cheerio. Always exceedingly well-organized, she had a weekly wardrobe battle plan for Trey throughout the year that included color-coordinating his clothes for each day, matching shirts, pants, and socks. On Monday he might go to school dressed in green, on Tuesday beige . . . Wednesday blue . . . then black. . . . When the family would go to Trey's grandparents' house on Hood Canal with friends, Mary would post dinner menus for the entire weekend on the refrigerator. Each meal was carefully planned out, along with dinner times. Everything fit into a schedule.

It is a trait she has passed on to her son, who brooks no wasted time either at work or play.

Were it not for a fateful decision by his parents in 1967, Bill Gates might well have ended up a mathematician or college professor. At 11 years of age, he was far ahead of his peers in math and science and in need of new academic challenges. His parents decided he should not continue in the public schools like his sister but instead enroll that coming fall at Lakeside, an all-boys private prep school noted for its rigorous academic environment. It was Seattle's most exclusive school, home to the sons of the rich and powerful. About 300 students a year attended Lakeside, for a tuition that at the time cost roughly $5,000. Gates would be able to go head-to-head against the best and brightest of the next generation of Seattle's leaders.

Lakeside was a crucible that would fire his creative genius in ways his parents never imagined. It was here that the proper mix of ingredients needed to forge Gates' inner fire came together: energy, intelligence, intensity, competitiveness, obsessiveness, drive, desire, business acumen, entrepreneurship, and luck. He would cut his first business deals at Lakeside, and form his first money-making company. He would develop lasting friendships with a handful of Lakeside computer whiz kids like himself, who would become the first to join him in his crusade to build a software empire.

In 1967, students in the seventh and eighth grades made up the Lower School. The Upper School consisted of students in the ninth through twelfth grades. Those who started in the seventh grade and survived Lakeside's academic pressure cooker until they graduated were called "lifers." Trey Gates became a lifer.

Until the 1960s, Lakeside was a very traditional prep school. Boys wore coats, ties, and wingtip shoes. The seniors had special privileges—only seniors, for example, could use the front doors or smoke. But with the Vietnam War came protest and change. The coats and ties came off, hair grew longer, and many of the boys started coming to school in beards, blue jeans, and army fatigue jackets.

"The Sixties loosened up what had been a classic boys' school," recalled Robert Fulghum, the bestselling author of *All I Really Need to Know I Learned in Kindergarten*, who was an

18

art teacher at Lakeside. Fulghum represented Lakeside's alternative side. He was the kind of teacher who would show up for his class in a gorilla suit to illustrate a point, and whose exams included questions like, "Suppose all humans had tails. Describe yours." Fulghum knew Gates fairly well, although the boy was never in any of his art classes.

Lakeside always drew on the city's big-money establishment. Many of the boys who had passed through the school over the years were the movers and shakers of the community. It was a fiercely competitive environment at every level. "Even the dumb kids were smart," said one member of Gates' graduating class of 1973. Among the students at Lakeside were the McCaw brothers, who together built a billion-dollar cellular phone empire.

Although the school rewarded the marchers and the saluters, the students who really attracted attention were those who were unusual in some way. These kids got a lot of support and encouragement from the administration and faculty.

"You could, if you looked at Lakeside superficially, think of it as an elitist school with high requirements and strictly focused on college preparation," said Fulghum. "But in fact, it tended to look very, very carefully at individual students, especially ones who stuck out in any direction, and it would give those students lots and lots of privilege and rope and space to do whatever they could do, even if it was far out of the usual constraints of the school."

In that sense, Lakeside was extraordinary: it allowed students to develop their own interests, and Gates quickly did just that.

There would come a time when every student in school knew his name, knew that he was the best of the best at Lakeside. But the only thing remarkable about Bill Gates when he began the seventh grade were his big feet. Although he was the smallest boy in the seventh grade, Gates wore size 13 wingtips. "We all wondered if he would grow into his feet," a classmate recalled.

Of all the friendships he would develop at Lakeside, none would be as strong or as close as his friendship with Kent Evans. The two were inseparable from the seventh grade. Both were gifted, both shared a passion for mathematics, and both would soon share an even greater passion for computers.

Gates and Evans had very different personalities. While Gates could be cold and aloof like his father, Kent was warm and outgoing. A minister's son with a harelip and thick black hair, there was a down-to-earth quality to Evans. Lakeside students would remember him as "the nicest boy in school."

Toward the end of Gates' first year at Lakeside, in the early spring of 1968, the school made a decision that would prove decisive to Bill Gates' future. America was preparing to send astronauts to the moon, a technological feat made possible by the development of the computer. Lakeside had decided to expose its students to this new and exciting world of computers. The question was how to buy a computer on a school budget, even the budget of a well-to-do private school. The "Giant Brain" mainframe computers of the day cost millions of dollars and were out of reach of all but the government, universities, and the largest corporations. Digital Equipment Corporation, better known as DEC, had recently begun marketing a minicomputer, but even this refrigerator-size machine was out of reach of the Lakeside budget. So the school bought itself a relatively inexpensive teletype machine. For a fee, users could type commands on the teletype and communicate via telephone line with a PDP-10 minicomputer in downtown Seattle (PDP stands for Program Data Processor). The PDP-10, one in a series of very famous computers built by Digital Equipment Corporation, would play a significant role in Gates' development as a computer programmer. The PDP-10 Lakeside used was owned by General Electric, which billed Lakeside for "computer time" used by its students. And computer time was very costly.

A group of mothers, the Lakeside Mothers Club, held a rummage sale to buy computer time and raised about $3,000, figuring the amount would be enough to last the rest of the school year. What they didn't realize was how seductive a mistress The Machine would become to a few precocious boys who liked math and science. Bill Gates and Evans were about to develop a very expensive addiction.

Lakeside became one of the first schools in the country with computer capability. The computer room soon became a powerful magnet for several of Lakeside's brightest students, especially Gates. Before long, the teletype would be his umbilical cord to a new and exciting universe.

Gates was in Paul Stocklin's math class when he got his first peek at the computer room. One spring day, Stocklin took his entire math class over to the Upper School to see it. Under Stocklin's supervision, Gates typed in a few instructions and watched in awe as the teletype, after communicating with the PDP-10 several miles away, typed back the response. It was better than science fiction.

"I knew more than he did for the first day, but only for that first day," said Stocklin, who now chairs the Lakeside math department. "We were really winging it . . . . None of us knew anything back then. This thing wasn't like a Macintosh."

Gates was immediately hooked. Whenever he had free time, he would run over to the Upper School to get more experience on the system. But Gates was not the only computer-crazed kid at Lakeside. He found he had to compete for time on the computer with a handful of others who were similarly drawn to the room as if by a powerful gravitational force. Among them was a soft-spoken, Upper School student by the name of Paul Allen, who was two years older than Gates.

Seven years later, the two classmates would form Microsoft, the most successful startup company in the history of American business.

When Albert Einstein was four or five years old and sick in bed, his father gave him a magnetic pocket compass. In his *Autobiographical Notes*, written 60 years later, Einstein described the compass as "a wonder." It may well have determined the direction of his life as a theoretical physicist. "That this needle behaved in such a determined way did not at all fit into the nature of events," he wrote. "I can still remember—at least I believe I can still remember—that this experience made a deep and lasting impression on me."

Bill Gates undoubtedly cannot explain why he reacted as he did to his own "wonder," the computer. But it triggered a deep passion, an obsession, in him. From that first day in the small computer room at Lakeside, its pull on him was inexorable.

Gates devoured everything he could get his hands on concerning computers and how to communicate with them, often teaching himself as he went. The faculty knew next to nothing about computers. Gates and the other kids hanging out day and night in the computer room were pretty much on their own.

"We were off in our own world," Gates recalled later. "Nobody quite understood the thing but us. I wanted to figure out exactly what it could do."

This insatiable appetite for computer time was very expensive. Within weeks, most of the $3,000 raised by the Mothers Club was gone. Eventually, parents were asked to help pay Lakeside's mounting bills from General Electric.

Gates' first computer program, a series of instructions telling the computer what to do, was a tick-tack-toe game. He then wrote a program for a lunar lander game, which required the user to make a soft landing on the moon before expending all fuel in the spacecraft and crashing on the moon's surface. (This game would prove somewhat prophetic. The Apollo 11 lunar lander carrying Neil Armstrong and Buzz Aldrin had only seconds of fuel remaining when it landed on the Sea of Tranquility, July 20, 1969.) As his programming skills developed, Gates taught the computer to play Monopoly™, commanding it to play thousands of games in search of winning strategies.

These early programs were written in a computer language known as BASIC (Beginner's All-purpose Symbolic Instruction Code.) It was developed by two Dartmouth College professors in 1964 under a grant from the National Science Foundation to teach their students an easier way to use computers. Gates was particularly interested in the mathematical foundations of computer science, the strange new binary world in which one communicated with the computer using only two words—usually designated zero and one. Gates talked about this relationship between computers and mathematics in the book *Programmers at Work* by Susan Lammers:

> "Most great programmers have some mathematical background, because it helps to have studied the purity of proving theorems, where you don't make soft statements, you only make precise statements. In mathematics, you develop complete characterizations, and you have to combine theorems in very nonobvious ways. You often have to prove that a problem can be solved in less time. Math relates very directly to programming, maybe more so in my mind than in other people's minds, because that's the angle that I came from. I think there is a very natural relationship between the two."

Gates had always been very good at math. In fact, he was gifted. On the math achievement test Lakeside gave its students, Gates was the number one student in the school. He later scored a perfect 800 on the math portion of his college boards.

While at Lakeside, he took advanced math courses at the University of Washington. "I read ahead in math, so I really didn't spend much time on math classes in school. Even when I got bad grades in everything else, which was up through the eighth grade, I always did well in math."

Fred Wright, chairman of the math department at Lakeside when Gates attended, said of Gates, "He could see shortcuts through an algebraic problem or a computer problem. He could see the simplest way to do things in mathematics. He's as good an analytical mathematician as I've worked with in all my years of teaching. But Bill was really good in all areas, not just math. He's got a lot of breadth. It's one of the unusual things about him."

Wright was in charge of the computer room in the Upper School, and has been given much of the credit for cultivating Lakeside's first crop of computer talent in the spring of 1968. He nourished, encouraged, and befriended not only Gates and Allen but a handful of others, including Marc McDonald, Richard Weiland, and Chris Larson, three of the first programmers hired to work for Microsoft.

"You have to understand what early age compulsions are like. They are all-consuming," said the Reverend Marvin Evans, Kent's father. "After Lakeside got that computer, Bill and Kent were in constant trouble with the faculty. Some of Kent's journals demonstrate this. Everything was late—chemistry workbooks were late, physics workbooks were late, history and English themes were late."

Wright, amused by the antics of his young charges, adopted the code name, "GYMFLKE," to log on to the computer, an inside joke on Gates, Evans, and some of the others who "flaked out" of gym to work on The Machine. While the kids all became experts at finding confidential user passwords and breaking computer security systems, none of them, Gates included, discovered Wright's secret password.

Although Gates was only in the lower school, before long some of the older boys were coming to him for help with the computer. Among them was Paul Allen, who would egg Gates on, challenging him to solve a difficult problem.

"Paul thought I had this attitude like I understood things," Gates said. "So when he got stuck he would say, 'Hey, I bet you can't figure this out!' He would kind of challenge me . . . and it was pretty hard stuff."

As they spent more and more time together in the computer room, Gates and Allen became friends. One day, Gates went to Allen's home, only to be amazed by Allen's collection of sci-fi books.

"He had read four times as much as I had," recalled Gates. "And he had all these other books that explained things. So I would ask him, 'How do guns work? How do nuclear reactors work?' Paul was good at explaining stuff. Later, we did some math stuff and physics stuff together. That's how we got to be friends."

It wasn't surprising that Allen should be well read. For more than twenty years his father, Kenneth Allen, was associate director of libraries for the University of Washington.

Although Allen could be just as intense and competitive as Gates, he was surprisingly soft-spoken, with an equally soft handshake. Allen talks so softly, in fact, that when reporters interview him, his voice sometimes fails to automatically activate their tape recorders.

The other kids at Lakeside liked Paul Allen. To many of his classmates, he seemed more personable than some of the others who had taken over the computer room. It was easy to like the boy with the blond Fu Manchu mustache and aviator sunglasses who habitually carried a briefcase. There was no pretentiousness in Allen, none of the I'm-smarter-than-you attitude.

"Paul was cool," said a classmate who was not one of the computer room crowd. "He was a nerd who didn't look like a nerd. He was always more approachable and friendlier than Bill. . . . You would run into him in the hallways and he would actually stop and talk to you."

Allen and Gates not only spent a lot of time working together in the computer room but also a lot of time talking about the future of computer technology.

"We both were fascinated with the different possibilites of what you could do with computers," Allen said. "It was a vast area of knowledge we were trying to absorb. . . . Bill and I always had big dreams of what we could do with computers."

While Allen liked to read magazines like *Popular Electronics*, Gates read the business magazines that came into his family's home. As a prelude to doing business in the "real world," Gates and Allen formed the Lakeside Programmers Group, along with two of their friends, Richard Weiland and Kent Evans. Weiland and Allen were in the tenth grade, while Gates and Evans were in the eighth grade. The Lakeside Programmers Group was dedicated to finding money-making opportunities to use The Machine in the real world.

"I was the mover," Gates said. "I was the guy who said, 'Let's call the real world and try to sell something to it.'"

As it turned out, the real world called them first. And what a deal it was—all the free computer time they wanted.

———————

Founded by four University of Washington computer experts in the fall of 1968 with the backing of several Seattle investors, Computer Center Corporation was a private Seattle firm offering the largest concentration of timesharing computer power on the West Coast. The company (which Gates referred to as "C-Cubed") had leased several computers from Digital Equipment Corporation, including a PDP-10 like the one Gates and the other Lakeside students used.

Computer Center Corporation attempted to sell its timesharing services to scientific and engineering businesses in the region—or any other customer in need of computer power at an affordable price.

One of the firm's founders and chief scientific programmer, Monique Rona, had a son in the eighth grade at Lakeside—the same grade as Gates. She knew about the school's teletype machine and its deal with General Electric for computer time. A representative from her company contacted Lakeside to inquire whether the school would be interested in making a similar arrangement with Computer Center Corporation. The students would have an even greater opportunity to learn about computers, the representative argued.

Lakeside concurred, and once again asked parents to help pay for the computer time used by their sons.

Gates and some of the other boys soon discovered all kinds of "neat" programs hidden in the C-Cubed PDP-10 software—programs they had not encountered with the General Electric computer. One trick the boys learned was something called "detach and leave job running." This meant that even though they were logged off the system, the machine was still working on their program . . . and keeping a record of the computing time used. Computer bills soon ran into the hundreds of dollars.

"These kids were very hungry for time," recalled Dick Wilkinson, one of the partners who organized Computer Center Corporation. "Every time we would get a new version of software, they would go poking around in the system, and we would have to forgive some bills because they would be running programs they were not supposed to. They found chess on the system, when they should not have. So they would play a half game of chess, and then leave the Lakeside terminal and go off to class or something. They didn't understand they were using computer time like it was going out of style."

The electronic mischief eventually got out of hand. Gates and a couple other boys broke the PDP-10 security system and obtained access to the company's accounting files. They found their personal accounts and substantially reduced the amount of the time the computer showed they had used. They were quite proud of this ingenious accomplishment—until they got caught.

Wilkinson drove out to Lakeside for a talk with Fred Wright, the math teacher in charge of the school's computer project. Like naughty boys, Gates and the others were marched into the principal's office.

"We told them they were off the system for six weeks," Wilkinson said, "and if we caught them on it we would call the police, because what they were doing was illegal. They were all very contrite. They were pretty good kids from then on."

Gates became even more of a problem for Computer Center Corporation shortly afterward. The very first BASIC program Gates wrote using the PDP-10 computer at C-Cubed was called "Bill." The next time Gates dialed up the computer and tried to load his program, however, the system crashed.

Gates tried it again the next day. "New or old program?" the computer asked via the teletype machine.

Gates punched out the answer on the teletype keyboard: "Old program."

The computer then asked, "Old program name?"

Gates punched out the answer: "Old program name is Bill."

Bam! Just like that, the system crashed again. Gates attempted to load up his program several times over the next few days, and each time the C-Cubed computer would break down.

This was not good news for Computer Center Corporation, which was trying to pay bills, attract new customers, and keep old ones. Whenever the computer went down, other paying customers were also knocked off the system. Worse, the computer "lost" everything it had been working on—a case of electronic Alzheimer's. When the machine came back up, its memory banks were blank.

Frustrated programmers at C-Cubed eventually figured out what Gates was doing wrong. When the computer asked him the name of his program, he was supposed to type only the word, "Bill." The string of characters he was typing, "Old program name is Bill," was too long for the machine, an anomaly that caused it to crash.

It was an exhilarating feeling for Gates, knowing he could single-handedly bring down the huge computer by typing a string of letters. He soon learned, however, just how easy it was to crash the PDP-10.

The software that Digital Equipment Corporation supplied with its PDP-10 was "flaky" at best. On good days, the C-Cubed system might stay up four hours before crashing. On bad days, when there were lots of paying customers on line, it was usually down within half an hour. Clearly, something would have to be done if the firm were going to stay in business.

"We knew we had this reliability problem," recalled Steve Russell, one of the programmers working for C-Cubed. "We knew how to turn the crashes on and off to some extent . . . simply by having lots of users and not having lots of users. What we wanted to do was get a herd of friendly users that we could turn on and off, so that we could turn them on to test the system and turn them off when we wanted the system to be reliable, because there were paying customers on the machines making money for us."

So the company hired a herd of friendly users, and they became the unofficial "night shift." C-Cubed offered Gates and the other Lakeside computer junkies an opportunity to try to crash the system. In exchange, they would get all the free computer time they wanted. They were simply to come down to C-Cubed in the evening and on weekends, after the paying customers were off the computer, log onto the system and have fun. The only requirement was that they were to carefully document each "bug" they found that caused the system to crash.

Computer bugs were appropriately named. In August of 1945, while working on an experimental computer known as the Mark 1 at Harvard University, a circuit malfunctioned, and a research assistant went looking for the problem in the tangled mess of vacuum tubes and wires. He found the problem, and removed it with a pair of tweezers—it was a 2-inch long moth.

"From then on," Grace Hopper, a member of the Mark 1 research team, told *Time* magazine in 1984, "when anything went wrong with a computer, we said it had bugs in it." (The famous moth is preserved at the U.S. Naval Surface Weapons Center in Dahlgren, Virginia.)

Finding bugs in the C-Cubed computer system proved to be a fertile field of investigation for Gates and the other boys. They were given what became known as the "Problem Report Book," a journal of their discoveries and investigations. Over the next six months, the "bug" book grew to more than 300 pages. Most of the entries were made by just two boys—Bill Gates and Paul Allen.

Computer Center Corporation was located in the city's University District, in what had been an old Buick dealership. After school, Gates would rush home to Laurelhurst for dinner, then run to nearby Children's Hospital to catch the No. 30 bus for the short ride to C-Cubed.

It was often past midnight when the boys finished their work. Gates would usually walk home. Sometimes, one of the parents would come by and drive all the boys home.

"It was when we got free time at C-Cubed that we really got into computers," Gates said. "I mean, then I became hard core. It was day and night."

At this point, Gates was 13 years old, and finishing up the eighth grade.

"We stayed up until all hours of the night. . . . It was a fun time," recalled Allen.

Gates and Allen not only looked for bugs but they also looked for any information that might help them learn more about computers, operating systems, and software. Allen would hoist Gates on garbage cans so he could poke around for important tidbits of information left behind by the "day shift."

"I'd get the notes out with the coffee grounds on them and study the operating systems," Gates said.

Kent Evans was often there late into the night with Gates and Allen, as was Rick Weiland. After four or five hours working in front of a computer, the boys would send out for pizza and Coke. It was a hacker's heaven.

Occasionally, a tall, quiet, bearded fellow by the name of Gary Kildall dropped by in the evenings to use the computers and talk to some of the programmers. Kildall was finishing work on his Ph.D. in computer science at the University of Washington. Ten years later, he would fumble one of the biggest business opportunities of the personal computer revolution and in the process help to make Bill Gates a very rich man.

The ground rules set down by C-Cubed for the night shift were pretty straightforward. The boys could use the system as much as they wanted, at no charge. They were encouraged to try to crash the system, and when it went down, they were to tell C-Cubed what they had input when it crashed. The deal was they could find any bug once, but only once. C-Cubed would then "de-bug" that part of the program.

"On occasion we had to give some verbal reprimands for violating our rules, which was using the same bug more than once before we fixed it," said Steve Russell. "Since we were giving them time, they had considerable motivation to play the game our way."

Russell, in his early thirties, was there at night to ride herd on the boys.

"Usually, when I stuck my nose in on them, I'd get asked a question or five, and my natural inclination was to answer questions at considerable length," he said. "They got some useful info from that."

Steve Russell was famous as a computer programmer, and the kids eagerly plied him for information. Russell had gone to college at Dartmouth but left in 1958 to work as a computer programmer at the Massachusetts Institute of Technology, where professor John McCarthy had set up an artifical intelligence research center in order to get funding from the federal government. It was McCarthy, an absent-minded professor and master mathematician who came up with the term "artificial intelligence," or AI. He later went to Stanford's AI research center on the West Coast, and Russell followed.

In 1961, using a PDP-1, the first in Digital's PDP series of computers, Russell had hacked out the first computer video game called "Space Wars." The PDP-1 had a CRT or cathode ray tube screen. Russell worked for hours just to produce a dot on the screen, which would be commanded to change directions and accelerate by flipping toggle switches on the front of the computer. Eventually, his game took shape—a battle in outer space involving two rocket ships, each with 31 torpedoes. (Russell was another big science fiction fan.) Random dots on the screen represented stars. A subsequent program turned the stars into constellations. Other hackers improved on his game. A player could jump into hyperspace with the flick of a switch.

"Space Wars" became the mother of all computer games. Before long, a generation of new games followed.

At Stanford, Russell worked on multi-user computer systems, using DEC's PDP-6. C-Cubed was created to take the next version of that multi-user system, the PDP-10, and make a commercial service out of it. Russell was recruited by the C-Cubed company from Stanford's Artificial Intelligence Research Center in late 1968 because of his experience with multi-user computer systems.

Russell sometimes gave Gates and Allen computer manuals, with instructions to return them the next morning. Instead of going home, the boys would remain at C-Cubed all night reading.

Gates and Allen stood out from the other kids, Russell recalled, because of their enthusiasm. "They also seemed to have a lot more interest in breaking the system than the others." Gates earned a reputation at C-Cubed as an expert in the art of breaking into other computer security systems. He was particularly good at finding a bug known as the "one liner." This was a pathological string of characters that could be typed on one line, allowing Gates to take over the system or cause it to crash. Legend has it that Gates was severely reprimanded at C-Cubed for breaking into security systems. However, other than the one time he altered his account from Lakeside, those stories are apocryphal. The company encouraged Gates and the other boys to try to poke around in files they were not supposed to be able to get into. After all, C-Cubed couldn't fix a security leak unless it knew about it. Digital had supplied an elaborate security system with the PDP-10, for which the C-Cubed staff added a few bells and whistles of their own. They wanted to know if someone was able to get past the security system, and they were more than happy to have Gates try to do this. He did so with the knowledge and permission of C-Cubed.

"We wanted to know about these bugs so we could get rid of them," Russell said.

Another programmer at C-Cubed, Dick Gruen, said, "I would not call it breaking in if I said, 'See if you can find a way around this.' I'd call it asking people to see whether the watchman was doing his job. The distinction is they were not stealing anything from us, and they were doing it not just with our approval but on our behalf. We wanted them to tell us about holes that they found."

Despite the work of Gates, Allen, and the other kids from Lakeside, DEC continued to have problems with the multi-user software it used. It would take another seven years before all the bugs were gone. By then, C-Cubed was no longer in existence, and Bill Gates and Paul Allen were a lot more famous than Steve Russell.

Computer Center Corporation first began struggling in late 1969; in March of 1970 the company went out of business.

Gates was finishing up the ninth grade when C-Cubed went under. When it did, he made the first of what would be many smart, profitable deals while at Lakeside. In the process, he showed that when it came to business, he didn't allow anything, even friendship, to stand in the way.

Without discussing the matter with Allen and Weiland, their partners in the Lakeside Programmers Group, Gates and Evans negotiated to buy the valuable DEC computer tapes from C-Cubed at a cut-rate price. They hid the tapes in the Lakeside teletype machine. When an angry Allen found out, he took the tapes. Gates and Evans threatened legal action, despite the fact that they were barely teenagers.

"There was definitely some tension there," Allen said, "but it got resolved." Gates and Evans eventually sold the tapes and made a nice profit.

Mary and Bill, Jr., were not pleased with such shenanigans. They became increasingly concerned about their son. The Machine seemed to them to have an almost supernatural hold on him. Although he was only in the ninth grade, he already seemed obsessed with the computer, ignoring everything else, staying out all night. Gates was turning into what MIT professor Joseph Weizenbaum, in his book *Computer Power and Human Reason*, described as a computer bum:

> "Bright young men of disheveled appearance, often with sunken glowing eyes, can be seen sitting at computer consoles, their arms tensed and waiting to fire their fingers, already poised to strike, at the buttons and keys on which their attention seems to be riveted as a gambler's on the rolling dice. When not so transfixed, they often sit at tables strewn with computer printouts over which they pore like possessed students of a cabalistic text. They work until they nearly drop, twenty, thirty hours at a time. Their food, if they arrange it, is brought to them: coffee, Cokes, sandwiches. If possible, they sleep on cots near the printouts. Their rumpled clothes, their unwashed and unshaven faces, and their uncombed hair all testify that they are oblivious to their bodies and to the world in which they move. These are computer bums, compulsive programmers. . . ."

Weizenbaum was describing young men at MIT in the late sixties, at the artificial intelligence lab. The passage in his book became infamous in computer circles. Hackers considered it unfounded and vicious. They saw the computer as a revolutionary tool that could change the world. But Weizenbaum considered it dehumanizing. Young men addicted to The Machine had no sense of limits, he said. They had tunnel vision, unable to see the real world.

Mary and Bill, Jr., were beginnning to see this dehumanizing, addictive behavior in their son. Although they had never pushed him in any direction before, they did so now. They ordered him to give up computers, at least for a while.

"It was a combination of things," Gates explained, "where people thought, hey, maybe we are out of control, and people thought we weren't paying attention to anything else, and that it was a kind of abnormal situation. So my parents said, 'Why don't you give this stuff up.' So I did."

It was no big deal, he said. "I just went off and did some other stuff . . . science, math. There was an infinite amount to read. There was at least nine months there when I did nothing with computers."

Read he did, with the same kind of commitment he had made to computers. He consumed a number of biographies—Franklin Roosevelt's and Napoleon's, among others—to understand, he said, how the great figures of history thought. He read business and science books, along with novels. His favorites were *Catcher in the Rye* and *A Separate Peace*. He would later recite long passages from those two books to girlfriends. Holden Caulfield, the main character in *Catcher in the Rye*, became one of his heroes.

And so Bill Gates, the biggest computer junkie in the Lakeside computer room, swore off computers for nearly a year, from the end of the ninth grade through the first half of the tenth.

"I tried to be normal," he said, "the best I could."

―――――――

As a student at Lakeside School, Bill Gates was never just one of the boys. His drive, intensity, attitude, and intelligence made him stand out from the crowd. In fact, nothing about Bill Gates was normal. Gates used to be teased at Lakeside because he was clearly so much brighter than the other students. Even in an environment like Lakeside, where smart kids tended to command respect, anyone as smart as Gates got teased by some of the others. In a school carpool, Gates, who was younger and smaller than the other boys, always sat in the back and was usually left out of conversations. Occasionally, he would attempt to win their approval by telling a joke. When he did, one older boy who always sat in the front usually turned around, put his hand in Gates' face, spread his thumb and forefinger about an inch apart, and with a smirk, told him, "Small man . . . small joke."

After a nine month hiatus, Gates resumed his love affair with the computer. It didn't take long for other students to notice that the same kids always seemed to crowd the small computer room at Lakeside. The floor was often littered with folded, spindled, or mutilated punch cards, and punched out pieces of teletype tape. The teletype was usually hammering away. Gates and his friends often sat at a long table, drinking from two-liter bottles of Coke, playing chess or the ancient Chinese game of Go to while away the time until the computer had finished the job it was running. With all the time he spent in the computer room, Gates became a master of Go and could beat anyone in the school.

"Gates mostly associated with the kids in the computer room," recalled one classmate, who today is a prominent Seattle architect and community leader. "He was socially inept and uncomfortable around others. The guy was totally obsessed with his interest in computers. . . . You would see him playing tennis occasionally, but not much else. Initially I was in awe of Gates and the others in that room. I even idolized them to some extent. But I found that they were such turkeys that I didn't want to be like them. They were part of the reason I got out of computer work. . . . They had developed very narrowly socially and they were arrogant, and I just didn't want to be like that. . . ."

By his junior year, Gates was something of a computer guru to the younger Lakeside computer hacks. He would often hold court in the computer room for hours, talking shop and telling stories about industry hackers and "phone phreaks" like Captain Crunch, who had gained national notoriety by building so-called blue boxes, which allowed the user to make free long-distance phone calls. One of these computer groupies who came to hear Gates was Brad Augustine, four years his junior.

"He lived and breathed computers to the point he would forget to clip his fingernails," Augustine recalled. "His nails would be a half an inch long. He was a slob in that sense, just so much into whatever he was doing."

The school annual of his graduating year at Lakeside contains a picture of Gates lying on the table in the computer room, phone to his ear, ski cap pulled low over his head. "Who is this man?" the caption asks.

"Bill stood out," said one former classmate, who is now a successful businessperson. "Everyone knew who Bill Gates was. I don't think there was anyone in the school who didn't. There were nerd types that no one ever noticed, and there were nerd types that everyone knew. Bill fit that latter category. He looked like a little kid, for one thing. He looked much younger than he was. He was also incredibly obnoxious. He was also considered the brightest kid in school. If you had asked anybody at Lakeside, 'Who is the real genius among geniuses?' everyone would have said 'Bill Gates.' He was obnoxious, he was sure of himself, he was aggressively, intimidatingly smart. When people thought of Bill they thought, well, this guy is going to win a Nobel Prize. But he didn't have any social graces. He just wasn't a personable kind of person. He was one of those guys who knew he was smarter than everyone else and knew he was right all the time. . . ."

He had a hard-nosed, confrontational style even with his teachers—a style he is noted for today. His intensity at times simply boiled over into raw, unthrottled emotion, and occasionally childlike temper tantrums. Several former classmates vividly remember a volatile exchange between Gates and physics teacher Gary Maestretti in the tenth grade. The two were heatedly arguing with one another, jaw to jaw, in front of the class on a raised stage that was used for class demonstrations. Gates was yelling at the top of his lungs, waving his finger, hammering away at Maestretti, telling him he was wrong about a physics point . . . and Gates was winning the argument.

Maestretti, who now chairs the school's science department, has no recollection of the argument, but he certainly remembers Gates, and his best friend Kent Evans.

"Written work from Bill didn't come across with a lot of polish," Maestretti said. "Kent Evans would produce copious explorations of things. Bill wasn't one to produce a lot of writing." At one point Maestretti tried to encourage Gates to use his hands as well as his intellect. As a project, Maestretti asked him to assemble a Radio Shack electronics kit, in order to force him to build something correctly and make it work.

"I can remember when he brought it to me, telling me, 'Okay, now I've satisfied my project.' And of course solder was dripping all over the back. . . ." Needless to say, it didn't work. "He was clearly much more ethereal and intellectual than practical. . . ."

The classroom, not the workshop, was Gates' competitive arena, the intellectual battleground where he would strive for the best test score or compete to solve math and physics problems faster than anyone else. He was legendary in his classes for correctly answering trick questions—he almost always saw the hidden meaning or spotted the red herring thrown out by the teacher.

"He was always one step ahead," said Carl Edmark, his childhood friend. "You couldn't fool him."

Gates was impatient with those not as quick as he was, teachers included. His science teacher, William Dougal, once commented, "If a teacher was slow, Bill always seemed on the verge of saying, 'But that's *obvious.*' "

His superior attitude rubbed some of his classmates the wrong way. Colby Atwood, who was a year ahead of Gates, sat in front of Gates in a law class taught by lawyer Gary Little. Gates, at this point, was a junior. One day Gates laughed at a student who was slow to answer a question put to him by Little. When Atwood, who didn't particularly care for Gates, heard him snicker at his friend, he turned around, grabbed Gates by his shirt, and told him off. Little had to jump in and break it up.

"It was a response not to just that one incident but to an attitude that Gates had had for some time in the class," said Atwood. Atwood saw Gates again on a plane 20 years later, when Gates boarded at the last moment.

"He looked rumpled . . . tired . . . hair uncombed . . . just the way he used to look in school."

While some classmates remember Gates as socially awkward and completely absorbed by the world of the Lakeside computer room, to those who knew him best Gates was hardly the social outcast he may have appeared to be from a distance. He had a sense of humor and adventure. He was a risk taker, a guy who liked to have fun and who was fun to be with. He had an immense range of knowledge and interests and could talk at length on any number of subjects.

"Anyone who remembers him as a nerdy person either didn't deal with him closely or is remembering wrong," said friend Paul Carlson, whose passion was politics, not computers.

When he was 16, Gates bought a new, red 1970 Mustang that he and his friends would use to cut afternoon classes and go joy riding.

"He liked to drive fast," recalled Peter Randlett, one of his friends who often went on the rides. "He was a typical, privileged, adolescent kid who liked to goof off and take a break from the competitiveness of Lakeside. We would often just rap for hours."

Other than Kent Evans, probably no one was closer to Gates in high school than Carl Edmark, his friend since the fourth grade. Throughout high school, Gates and Edmark did practically everything together—saw new movies, cruised in the Mustang, hung out at hamburger stands, and played endless games of pinball. On weekends in the summer months, they went water skiing on Hood Canal. They also learned to hang glide on Hood Canal behind a speedboat with a 1,000-foot tow line attached to a 16-foot kite.

"We did all the normal, nutty things that kids do as teenagers," said Edmark. "Bill . . . was exceptionally normal. . . . We would talk about CD technology. We were both interested in technical things. . . . But we would never say, 'I'm going to be this' or 'I'm going to be that.' We really didn't know what we were going to do with our lives."

In their sophomore year, Edmark had a summer job working in a Seattle bank. One day, an elderly woman came in and deposited several thousand-dollar bills into her account. Edmark had never seen a thousand-dollar bill before. That night, he told Gates. "Well, let's get one," Gates said. The next day, he gave Edmark a huge wad of twenty-dollar bills, and Edmark took the money to one of the bank's managers, who gave him a thousand-dollar bill.

That night, Edmark and Gates went to Dick's, a popular hamburger hangout noted for serving the greasiest fries in town. The two boys ordered cheeseburgers and fries. When the order came, Gates nonchalantly opened his wallet and handed the cashier the crisp thousand-dollar bill. She looked at the bill, then looked up at Gates, repeating her eye motion several times. Finally she went to get the manager.

"Got anything smaller?" the manager asked with a straight face when he came out. Gates, looking five years younger than his age, shook his head solemnly. "No, nothing else," he said, determined to play out the scene for all it was worth.

"Well, after lunch we might have been able to break this. But not now," replied the manager.

Gates and Edmark burst into laughter. They finally paid for their food with a couple of bucks and headed off in the Mustang into the night.

Although Gates may not have known what he was going to do with his life during high school, he seemed confident that whatever he did would make him a lot of money. He made just such a prediction about his future on several occasions to other students and teachers at Lakeside. In the 11th grade, Gates told his friend Paul Carlson that he would be a millionaire by the time he was 30 years old.

"That is something that might sound like arrogance," said Carlson. "Some might just say it to brag. Some might say it as if they had the measure of themselves. Bill was in that second category."

When Gates got back into computers in late 1970, he began exploring new ways to make money. While Gates was on his nine month sabbatical, Paul Allen had been busy finding new computers to play on at the University of Washington, where his father worked at the campus library. Allen knew his way around. He found a PDP-10 computer in the physics department, and a PDP-11 in the university's hosptial. He discovered other computers in the engineering department. By the time Gates was back in the fold, the Lakeside Programmers Group had moved operations to the university, where the boys were keeping hours all night.

"We hacked around on all of those machines," Gates said. "We hung around the university to find any computer we could get free time on. Once C-Cubed went out of business, it was just finding time on anything."

There were rumors that Gates crashed Cybernet, a national computer network run by Control Data Corporation, by hacking his way into the system on a CDC computer at the university.

Two books, *Fire in the Valley* and *The Making of Microsoft*, reported that Gates received strong reprimands from CDC engineers who discovered his tracks. But like the stories of his hacking exploits at C-Cubed, this story appears more apocryphal than factual. Control Data Corporation was one of the so-called Seven Dwarfs that made mainframe computers in the 1960s in the shadow of the Giant, IBM. The University of Washington did indeed have a CDC computer that Gates had access to. But it was not connected to Cybernet, so there would have been no way for Gates to break the network, according to a systems programmer who installed the CDC computer at the university in 1968.

Said Gates of the story: "We learned about peripheral processors on the CDC at the university. But I was not involved in crashing the Cybernet . . . although I know some people who say they did."

The Lakeside Programmers Group received an important business opportunity in early 1971. Information Sciences Inc., a Portland, Oregon, timesharing computer company similar to C-Cubed, contacted the group about writing a payroll program for one of its clients. ISI had a PDP-10 computer and its president, Tom McLain, was aware the Lakeside kids had a lot of experience writing programs on the machine. Dick Wilkinson, one of the partners who organized C-Cubed, had sold the PDP-10 computer system to ISI while he was regional sales manager for Digital Equipment Corporation. Allen and Richard Weiland decided they didn't need their younger colleagues and asked Gates and Kent Evans to bow out of the ISI project.

Recalled Gates: "Paul and Rick decided there wasn't enough work to go around so they told us 'We don't need you guys.' But then they got sidetracked. They weren't even writing the payroll program. So they asked me to come back in and I said to them, 'Okay, you want me to come back in, then I'll be in charge of this thing. . . . Kent and I ended up writing most of the payroll program, a COBOL program. We got free computer

puter time to do the work, and as compensation we got free computer time. It ended up being a good deal for everybody."

The payroll project was actually "pretty boring," according to Gates. "You had to understand state taxes, payroll deductions . . . that kind of stuff."

The business deal with ISI meant the Lakeside Programmers Group would have to become a formal partnership. Gates' dad helped with the legal formalities and also assisted with the ISI contract. He became the group's principal legal adviser. Gates and Evans were 15 years old. Evans kept a journal of the ISI project, and it gives a rare insight into kids who, when it came to business, were wise beyond their years. Wrote Evans in one entry: "We've been writing a very complicated payroll program. March 16 is our deadline. This is very educational because we've learned a lot by working in a business environment and dealing with government agencies. During the past few weeks we've been frantically trying to get it done. Tuesday we go to Portland to deliver the program, and as they have put it, 'Hammer out an agreement on future work.' Everything so far has been done for its educational benefits and for large amounts of expensive computer time. Now we want to get some monetary benefits, too."

Gates, Allen, Evans, and Weiland boarded a bus to Portland when the program was done for a meeting with ISI's executives. After the meeting, Kent wrote, ". . . we all were given pencil and paper to write resumes to aid them in hiring us . . . money had not been mentioned. Paul, Bill and I didn't want to be paid hourly rates, so we mentioned piece rates for programmed products or royalty arrangements. The royalty scheme went over big. We get about ten percent of the money ISI gets because of one of our programs—we get more in the long run and the company doesn't need to tie up any of its capital."

It's not clear how much, if anything, the group made in royalties from their payroll project, but ISI gave them about $10,000 worth of free computer time.

"If anybody wants to know why Bill Gates is where he is today, in my judgment it's because of this early experience cutting deals," said Marvin Evans, Kent's father.

Allen graduated from Lakeside in 1971 and enrolled that fall at Washington State University, majoring in computer science. But he and Gates were already working on another money-making project involving their own company, which they called Traf-O-Data.

The idea behind their enterprise was ingenious. Almost every municipality used metal boxes linked to rubber hoses that stretched across the roadway to count cars. These traffic boxes contained a 16-channel paper tape (twice as wide as the 8-channel tape used in old teletype machines), and each time a car passed over the rubber hose, the machine punched the tape with the binary numbers zero and one. The numbers reflected time and volume. Municipalities hired private companies to translate this raw data into information city engineers could then use, for example, to determine how long a traffic light needed to be red or green for the best traffic flow.

But the companies providing these services were slow and expensive. Gates and Allen figured they could program a computer to analyze the traffic-counter tapes, then sell the information to municipalities faster and cheaper than the competition. Gates recruited seventh and eighth graders at Lakeside to transcribe the numbers from the traffic tapes onto computer cards, which he then punched into the CDC computer at the University of Washington. His software program turned the data into easily readable traffic-flow charts.

Chris Larson, four years behind Gates, was one of a handful of students hired at low wages to transcribe numbers from the traffic tapes onto the computer punch cards. His cousin, Brad Augustine, was also hired for the Traf-O-Data work. Several other students helped out, as did a few mothers when the kids were overwhelmed with homework.

Once Traf-O-Data was up and running, Allen decided he and Gates should build their own computer to analyze the traffic tapes directly, thus eliminating the need for manual work. It proved a difficult task. They hired a Boeing engineer to help with the hardware design. Gates came up with $360, and he and Allen purchased one of Intel's new 8008 microprocessor chips, one of the first of the chips sold through a distributor anywhere in the country. They connected a 16-channel paper tape reader to their "computer," and fed traffic-counter tapes directly into the machine.

It was not nearly as capable as the microcomputers that would come later, but the Traf-O-Data machine worked—most of the time. Mary Gates once recalled her son demonstrating his traffic machine to a city official in her dining room. When the computer crashed, and the official lost interest, Bill pleaded with his mother, "Tell him mom, tell him it really works!"

Gates and Allen reportedly grossed about $20,000 from Traf-O-Data. But the enterprise was never a great success, and it eventually folded after Gates went off to college.

During his junior year at Lakeside, while finding business for Traf-O-Data, Gates came up with other money-making schemes. He and Evans formed another computer group, called Logic Simulation Company, and they sent out student flyers to drum up business and a cheap labor force.

One of their letters to Lakeside students said: "LPG and LSC are two computer-oriented computer organizations involved in a number of attempts to make money. These include class scheduling, working on traffic volume studies, producing cookbooks. . . . We want to expand our work force, which now has five Lakesiders. It's not just for computer freaks. We think we will need people who can type and do drafting and architectural drawings. If interested, see Kent Evans or Bill Gates or Chris Larson."

The letter mentioned "equal opportunity for males and females," and included a form for interested students to note how many hours they might be able to work, their availability for summer employment, and their computer experience.

In May 1972, near the end of their junior year, Gates and Evans were approached by the Lakeside administration about computerizing the school's class schedule for its nearly 400 students. The scheduling system had long been a time-consuming mess. Lakeside wanted the new computer program ready for the start of the 1972–73 school year in the fall. A former Boeing engineer who had been hired as a math teacher at Lakeside had been working on the project, but he was killed in a plane crash. The job now fell to Gates and Evans.

Tragically, less than a week later, on May 28, Memorial Day weekend, Kent Evans was killed in a mountain-climbing accident. A few months after Evans died, the school learned he was among its 11 semifinalists in the National Merit Scholarship Test. Gates, too, made the list (the next year he would be a finalist). After Evans died, a shaken Gates asked Allen to help him with the class scheduling project. They agreed to do it that summer when Allen returned from Washington State University.

(In 1986, Gates and Allen gave Lakeside $2.2 million to build a science and math center named after them, dedicating the building's auditorium to Evans.)

The first month or so of that summer, as a kind of farewell tribute to Evans, who loved politics as much as computers, Gates went to Washington, D.C., as a page in the U.S. House of Representatives. His parents had gotten him the job through Brock Adams, who was now a congressional representative. Gates quickly showed his talent for making business deals. He bought 5,000 McGovern-Eagleton buttons for a nickel each—$250 worth. When George McGovern dropped Thomas Eagleton from the presidential ticket, Gates sold the scarce buttons as collector's items for $25 each, making several thousand dollars in profit.

When Congress adjourned for the summer recess, Gates returned to Seattle to help Allen with the class-scheduling work. They wrote their program using the free computer time they had accrued from Information Sciences Inc. Lakeside paid them for that computer time as well, and they made a couple thousand dollars in spending money. The scheduling program they designed is still used at Lakeside, although it has been refined over the years.

The schedule proved a big hit with students that fall, particularly to some members of the senior class who—thanks to Gates and some creative scheduling—didn't have any classes on Tuesday afternoon. The group of seniors wore silk-screen T-shirts, with "Tuesday Club" printed on the shirts over the outline of a keg of beer.

Girls had been admitted to Lakeside at the start of Gates' junior year, when Lakeside merged with St. Nicholas, an all-girls school. Gates signed up for a drama class during his senior year that included some of the first female students to attend Lakeside. As a result, Gates landed leading roles in two school plays, *The Night the Bed Fell*, by James Thurber, and *Black Comedy*, by English playwright Peter Shaffer. The Thurber play required that Gates memorize a three-page monologue. Gates, with a nearly photographic memory, merely glanced at the pages for a few seconds and had the material memorized.

"I thought to myself," recalled Anne Stephens, who directed Gates in both plays, "how's this gawky guy going to carry this off? It's a very dry piece. But he did a delightful job in the play. He was absolutely charming."

With the success of the class-scheduling project, Gates continued to look for money-making opportunities during his senior year. He sent letters to area schools, offering to computerize their schedule. He offered a system that he said was 95 percent conflict-free.

"We use a unique scheduling service developed by Lakeside," his letter said. "We would like to provide scheduling for your school as well. A good job at a reasonable cost—$2 to $2.50 per student. We would appreciate opportunities to discuss this with you."

Gates was able to land a job writing the first computer program for class registration at what was known as the Experimental College at the University of Washington. The school was staffed by UW students and provided alternative courses at affordable fees. It was run not by the university but by the university's student government association.

Gates was hired for the programming job by the association. One problem arose, however, and it did not have to do with the program he wrote. His sister Kristi, a student at the University of Washington at the time, was an officer on the student government association. When the campus paper learned her brother had received the scheduling contract, it accused the association of nepotism. In the end, Gates made very little money from the project, about $500.

As he entered the second trimester of his senior year, Gates was still looking for a way to use his computer experiences to earn "real" money. He didn't have to wait long.

One day Gates received a call from a man from TRW, the giant defense contractor. Moments later, Gates was on the phone to Washington State University in Pullman, trying to reach Paul Allen with the news.

TRW, Gates hurriedly explained to Allen, wanted the two of them to go down to Vancouver for a job interview as soon as possible. "Paul, it's our chance to finally make some real money! We gotta do it."

Paul Allen didn't need any coaxing. Although he was only in his second year at Washington State University, Allen was weary of college life, and restless. He wanted to get out in the real world, apply what he knew about computers, and make some money. Perhaps he and Bill might form their own software company. They had talked about doing just that many times.

Up to now the payback from their business ventures had been mostly in the form of free computer time, first at C-Cubed and then at Information Sciences. But TRW offered a full-time job with a salary.

The giant government defense contractor was in trouble. TRW was in the midst of a project to computerize the Bonneville

Power Administration's power grid for the Northwest. Computers would analyze the power needs of the region and control the amount of electricity generated by hydroelectric dams on the Columbia River. TRW had set up offices in Vancouver, across the Columbia River from Portland. The power-monitoring system would use several PDP-10 computers, and TRW was to write the software. But the project soon fell behind schedule. As usual, the PDP-10 software was infested with bugs. The contract called for a real-time control system with 99.9 percent reliability; if TRW couldn't get the software problems fixed, and soon, it would have to pay substantial contract penalties.

It was time to call in the exterminators.

An urgent request was made from TRW's headquarters in Cleveland for bug-hunting experts with PDP-10 software. Following a lead from Digital Equipment Corporation, a TRW technician discovered the Problem Report Book at the bankrupt Computer Center Corporation in Seattle. The names of two bug hunters appeared on nearly every page—Bill Gates and Paul Allen. TRW contacted Gates by phone at his home, suggesting he and Allen come down to Vancouver for an interview.

"Bill and I went down there dressed in the best suits we could find," Allen said.

Despite their youth, Gates and Allen were offered jobs, at $165 a week.

"We were just thrilled," Allen said. "Up to that point, we had never been paid real money for doing anything on a computer. . . . To get paid for something we loved doing . . . we thought that was great."

Instead of crashing the PDP-10 as they had done at C-Cubed, they were hired to work on restoring the system when it did crash.

Gates received permission from Lakeside to miss the second trimester of his senior year so he could work full-time at TRW. Allen dropped out of Washington State University, and the two found an apartment in Vancouver, 160 miles from Seattle.

It was at TRW that Gates began to develop as a serious computer programmer. Computer programming is more of an art than a science. The best programmers have a style as recognizable to other programmers as the brush stroke of a great painter. Gates fancies himself a master programmer, although today he hasn't written code in years because he's too busy running his company.

There were several top-notch programmers on the TRW project. One of the best was John Norton. He liked to write endless memos commenting on a programmer's code. It was the first time Gates had seen anyone respond that way before, and it left a lasting impression. To this day, Gates sends his own electronic memos to his programmers at Microsoft, commenting on their codes. Often they are critical and sarcastic. More than one unlucky programmer at Microsoft has received E-mail at 2:00 A.M. that began, "This is the stupidest piece of code ever written."

Norton liked Gates and became something of a mentor, helping the intense, inquisitive teenager hone his programming skills. Whenever Gates made a mistake or did sloppy work, Norton would review his code and explain what he had done wrong or how he could do it better and more efficiently.

There was, however, still the matter of finishing high school. In the spring of 1973, having already been accepted at Harvard for the fall, Gates returned to Seattle for his final trimester at Lakeside. Although he had missed three months of school work, he quickly caught up. In a calculus class, he made his only appearance to take the final exam, which he aced. He received a "B" in the course, however, because the teacher felt that by never showing up, Gates had not displayed the "right attitude."

Gates' self-confidence was at an all-time high. Bill Hucks, also in the class of '73 at Lakeside, remembers a squash match with Gates in the school gym shortly before they graduated in June. After the match, which Gates won, Hucks asked him, "So what's your story? Where do you go from here?"

Gates said he was heading off to Harvard in the fall. Then he added, in a very matter-of-fact way: "I'm going to make my first million by the time I'm 25." It was not said as a boast, or even a prediction. He talked about the future as if his success was predestined, a given, as certain as the mathematical proof that one plus one equals two.

"I remember it not surprising me," said Hucks, who later went into journalism and now sells medical equipment in the Seattle area. "It was no big deal that this Gates guy was ambitious and was going to make money. Everyone at school knew his background."

Following graduation, Gates returned to Vancouver to continue working with Allen on the TRW project. But his summer wasn't completely a binary existence of zeros and ones, of late-night pizza and Coke in front of a computer terminal. He used part of his salary to buy a speed boat, and he and his friends water-skied on nearby lakes in Oregon and Washington when time allowed on weekends.

As the summer wore on and it was nearly time for Gates to leave Vancouver to attend college, he and Allen began to talk seriously about forming their own software company. For some time now they had shared the same vision, that one day the computer would be as commonplace in the home as a television set, and that these computers would need software—their software.

"We always had big dreams," Allen said.

CHAPTER 2

"It's Going to Happen"

Bill Gates would later tell a friend he went to Harvard University to learn from people smarter than he was . . . and left disappointed.

He had arrived in Cambridge in the fall of 1973 with no real sense of what he wanted to do with his life. Although he listed his academic major as prelaw, he had little interest in becoming a lawyer like his father. Nor did his parents have any expectations that he would. There was no pressure on him to be this or that. They only insisted he go to college and mix with other students. And what better environment for their son than Harvard, America's oldest institution of higher learning? There was a mystique about the place. It conjured up images of success, power, influence . . . greatness. Supreme Court justices went to Harvard. So did presidents. Now their son had ascended into this rarefied intellectual atmosphere. Any plans he had to form a software company with Paul Allen would have to wait, his parents insisted.

"I was always vague about what I was going to do, but my parents wanted me to go to undergraduate school," Gates said.

"They didn't want me to go start a company or just go do graduate work. They didn't have a specific plan in mind, but they thought I should live with other undergraduates, take normal undergraduate courses . . . which is exactly what I did."

At Harvard, most first-year students live in dormitories in and near what is known as the Yard, next to Harvard Square in Cambridge. The Yard is the center of what was the original college, founded in 1636, just 16 years after the Pilgrims landed at Plymouth. At the end of their first year, students can apply to live in twelve residential houses.

Gates was assigned to one of the dorms his freshman year and roomed with two other students, Sam Znaimer and Jim Jenkins. They had been assigned the same room by chance. They didn't know each other. The three came from vastly different backgrounds and cultures—just the kind of environment Gates' parents were hoping for. Gates was a rich white kid from Seattle. Znaimer was a poor Jewish kid from Canada whose parents had immigrated to Montreal after the Holocaust. He was attending Harvard on a scholarship, majoring in chemistry. Jenkins was a middle-class black kid from Chattanooga, Tennessee, whose father was in the service.

"I found Bill fascinating," recalled Znaimer, who today is a venture capitalist in Vancouver, British Columbia. "I had not run into too many people from fairly affluent, WASP backgrounds. I didn't know those kinds of people in Montreal. Bill was someone who came from a comfortable family and had gone to a private school. He would talk about how some governor of the state of Washington used to hang out with his grandfather . . . which was not the world I was used to. On the other hand, Bill was very down-to-earth. There was not a lot of bullshit or pompousness about him. We all lived more or less the same lifestyle. We all ate together, worked together, and as a group we were all interested in science, engineering and that kind of stuff. We also all loved science fiction."

When he enrolled at Harvard, Gates received permission to take both graduate and undergraduate courses. That was not unusual for gifted students. What was unusual was that he was allowed to set aside those graduate-level courses in math, physics, and computer science and apply the credits toward a graduate degree later. "About two-thirds of my courses were toward my undergraduate degree and about a third were set aside for my graduate degree, although it all doesn't matter now since I didn't complete either one," said Gates.

That first year he took one of Harvard's most difficult math courses, called "Math 55." Almost everyone in the class had scored a perfect 800 on the math portion of the Scholastic Aptitude Test. Gates did well in the course, but he was not the best. Two other students finished ahead of him, including Andy Braiterman, who lived in the same dorm as Gates. Braiterman had entered Harvard as a sophomore. He and Gates became good friends and later roomed together.

Gates took the typical undergraduate courses in economics, history, literature, and psychology. His attitude toward class work was much the same as it had been at Lakeside. He worked hard and did well in those courses he cared about. He didn't work hard in courses that didn't interest him. However, he still did well because he was so smart. In Greek literature his freshman year, Gates fell asleep during the final exam but still managed to receive a "B" in the class. "He was really very proud of that," recalled Braiterman. "It was a story he liked to tell on himself."

That Gates would fall asleep in class was not surprising. He was living on the edge. It was not unusual for him to go as long as three days without sleep. "How he coped with lack of sleep I never figured out," said Znaimer. "I would kind of wimp out after 18 to 24 hours, but his habit was to do 36 hours or more at a stretch, collapse for ten hours, then go out, get a pizza, and go back at it. And if that meant he was starting again at three o'clock in the morning, so be it."

His sleeping habits were just as bizarre. Gates never slept on sheets. He would collapse on his unmade bed, pull an electric blanket over his head and fall asleep instantly and soundly, regardless of the hour or activity in his room. (Gates still falls asleep instantaneously. When he flies, he often puts a blanket over his head and sleeps for the entire flight.)

"He didn't seem to pay much attention to things he didn't care about, whether it was clothes or sleep," said Znaimer.

To his roommates and the small group of students he hung out with, Gates was a very intense character. He would often work himself into a frenzy of energy and start rocking back and forth, head in his hands, during a conversation or while reading or concentrating on a mental problem. Sometimes, he would wave his arms madly about to make a point in conversations.

Much of this energy was directed toward computers, just as it had been at Lakeside. Although Gates may not have decided what he was going to do with his life when he entered Harvard, to those who knew him there was little doubt about his real passion. He worked for weeks during his first year there on a BASIC program for a computer baseball game, which required that he figure out highly complex algorithms that would represent figures on the computer screen hitting, throwing, and catching a baseball. Even when he was sound asleep under his electric blanket, Gates was dreaming about computers. Once, about three o'clock in the morning, Gates began talking in his sleep, repeating over and over again, "One comma, one comma, one comma, one comma . . ."

He spent many nights that year in the Aiken Computer Center at Harvard, which also had a PDP-10. Znaimer would sometimes drop by the computer building and find Gates hacking away at one of the machines. There were several games on the computers, including Steve Russell's "Space Wars," and Gates and Znaimer would play computer games into the early morning hours.

To unwind and relax, Gates, Znaimer, and Braiterman would go to movies in Cambridge or play pinball in an upstairs lounge in their dorm. The lounge also had an early version of the video game "Pong." (This game had been designed by Nolan Bushnell, and it made him rich and famous. He sold the game through his startup company, Atari.)

As usual, when it came to games the competitive Gates almost always won. He became an exceptional player at both pinball and "Pong."

"Other than playing pinball and going to a lot of movies," said Znaimer, "we were all doing our share of sex, drugs and rock 'n' roll . . . with the exception that the rest of us were more overwhelmed by our hormones than Bill. I don't remember him chasing any women, and there were lots of opportunities."

No one who knew Gates at Harvard can recall him ever dating anyone while he was there. He did see one young woman occasionally when he returned home on holiday breaks to Seattle, but they were not romantically involved. The woman was Karen Gloyd, a freshman at Whitman College in Washington State. Gloyd was a couple years younger than Gates, having entered college early, at age 16. They met through their parents. Her stepfather was on the state bar association's board of governors, as was Gates' father. Gates did not make a very good impression on Gloyd. He lacked the social graces a young lady would have expected of a Harvard man. It was clear to Gloyd that Gates had had little experience with women. The first thing he wanted to know when they met was the score she made on her college SAT.

"It didn't strike me as being a great pickup line at the time," recalled Gloyd, now married. "It's kind of amusing looking back on it, but at the time I really wasn't that amused. I thought maybe I hadn't heard him right. I thought it rather odd to say the least." Gates then proceeded to explain to Gloyd that he had taken his Scholastic Aptitude Test twice so he could make a perfect score of 1600. (Math and verbal scores each count a maximum of 800 points.) Gates told her that when he first took the test, he breezed through the math portion but made a silly mistake and ended up with 790 points. The second time he took the test he got a perfect math score of 800. "At that point in the conversation," said Gloyd, "I assumed we had very little in common."

They did see each other a few more times. Once, when both were home from college, they accompanied their fathers on a bar association trip to Friday Harbor in the scenic San Juan Islands. Gloyd and several other young people on the trip took off in their parents' cars and went into town at night to dance and party. Gates, however, stayed behind and played poker with the adults.

"Bill and I played tennis together a few times, but we really didn't have much in common socially," said Gloyd. "I always thought he was really nice, but I just thought he was sort of a brain, and I was more into partying, sororities, and that kind of thing. Bill was real shy. I didn't get the impression at the time that he had a lot of experience dating girls and going out and doing social things. I may have thought of him then as being nerdy, but I think he just didn't want to spend a lot of time doing things he wasn't interested in."

Although Gates may not have had much experience with girls, he did have experiences of another kind that set him apart from many of his peers at Harvard. He had already been out there in the "real world." He even had his own company, Traf-O-Data.

"That was one of the more interesting things about Bill," said Znaimer. "Compared to the rest of us at Harvard, he was much more broadly grounded. You could find other people who were really good mathematicians or really good physicists. But Bill had a lot more hands-on experience. He had gone and worked in various environments, like TRW."

Znaimer remembered Gates spending several nights in his dorm room in early 1974 working on an IRS tax return for his Traf-O-Data business. "I could not have told you which way was up on a tax form. It was something my parents did," Znaimer said. "But Bill sure knew."

While Gates was finishing his first year at Harvard, Paul Allen was back in Washington State trying to find new business for Traf-O-Data. He had negotiated deals with municipalities in several states, as well as Canada. But the enterprise was being undercut by the federal government, which had decided to help cities and counties analyze traffic statistics.

No one was going to pay Gates and Allen for this service when the feds would do it for nothing. Their contracts in Canada were not enough to keep the business going. At one point, they even considered selling Traf-O-Data machines to a firm in Brazil, but the deal fell through. With their company on the skids, Gates and Allen began having long telephone discussions about what they should do next. Allen decided he would join his friend after Gates completed his first year. They would work together and "brainstorm" about future projects. Much to his parents' dismay, Gates was even thinking about dropping out of Harvard. He and Allen were serious about starting their own computer company, he told his parents. That summer of 1974, Gates interviewed for a job at various places around Boston, including Honeywell, one of the so-called Seven Dwarfs that made mainframe computers in the shadow of Snow White—mighty IBM. A manager at Honeywell who interviewed Gates telephoned Allen in Seattle.

"I've just seen this friend of yours, and he really impressed me with his abilities," the guy told Allen. "We'd like to offer you a job, too. Come on out to Boston and we'll finalize the deal."

Allen packed up his Chrysler New Yorker and headed east, driving across the country in three days to join Gates. But when Allen got to Boston, he was in for a surprise. He went to Honeywell dressed in his best suit to talk with the manager who had called him in Seattle. "That was a great discussion we had on the phone," the man told a startled Allen, "but we really didn't offer you a job." It took some tense negotiating, but Allen got the job. He and Gates worked together at Honeywell for the rest of the summer.

Gates and Allen were convinced the computer industry was about to reach critical mass, and when it exploded it would usher in a technological revolution of astounding magnitude. They were on the threshold of one of those moments when history held its breath . . . and jumped, as it had done with the development of the car and the airplane. Computer power was about to come to the masses. Their vision of a computer in every home was no longer a wild dream. "It's going to happen," Allen kept telling his friend. And they could either lead the revolution or be swept along by it. Allen was much more eager to start a company than Gates, who was worried about the reaction from his family if he dropped out of school.

"Paul kept saying, let's start a company, let's do it," Gates recalled. "Paul saw that the technology was there. He kept saying, 'It's gonna be too late. We'll miss it.' "

For a while, they considered building their own computer. Allen was more interested in computer hardware than Gates, whose interest was pure software—the "soul" of The Machine. As a boy, Allen had read electronics magazines and built radio and shortwave sets. He had worked with vacuum tubes, transistors, and finally with integrated circuits when he helped design the Traf-O-Data machine. But that experience also taught him what it took to build a computer. He and Gates soon abandoned the idea. They decided to stick with what they knew best—software. Building a computer was too hair-raising.

"We saw that hardware was a black art," Allen said. "That was not our area of expertise. Our forte was software."

By the fall of 1974, Gates had decided he would remain in school. The time just wasn't right to start their company. Allen stayed on at Honeywell while Gates returned to Harvard to begin his sophomore year.

Gates landed in Currier House, where he roomed with his friend Andy Braiterman. These residential houses at Harvard, each with its own dining facility, are modeled after the residential colleges of Oxford and Cambridge universities. Gates' former roommate, Znaimer, ended up at North House, about a hundred yards from Currier House.

Clearly, Gates was confused about his academic future. He would later say that he spent many hours sitting in his room "being a philosophical depressed guy, trying to figure out what I was doing with my life." He started playing poker. Lots of poker. This great American game of riverboat gamblers and U.S. presidents became as all-consuming to Gates as computers. He put the same intensity into his poker playing as he did anything else that mattered. When he first started playing poker, Gates was terrible. But he was very determined, and eventually became a pretty good player. "Bill had a monomaniacal quality," said Braiterman, his roommate. "He would focus on something and really stick with it. He had a determination to master whatever it was he was doing. Perhaps it's silly to compare poker and Microsoft, but in each case, Bill was sort of deciding where he was going to put his energy and to hell with what anyone else thought."

This was serious poker the boys played, not a friendly penny-ante family game. It was not unusual for players to win or lose several hundred dollars a night. A $2,000 loss was not unheard of. The game of choice was Seven Card Stud, high-low split, meaning the player with the best poker hand splits the pot with the player with the worst hand.

The games were played nightly in Currier House in a room that was hardly ever used for anything else. It became known as the "poker room." Regulars at the table were some of the best and brightest at Currier House, including Tom Wolf, Greg Nelson, Scott Drill, and Brad Leithauser. Braiterman also played, although not nearly as much as his roommate. Other than Gates, none of the poker crowd went on to become billionaires, but they didn't do badly, either. Wolf, known as the "Captain" of the games, is a mathematics professor at the California Institute of Technology in Pasadena. Nelson is with Digital Equipment Corporation's research center in Palo Alto. Drill is president of Varitronics Systems, an office machine firm in Minneapolis. Leithauser is a poet, author, and frequent contributor to *The New Yorker*. He teaches at Mt. Holyoke College. Braiterman is a top Wall Street tax attorney.

By most accounts, Gates became a good enough player to hold his own with this crowd. "He was a fine player—when he could pry himself away from his beloved PDP-10 computer," recalled Nelson.

"I was good," said Gates. "But what happened was that when we first started out, all these guys from the business school and the medical school would come in, and they weren't very good. So we would raise the stakes, and people would lose their money and they would leave. Toward the end of the poker games at Harvard, it was guys who all we did full-time was play poker. By the very end, I was just able to hold my own."

There were a few games that went on for 24 hours. Trying to break his addiction, Gates once gave Allen custody of his checkbook. Then he asked for it back.

Drill said he often got the best of Gates in big pots when they went *mano-a-mano*. Gates, he said, had a tendency to play out his hand to the costly end whenever he believed he had correctly "read" other players at the table. Because of this tendency, Drill would sometimes razz Gates. He came up with a nickname for Gates from a popular dog food commercial of the day. "Here comes the Gravy Train," Drill would say, as Gates relentlessly threw more and more chips into the pot, refusing to fold his hand.

"My perception of Bill's lifestyle, and it was a lot of people's perception, was that he spent his time either playing poker or in the computer room," recalled Drill.

One student at Currier House who heard all about Gates' poker exploits was Steve Ballmer, who lived just down the hall. After a long night of gambling, Gates would sometimes drop by

Ballmer's room to recount his adventures at the poker table. Ballmer was usually awake. He was able to go without sleep as long as Gates could. They had the same intensity level, the same unlimited energy source. They were on the same wavelength. In Gatesspeak, it's known as "high bandwidth communication," or the amount of information one can absorb. The two would often engage in heated debates, exchanging information at a high band rate like two computers connected by modem. A short while into most conversations, Gates and Ballmer would start rocking in sync, talking at the same time but hearing every word the other said.

Several years later, Gates would ask Ballmer to join him at the controls of the Microsoft joyride. He would become the second most influential person in the company, next to Chairman Bill.

Ballmer was much more social than Gates. He seemed to know everyone at Harvard. He convinced Gates to join the Men's Club at Currier House. As an initiation rite, Gates was blindfolded, dressed in a tuxedo, and brought to the dining room table, where he was ordered to talk about computers.

Just as Gates wanted to be accepted as one of the boys back at Lakeside in Seattle, he also wanted to fit in at Harvard . . . to belong to a fraternity and be part of "the group." But it wasn't in his nature. Despite his association with the outgoing Ballmer, Gates was very much a loner with only a small group of friends. His shyness often came across as aloofness.

"Bill and Steve were polar opposites," said Braiterman. "Bill was really not a social kind of guy. He was not the sort of person who hung out with a lot of people. I don't mean he wasn't social in the sense of being unfriendly or anything. He just wasn't very outgoing. Steve was."

Ballmer did not have the passion for computers or the technical background that Gates had, but he did share his interest in mathematics. Ballmer was working on a degree in applied mathematics. At one time in high school, Gates had thought about becoming a mathematician. It was one of many career possibilities. Now, at Harvard, he was having second thoughts as he sized up his competition. Still, he continued to take graduate-level math courses his sophomore year.

"He would sit in class without even a pad of paper, resting his head on his hands," recalled Henry Leitner, who took a graduate math course with Gates on the theory of computations. "He would look very bored, then a half hour into a proof on the blackboard, Bill would raise his hand and blurt out, 'You made a mistake, I'll show you.' Then he would trace the mistake back. He would stump the teacher. He seemed to take great joy in that." Leitner, now a senior lecturer in computer science at Harvard, was a graduate student at the time. He and Gates sat next to each other in class, and were supposed to collaborate on homework problems. But Leitner couldn't get the younger Gates to work on problems he didn't think worthy of his time. Gates only liked the challenge of the most difficult problems. "I used to wonder what I was doing trying to work with this guy," said Leitner. "He would only do about 20 percent of the work. But it was worth it. A couple minutes on the phone with him and he would straighten me out on a complex math problem. He was a real character."

At Lakeside, Gates had been the best student in the school at math. Even at Harvard, he was one of the top math students. But he was not *the* best. He had met several students better than he was at math, including Fred Commoner, the son of scientist-author Barry Commoner. Gates eventually gave up any thoughts of becoming a mathematician. If he couldn't be the best in his field, why risk failure?

"I met several people in the math department who were quite a bit better than I was at math," said Gates. "It changed my view about going into math. You can persevere in the field of math and make incredible breakthroughs, but it probably discouraged me. It made the odds much longer that I could do some world-class thing. I had to really think about it: Hey, I'm going to sit in a room, staring at a wall for five years, and even if I come up with something, who knows. So it made me think about whether math was something I wanted to do or not. But there were so many choices. My mind was pretty much open. I thought law would be fun. . . . I thought physiological psychology—the study of the brain—would be fun. . . . I thought working in artificial intelligence would be fun. . . . I thought theoretical computer science would be fun. . . . I really had not zeroed in on something. . . ."

It's not well known outside a few of his professors, but Gates did make one small but noteworthy contribution in the field of mathematics while at Harvard. He helped advance the solution to a mathematical puzzle that had been around for some time. No one had come up with a definitive solution.

This was the puzzle, as it had appeared in several mathematical journals: "The chef in our place is sloppy, and when he prepares a stack of pancakes they come out all different sizes. Therefore, when I deliver them to a customer, on the way to the table I rearrange them (so that the smallest winds up on top, and so on, down to the largest at the bottom) by grabbing several from the top and flipping them over, repeating this (varying the number I flip) as many times as necessary. If there are "n" pancakes, what is the maximum number of flips (as a function of "n") that I will ever have to use to rearrange them?"

Gates was assisted in his work on the puzzle by then Harvard professor Christos Papadimitriou, who taught computer science. Gates considered the math puzzle very similar to the kind of challenges he faced when working on a complicated computer program in which he had to design algorithms to solve a specific problem.

"This was a simple problem that had proved very stubborn," said Papadimitriou. "Bill claimed to have a way of doing it better than anyone else, and I was patient enough to suffer through his long and ingenious explanation." Later, Papadimitriou decided to write up Bill's solution, and it was published in 1979 in the journal *Discrete Mathematics*. The breakthrough Gates made on the puzzle has remained on the cutting edge of the field for the past 15 or so years, according to Papadimitriou, who is now at the University of California in San Diego. The professor occasionally gives the puzzle to some of his students and tells them if they solve it, he will quit his job and work for them. "I should have done this with Bill," he said.

Gates may not have been the best math student at Harvard, but he had no peers in computer science. His professors were impressed not only by his smarts, but his enormous energy. "There's one in a handful who come through in computer science that you know from the day they show up on the doorstep they will be very, very good," said professor Tom Cheatham, director of the Center for Research and Computing Technology at Harvard. "No doubt, he was going to go places."

Although Gates took several computer science classes from Cheatham, they did not like each other. "Gates had a bad personality and a great intellect," recalled Cheatham. "In a place like Harvard, where there are a lot of bright kids, when you are better than your peers, some tend to be nice and others obnoxious. He was the latter."

When Gates wasn't playing poker at night, he was usually working in the Aiken Computer Center. That was when the machines were least used. Sometimes, an exhausted Gates would fall asleep on computer work tables instead of returning to his room at Currier House. "There were many mornings when I would find him dead asleep on the tables," recalled Leitner, the graduate math student who was also interested in computers. "I remember thinking he was not going to amount to anything. He seemed like a hacker, a nerd. I knew he was bright, but with those glasses, his dandruff, sleeping on tables, you sort of formed that impression. I obviously didn't see the future as clearly as he did."

But Paul Allen saw the future. He may have seen it even more clearly than Gates.

On a cold winter day in December 1974, Allen was walking across Harvard Square in Cambridge on his way to visit Gates, when he stopped at a kiosk and spotted the upcoming January issue of *Popular Electronics*, a magazine he had read regularly since childhood. This issue, however, sent his heart pounding. On the cover was a picture of the Altair 8080, a rectangular metal machine with toggle switches and lights on the front. "World's First Microcomputer Kit to Rival Commercial Models," screamed the magazine cover headline.

"I bought a copy, read it, and raced back to Bill's dorm to talk to him," said Allen, who was still working at Honeywell in nearby Boston. "I told Bill, 'Well here's our opportunity to do something with BASIC.' "

He convinced his younger friend to stop playing poker long enough to finally do something with this new technology. Allen, a student of Shakespeare, was reminded of what the Bard himself wrote, in *Julius Caesar:* "There is a tide in the affairs of men, which, taken at the flood, leads on to fortune. Omitted, all the voyage of their life is bound in shallows and in miseries. On such a full sea are we now afloat, and we must take the current when it serves, or lose our ventures."

Gates knew Allen was right. It was time. The personal computer miracle was going to happen.

———————

It was named after a star and had only enough memory to hold about a paragraph's worth of information. But the Altair, the people's entry into the dazzling new world of computers, represented nearly 150 years of technological evolution and thought.

Although what we know as the modern computer had arrived some 30 years before the Altair, in the 1940s during World War II, the concept of such a machine came from the mind of an eccentric 19th century mathematical genius named Charles

Babbage, who developed the first reliable life-expectancy tables. In 1834, having already invented the speedometer and the cow-catcher for locomotives, Babbage put all his creative energies into the design of a steam-powered machine he called the "Analytical Engine." Frustrated by inaccuracies he found in the mathematical tables of the day, Babbage wanted to build a machine to solve mathematical equations. On paper, his Analytical Engine consisted of thousands of gears and cogs turned by steam, and a logic center that Babbage called "the mill." His design called for a machine the size of a football field. Such an undertaking also called for huge sums of money, and when the government stopped backing the project, Babbage was helped financially by Augusta Ada, the Countess of Lovelace and daughter of the poet Lord Byron. The beautiful and scientific-minded countess was a fine mathematician herself and is now considered the first computer programmer. The countess planned to use punch cards to instruct the Analytical Engine what to do. She got the idea from the cards used on Jacquard looms to determine the design on cloth. "The Analytical Engine weaves algebraic patterns just as the Jacquard loom weaves flowers and leaves," she wrote.

Although Babbage devoted almost 40 years of his life to the project, his Analytical Engine was never completed. The technology just wasn't there to make it possible.

By the end of the century, however, punch cards were used in a test to help tabulate information from the 1890 Census. The electric tabulating machine used in this experiment was designed by a young engineer named Herman Hollerith. Soon, punch cards were widely used in all kinds of office machines, and Hollerith's company was absorbed by a New York firm that would later become the biggest name in computers—International Business Machines.

In the 1930s, IBM agreed to finance the development of a large computing machine. It gave Howard Aiken, a Harvard professor for whom the university's computer center was later named, $500,000 to develop the Mark 1. When it was finally completed in 1944, the Mark 1 could multiply two 23-digit numbers in about five seconds. But it was an electromechanical machine, which meant that thousands of noisy relays served as switching units, opening and closing as the machine performed its dim-witted calculations.

The vacuum tube soon replaced electromechanical relay switches and gave birth to ENIAC, the first electronic digital computer in the United States. It was unveiled in 1946 at the University of Pennsylvania. Built to calculate artillery firing tables for the military, ENIAC (for Electronic Numerical Integrator and Calculator) weighed 30 tons and contained 18,000 vacuum tubes, 70,000 resistors, and 10,000 capacitors. It took up more space than the average two-car garage. The ENIAC cost about a half-million dollars to develop and could handle about 5,000 additions and subtractions per second. Today, any inexpensive home computer can outperform the ENIAC. The machine was not very reliable. Its tubes failed on the average of once every seven minutes. Still, it was used during final stages of completion to do mathematical calculations for the physicists at Los Alamos who were building the first atomic bomb.

The big breakthrough in computing technology came two days before Christmas in 1947, when three scientists working at Bell Labs tested a crystal device known as the transistor, short for "transfer resistance." (They would win the Nobel Prize for the invention.) These tiny crystals, or semiconductors as they became known, acted like switches, controlling the flow of electricity in circuits. Semiconductors replaced the vacuum tube. They were much smaller and more reliable. They didn't give off as much heat as tubes did, so they could be packaged close together. They had no moving parts, so they were less likely to fail. And perhaps most important of all, semiconductors were cheap to make. The first ones were made out of crystals of germanium. Later, silicon became more popular.

William Shockley, one of the inventors of the transistor, left Bell Labs to return home to Palo Alto in the Santa Clara Valley of California to form his own company in the heart of what would become known as the Silicon Valley. Other companies soon hired away the Bell Lab's star scientists and began turning out semiconductors, including Texas Instruments.

Another technological leap came in the late 1950s, when networks of transistors were etched on a single piece of silicon with thin metallic connectors. These integrated circuits, or chips, became the foundation of all modern electronics.

Computers, meanwhile, got smaller, faster, and more powerful. IBM dominated the playing field in the 1950s. Business writers referred to the other makers of large, mainframe computers as the Seven Dwarfs—RCA, General Electric, Honeywell, Burroughs, NCR, Sperry Univac, and Control Data Corporation. The so-called giant brain computers made by these corporations were big and expensive. They could easily fill several rooms and cost hundreds of thousands of dollars. A priesthood of technicians was needed to watch over them. The machine had to be pampered with air conditioning. Access was usually through intermediaries. Scientists and engineers wanted a computer they could operate themselves, one that would be smaller, cheaper, and easier to maintain. The development of the semiconductor made possible just such a machine—the minicomputer. When IBM decided not to enter this new market, it left a fertile field of opportunity to be plowed by new computer companies such as Digital Equipment Corporation, which quickly became the leader. DEC established the minicomputer market in 1965 when it introduced its PDP-8 (shorthand for Program Data Processor). It cost $18,500. The price included a teletype. Digital called its machine a "small computer." The press, looking for a sexier name, tagged it the "minicomputer," after the fashionable miniskirt. "We fought the name for years and finally threw up our hands," recalled one engineer at Digital. The minicomputer was a highly interactive machine. Instead of feeding punch cards into the machine, the user communicated with the computer via keyboard—a novel idea at the time.

When engineers working at a Santa Clara company known as Intel developed the microprocessor in 1971, the next evolutionary step for the incredible shrinking computer was inevitable. The microchip allowed the entire central processing unit of a computer to be encoded onto a silicon chip no larger than a thumbnail. But this next step would not be taken by large corporations like DEC or IBM with money and expertise. Instead, it would be taken by entrepreneurs and hobbyists with vision and dreams . . . dreams of one day owning their own computer. A personal computer. A pretty radical idea.

One of these hobbyists was a hulking bear of a man by the name of Ed Roberts. He stood about six feet four and weighed nearly 300 pounds. Roberts had enormous energy and an insatiable appetite for food and information. If he became interested in a subject, be it photography or beekeeping, Roberts would read everything he could find in the library on the topic.

Roberts was something of a gadget nut. He loved tinkering with electronic hardware. He had joined the Air Force to learn more about electronics and ended up stationed at Kirtland Field outside Albuquerque. There, he formed a company called Model Instrumentation and Telemetry Systems. (Later, the word "Model" would be changed to "Micro.") At first, Roberts operated MITS out of his garage, selling mail-order model rocket equipment. He also sold radio transmitters for model planes. After Roberts left the service, he started selling electronic equipment. In 1969, he moved MITS out of the garage and into a former Albuquerque restaurant called "The Enchanted Sandwich Shop." Roberts sunk all of his company's capital into the commercial calculator market. MITS was the first company in the United States to build calculator kits. Business was good. MITS quickly expanded to more than 100 employees. Then the bottom fell out. In the early 1970s, Texas Instruments entered the calculator market. Other semiconductor companies did the same. Pricing wars followed. MITS could no longer compete.

By 1974, MITS was more than a quarter of a million dollars in the red. Desperate to save his failing company, Roberts decided to take advantage of the new microprocessors and build computer hobby kits. Roberts knew that Intel's 8008 chip was too slow. He was banking on the next generation of chip, known as the 8080. It came out in early 1974. The 8080 was an exciting successor. It was much faster and had much more brainpower than the 8008. The new chip could certainly support a small computer. Or so Roberts believed.

He decided he would sell his machine for $397. This was a mind-boggling figure, and Roberts knew it. After all, Intel's 8080 chip alone was selling for $350. But Roberts had been able to browbeat Intel into selling him the chips in volume, at $75 apiece.

Although the machine had a price, it still lacked a name. David Bunnell, MITS technical writer, suggested the Orwellian-sounding "Little Brother." Roberts didn't much care for the name. With the name still up in the air, Roberts and his small team of engineers went to work building a prototype machine. He was soon contacted by Les Solomon, technical editor of *Popular Electronics*. Solomon was looking for a good computer story to put on the cover of his magazine. He knew Roberts and had heard about his plan for a home computer kit. Solomon flew to Albuquerque to talk with Roberts. Could Roberts have the prototype ready by the end of the year? Roberts assured Solomon he could.

After he returned to New York, Solomon scratched his bald head for days trying to come up with a name for the computer. One night, he asked his 12-year-old daughter, who was watching "Star Trek" on television. Why not call it "Altair," she said. That's where the Starship *Enterprise* was heading.

Roberts, a sci-fi fan, liked the name, too. Altair was also the name of the planet visited by the spaceship in the classic science fiction movie, *Forbidden Planet*.

Although Solomon's daughter came up with the computer's name, it was Roberts who coined the term "personal computer" as part of an ad campaign for Altair. "I was trying to convey a small machine you could afford to buy that didn't sound like a toy," he said.

Before *Popular Electronics* could publish the articles on the Altair, Solomon needed to see the prototype to test it and make sure it worked as advertised. Roberts shipped his only working model to New York City by rail. It never arrived. The world's first home computer—lost in transit! Solomon was in a panic. It was too late to change the planned January 1975 cover. And there was not enough time to build another computer. MITS engineers hurriedly put together a metal shell with the proper, eye-catching switches and lights on the front and shipped the empty machine to New York. And that's what appeared on the magazine's cover. The magazine's nearly half-million hobbyist-subscribers never knew—although they would soon learn that things didn't always work right at MITS.

The article on the Altair explained that the computer had only 256 bytes of memory, although it had 18 slots for additional memory boards that could increase its capacity to about 4K, or 4,096 bytes. There was no screen or keyboard. Since no one had developed a high-level language for the 8080 microchip, the Altair could only be programmed in complex 8080 machine language. This was painstakingly accomplished by flipping the switches on the front panel. One flip of a switch equaled one bit of information. (A series of 8 bits equals a byte, or one character of ordinary language.) The Altair "talked" back by flashing red lights on the front panel.

There were about a dozen high-level software languages available for mainframe and minicomputers when the Altair came along. These languages were each designed for different kinds of applications. The first widely accepted language was FORTRAN, or formula transition. Developed by an IBM team in 1956, FORTRAN was widely used in scientific circles and involved complex programming. Another language was COBOL, or common business-oriented language. It was mostly used for programming on mainframes. It, too, was difficult to master. But

BASIC was easy to learn. It was even taught in some elementary schools. As John Kemeny, one of the two Dartmouth professors who developed BASIC, wrote: "Profiting from years of experience with FORTRAN, we designed a new language that was particularly easy for the layman to learn." BASIC, he went on to explain, "facilitated communication between man and machine."

Roberts had decided in the summer of 1974 that BASIC would be the language for the Altair, the people's computer. But Intel had never expected its 8080 chip to be used as a microcomputer. Some engineers had told Roberts they didn't believe it was possible to develop a working BASIC for the chip.

At Harvard, two young men went to work to prove these experts wrong.

Wired from excitement and lack of sleep, Gates and Allen made the long-distance call to MITS in Albuquerque from Gates' room in Currier House. It had been only a few days since he and Allen had read the *Popular Electronics* article on the Altair. They had done little but talk since.

A man with a deep, gruff-sounding voice came on the phone at the other end. "Hello, is this Ed Roberts?" Gates asked in his high-pitched, boyish voice. Told it was, Gates proceeded to explain, with youthful bravado, that he and his friend had developed a BASIC that could be adapted for the Altair computer.

In fact, they didn't have a program at all, and Roberts suspected as much. He had heard such boasts already. "We had at least 50 people approach us saying they had a BASIC," recalled Roberts. "We just told everyone, including those guys, whoever showed up first with a working BASIC had the deal."

Gates and Allen followed up the phone call with a letter to Roberts, reiterating that they did indeed have a BASIC that worked with the 8080 Intel chip. They proposed an arrangement whereby they would license MITS to sell their software with the Altair to hobbyists, and in return they would be paid royalties. They sent the letter on Traf-O-Data letterhead. When Roberts received the letter and called the number on the letterhead, he found he had reached a private school in Seattle. No one at Lakeside knew anything about a BASIC for the Altair. What *was* an Altair, someone wanted to know. This was curious indeed, Roberts thought. Who are these guys? High school pranksters?

Back at Harvard, Gates and Allen had hunkered down in the Aiken Computer Center. Like a couple of school boys caught in a lie, they were furiously trying to cover their tracks. They had told Roberts they had a BASIC, and now they had to produce one—before all those other competitors who undoubtedly were also trying to make good on their exaggerated claims.

For the next eight weeks, the two would work day and night in the computer room, trying to do what some experts at Intel said couldn't be done—develop a high-level computer language for the 8080 chip. Gates not only stopped going to all his classes, he even gave up his beloved poker games. His poker pals knew something was going on. "As soon as Bill started missing the games, it was obvious he was up to something, but none of us knew what it was," said Greg Nelson, one of the poker regulars.

Gates and Allen didn't have an Altair, which made their task especially difficult. Roberts had the only up-and-running Altair in existence. And he was in New Mexico. The *Popular Electronics* article contained the computer's schematics, which would help. But what they really needed was detailed information about the 8080 chip. So they went to an electronics shop in Cambridge and bought a manual on the 8080 written by Adam Osborne, an Intel engineer whose job was to write technical manuals for the company's new microcomputer chips. Osborne, a stately, Bangkok-born Englishman, would soon become a very famous player in this new revolution. He would make a fortune publishing the first microcomputer books before building his own version of the Altair.

While Gates concentrated his efforts on writing code for the BASIC, Allen did the more technical work with the PDP-10 in the Aiken Computer Center.

They would have to create their BASIC with some brilliant innovation. Since they didn't have an Altair, Allen had to make the PDP-10 mimic the 8080 chip. It required all his technical knowledge and skills. But he eagerly accepted this new challenge. All those days in the computer room at Lakeside . . . those all-nighters at C-Cubed . . . hacking away on computers at the University of Washington . . . building the Traf-O-Data machine . . . learning about the 8008 chip . . . all his previous experience with computers had prepared Allen for what he and Gates now faced. "We were in the right place at the right time," Allen would say later. "Because of our previous experience, Bill and I had the tools to be able to take advantage of this new situation."

Gates faced different challenges than his friend. He had to write slick, tight code and make it fit into the maximum 4K memory of the Altair. It was like trying to squeeze his size 13 feet into size eight shoes. Actually, it was a tighter fit than that. Their BASIC not only had to fit in the limited memory space, but room had to be left over to run programs. What was the use of having a BASIC if there were no memory left in the computer to do anything?

"It wasn't a question of whether I could write the program," Gates said, "but rather a question of whether I could squeeze it into 4K and make it super fast."

He did. Gates said later that of all the code he ever wrote, he was most proud of the BASIC program developed in those eight weeks at Harvard. "It was the coolest program I ever wrote," Gates said.

No one had ever written a BASIC for a microcomputer. In that sense, Gates and Allen were blazing the trail for future software developers and establishing the industry standard. *They* would decide, rather than the marketplace, the minimum features their BASIC needed. The two worked at a frantic pace in the computer lab, often for days at a stretch with only an hour or two of sleep. When he was so exhausted he could no longer program, Gates would lay down behind the PDP-10 for short catnaps. Occasionally, he would nod off at the computer keyboard, then wake up with a start and immediately start typing again.

He and Allen took about as much time to eat as they did to sleep. One day, during a quick meal break in the dining hall at Currier House, they were talking about the math package that would be needed as part of the BASIC. This was a subprogram known as "floating point routines," which manipulate the numbers in a computer. The routines implement basic operations like addition, subtraction, multiplication, and division. Both Gates and Allen knew how to write this subprogram, but neither wanted to spend the time doing so.

Sitting at their table and overhearing the conversation about floating point routines was another student, Monte Davidoff. The talk had caught his ear because he had done this kind of programming before. Davidoff spoke up.

"I know how to do that," he said.

Gates and Allen wanted to know more. After talking with Davidoff for awhile, they told him about the Altair project they were working on. Davidoff said he would like to help. Several days later, they gave him the word—he was in. But payment for his work was left up in the air. "We just had an oral agreement," recalled Davidoff, who now works for a computer and electronics firm in Cupertino, California. "They didn't know if the thing was going to make any money. They felt there was the potential to make some money, and if they did make money, they would pay me. . . . So I just trusted them and left it loose."

Like Gates, Davidoff neglected his studies to work full-time on his part of the project. He would become the forgotten man of BASIC. Years later, when Gates began appearing on the cover of national magazines, and reporters wrote stories about how the Harvard dropout and his sidekick Allen developed the industry's first BASIC and became rich and famous, there was never any word of Monte Davidoff. He *was* mentioned once, just briefly, in the book *Fire in the Valley*. But even then, his first name was misspelled as "Marty."

"The first time I saw Bill on the cover of *Time* magazine, and it said he and Paul wrote this and it didn't mention me, I was a little upset," said Davidoff. "But I've gotten over it."

Gates and Allen were about four weeks into the project when Davidoff joined the team. They had already talked several times with MITS engineers in Albuquerque, seeking information about the Altair not found in the *Popular Electronics* article. Roberts wanted to know how soon they could come to Albuquerque to demonstrate a working BASIC. Gates had initially told Roberts he could have the BASIC to him in three or four weeks. It would not be the last time he seriously underestimated how long it would take to develop a product. Gates did write the initial program in about three weeks, but he spent four more weeks polishing the rough edges until it was as tight and fast as he wanted it. But since they didn't have an Altair, they had no way of knowing if it would really work.

By late February they felt they were ready. Allen would be the one to fly out to MITS. On the eve of Allen's appointment with Roberts, Gates told his friend to go home and get some sleep so he would have his wits about him the next day. Gates remained in the computer room, making last-minute fixes in the program. He barely had it ready in time for Allen to catch his early morning flight out of Boston's Logan International Airport.

As his plane was on its final approach into Albuquerque, Allen suddenly had a horrible thought. "Oh my God!" he cried out loud, startling the passenger seated next to him. He and Gates had forgotten to write what's known as a "bootstrap," a program that would instruct the Altair how to load BASIC. Writing on a piece of paper in complicated 8080 machine language, Allen had the program completed before the jet's wheels peeled rubber on the runway of the Albuquerque airport. (Later, Allen and the always competitive Gates would have a contest to see who could write the shortest loader program. Gates won.)

Ed Roberts met Allen at the airport. He was driving an old pickup truck.

Allen had not been sure what he would find when he arrived in Albuquerque. He certainly wasn't prepared for the giant who was there to greet him. But he was in for an even greater shock when Roberts took him to MITS.

Micro Instrumentations & Telemetry Systems Inc. was located just off famous Route 66, in a string of businesses that passed as a downtown mall. There was a massage parlor on one side, a laundromat on the other. Roberts told Allen he wanted to wait until the next morning to test the BASIC, so after a short visit he drove Allen to the most expensive hotel in town. The future billionaire didn't have enough money to pay for his hotel room. He had to borrow extra cash from Roberts.

That night, Allen called an anxious Gates waiting back in Cambridge. He told his friend about the guy who had picked him up in a run-down pickup, told him about the low-budget operation he had seen that afternoon. They were both disappointed . . . and worried. They had thought all along they were doing business with a big, successful company. Had their efforts been wasted?

The next morning, Roberts came by to get Allen, and they returned to MITS. It was time to test the BASIC. The code was on a paper tape. Unlike the Altair kits that would be sold to the public, the machine at MITS had several perks unavailable on the public models. This Altair was running on 7K of memory. And it was connected to a teletype. Allen would not have to read the flashing lights to understand output from the Altair. But best of all, this Altair was hooked into a paper tape reader. Allen could feed his BASIC tape directly into the machine. Otherwise, it would have meant flipping the toggle switches on the front of the Altair approximately 30,000 times in proper sequence. The only thing Allen had to key into the machine was the loader program.

Allen crossed his fingers. This was the first time he had ever touched the Altair. Any mistake he and Gates had made along the way, either in designing the 8080 simulator or coding the BASIC itself, would now mean failure.

Suddenly, the Altair came to life. It printed "memory size?" Allen entered "7K." The machine was ready for its first instruction. Allen typed "print 2 + 2." The Altair printed out the correct answer: "4."

"Those guys were really stunned to see their computer work," Allen said. "This was a fly-by-night computer company. I was pretty stunned myself that it worked the first time. But I tried not to show much surprise."

Recalled Roberts of that historic moment when his machine was turned into a useful computer: "I was dazzled. It was certainly impressive. The Altair was a complex system, and they had never seen it before. What they had done went a lot further than you could have reasonably expected. I'd been involved with the development of programs for computers for a long time, and I was very impressed that we got anywhere near as far as we did that day."

Later that morning, Allen found a book of 101 computer games, and ran a Lunar Lander program on the Altair. It was very similar to the program Gates had written back at Lakeside when his interest in computers was first piqued by the teletype machine in the school's computer room. The game required the user to make a soft landing on the moon before expending all the fuel in the spacecraft. It was the first software program ever run on what would become known as Microsoft BASIC.

The personal computer revolution had begun with a game played on a small blue box with blinking lights named after the brightest star in the constellation Aquila. Thirty years earlier, people in Albuquerque had witnessed the sun come up in the south when the world's first atomic bomb exploded in the predawn darkness near Alamogordo a hundred miles away, heralding the nuclear age. Now, another age had dawned in Albuquerque. It began at a ragtag company located next to a massage parlor. Its prophets were two young men not yet old enough to drink, whose computer software would soon bring executives in threepiece suits from around the country to a highway desert town to make million-dollar deals with kids in blue jeans and t-shirts. Gates and Allen had ignited a technological revolution that would spread like wildfire, from the apricot and plum orchards of the Santa Clara Valley, where dreams born in garages would flourish in a great concrete expanse known as the Silicon Valley, to the lush forests of the Pacific Northwest, where Gates would eventually return home to become the youngest billionaire in the history of America.

When Allen got back to Boston, he and Gates celebrated by going out for ice cream and softdrinks. Gates had his usual Shirley Temple, the liquorless drink of 7 Up and grenadine usually given to kids who want to feel more grown up.

"We were both real, real excited," said Allen.

They talked about what kind of licensing agreement they should make with Roberts for their BASIC. They had worked 20-hour days, sometimes longer, for eight weeks. Now it was time to make some money.

As he ate his ice cream and sipped his Shirley Temple that day in Cambridge, Gates knew there was still a lot of work to do before BASIC was ready for the marketplace. Bugs needed to be found and removed. Refinements and enhancements had to be made. Gates returned to the Aiken Computer Center, while Allen went back to work at Honeywell. But Gates soon faced a problem that could not be solved with his programming wizardry. Harvard officials had found out that he and Allen had been making extensive use of the university's PDP-10 to develop a commercial product. The officials were not pleased.

The PDP-10 that Gates and Allen had used to develop their BASIC had an interesting history. In 1969 it was destined for shipment to Vietnam when Professor Cheatham got a call asking if Harvard wanted the machine. Since a PDP-10 cost several hundred thousand dollars, and the university didn't have one, Cheatham naturally said yes. But how to get it on campus without causing a riot? The computer was crated and packed away in the back of a two-and-a-half-ton U.S. Army truck. This was at the height of the Vietnam War. The Army was not exactly Big Man On Campus. At Harvard, glass windows had been replaced with plastic after repeated antiwar demonstrations. An Army truck rolling down these Ivy League streets was the last thing the Harvard administration wanted to see. So the truck snuck in on a Sunday morning, about 4:00 A.M. It pulled up in front of the Aiken Computer Center, unloaded its cargo, and left before the first student saw the crimson rays of the morning sun.

Even though Harvard now had possession of the PDP-10, the military strings had not been cut. The computer was being funded by the Department of Defense through its Defense Advanced Research Projects Agency, better known as ARPA. The little-known agency was created in 1958 to find long-term military applications from civilian research projects. For a while, it was known as ARPA. The word "Defense" was later added by Congress to underscore its military mission. Many of the military's high-tech toys have come from DARPA-funded computer research, including the Stealth fighter and so-called smart weapons used in the recent Persian Gulf War.

Although DARPA was funding the PDP-10 at Harvard, there was no written policy regarding its use.

"The attitude here was that the kids could use the machine for personal use," said Cheatham. "But after the Gates incident, there was tighter supervision."

It's not clear how much trouble Gates got into for using the computer for personal gain, or for allowing Allen, an outsider with no connection to Harvard, to use the machine. Cheatham refused to talk about the incident. But another professor said Gates was reprimanded and threatened with expulsion. Gates, however, denies this.

"There was no formal reprimand, just an admonishment for bringing Paul in on a regular basis," said Gates. He later wrote a letter to the university administration, complaining about the lack of guidelines. Why could professors use the Harvard library to do research for books that brought them royalties, but students could not use the computer for commercial work? asked Gates in his letter. By the next year, a written policy was in place: If a student used the computers for a commercial product, Harvard had to be cut in on any profits that resulted.

After the computer flap, Gates and Allen bought computer time from a timesharing service in Boston to put the finishing touches on their BASIC.

Allen had been in constant touch with Roberts since flying to Albuquerque to test the BASIC. Soon after the trip, Roberts had asked Allen if he wanted to come work for MITS. In the spring of 1975, Roberts offered Allen the job of MITS software director. Allen accepted and left for Albuquerque. Gates went back to playing poker with the boys, and thinking more seriously than ever before about his future.

CHAPTER 3

The Microkids

T he Sundowner Motel in Albuquerque New Mexico was in a sleazy part of town noted for its prostitutes and all-night coffee shops rather than its high-tech businesses. It was located just off Central Avenue, which is what Route 66 was called as it passed through this torrid desert town on the Rio Grande. When Paul Allen checked into the budget motel in the spring of 1975, he told the manager he was not sure how long he would be staying, but thought likely until his friend at Harvard could join him in a couple of months. Allen didn't care about the cheap accommodations or the motel's seedy surroundings. The important thing was that he was only a five-minute walk from MITS, where he would be spending most of his time getting BASIC ready for the Altair. Bugs had to be found and removed from the language before it was ready to be sold commercially.

Compared to his job at Honeywell in Boston, Allen had walked into a buzzing hive of disorder at MITS. Although his title was MITS' software director, in fact Allen was the entire software department. The others employed by the company were furiously working on hardware for the Altair. The response to the *Popular Electronics* article had been nothing short of phenomenal, firing the imagination of electronics hobbyists and computer hackers across the country who had dreamed of one day owning a computer. And now they could, for the very affordable price of $397.

"You've got to remember that in those days, the idea that you could own a computer, your own computer, was about as wild as the idea today of owning your own nuclear submarine. It was beyond comprehension," said Eddie Curry, who joined MITS as executive vice-president soon after Allen arrived. They quickly became friends. "Computers were things that were housed in big buildings and took up several floors and had a staff to maintain them and a priesthood to watch over them. A large part of the success of the Altair and the microcomputers that followed was the desire of people just to own one. It didn't really matter if they could do anything with the computer. Everybody knew you could do something with them, but nobody knew what. The mere fact that you owned a computer was very prestigious."

Curry, a childhood friend of Roberts, was in graduate school when Roberts told him his idea of a small computer for the masses. They talked a lot on the phone, running up hundred-dollar-a-month bills. Although they alternated payment of the bills, Curry couldn't afford such extravagance while in school, so he and Roberts began exchanging tapes, which turned into sizeable creative productions, complete with sound effects, background music, comedy skits, and dramatic readings.

"We got into this sort of running discussion of where we were going in life," said Curry, "and I asked him on one tape what his goals were for MITS and what he wanted to do with MITS. He told me his dream was to build a computer kit so everyone could have their own computer." He and Roberts had detailed, technical discussions via tape throughout the development of the computer, even down to how much Roberts should charge for the Altair.

With MITS near bankruptcy, Roberts gambled everything on the Altair. He had secured a $65,000 development loan by assuring his bankers in Albuquerque there was a market for several hundred of the machines. As it turned out, MITS received that many requests for the Altair within days after the *Popular Electronics* issue featuring the Altair hit the newsstands. Within a few weeks, more than 4,000 orders had poured in for the computer. Almost overnight, the company's cash balance went from about $300,000 in the red to about a quarter million in the black. The chance to own a personal computer was so appealing that thousands of people sent checks and money orders to a company they had never heard of. A few fanatics flew to Albuquerque by private plane, hoping to get their Altair faster by showing up in person.

Les Solomon, the short, bald-headed technical editor of *Popular Electronics* who had put the dummy Altair on his magazine's cover, described the reaction that followed publication this way in the book *Hackers*, by Steven Levy:

"The only word which could come to mind was 'magic.' . . . Most people wouldn't send fifteen cents to a company for a flashlight dial, right? About two-thousand people, sight unseen, sent checks, money orders, three, four, five hundred dollars apiece, to an unknown company in a relatively unknown city, in a technologically unknown state. These people were different. They were adventurers in a new land. They were the same people who went West in the early days of America. The weirdos who decided they were going to California, or Oregon or Christ knows where."

In its ads, MITS promised delivery of a computer kit within two months. But the company was unprepared for the staggering number of orders it received. It could not possibly keep up with demand. Anxious customers who sent in money for an Altair called repeatedly to find out what had happened when their machine did not arrive in the mail as promised. They were told MITS had a huge delivery backlog and they would have to wait. One frustrated hacker drove across the country and lived for several weeks in a trailer parked near MITS, waiting to take delivery of his Altair.

For their $397, these adventurers didn't get much. The Altair came in a kit, which wasn't for the faint of heart. The customer had to figure out how to put it together, which took many hours and was not easy. Most of the kits were never properly assembled. And even if the computer did work when it was assembled, the Altair couldn't do very much. The first machines sold in early 1975 did not have interface boards that allowed for a teletype hookup. Memory expansion boards also were not yet available, so the Altair was all but brainless, with only 256 bytes of memory. Crude programs in complicated binary machine language could only be entered into the computer by flipping the toggle switches on the front panel hundreds of times in proper sequence. One mistake meant the user had to start over from scratch.

The 8080 BASIC computer language that Gates and Allen were creating at Harvard was not yet finished when the first Altair computer kits were shipped. Even if the software had been ready, MITS hadn't yet designed working memory boards that would provide Altair owners enough additional memory to run BASIC. Paul Allen's responsibility as the MITS' software director in 1975 was to continue making enhancements to BASIC and get it ready for shipment. He and Gates talked constantly by phone on technical problems that cropped up. They both realized a new software market had been born with the Altair, and they hoped to make a lot of money from the sale of their BASIC. What they now needed was a formal partnership.

For some time, Gates had tried to prepare his parents for the fact that he might eventually drop out of Harvard to form a computer business with Allen. But this latest news took his parents by surprise. He wanted to start a company not in Seattle, his hometown, where he would be close to his family, but in

Albuquerque, of all places, way out in the deserts of New Mexico.

As Mary Gates saw it, her 19-year-old son was about to commit what amounted to academic suicide. She was dead set against her son leaving school before getting his degree. Dan Evans, the governor of Washington (and a close family friend who had once helped Gates paint the lines on the family's pickleball court), had just named Mary Gates to the University of Washington Board of Regents, one of the most prestigious political appointments in the state. How would it look for her son to drop out of Harvard now, she wondered. His father was also strongly opposed to Gates starting a company before finishing his education. But though he and Mary urged their son to remain in school, both recognized that they did not have the technical background to analyze the business soundness of starting a software company.

So Mary Gates turned to a new friend, Samuel Stroum, an influential and respected business leader she had met during a United Way campaign, for help with her son. She arranged for Bill to talk with Stroum, in the hope that Stroum would convince her son to drop the idea of starting a company, at least for the time being, and continue his education at Harvard.

A self-made multimillionaire, philanthropist, and civic leader, Samuel Stroum's advice was often sought, even by the region's most powerful movers and shakers. Like Mary Gates, he is a regent at the University of Washington. Stroum never went to college. After World War II, he founded an electronics distribution company in Seattle and later amassed a fortune from the sale of Shuck's Auto Supply, the Northwest's most popular auto-parts chain. In 1975, he was one of the few people in Seattle's business community who not only understood computer technology but had the vision to see where the computer industry was heading.

While Gates was home from Harvard on break, Stroum took him to lunch at the Rainier Club, the city's center of power and business. Founded in 1888 and steeped in tradition, the private club was considered *the* place for lunch among Seattle politicians, powerbrokers, and corporate high-flyers. "I was clearly on a mission," recalled Stroum of the couple hours he spent picking Gates' brain. "He explained to me what he was doing, what he hoped to do. I had been involved in that industry since I was a young boy. He just talked about the things he was doing. . . Hell, anybody who was near electronics had to know it was exciting and a new era was emerging."

Gates talked about the vision he and Paul Allen shared. The personal computer revolution was just beginnning, he told Stroum. Eventually, everyone would own a computer. Imagine the money-making possibilities. . . . a zillion machines all running on his software.

Not only did Stroum not try to talk Gates out of his plans to start a business, but after listening to the enthusiastic teenager he encouraged Gates to do so. "Mary and I have kidded about it for years," said Stroum, now 70. "I told her I made one terrible mistake—I didn't give him a blank check to fill out the numbers. I've been known as an astute venture capitalist, but I sure didn't read that one right."

When Gates finished his sophomore year at Harvard, he joined Allen in Albuquerque, though he still had not made up his mind about dropping out of school. It was a decision he would not finally make for another year and a half.

Microsoft—an abbreviation for microcomputer sofware—was born in the summer of 1975. (The name was originally "Micro-Soft;" the hyphen in the name was soon dropped.) Some accounts have reported that Gates and Allen created Microsoft out of Traf-O-Data by simply changing the name. That was not the case. The two companies were always separate legal partnerships. The initial Microsoft partnership agreement called for a 60/40 split in favor of Gates, since he argued that he had done more of the initial development work on BASIC. This was later changed to a 64/36 split. (By the time Microsoft went public in

1986, Gates owned more than 11 million shares of the company's stock and Allen more than six million shares.)

Although Gates was independently wealthy from his parents and the trust fund left him by his grandparents, he was determined to make it on his own and not dip into that money to help finance his and Paul Allen's new business. His parents and grandparents had taught him to be financially conservative, and that was the way he intended to run his company. There would be no unecessary overhead or extravagant spending habits with Microsoft. When Gates arrived in Albuquerque, he and Allen shared a room at the Sand and Sage Motel, which was only a slight improvement over the Sundowner. Later, they moved into an inexpensive downtown apartment.

Early that summer, MITS took the Altair on a show-and-tell road tour. Several of the company's hardware engineers crowded into Roberts' blue mobile home and headed across America, travelling from city to city to spread the word about Altair. The MITS-mobile, or Blue Goose, as it was quickly dubbed, carried a working Altair complete with bells and whistles not available with the computer kits being sold to hobbyists. This Altair was connected to a teletype and paper tape reader, and ran the 4K version of BASIC developed by Gates and Allen. It was a public relations show on wheels. Wherever the MITS-mobile stopped, Altair demonstrations were set up. Seminars were held in motel rooms. Hobbyists who turned out were encouraged to form computer clubs, and many did, in garages, basements, wherever they could meet to feed an insatiable appetite for information about computers and to share a passion for this new revolution and its possibilities. The MITS caravan also served as a kind of traveling MASH unit, with hardware experts offering technical surgery to frustrated Altair owners who could not get their machines to work. Gates himself made one of the song-and-dance tours in the MITS-mobile his first summer in Albuquerque. He felt it was a good marketing strategy to spread the word about BASIC as well.

The MITS-mobile was not the only marketing tactic used by Roberts to promote the Altair. He and David Bunnell, the company's technical writer, formed a nationwide computer club with free memberships to Altair owners. Bunnell also began publishing a newsletter called *Computer Notes*. Roberts wrote a regular column for the newsletter, and Gates and Allen became frequent contributors with articles about their software. Bunnell, who had left a teaching job on a Sioux Indian reservation in South Dakota to join MITS in 1972, became good friends with Gates. Bunnell designed Microsoft's first logo and letterhead. He would go on to become one of the country's leading publishers of personal computer magazines.

Gates, when he was not on the road in the MITS-mobile, pulled all-nighters with Allen to further enhance BASIC. By midsummer, they had an 8K BASIC to go with the 4K version, and they were working on an "extended" BASIC that required 12K or 16K of memory. On July 22, 1975 they signed a formal licensing agreement with Ed Roberts regarding the rights to their BASIC for the 8080 computer chip. The agreement, prepared by Gates with help from his father and an Albuquerque attorney, broke new legal ground. Gates, only 19 years old, understood not only the complex technology but the cutting-edge legal issues involved in licensing software. The agreement, which was to run for ten years, gave MITS exclusive, worldwide rights to use and license BASIC, including the right to sublicense BASIC to third parties. MITS agreed not to license BASIC to any third party without first obtaining a secrecy agreement that prohibited the unauthorized disclosure of BASIC. What would later turn out to be the most important part of the agreement was a paragraph that stated: "The Company (MITS) agrees to use its best efforts to license, promote, and commercialize the Program (BASIC). The Company's failure to use its best efforts . . . shall constitute sufficient grounds and reasons to terminate this agreement. . . ." The contract with MITS would serve as a model for future software licensing agreements in the growing microcomputer business, and it helped establish industry standards.

Gates and Allen received $3,000 from MITS on the signing of the agreement. The agreement provided for royalties from the licensing of BASIC, with or without the accompanying sale of MITS hardware. Microsoft received $30 for each copy of its 4K version of BASIC licensed by MITS as part of a hardware sale, $35 for each copy of their 8K version, and $60 for each copy of the "extended" verion. When MITS licensed any version of BASIC without hardware, Gates and Allen received 50 percent of the sale. They also received 50 percent of the money received from the licensing of the BASIC source code. The source code would allow companies that licensed BASIC to modify it to their needs and develop application software to run on top of the high-level language.

Although the licensing agreement was a good one for Microsoft, it would never make Gates or Allen rich men. They could only earn a maximum of $180,000 in royalties according to the terms of the contract. But for the time being, they needed MITS to help market BASIC with the Altair.

―――――――

As Microsoft grew, Gates sought out trusted friends to join him in his crusade. His recruiting forays often led back to Lakeside School in Seattle and to his old friends from the computer room.

That first summer in Albuquerque, when it became clear he and Allen couldn't do all the programming work themselves on BASIC, Gates contacted Chris Larson, his young protégé at Lakeside. Larson was only a sophmore, but he had the same energy, passion, and commitment as his mentor. In the two years since Gates had left Lakeside for Harvard, Larson had taken over Lakeside's computerized scheduling project. He was also looking after Bill's sister Libby, who now attended Lakeside.

Larson, four years ahead of Libby, saw to it that she got the classes she wanted. Larson and his friends got the classes they wanted, as well. "I guess there was an unwritten understanding between us and the faculty that we wouldn't overly abuse the situation, or obviously we would have had the job taken away from us," recalled Larson. (Two years later, as a senior at Lakeside, Larson scheduled himself in a class with all girls—a nifty bit of programming wrongly credited to Bill Gates.)

Gates recruited Larson for the summer, and found a second programmer for the summer from Harvard—Monte Davidoff, who had developed the math package for BASIC. When Larson and Davidoff arrived in Albuquerque, they shared an apartment with Gates and Allen, often sleeping on the living room floor. All four kept late hours, and became familiar with every late-night pizza place and coffee shop in the neighborhood. The MITS software office where the Microsoft employees worked was separate from the company's main administrative office, located next to a vacuum cleaner shop. While MITS hardware engineers worked on memory boards and refinements for the Altair, Gates and his team worked on BASIC and various software programs that allowed the Altair to be used with a teletype, printer, or paper-tape reader.

The people employed by MITS and Microsoft were youthful computer fanatics, religious zealots who worshipped The Machine. "It was almost a missionary kind of work in the sense that we were delivering something to someone they never thought they could have," recalled Eddie Curry. "There was a kinship that you wouldn't normally see in commerical enterprise between not only the people in the company but between the people in the company and the customer base. People would work from early in the morning until the end of the day. Then they'd rush home to get dinner, come back and work until late at night. Typically, there were people at MITS 24 hours a day, seven days a week."

Curry got a call one day from an executive who said he had been trying for a week to get hold of Gates or Allen. The executive was excited because he felt he had stumbled upon what he thought was a little known industry secret—software people only came out at night. Gates sometimes slept at the Microsoft offices, just as he had slept in the computer lab at Harvard at times rather than returning to his room at the Currier House. One day Ed Roberts was taking a group of visitors on a tour through MITS when he stepped over a body in the software area. It was Gates, curled up on the the floor, sound asleep.

"Bill and Paul were very, very intense," said Curry. "They had a clear understanding of what they were doing, in the sense that they had a vision of where they were going. It wasn't just that they were developing BASIC. I don't think most people ever really understood this, but Bill, certainly, always had the vision from the time that I met him that Microsoft's mission in life was to provide all the software for microcomputers."

Gates, Allen, and the other programmers got along with Curry, but not, curiously, with Roberts. The Microsoft employees had long hair and kept strange hours. They listened to rock'n'roll music while Roberts preferred easy-listening music. "As soon as Roberts would leave," recalled David Bunnell, "they'd switch to rock'n'roll. I couldn't see how they ever got any work done with that acid rock music blaring out all the time, day and night."

In addition, Roberts considered Gates something of a smart-ass. They were both extraordinarily well-read, and would often debate issues unrelated to computers. Should the United States have dropped the atomic bomb on Japan? Regardless of what side Gates took on an issue, Roberts took the opposite . . . seemingly out of spite rather than conviction. The gangly teenager clearly got under Roberts' skin. It was inevitable the two would clash about more serious matters, as well, and they did, often and angrily. The burly Roberts, who could be surly, authoritative, and intimidating, was used to getting his way. No one at MITS got along in complete harmony with Roberts. Employees either did things his way, or encountered fierce opposition.

Gates, on the other hand, didn't back down regardless of how formidable Roberts could be.

"Bill could be fairly prickly," said Nelson Winkless, the first editor of *Personal Computing* magazine. "He had his own view of what MITS ought to be doing and how they should do it. He was very much self-possessed."

Although he wasn't old enough yet to order a beer legally, the 5-feet-11 Gates stood his ground with Roberts, often going jaw to jaw with the huge, gruff man 13 years his senior. Roberts weighed close to 300 pounds, and at 6-feet-4 towered over Gates. "Bill was brash, very intelligent, and energetic," recalled Bunnell. "I knew of no one who would go to the wall with Ed until I met Bill Gates."

In Gates' mind, every good idea at MITS was only half-executed, and he didn't hesitate to let Roberts know how he felt. "MITS was run in a very strange way," he said, "and everyone there felt very poorly. . . . We all thought, gee, this thing is a mess. And there was a vacuum of leadership. It was actually kind of unusual. Even though I was never formally an employee or anything—I was just doing my software stuff—I had some thoughts on how it ought to be run, so we'd all sit around and talk about this stuff and people would actually kind of egg me on to stand up to Ed. We always thought we might do something to improve the way things were run."

The company's foul-ups drove the business-minded Gates up the wall, especially the problem MITS was having with dynamic memory boards for the Altair. These high-tech circuit boards gave the Altair enough brain power to run BASIC, and were essential to the sale of BASIC, which required a minimum of 4K of memory. But the boards seldom worked. Gates wrote a software program to test the boards and didn't find one that worked as advertised. "It was irritating, as well as an embarassment to everybody, including us," said Curry. This was particularly so since many of the faulty memory boards were delivered to Altair customers already frustrated that it had taken so long to get one of the computer kits. Other hardware companies, seeing an opportunity in the young microcomputer field, were soon making and shipping memory boards that did work, which irritated and embarrassed Roberts enormously. Gates ranted and raved at Roberts about the problems he saw. He and Allen needed cash flow to fund their young company's growth. How could they expect royalties from their agreement with MITS when things at MITS were so screwed up?

Although Roberts respected Gates' technical abilities, he didn't care for Gates' confrontational style. "We got so we didn't even invite him to meetings where we were trying to come up with a new software approach or something like that because he was impossible to deal with," Roberts recalled. "He was a spoiled kid. He literally was a spoiled kid, that's what the problem was. Paul Allen was much more creative than Bill. Bill spent his whole time trying to be argumentative and not trying to come up with solutions. Paul was exactly the opposite."

At the end of that first summer in Albuquerque, Larson went back to school at Lakeside, and Davidoff returned to Harvard. Gates, too, decided to go back to Harvard that fall. He was still wrestling with his future, and his parents continued to pressure him to finish his education. For the next year and a half, Gates would divide his time between school and poker at Harvard and creating software and negotiating deals for his new business in Albuquerque.

With Gates, Larson, and Davidoff back in school, Allen was left alone to deal with Roberts and MITS. He had his hands full. MITS had been the first company to hit the market with an affordable microcomputer, but others quickly followed. A couple startup companies were working on a microcomputer that used Motorola's new MC6800 microchip instead of the Intel 8080, the mathematical engine in the Altair. Roberts wanted MITS to build a new Altair around the Motorola chip. Allen argued otherwise. It would mean rewriting the BASIC software, and putting out competing hardware products in the marketplace. But Roberts, as usual, got his way. Allen brought in Richard Weiland, one of the founding members of the Lakeside Programmers Group, to write the 6800 version of BASIC. MITS later did produce an Altair known as the 680b, though as Allen had predicted, it was not very successful.

In late 1975, MITS decided to release a floppy disk–storage system for the Altair 8800. As a result Allen, as software director, was asked to develop a disk BASIC, quickly. Magnetic disks that stored data had been used for years in mainframe machines and minicomputers, but it was not until after the Altair hit the market that floppy diskettes were designed for microcomputers. Disks were a much more efficient way to store data than paper tape.

Even before MITS had announced its intentions to market a disk-based version of Altair BASIC, Allen, anticipating the need for such a product, had asked Gates to write the new software code. But Gates had been busy on other projects and pushed the request aside. Now Gates had no choice. When the fall semester ended, Gates flew to Albuquerque and checked into the Hilton Hotel with a stack of yellow legal pads. Five days later he emerged, the yellow pads filled with the code of the new version of BASIC. Gates then went to the software lab at MITS to iron out the new BASIC, instructing the others that he was to be left alone. In another five days, Gates had what would become known as DISK BASIC running on the Altair. That, at least, is the "official" version of Chairman Bill's feat of programming prowess, as recounted in the preface to the company's bible, the MS-DOS Encyclopedia. Although Gates is generally thought of as the father of Microsoft BASIC, which became an industry standard and was the foundation on which his software company was built, there are those in the industry who believe Allen deserves at least as much credit as Gates, and possibly more. According to them, the legend of Gates has risen to such Olympian heights that it sometimes overshadows reality. Ed Curry, for one, felt Allen never got the credit he should have for his work on BASIC.

"What was delivered to us initially there in Albuquerque," said Curry, "was what came to be known as the 4K version. And it had no file management capability and was, you know, very restrictive, about as restrictive a subset of BASIC as you could have and still call it BASIC. It was Paul who began to flesh it out. . . . When you read things about Bill writing BASIC, for example, to me, that's a little bit of a joke. He was part of a team. I think it's accurate to say that if you went back and looked at BASIC three or four years later and said, 'Okay, who made the most significant contribution?' it was Paul Allen. The initial hack was a very important piece of work. Undoubtedly it was very challenging and very difficult, but . . . You know, I don't want this to come out that I said Bill Gates didn't write BASIC. That's not what I'm saying. Bill was part of a team effort. He made very imporant contributions. But if any one person were to be said to be the author of BASIC, I would think it would be Paul. If you asked who was the driving force behind BASIC, it was Bill and Paul. If you asked who solved the hard problems, it was Bill and Paul. But in terms of who sat down and did the work for BASIC as we know it today, it's got to be Paul who did the lion's share."

Those patient enough to have actually received an Altair kit, skilled enough to have assembled the pieces, and lucky enough to have gotten the machine up and running could have cared less who authored BASIC. They just wanted to use it, and when they couldn't get it, many resorted to "stealing" this prized piece of software that gave them the programming power to turn $397 worth of electronic parts and an Intel 8080 chip into a useful computer that could do more than just flash two rows of red LED lights.

These computer hackers were the first "software pirates," a somewhat romantic description suggesting high-tech swashbucklers who hack their way across computer screens like Errol Flynn. But as far as Bill Gates was concerned, they were unprincipled thieves. And he called them as much in an infamous letter published in the Altair newsletter, which was reprinted in other computer magazines and ended up as dartboard material in computer clubs from New York to California.

Gates wrote his stinging denunciation in early February of 1976, but the larceny problem and what to do about it had been eating away at him for months, after he learned that unauthorized copies of BASIC were being handed out like so many free raffle tickets at computer club meetings across the country. What happened one night at a gathering of the Homebrew Computer Club in Northern California was typical.

The computer clubs fueled the revolution that had begun in Albuquerque with the Altair and was sweeping across the country like an out-of-control prairie fire. The clubs were technological communes for those who loved computers. Gates himself had toured in the MITS-mobile to encourage some of the clubs to organize. And they did, in garages, warehouses, homes, schools, offices . . . anyplace members could meet and talk about computers. The clubs were organized by engineers, technicians, hobbyists, hackers, electronics buffs, gadget freaks . . . energetic people fascinated by the seemingly limitless possibilities for microcomputers. Probably no computer club in the country reflected this communal spirit more than Homebrew. From its ranks would come numerous industry pioneers who blazed their own trails through the Silicon Valley and a new multibillion-dollar industry.

Homebrew started in a garage on a rainy night in early March of 1975, in the town of Menlo Park, next to Palo Alto and Stanford University, on the edge of the Silicon Valley. More than thirty people turned out for the first meeting, including an electronics whiz kid working in the calculator division of Hewlett-Packard named Steve Wozniak. Within a year, Wozniak, with Steve Jobs, would build a personal computer of his own, the Apple I, which would transform the computer industry.

In June of 1975, the MITS Mobile Caravan was out on the West Coast for the National Computer Conference. One of its stops was Rickey's Hyatt House in Palo Alto. By then, a number of Homebrew members had ordered an Altair. When the MITS-mobile arrived, about two hundred people crowded into the Hyatt's Edwards Room to look at the Altair. They discovered an Altair with features not available on the machines they had ordered. It was connected to a teletype and a paper-tape reader, and was running the 4K version of BASIC developed by Gates and Allen. At this point, no one at Homebrew who had ordered an Altair had received a copy of BASIC, though they had sent MITS their money for the program. According to one account, someone from Homebrew picked up the punched paper tape containing BASIC lying on the floor near the Altair. Someone else later ran off copies of the tape, and at the next Homebrew meeting a large box of tapes were passed out to anyone who wanted one. Gradually, then exponentially, BASIC spread from computer club to computer club like a virus. And no one was paying for it.

When Gates learned what was going on, he was beside himself. No wonder he and Allen were receiving so little money from their royalty agreement with MITS, he thought. One day he stormed into Roberts' office and threw one of his fits that many around MITS had become accustomed to. "I vividly remember the conversation," recalled Roberts, "him coming into my office that first summer and screaming and yelling at the top of his lungs that everyone was stealing his software, and he was never going to make any money, and he wasn't going to do another thing unless we put him on the payroll."

Roberts said he put Gates on the company's payroll for about a year, and paid him about $10 an hour. Gates, however, later claimed he never worked for MITS. Technically, he was right. According to David Bunnell, the salary Gates received for the hours he worked enhancing and selling BASIC was actually an advance against royalties. He was never on the MITS staff.

Gates eventually became convinced that BASIC wasn't selling very well because so many people had obtained copies without paying for them. At one point, frustrated and demoralized, Gates offered to sell Roberts all rights and ownership to BASIC for about $6,500. In hindsight, it would have been the bonehead deal of the century. "Clearly, it would have been a bad decision on Bill's part, because there might not be a Microsoft today," said Eddie Curry. But Roberts decided not to take Gates up on the offer. He later told Curry that he liked both Gates and Allen and didn't want to take advantage of them because they were so young. In truth, Roberts decided it made better business sense to continue paying royalties to the two, and reap whatever benefits came from the enhancements they were making with BASIC. Had Allen quit as MITS' software director, which he almost certainly would have done if he and Gates no longer had a financial interest in BASIC, then there would have been no one to make the badly needed upgrades in the language. "In retrospect," said Curry, "it worked out in a way that I don't think Ed is very happy about today, but at the time was the right decision based on what everybody knew."

Gates decided the best thing he could do to stop people from stealing his software was to strike back publicly at the thieves. He asked Bunnell to publish a letter in the Altair newsletter, *Computer Notes*. Entitled "An Open Letter to Hobbyists," Gates noted that the most important thing inhibiting computer hobbyists was the lack of good software.

"Almost a year ago, Paul Allen and myself, expecting the hobby market to expand, hired Monte Davidoff and developed Altair BASIC. Though the initial work took only two months, the three of us have spent most of the last year documenting, improving, and adding features to BASIC. Now we have 4K, 8K, EXTENDED, ROM and DISK BASIC. The value of the computer time we have used exceeds $40,000."

Gates noted that while feedback from enthusiasts was strong, he'd noticed two things: "1) Most of these "users" never bought BASIC (less than 10 percent of all Altair owners have bought BASIC), and 2) The amount of royalties we have received from sales to hobbyists makes the time spent on Altair BASIC worth less than $2 an hour."

He then accused hobbyists of stealing software programs. "Is this fair? One thing you don't do by stealing software is get back at MITS for some problem you may have had. MITS doesn't make money selling software. The royalties paid to us, the manual, the tape and the overhead make it a break-even-operation. One thing you can do is prevent good software from being written. Who can afford to do professional work for nothing? . . . The fact is, no one besides us has invested a lot of money in hobby software . . . but there is very little incentive to make this software available to hobbyists."

He went on to add that those who resell BASIC software "give hobbyists a bad name, and should be kicked out of any club meeting they show up at.

"I would appreciate letters from any one who wants to pay up, or has a suggestion or comment. . . . Nothing would please me more than being able to hire ten programmers, and deluge the hobby market with good software." The letter was published on February 3, 1976. Bunnell not only printed the diatribe in the Altair newsletter, but he made sure it ran in most of the major industry publications, including the newsletter of the Homebrew Computer Club.

Gates' letter caused quite a stir. The Southern California Computer Society, which had been visited by the MITS-mobile in early 1975 and by now had several thousand members, threatened to sue him. "They were upset that Gates had called them thieves," said Bunnell. "They were not all thieves . . . just most of them." Only a handful of people who possessed pirated copies of BASIC sent Gates money as he had asked them to do in his letter. Some fired off their own angry letters in return. What was the difference between making copies of BASIC and taping music off the air rather than buying the recording artist's music, some wanted to know? Others argued the altruistic position that BASIC belonged in the public domain, an argument that had some merit since Gates and Allen had created BASIC using the PDP-10 at Harvard, a computer funded by the Defense Advanced Research Projects Agency. In other words, these people argued, the computer time they had used was paid for with taxpayers' money.

Regardless of what philosophical rationalizations hobbyists used to justify why they had not paid for BASIC, they did have one legitimate beef: MITS was partly to blame by engaging in a pricing policy that all but assured Altair owners would do anything possible to avoid paying for BASIC. No one wanted the memory boards MITS was turning out. But everyone wanted BASIC. So early on the company had decided to charge $500 for BASIC alone, about a hundred dollars more than the Altair itself cost. But for only $150, a customer could get a memory board plus BASIC. Of course, word quickly got around that most of the boards didn't work, and MITS knew this, which is why it priced BASIC out of reach of many hobbyists. MITS was forcing customers who wanted BASIC to buy the atrocious circuit boards.

Gates did not stop the antipiracy campaign with his letter. In late March, he spoke out on the piracy issue at the World Altair Computer Convention in Albuquerque in his first industry speech. The convention, the first ever for microcomputers, was the brainchild of Roberts and Bunnell. By then, MITS had annual sales of well over a million dollars and Roberts wanted to showcase the company with a convention that would bring together key people in the industry. Bunnell organized and promoted the convention, which was held March 26–28, 1976, in a hotel near the Albuquerque airport. Several hundred people came, including a few uninivited competitors who crashed the party. One of these competitors was Processsor Technology, a startup hardware firm producing 4K memory boards that could be used with the Altair. The company had wanted to set up a display booth at the convention, but Roberts, who had become increasingly paranoid about competition, vetoed their request. The boards produced by Processor Technology not only worked, but were selling very well, much better than the faulty circuit boards designed by MITS. The only reason customers bought a MITS board at all was to get a copy of BASIC for the $150 package price.

When Roberts told Processor Technology founder Bob Marsh he could not have a display booth at the MITS-sponsored Altair convention, Marsh rented the hotel's penthouse suite and posted hand-written signs in the hotel lobby directing convention goers to his company's suite. Later, Roberts published his own diatribe in the Altair newsletter, describing Processor Technology and other companies who dared produce memory boards for his computer as "parasites." In the end, he only damaged himself in the industry further.

The three-day convention, which included guided tours of MITS, was more of a conference than a trade show. There was no hardware on display, except in the penthouse suite. Most sessions were held in a large room in the hotel where attendees listened to speeches and talked about microcomputers. When Gates spoke, his speech was another belligerent attack on those hobbyists who he said were "ripping off" his software. At the time, Gates was fairly unknown in the industry. He was better known as the author of the scathing letter in *Computer Notes* than as the author of BASIC. Now twenty years old, he looked more like fourteen. His hair was uncombed and hung helter-skelter over his eyebrows and ears, and his thick, oversized glasses accentuated his childlike appearance. His high-pitched voice underscored his youthfulness. But Gates did have a certain charisma. His words crackled with the authority of someone much older and wiser. After his talk, people crowded around him to ask questions. Although he came off as brash and arrogant to many, Gates did have his supporters. "I was very much in sympathy with his attitude," recalled Winkless, the *Personal*

Computing magazine editor. "How do you get your investment back?"

Roberts later asked his friend Eddie Curry to talk with Gates and persuade him to write a second letter, in the hopes of undoing some of the public relations damage. Roberts had been furious with Gates over the first letter because it had been written on the MITS stationery. "It looked like we were accusing all our customers of being crooks. . . . I was very, very upset," Roberts said.

Gates acknowledged that he had made a mistake by using MITS letterhead, and he agreed to work with Curry on a suitable second letter. "In retrospect, it really didn't help anything to accuse people of being thieves," said Curry. "All it did was to work against Bill. He didn't feel he had done some terrible thing, but in the calm light of day he understood it was not the most prudent thing to have done."

Gates'subsequent effort, entitled "A Second and Final Letter," ran in the Altair newsletter in April:

"Since sending out my "Open Letter to Hobbyists" of February 3rd, I have had innumerable replies and an opportunity to speak directly with hobbyists, editors and MITS employees at MITS' World Altair Computer Convention, March 26–28," Gates wrote. "I was surprised at the wide coverage given the letter, and I hope it means that serious consideration is being given to the issue of the future of software development and distribution for the hobbyists. . . ."

Gates then went on to say, "Unfortunately, some of the controversy raised by my letter focused upon me personally and even more inappropriately upon MITS. I am not a MITS employee and perhaps no one at MITS agrees with me absolutely, but I believe all were glad to see the issue I raised discussed. The three negative letters I received objected to the fact that I stated that a large percentage of computer hobbyists have stolen software in their possession. My intent was to indicate that a significant number of the copies of BASIC currently in use were not obtained legitimately and not to issue a blanket indictment of computer hobbyists. On the contrary, I find the majority are intelligent and honest individuals who share my concern for the future of software development. . . . Perhaps the present dilemma has resulted from a failure by many to realize that neither Microsoft nor anyone else can develop extensive software without a reasonable return on the huge investment in time that is necessary."

Gates ended by saying he considered the pirating matter closed. He predicted BASIC would become the foundation for the development of new and exciting application programs for microcomputers.

The BASIC that Gates and Allen had written in those eight frantic weeks at Harvard a year earlier had now spread all over the country, thanks in large measure to the very actions of hobbyists Gates had so bitterly denounced. BASIC *had* become a *de facto* standard in the young microcomputer industry. When new computer companies joined the revolution and needed a BASIC langauge, they came to Albuquerque and did business with Gates and Microsoft. And they came with pockets stuffed with money.

Part of what made Microsoft so successful during the company's infancy was the team of programmers that Gates and Allen began to assemble in the spring of 1976. They became known as the Microkids—high-IQ insomniacs who wanted to join the personal computer crusade, kids with a passion for computers who would drive themselves to the limits of their ability and endurance, pushing the outside of the software envelope.

Chris Larson, the first of the programmers, was still in high school and could only work summers. Richard Weiland came and went for a couple years before he left for good. Marc McDonald, however, was hired as Microsoft's first permanent programmer, and thus became the first of the Microkids. McDonald, who arrived in Albuquerque in April, was a 1974 graduate of the Lakeside computer room. He and Gates had known each other since their days at C-Cubed trying to crash the PDP-10 computer system. Since Microsoft did not yet have its own offices, McDonald worked on a computer terminal in the apartment he shared with Allen, or he used one of the terminals at MITS. Not long after McDonald joined the team, Weiland returned. He had left several months earlier after developing BASIC for the 6800 chip. Weiland, who moved in with Allen and McDonald, took on the role of Microsoft's general manager. He would eventually be offered part of the company by Gates and Allen as an inducement to stay, but instead he decided to go to business school at Stanford University.

Two more programmers arrived in the fall of 1976: Steve Wood and Albert Chu. Wood had grown up in Seattle, but went to public schools and did not know Gates or Allen. He had been finishing his master's degree at Stanford University in electrical engineering and looking for a job when he noticed a Microsoft recruitment poster in the placement office of the Stanford Linear Accelerator Center, where he worked as a research assistant. The center was one of the first facilities in the country to acquire a microcomupter lab; it had also become the regular meeting place for the Homebrew Computer Club.

Unlike the others already working for Microsoft, Wood was married. He was a year older than Allen and Weiland. After Wood interviewed for the job and returned home with an offer, he and his wife threw their belongings in a small U-Haul trailer and headed for Albuquerque. Microsoft had just rented its first offices on the eighth floor of a bank building near the airport. The address, Two Park Central Tower, would be Microsoft's home for the next two and a half years.

Although Microsoft now had offices, it did not have its own computers. Instead, the company contracted to timeshare with the Albuquerque city schools, which used a DEC PDP-10 system. Microsoft's programmers worked at so-called dumb terminals without a printer and each day someone had to go down to the school adminstration building and pick up computer printouts.

Gates and Allen had decided that FORTRAN was the next high-level language to develop as Microsoft expanded its product line; when Wood and Chu arrived they immediately went to work writing FORTRAN code for the 8080 microchip. At the time, FORTRAN was probably the second most popular computer language after BASIC. This strategy of anticipating the market and being the first out with a new product was a competitive edge Microsoft would hone in the years ahead. Allen, even more than Gates, had a knack for figuring out the direction of the industry three or four years down the road. The question constantly before the young company was whether Microsoft should invest in this product or that product, this set of software features or that set of features. Gates and Allen had to determine where the market was heading, what the technology would be like. "Microsoft definitely has a vision of where it wants to go. It's very broad compared to some companies that have a narrow focus on only one product," said Allen later. "Part of this goes back to when Bill and I were working on new languages in Albuquerque. Every time there was a new language we thought was going to be popular, we'd see that as another possible market for our software technology."

In late 1976, Microsoft landed its two biggest customers and most lucrative accounts to date, National Cash Register and General Electric. Both wanted BASIC. General Electric only wanted to buy the source code. But NCR needed a digital cassette BASIC that would work with its 8080 file system. That job was given to Marc McDonald, who later developed what became known as Stand-alone Disk BASIC for NCR. It was one of Microsoft's most successful and important software products to date, although Gates, rather than McDonald, would get the credit.

Allen remained as MITS software director until November, when he quit to work fulltime for Microsoft. The company was growing fast. Revenues for its first full year were more than $100,000. This was expected to triple in the next year. Things were working out just as Allen and Gates had imagined that summer at TRW in Vancouver when they talked about one day owning a software company.

In January of 1977, two months after Allen quit MITS, Gates dropped out of Harvard, this time for good. Sam Znaimer, who had roomed with Gates when they were freshmen, recalled that Gates told him shortly before he left school that he had come to Harvard because he was looking for people smarter than he was. "He told me he had not found them," Znaimer said. "I think Bill just got bored." But Andy Braiterman, who was rooming with Gates at the end, said Gates realized even he had limitations. "Bill was trying to do too much. He really did have a sense that things were out of control. He didn't have time for both his business and school, not to mention trying to keep up with poker playing. He was really worn out by the end. . . . If he had stayed in school, it would have been a tremendous mistake."

Because Braiterman had entered Harvard as a sophomore, he graduated at the same time Gates dropped out. During their final semester together, they had talked often about computers and the future. "Bill was one of the first people I ever knew who really had this concept of computers being everywhere," said Braiterman. "He saw that as being the future. I'm not sure he really saw things quite the way they turned out, though. He saw personal computers as being omnipresent in people's homes, as opposed to offices. But he was clearly thinking in the right direction. He also talked to me about the concept of everyone being able to discard all their books and paper materials and access everything they wanted to know by computer—to do all communication by computers."

Back in Seattle, Gates' parents took the news hard that he was dropping out of Harvard to work fulltime at Microsoft.

"They were very distraught," remembered the Reverend Dale Turner. They might have taken comfort, however, in knowing that Harvard's official records listed their son as having left "in good standing." In fact, he is still considered by the university to be on a leave of absence. Harvard, it seems, does not like to admit someone would drop out and not intend to come back and graduate someday.

After leaving Harvard, Bill Gates put all his considerable talent and energy into Microsoft. There were no more distractions to divert his focus from the company. Over the next five years, in fact, he would take only two vacations of a few days each.

The most pressing problem at Microsoft when he arrived in Albuquerque in January of 1977 was the business relationship with MITS, which he found more and more frustrating. There was so much money to be made, he felt, were it not for the fact that Microsoft was still a legal and financial captive of MITS. The imposing figure of Ed Roberts had cast a giant shadow over Microsoft's otherwise bright future.

The licensing agreement with MITS prevented Microsoft from selling 8080 BASIC to companies without the approval of MITS. Roberts had said he would not block a sale unless it were to a competitor. This was not a problem at first because the Altair had no rivals. But within two years of the *Popular Electronics* article, dozens of computer hardware companies had joined the revolution. In early 1977, Commodore hit the market with its PET computer, named after the trendy and popular pet rocks of the day. And down in Texas, the huge Tandy corporation was running tests on a microcomputer called the Radio Shack TRS-80, which was expected on the market soon. Out in the Silicon Valley of California, a new company that had been started in a garage was about to offer the fruit of its labors—the

Apple II. The industry was growing up fast, and a language company like Microsoft that allowed computer users to utilize their machines more effectively stood to reap a financial harvest.

While Gates looked at these new computer hardware companies and saw new markets for Microsoft's products, Roberts saw them as a threat. Inevitably, he and Gates were headed for a collision. Although the two had argued, yelled, and screamed at each other almost since the day they met two years earlier, Roberts realized he was dependent on Gates. Had the young software creator left MITS and taken Allen with him, MITS would have been in serious trouble, particularly if Microsoft forged an alliance with a new hardware company. So there were limits on how far Roberts could go in arguing with Gates. On the other hand, Gates knew Roberts was not his equal when it came to understanding computer software. Arguably, no one was. Part of the problem for Roberts in dealing with Gates was that Gates knew he was good, and at times he could be obnoxious. He did not hesitate to call someone "stupid," or an "idiot," including Roberts.

One heated blow-up between the two had occurred in 1976, when a company called Intelligent Systems Corporation approached MITS about licensing BASIC. Roberts considered the firm a competitor and jacked the price of BASIC up so high that the deal fell through. Later that year, Microsoft negotiated deals for BASIC with several other companies, including Zilog and Rydacom. Zilog had recently come out with the Z80 microchip, which was a clone of Intel's 8080. But once again Roberts interfered, refusing to sign licensing agreements. By early 1977, Gates' tireless salesmanship, browbeating, and haggling had resulted in tentative agreements to license BASIC to a number of computer companies, including ADDS, Delta Data, Courier, Control Data, Lexar, Astro, Rand, Lawrence Livermore, Isyx, and Magnavox. Microsoft and MITS stood to make more than $100,000 each. But Roberts again refused to sign the agreements. A letter Roberts sent to ADDS (Applied Digital Data Systems) was typical of his position:

"During our recent discussions involving the potential of granting ADDS a license to market MITS Extended BASIC, we were having difficulty establishing terms that would mutually satisfy the long-range marketing objectives of both companies. After further consideration of the potential problems, we feel that it is in the best interests of both ADDS and MITS to discontinue our efforts to try to enter into a license agreement." Roberts went on to note that ADDS "should be aware that MITS holds exclusive rights to the BASIC software programs developed by Mr. Gates and his partners, and that any commitments regarding the rights to the BASIC program, or any modified versions or portions of it, by anyone other than MITS personnel, are not authorized."

Roberts also fired off a letter to Microsoft, notifying Gates and Allen that he had told ADDS and Delta Data that MITS would not license BASIC to them because of "market conflicts." Roberts also added in his letter, "All other third party deals, e.g., Intel, Motorola, etc., appear to be at a standstill due to a variety of reasons. Let me again reiterate my desire that you not contact directly any potential third party customer without our approval and involvement."

Microsoft faced an even more serious problem. Roberts was thinking of selling MITS and moving to Georgia to buy a farm. The likely buyer, Pertec, a company specializing in disk and tape drives for microcomputers and mainframe computers, had made it clear that the licensing agreement with Microsoft was part of any sale. MITS had grossed about $13 million in 1976, but the Altair, which had gone supernova, was now a collapsing star. Without the licensing agreement, MITS had little value. BASIC, not the Altair, was the MITS cash cow.

When Gates learned of the pending sale, he knew he and Allen had to do whatever it took to get BASIC back. Since signing the agrement with MITS, Gates and Allen had received almost $180,000 in royalties, including roughly $105,000 for the licensing of BASIC when accompanied with the sale of MITS hardware; $10,000 from the licensing of BASIC without the sale of hardware; and $55,000 from the licensing of the BASIC source code. Because the agreement provided for a $180,000 royalty cap, Microsoft could not make much more money from BASIC unless they could break away from MITS. On April 20, 1977, after consulting with Gates' father in Seattle, and hiring an attorney in Albuquerque, Gates and Allen notified Roberts by letter that they were terminating the licensing agreement for BASIC, effective in ten days. They cited several reasons: MITS had failed to account for thousands of dollars in royalty payments, failed to make its "best efforts" to promote and commericialize BASIC, and failed to secure secrecy agreements when BASIC was licensed to certain third parties, mostly hobbyists.

The licensing agreement required that any disputes that arose would be settled by arbitration. But a couple weeks after receiving Microsoft's letter, Roberts filed for a restraining order in Bernalillo County District Court in Albuquerque. A judge granted his motion: Until the licensing dispute was resolved, Microsoft could not license its 8080 BASIC. Roberts said he went to court when he found out Microsoft was negotiating to license BASIC to Texas Instruments, which was about to come out with a microcomputer of its own. Texas Instruments, of course, had helped to undercut the market when MITS was a struggling calculator kit company.

It would take several months to resolve the matter, and for what would be the only time in the company's history, Microsoft faced money problems.

"It was tough that spring and summer," recalled Steve Wood. "There wasn't any revenue coming in. We had a little coming in from FORTRAN, which we had just started shipping, and we had a little coming in from 6800 and 6502 versions of BASIC. But those were not huge revenue streams."

On May 22, 1977, Roberts sold MITS to Pertec. It was essentially a stock swap—Roberts walked away with several million dollars worth of Pertec stock.

When the chief counsel for Pertec came to Albuquerque to assess the situation and talk with Gates, he took one look at the long-haired, scraggly, 21-year-old and decided the legal battle against Microsoft was going to be easy. Roberts had warned Pertec that it would have its corporate hands full with Gates, but no one listened to him. "Pertec kept telling me I was being unreasonable and they could deal with this guy," Roberts said. "It was a little like Roosevelt telling Churchill that he could deal with Stalin."

Eddie Curry talked Gates into meeting with Roberts and the Pertec lawyer. They gathered in a conference room at MITS, while Curry waited outside. Within minutes, he could hear the three screaming and shouting. Curry was worried that Gates was taking a real beating. He placed a frantic call to Allen over at Microsoft, advising him to phone Gates and tell him they needed to discuss an urgent business matter. It was a ruse to get Gates out of the room. Allen made the call and rushed over to MITS to wait for Gates to come out. Curry recalled that when Gates emerged, "Bill told Paul in a very loud voice something like, 'These guys think they've got me over a barrel, but I'm holding my own.' And then he went right back in. Well, I didn't worry about him after that."

It was obvious that talking wasn't going to settle things. The dispute finally went to arbitration. In addition to underestimating Gates, Pertec made another mistake. The company wrote a very explicit letter to Microsoft, saying it would no longer market BASIC or allow it to be licensed because it considered all other hardware companies competitors. The letter turned out to be the key piece of evidence in the arbritration hearing, in that it went completely counter to the "best efforts" provision in the licensing agreement. "It weakened their case," said Wood. "They came in very arrogant, essentially saying, 'We are this huge multimillion dollar company and you are just a handful of kids and we are not going to take you seriously.' And that was a big mistake."

The hearing went on for three weeks, from eight in the morning until about five at night each day. "It looked like big giant Pertec was picking on these poor nineteen- and twenty-year-old guys and trying to steal their life's work," said Roberts. "That's how they played it and it played pretty well. . . . I told Pertec they needed to deal with Gates hard. But they didn't. It was a fatal mistake. It turns out he won everything."

It was a complex and highly technical case. If the arbitrator had had to decide the dispute based on his understanding of the technology, Microsoft might still be waiting for a ruling. "I don't think he had a clue to what anybody was talking about," said Curry. Instead, the arbitrator ruled on the legal merits. Microsoft, he decided, owned the rights to BASIC and could market the product as it saw fit.

"If Pertec had prevailed, there might not be a Microsoft today," said David Bunnell. "Whether Gates was right or wrong, it was in the best interest of the PC business that he prevailed."

After the Pertec decision came down and the log jam of customers waiting for BASIC broke loose, Microsoft never had to worry about money again.

Ed Roberts stayed on with Pertec for a couple years, then returned to his mother's birthplace in the quiet heart of Georgia, where he used some of his new wealth to buy a farm. A few years later, he sold the farm and entered medical school—he had always wanted to be a doctor. Today, he's a family physician in Cochran, a town of about 5,000 south of Macon. Few of the townspeople know that Roberts once built a tiny computer called the Altair, which shone like a Christmas star in the night sky during the early days of the personal computer revolution. A dozen years after the light went out and Roberts left Albuquerque, he is still bitter when he talks about Gates, perhaps because Gates went on to such great success, while Roberts became something of a Robert Goddard, the scientist who laid the foundation of modern rocketry and then was all but forgotten by history. The world will never appreciate what Ed

Roberts did for the computer industry, said his friend Eddie Curry.

Roberts still maintains that MITS was the rightful owner of the BASIC that helped make Gates a billionaire several times over. He does not dispute that Gates and Allen were the authors. But MITS, he said, footed the bill for the development costs that turned BASIC into a marketable product for microcomputers. He estimated that Gates and Allen used several hundred thousand dollars' worth of computing time while working on BASIC at MITS. "I was naive," Roberts said. "It sounds self-serving now, but I was really concerned with not trying to screw those guys. Bill was only 19 and Allen only a couple years older, but it turns out they were a lot older than I was—Bill was for sure. Paul is a totally honorable guy."

What Ed Roberts understood, and Pertec learned the hard way, was that Bill Gates' looks were deceiving. Although he looked more like a stockroom office boy than a corporate executive, Gates proved himself to be a formidable businessman. At age 21, he was as comfortable sitting in his office negotiating tough deals with much older executives in three-piece suits as he was programming long into the night in front of a computer terminal, eating cold pizza and swigging down Coke.

The skinny kid with the dandruff and uncombed mop haircut not only understood software as few in the industry did, but he had the business and marketing savvy to run a very profitable company in a highly competitve environment. He understood the underlying issues in negotiation that were not immediately apparent, and he was confident that he could handle them correctly. Given his white-hot drive, and his determination to trounce the opposition, to do whatever had to be done to dominate the software market, this rare combination of technical genius and managerial acumen was an unbeatable combination.

Steve Wood recalled executives coming to Albuquerque and being taken back by the long-haired Microkids. "Their reaction was, 'Who are these kids? Where's their leader?' Then Bill would take charge of the meeting and within ten minutes that wouldn't be an issue anymore." Typically, these business meetings were held with men in their thirties and forties, who came dressed in conservative business attire. With important visitors, some of the Microsoft programmers would wear slacks instead of jeans and try to get Marc McDonald to wear shoes instead of sandals. But that was the extent of their effort to conform to formal business etiquette.

"Looking back on it now, that must have been pretty funny," said Wood, "but at the time we pretty much ignored it. We didn't even think about it. We had the products these guys needed and wanted. We thought we knew what they needed to do in terms of their product development strategy and their hardware. And we felt we understood that better than most of them did, and we told them that and we just kind of expected they would listen and pay attention. And for the most part they did."

Although the legal battle with MITS and Pertec lasted throughout much of 1977, the pace of work at Microsoft never slowed. The company worked on new languages, such as COBOL, and continued to market FORTRAN, as well as BASIC for chips other than the 8080.

Gates spent much of his time farming the OEM market. An OEM, or original manufacturer, is the brand name under which a product is sold. When a car buyer purchases a General Motors car with Goodyear tires, General Motors is the OEM because it buys the tires to use on equipment General Motors sells. In the case of the computer industry, an OEM would buy a computer from another manufacturer, build it into their own equipment and then sell the complete package, ready to run. Many OEMs, for example, made high-tech computer equipment for hospitals, such as imaging systems. Others specialized in graphics or robotics. But they all needed a high-level language such as BASIC or FORTRAN for their machines. It was a very lucrative market, and Microsoft received a substantial portion of its early revenues from contracts with OEMs.

While Gates cut the OEM deals, Allen concentrated on programming and figuring out what needed to be done next. It was a synergistic relationship.

"I always focused on new ideas and creating new technology," Allen said. "Bill would occasionally jump in and get involved in that, but he was always more focused on the business side, more attracted to the business relationship side of things."

At Harvard, Gates had read business books like other male students read *Playboy*. He wanted to know everything he could about running a company, from managing people to marketing products. He even checked out books on corporate law. He put his studies to good use at Microsoft. He not only negotiated the deals, he also wrote the contracts, as Wood found out one day when he met with Gates to discuss a nondisclosure licensing agreement for FORTRAN, for which Wood had written the code. Gates quickly drafted the agreement. According to Wood, Gates seemed to know more than the lawyers did. Not only did Gates understand what needed to be done, but he was able to do a lot of the contract writing himself, saving Microsoft expensive expert legal advice.

"Bill did it all," said one of the programmers. "He was the salesman, the technical leader, the lawyer, the businessman. . . . You could go on and on." Gates did get legal help on some of the company's big-money contracts. One such contract was the one Gates closed with Tandy. Around the Fort Worth area in Texas, the Tandy Corporation was known as the "McDonald's of the Electronics World." Founded as a leather business in 1927, it had stores around the country by 1962, when it bought a chain of nine mail-order electronics stores called Radio Shack. By 1975, Radio Shack had hundreds of stores nationwide. After the Altair hit the market, Radio Shack hired a couple of engineers to develop a microcomputer. The TRS-80, built around Zilog's Z80 chip, made its debut in August in 1977 at New York City's Warwick Hotel. It cost $399 and was distributed through Radio Shack stores across America. In its first month, more than 10,000 of the computers were sold. They rolled off the assembly line at Tandy like fast-food hamburgers. The TRS-80 was not a kit like the Altair, but came ready to plug in.

In negotiating with Tandy to supply BASIC for the TRS-80, Gates had met John Roach, at the time a vice-president in charge of marketing. He and Gates hit it off. Roach became something of a mentor to Gates, teaching his young and eager student business and marketing strategy. Within four years, Roach became the president of Tandy.

Not only did Microsoft hook up with Tandy in 1977, but the company also licensed BASIC 6502 to Apple for the Apple II computer. Microsoft had begun to set the industry standard with its software. And that's exactly what Gates had wanted, what he pushed for in meetings with his programming team. "We Set the Standard" became the company's motto in Albuqueque. It represented Gates' basic business philosophy. Of course, trying to be first out of the gate with a new software product just to create an industry standard sometimes caused problems. Too often Gates set unrealistic goals for product development. Deadlines were missed, products weren't always well-designed, and contracts had to be revised due to unforeseen obstacles or delays.

"Bill's approach, and you can still see it now in things like Windows, was always to go for creating a standard, to get the market share," said Wood. "He just hated to turn down business. If it meant we had to drop our price to get the business, he was typically much more willing to argue that we do that. . . .

"In Albuquerque, whenever we had pricing discussions or arguments, the way we would decide how much to charge an OEM customer is we would sit down and say, okay, what are they asking for? How long is it going to take us to do that? Of course, we would always underestimate that. Then we'd sit down and say, okay, how much do we think these guys will pay? How much can we get out of these guys? How much is reaonable to expect them to pay? How bad do we want this business? Bill would always be arguing for a lower price and a more aggressive schedule. 'Oh, we can do that in three months. Let's just charge them fifty thousand because we really want to get the contract.' Paul would argue for a higher price, saying, 'Let's try and get more money from these guys.' We usually ended up somewhere in between."

Although Gates spent most of his time taking care of business, he still involved himself with some of the technical work at Microsoft. He loved programming and would compete with his employees, occasionally participating in some of the informal contests the Microkids held to see who could write a program in the fewest lines.

In the book *Programmers At Work*, Gates is quoted as saying: "In the first four years of the company, there was no Microsoft program that I wasn't involved in actually writing and designing. In all those intial products, whether it was BASIC, FORTRAN, BASIC 6800 or BASIC 6502, not a line of code went out that I didn't look over."

Gates acknowledged his style rubbed some of his programmers the wrong way. "It's kind of painful sometimes if you have somebody else working on the project. They never code stuff exactly the same way you like to see it coded. I remember when we were working on BASIC, I'd go back and recode other people's section of code, without making any dramatic improvements. That bothers people when you go in and do that, but sometimes you just feel like you have to do it."

It was bad enough that Gates rewrote other programmers' code. But at least once he also got credit for their work. When Microsoft published the MS-DOS Encyclopedia, the preface to this huge technical manual credited Gates for developing Stand-alone Disk BASIC. In fact, the program was developed by Marc

McDonald for National Cash Register in 1977. McDonald had since left the company, but when he read the preface he fired off a blistering letter to Gates. "When I saw that in the DOS Encyclopedia," McDonald recalled, "I said to myself, 'What is this bullshit!?' Bill knew damn well I did that." The Disk BASIC developed by McDonald used a revolutionary file management technique known as the FAT, or file allocation table. According to McDonald, Gates did not write any of the code for Stand-alone Disk BASIC. It was much faster and more efficient than the Disk BASIC Gates wrote for the Altair while holed up for five days at the Hilton Hotel in Albuquerque.

"Bill has a very convenient memory," McDonald said of Gates. Subsequent editions of the encyclopedia gave McDonald, rather than Gates, credit for Stand-alone Disk BASIC. Before he left Microsoft, McDonald helped develop a version of Stand-alone Disk BASIC that was widely used on Japanese computers, as well.

Gates began to go aggressively after the Japanese market in 1977 and got a huge jump on the competition. "I went into Japan only two years after I started Microsoft knowing that in terms of working with hardware companies, that was a great place to be," he said. "A lot of great research goes on there. And also, it was the most likely source of competition other than the U.S. itself. I didn't want to leave that market so that companies would grow up using the domestic market and then come and be that much stronger to compete with us on a worldwide basis." (Today, Japan is Microsoft's second largest market, after the U.S.)

The point man for Microsoft's push into Japan and the Far East was Kuzuhiko Nishi, a silver-tongued salesman and hyperactive computer whizkid the same age as Gates. Although physically short and chubby, Nishi was brilliant and flamboyant. He would become known as the "Bill Gates of Japan." For a while he and Gates were as close as brothers.

Their backgrounds were remarkably similar, and they travelled parallel paths on opposite sides of the planet until a fateful meeting in Dallas, Texas in 1977. Both came from well-to-do parents, developed an early passion for computers, and dropped out of college to form their own companies. Nishi grew up in the Japanese port city of Kobe, where his family founded a private girls' secondary school. At age nine, he would sneak into his father's study late at night and play with an old Wang computer. By the time he entered prestigious Waseda University, he had become as obsessed with computers as Gates. He dropped out after two years to start a computer magazine, but he sold the magazine after a dispute with the publisher. He then started another publication, ASCII, which would become the largest software company in Japan.

His friendship with Gates and partnership with Microsoft began in early 1977, when Nishi placed a call from Japan to New Mexico to talk with "the people who designed BASIC." Several companies in Japan were thinking of entering the microcomputer field and Nishi wanted to help design their computers and supply the software. He and Gates talked for a while, and Nishi offered him a first-class ticket to fly immediately to Japan to talk business. Gates explained that he could not get away, but they agreed to meet for an hour at the upcoming National Computer Conference in Dallas, Texas. When they met, they talked for eight hours. Gates had found a computer soul mate who shared the same vision of the personal computer as he and had the same intensity and energy. Afterwards, they signed a one-page agreement to do business together, and Nishi became Microsoft's first Far East agent. That agreement would soon produce millions of dollars for both Nishi and Microsoft.

The 1977 National Computer Conference had been cochaired by Portia Isaacson (who years later would join Microsoft's board of directors). She had bulldozed NCC organizers into allowing microcomputers into the Dallas show as well as the "real" computers. Booths displaying the microcomputers were located downstairs in a hot, miserable hall without windows, while the "real" machines were located in an air-conditioned hall upstairs. Most of the attendees at the convention, however, were to be found downstairs in the small hall.

"It was really interesting," said Nelson Winkless. "It finally penetrated the computer establishment that these things were for real."

When the show was over, a number of industry people took the same flight to Albuquerque to do business with either MITS or Microsoft. The flight was two hours late, so the microcomputer group, including Gates, passed the time on the airport terminal floor by playing a dice game called "Petal Around the Rose." Gates had not played the game before, but he was eager to try his competitive hand. The game had been developed by students at the University of Southern California. Five dice are thrown, and the player is told three things: the name of the game is "Petal Around the Rose," the answer is always even, and there is a correct answer for each throw of the dice. The player is told nothing else. If someone gets the right answer five times in a row, it's considered *prima facie* evidence they understand the game and they are then sworn to secrecy.

It's a difficult game. Some catch on after only a few throws of the dice, others need weeks, and a few never get it. Frustrated players falling into the last category have resorted to running computer simulations. Gates was one who never figured the game out. He did get the right answer five times in a row, but not because he understood what he was doing. He actually didn't have a clue. But with his photographic memory, Gates was able to remember each correct answer from a previous roll by another player. With five dice, it was quite a feat of memorization.

Nelson Winkless realized that Gates was faking it when he picked up a piece of paper Gates inadvertently dropped in the aisle of the plane near his seat. On it Gates had written, "peddle around the roses." Knowing the proper spelling of the name of the game was essential to solving the puzzle. His poor spelling guaranteed he would never figure it out.

The computer fairs and trade shows were very important to young companies like Microsoft. They were an opportunity to see what was happening in the industry, exchange information, promote catchy new products, meet people face to face, and do some valuable networking. They could also be a lot of fun. At a trade show in Las Vegas in 1977 that he attended with David Bunnell and Richard Weiland, Gates spent the night at the craps table. About four o'clock in the morning, with Gates down a couple thousand dollars, Bunnell and Weiland decided to go back to their hotel; Gates, however, had locked the car keys in the trunk of the rental car. A locksmith had to be summoned to cut a hole in the trunk to get it open, which did not please the employees at the car rental agency, who charged Gates an extra $300. "He thought it was very funny," said Bunnell.

They rented a private plane for the flight back to Albuquerque. Weiland flew, Bunnell navigated, and Gates curled up in the back seat, pulled a blanket over his head, and went to sleep.

The character and flavor of Microsoft today is not all that different from the character of the company in suite 819 at Two Park Central Tower in Albuquerque in 1977. The personality of the company very much reflected its youthful leader. Although the company has grown since these formative years, the corporate culture is still much the same: the work ethic, intensity, hard drive, creativity, youthfulness, and informality were woven into the very fabric of Microsoft from the start. People wore what they wanted to work, set their own hours, and had a variety of outside interests. But they were part of a team, a family. They shared a common goal and purpose, and it emanated first and foremost from Gates—work hard, make better products, and win.

"We were just having fun and working really hard," said Steve Wood, who took over as general manager in the fall of

1977 when Rick Weiland left. "When I think about it, I'm amazed. You look back then and we were just five or six people. Now, Microsoft is nearly a two-billion-dollar-a-year company."

In its first year, as noted previously, Microsoft made about $100,000. By the end of 1976, revenues had more than doubled. Even though the court restraining order sought by Ed Roberts and Pertec prevented Microsoft from licensing its popular 8080 BASIC for much of 1977, there was still enough money coming in for the company to hire several more people, including another full-time programmer, Bob Greenberg, whose father was president of Coleco Industries, an electronic game and toy company back East that was just getting into the microcomputer field. Also joining the Microsoft team in 1977 was Andrea Lewis, who had helped David Bunnell run *Computer Notes* over at MITS. She was hired by Microsoft to write the technical manuals for the company's software products. Chris Larson and Monte Davidoff came back for the summer as well.

One of the best hires Microsoft made in 1977 turned out to be Miriam Lubow, who didn't know a thing about computers and had never heard of software. Lubow was a 42-year-old mother of four who spotted a "help-wanted" ad in the local paper for a secretarial job at Microsoft. She became the office "den mother," who held everything together and took care of the young programmers almost half her age. Her duties included typing, filing, bookkeeping, purchasing, and payroll.

Gates had been away on business when Lubow interviewed for the job with Wood. One morning, after only a few days at work, Lubow rushed into Wood's office with the information that some "kid" had just zipped past her desk and gone into the office of "Mr. Gates" and was playing with the computer terminal. That kid, Wood told her, *was* Gates. A few minutes later, Lubow came back in to see Wood.

"How *old* is he, Steve?"

"Twenty-one," Wood replied.

Lubow took a special liking to Gates. She became his surrogate mother, reminding him to get an occasional haircut and making sure his hair was combed when he had important visitors. Worried that he never seemed to eat, she brought him his favorite food, hamburgers, for lunch. She also tried to make sure he got to the Albuquerque airport on time for his business trips.

Gates was travelling a lot by that time, making deals with OEM customers around the country. His habit was to leave the office for the airport, which was only a couple miles away, as close as possible to his departure time—never more than ten minutes and usually closer to five. He often caught the plane just as the flight attendant was closing the door. It was a game he played, one that he still plays today. Gates simply liked pushing things to the edge. "That's where you most often find high performance," he once said. "I don't like to waste time. I have a very full schedule, and I travel enough that I think I am very efficient at getting to the airport and understanding how much time to set aside. I'm not the kind of guy who goes an hour before the flight leaves, let's put it that way. That would seem like a waste of time." There is also the challenge of beating the clock. And winning. Lubow began to tell Gates that the departure time of his flight was 15 minutes earlier than it actually was so she would not have to worry about him.

Gates often would be gone two or three days negotiating deals and selling the company's software. He would then return to Albuquerque, work all night, and go to a meeting the next day. Lubow would sometimes find him sleeping on the floor of his office when she came to work.

"He could revive pretty fast," one of the Microkids recalled. "It would just take a cup of coffee or something like that and he'd be into whatever the meeting was about. It was a good thing he was only 21."

The atmosphere at Microsoft was extremely casual unless out-of-town "suits" were expected for an important meeting. All the employees, including Lubow, usually took off their shoes and went around barefoot. The guys wore jeans and sport shirts. There was always a supply of free Coca-Cola around, a tradition that continues at Microsoft today. (The company provides free soft-drinks, milk, and juice to its more than 8,000 employees.) There were personal computers of various sorts around the office and boxes scattered everywhere—companies shipped their hardware to Microsoft to be fitted with software, and later the hardware was shipped back in the same box. Typically, programmers would show up for work by late morning. Because the timesharing computer system was so slow, they wrote code on yellow legal pads and made sure it was reasonably well-organized before typing it into a terminal. Only four of the terminals were connected to the PDP-10 in the school administration building the company shared time with, so not everyone could work at the same time. Once or twice a day, an employee went down to the school to pick up computer printouts or "listings." Any program debugging had to be done directly on the PDP-10, and once the program was working properly it was downloaded to the computers at Microsoft.

Although the office atmosphere was casual, it could also be confrontational. Gates was very demanding and the work was intense.

"Bill was always pushing," said one programmer. "We'd do something I thought was very clever, and he would say, 'Why didn't you do this, or why didn't you do that two days ago?' That would get frustrating sometimes."

But the Microkids expected to be challenged. And they expected to be able to challenge Gates. In fact, he wanted them to argue with him. His confrontational style of management helped Microsoft maintain its edge, its mental toughness. It made those who worked for him think things through. These are qualities that continue to distinguish Microsoft to this day. It is a culture that never gives employees a chance to get complacent because as soon as they do, someone is going to challenge them. Gates was not afraid to change his mind if someone made a convincing argument, a quality that Steve Wood came to admire. "Bill is not dogmatic about things. He's very pragmatic," Wood said. "He can be extremely vocal and persuasive in arguing one side of an issue, and a day or two later he will say he was wrong and let's get on with it. There are not that many people who have the drive and the intensity and the entrepreneurial qualities to be that successful who also have the ability to put their ego aside. That's a rare trait."

Because the Albuquerque school computer would get busy in the afternoon, and the response time was so terrible, most of the Microkids worked late into the night. The work ethic at Microsoft did not come from Gates—it was self-imposed. There was an unstated expectation that the kids would work as many hours as it took to get the job done.

"There were times, not that infrequently, that I'd be going home for a few hours of sleep about the time Marla (Wood's wife) was getting up," recalled Wood. "We'd often be there 24 hours a day, trying to meet a deadline for another OEM or getting a new product out. We noticed the long hours, but it wasn't a burden. It was fun. We weren't doing it because someone was standing over us with a whip saying, 'You guys have to do this.' We were doing it because we had stuff to do and we had to get it done." But no one could sit in front of a computer terminal all night without a break. Gates and Allen became late-night movie buffs. Albuquerque was no cultural Mecca, but one thing it did seem to have was movie theaters, more in fact per capita than any other city in the country. Gates and Allen saw every new movie that came out. Murder mysteries were their favorites, and they competed to be the first to figure out "whodunit."

"We'd go out to see a movie and then go back to work again," said Allen.

Late night was also the time Gates hit the back roads of Albuquerque in the green Porsche 911 he had bought with some of the profits from Microsoft. Gates liked to drive fast, testing the limits of himself and his machine. It was his way of relaxing or thinking out a problem. Paul Allen relaxed by playing his guitar.

The Mustang Gates owned in high school had an automatic transmission. Neither Gates nor Allen knew how to drive a stick-shift when they first arrived in Albuquerque. They learned in a parking lot, after Allen went to a Chevy dealership and bought a Monza. The two spent an entire afternoon trying to learn to shift gears without making the Monza lurch forward and die. "It was hilarious," recalled Allen.

Not long after he bought the Porsche 911, Gates took it back to the Albuquerque dealer to complain that it would only do 125 miles per hour—not nearly as fast as the manual prom-ised. Gates had a very heavy foot. Miriam Lubow worried that she would pick up the newspaper one morning and find that Gates had been arrested for outstanding speeding tickets. She constantly found tickets for him in the mail.

Gates told a friend that he *was* hauled off to jail once when he was stopped for speeding in Albuquerque. Allen was a pas-senger in the Porsche, and he and Gates got out of the car and tried to confuse the officer about who was actually driving. As Gates was the registered owner, he was taken to jail, and bail was set at a thousand dollars. It so happened that Gates had more than enough money on him to post bail immediately. For several days afterwards, police tailed Gates around town, think-ing he was a drug dealer. They couldn't believe someone as young as Gates could drive a Porsche, have a wallet full of cash, and own a legitimate business.

Everyone who knew Gates in Albuquerque had at least one hair-raising adventure with him and his beloved Porsche 911. "Riding with Bill was a frightening experience," remembered Eddie Curry. "He never went anywhere at less than 80 miles an hour." Curry, who drove a lumbering station wagon, at-tempted to follow Gates out of Microsoft's parking lot one day for a meeting across town. "He went roaring out, and I went roaring out after him when suddenly I realized I was in the middle of an intersection driving an old Chevrolet, and he was rolling down the road in a Porsche, and I was going to get killed because I couldn't get out of the way of the traffic fast enough."

David Bunnell had a wild ride to the Albuquerque airport with Gates. "We were on a street where the speed limit was 35 miles an hour, and we were doing more than 80."

One day, Gates picked up an important Japanese visitor at the airport and drove him downtown to Microsoft's office. "He was white, just white," recalled Allen. "He asked me, 'Mister Gates, he always drive so fast?' "

With Gates, everything turned into some form of competition, and that included his skills as a driver. He and Allen had regular contests to see who was first to arrive at an Albuquerque destination. Since Allen drove a Monza, a much slower car, he got very good at figuring out back-alley shortcuts around town. "When Bill drives a car, he really likes to test the limits of what it can do," said Allen. "But he's an incredible driver. He would push things to the limit but he was always in control."

During the summer of 1977, Gates often went out at 3:00 A.M. after hours of programming and drove around for an hour with his friend Chris Larson. One of his favorite roads was a narrow, twisting two-lane ribbon of highway a few miles east of town off Interstate 40 that led to an abandoned cement plant. Here, the finely tuned engine of the green Porsche could often be heard whining into the desert night as Gates smoothly negotiated one curve after another with each high-pitched shift of gears. On one of these wild summer rides with Larson, however, Gates did not maintain control. He spun out, and the Porsche crashed into a dirt embankment. "The way Chris described it," said Steve Wood, "they were going about 120 miles an hour [forward] and then they were going 120 sideways." Neither Gates nor Larson was injured, and there was only minor damage to the car.

Larson was Gates' partner again on late-night shenanigans at a road construction site east of Albuquerque in the Sandia foothills, where unsuspecting workers would leave the keys in the heavy equipment when they went home for the day. Gates and Larson would sneak into the site, and by trial and error they learned to operate the complex machinery and drive it around the site. Usually, it was by error. Gates once came within a few inches of backing over his Porsche with a bulldozer. After they mastered the machinery, there was the usual friendly competition. One night, Gates and Larson held a bulldozer race, engines revving, stacks belching black smoke, determined to find out whose machine was faster. Neither would claim to be the winner. The bulldozer race became part of Microsoft folklore.

"I kept thinking one of these days we would get a phone call in the morning and have to go bail him out of jail," said Wood.

The New Mexico desert around Albuquerque may have been an ideal place for late-night drives in fast cars, but it was a bad location for a fast-growing software company like Microsoft. Toward the end of 1977, Gates, Allen, and Wood, who was now general manager, talked about moving the company. The question was: where? The Silicon Valley, south of San Francisco, which had given birth to the semiconductor industry, was one obvious choice. It was now the heart of the new microcomputer industry, the world capital of high technology, synonymous with bright ideas, overnight millionaires, and smart upstart companies like Apple. Hardly a week went by without another Silicon Valley computer company opening its doors for business or going public.

"We talked for quite a while about whether we should move to the Bay Area," recalled Wood. "There was very little discussion about whether we were going to move. We knew we were going to move. It was hard to get people to move down to Albuquerque when we were recruiting. It was an inconvenience to travel in and out of. It was just not the right place to be."

Allen wanted to return home to Seattle. "After being in the desert, you want to see trees and water again," he said. Allen missed his family, as did Gates. Seattle was their home, their roots. They would have no problem recruiting talented people to come to the Northwest and work for Microsoft, Allen argued. Seattle was a great place to live. Besides, with all the rain it was an ideal environment for creative programmers who had to work indoors. Knowing that Gates was very close to his family, Allen asked Mary and Bill, Jr., to work on their son and encourage him to move Microsoft to Seattle.

"We talked for several months about whether the Bay Area or Seattle was the best place to go," said Wood.

Gates reportedly didn't care whether Microsoft moved to Washington or California, as long as the company's continued growth was assured. Either location seemed fine with him. In the end, Gates sided with Allen—they would head home to Seattle at the end of 1978. It was almost a year off, but a lot of planning had to take place first.

One person who benefitted from Microsoft's decision to move to Seattle was Bob Wallace. In late 1977, Wallace was working at a computer store in Seattle when he spotted a hand-drawn recruitment flier for Microsoft that had been left by Paul Allen on a recent visit to Seattle.

"I figured every programmer in the world must want to work for Microsoft, because obviously they are going to take over the world, or I thought so at that point," said Wallace.

Although Wallace, who was finishing his master's degree in computer science at the University of Washington, wanted desperately to work for Microsoft, he didn't want to leave Seattle and move to Albuquerque. When Allen told him the company would be moving back to Seattle within a year, Wallace was sold. And Allen was sold on Wallace, as well. Wallace agreed to start work at Microsoft in late spring of 1978 at a salary of about $20,000. Before Wallace arrived in Albuquerque, another programmer, Bob O'Rear, joined the team. The 35 year-old O'Rear had been working in Texas at a company called Texometrix, which he formed with a friend. The company built automated, custom machinery; its biggest project was a machine that assembled polyurethane bottlecaps. The machines used optics and a microcomputer to ensure the caps were assembled correctly. It was state of the art machinery, and O'Rear was the software wizard for the company. But Texometrix was winding down when O'Rear interviewed with Microsoft. "We were great engineers and lousy financiers," he said. When O'Rear joined Microsoft in January of 1978, he was assigned to clean up some remaining problems with BASIC for the Radio Shack TRS-80. Most of the work had already been done, but there were problems with the floating-point mathematical routines.

O'Rear did not like working nights. Ten years older than the next oldest employee, he had a wife, two dogs, and a cat, and he preferred to come to work early. He was usually at the office long before Miriam Lubow arrived.

"I was the guy that liked to come in real early and get my things done and leave at a normal time," said O'Rear. "I can remember occasions where I had a lot to do and I would come in at like four o'clock in the morning and sometimes I'd meet those other guys leaving, because they were working all night. I was a little bit the odd duck."

Wallace arrived in May and went to work developing BASIC for Texas Instruments. Another programmer was hired as well. With the Pertec mess finally settled, and Microsoft free to license BASIC, the money flowed in at warp speed from such companies as Commodore, Apple, Radio Shack, NCR, General Electric, Texas Instruments, Intel, and various OEM customers.

"Just a plain version of Disk BASIC went for $50,000, and we could make the thing in a couple of hours," recalled Marc McDonald.

Every couple months, Microsoft's bank account grew by $150,000 or more, and Wood would buy a $100,000 certificate of deposit. (Microsoft put all its early money in CDs.) In addition, the market in Japan was about to open up. Since signing the one-page agreement with Gates the year before, Nishi had been doing missionary work in Japan for himself and Microsoft. His biggest sale came when he convinced Kazuya Watanabe, a manager with the electronics giant NEC, to build Japan's first personal computer. He then persuaded Watanabe to fly to Albuquerque in 1978 to talk with Gates and Allen about software for the computer.

Gates met him at the airport in his Porsche. The visit was short, but Watanabe was impressed with Gates and Allen and the work Microsoft had done developing languages for American computers. When he returned to Tokyo, he sold the NEC executives on producing the country's first microcomputer and convinced them that they should hire Microsoft to supply the software. The NEC PC 8001 debuted the next year. Within three years, virtually every brand of Japanese computers available had some form of Microsoft software running on it.

"Microsoft played a big role in our decision making," Watanabe later told the *Wall Street Journal*. "I always felt that only young people could develop software for personal computers— people with no tie, working with a Coke and a hamburger— only such people could make a personal computer adequate for other young people."

And that pretty much described the atmosphere Watanabe had found at Microsoft. Looking back on those times 14 years later, Wood tried to explain Microsoft's phenomenal early success: "It was more the character of the people than any particular moment. One of the real keys, and this has always been true of Microsoft, was we were able to anticipate the markets pretty effectively. . . . We were always a year or two ahead of where the demand was really going to be. But we were generally guessing right. A lot of it was Bill's and particularly Paul's ability to see where some of the stuff was going to go. A lot of people are able to see things like that, but we had just an enthusiasm, a real high level of drive and ambition. There wasn't anything we couldn't do. Okay, so no one has done this for a personal computer before, so what? We can do it. No big deal. And nobody even thought about whether some of the things we were doing were feasible or not. We just said we can do them. We overcommitted ourselves. We missed deadlines. We consistently underestimated the time it would take to do a project, and we committed to too many of those projects at a time. But we always got it done. And it generally tended to be pretty successful."

Because of that success, Gates never had to use his family's wealth or venture capital to bankroll the company. Microsoft was bootstrapped from the beginning. By the time Gates began scouting for a new location for the company in Seattle in the summer of 1978, Microsoft's revenues for the year were closing in on the million dollar mark.

"We were driving hard," said O'Rear. "But we played hard, too." Before the summer ended, the last one they would spend in Albuquerque, the entire Microsoft team took time off for a camping and water-skiing trip to Elephant Butte Reservoir on the Rio Grande south of Albuquerque near Truth or Consequences. The break was needed. The upcoming move to Seattle would make great demands on everyone. Shortly before the picnic, Gates leased new offices in the Old National Bank building in Bellevue, across Lake Washington from Seattle. Microsoft would again be on the eighth floor—suite 819. The new phone number was an easy one to remember—8080, the number of the Intel chip that had made it all possible only four years earlier. Getting that telephone number from the phone company may have been made easier by the fact that Mary Gates served on the board of Pacific Northwest Bell.

Everyone working for Microsoft in Albuquerque planned to make the move to Bellevue except for Miriam Lubow, who decided to stay behind because of her husband's business. Steve Wood's wife, Marla, had been working at Microsoft as a clerk since spring, and she was being groomed to take Lubow's place. Marla had no secretarial skills and didn't know a thing about bookkeeping, which at Microsoft was still done on a ledger. Shortly before the move to Bellevue, she "lost" one of the hundred-grand certificates of deposit.

"There was a little bit of a panic trying to figure out where it was," she recalled. "It was in there somewhere, we just couldn't put our hands on it."

One more programmer was hired before the big move—Gordon Letwin, who was recruited personally by Gates. Letwin had designed a BASIC for Heath-kit, and during a Gates presentation to a roomful of Heath-kit managers, Letwin had brashly suggested that his BASIC was better. Clearly, Letwin had the right stuff to work for Microsoft, and Gates later suggested as much. When Heath-kit ended up licensing BASIC from Gates, Letwin made the move to Microsoft. Some years later, he would become the architect of Microsoft's OS/2 operating system.

A few weeks before the move, Bob Greenberg, who had won a free photo session, decided Microsoft needed a company portrait. Everyone paid the studio photographer an extra 50 cents to be included. The picture of the Microsoft Eleven taken that day would later become famous, appearing in *People, Time, Newsweek, Fortune, Money,* and other magazines across the country. With the exception of Gates, who looked like a high school freshman, the nine men in the picture looked more like part of a Berkeley peace march in the 1960s than employees in a computer software company.

The move to Seattle took place in December and January. Steve Wood supervised the installation of a new computer at the Seattle office—Microsoft was finally getting its own computer system, a quarter-million-dollar, high-end DEC 20. Microsoft had to cash in some of its certificates of deposit to pay for the new computer because Digital would not extend the company a line of credit. Microsoft was too new a company to have any real assets, according to Digital.

Once the computer was installed, several programmers, including McDonald and Allen, went on ahead to get the system

up and runnng. Gates and the others stayed behind in Albuquerque to keep things running there. Finally, in January, it was
their turn to leave, too. One of the last employees to leave, Bob
Wallace, while driving along Route 66 towards Seattle in his
Honda Civic, noticed a green dot appear in his rearview mirror.
Moments later, it shot past him at well over a hundred miles
per hour. It was Bill Gates in his Porsche.

"He was anxious to get moving," Wallace recalled. "All this
driving was a waste of time. You couldn't be programming."

Gates did make two unscheduled stops on the 1400-mile
trip back home to Seattle. He was pulled over twice for speeding, caught both times by the same airplane flying above the
stretch of highway, an unseen speedtrap in the sky for which
the radar detector in Gates' car was of no use. But one ticket
or two didn't matter to him. Microsoft was in high gear, just
like the Porsche, and Gates was not going to let anything slow
him down.

CHAPTER 4

Hitching a Ride with Big Blue

I t would prove to be the most important business meeting of his career, and Bill Gates didn't have a tie.

He had spent a sleepless night on Delta's red-eye flight from Seattle to Miami, memorizing business and technical information for his meeting with IBM. He, Steve Ballmer, and Bob O'Rear were scheduled to meet with IBM executives at their Entry Level Systems facility in Boca Raton. Gates carried with him the final report on how the jeans-and-tennis-shoe programmers at Microsoft could work with the white-shirt-and-wingtip crowd at IBM on Project Chess, codename for the top secret IBM effort to develop a personal computer.

The meeting was scheduled to begin that morning at ten o'clock, and it would determine once and for all whether IBM and Microsoft were to do business together. For two months, the companies had been holding unprecedented secret talks.

Never before had Big Blue, as IBM was known, considered letting an outsider play such a critical role in developing one of its computers. Now it was time for Gates to deliver the consulting report that IBM officials had been waiting for. Time was short. The personal computer that IBM was developing had to be ready in ten months. Could a small language company like Microsoft meet such a demanding schedule?

Gates faced two days of tough questioning from the IBM task force. At age 24, he would have to hold his own against much older and more experienced executives. Ballmer, his pal from Harvard who used to listen to him unwind after those late-night poker games, had come along to provide support, along with O'Rear, the "old man" among Microsoft's programmers. Although Ballmer had been part of the Microsoft team for only a few months, and did not have a technical background in computers, he did have street-smart business instincts. He was also someone Gates could confide in.

On the nonstop, overnight flight to Miami, the three friends, wired from excitement and lack of sleep, poured over the final report, making last-minute revisions and corrections. Part of the report had been prepared by Kay Nishi, and his contribution needed a lot of editing. It had been written in what was jokingly referred to at Microsoft as "Nishi English." There had been no time to polish the document before leaving Seattle. "We'd been working for a day or two on the proposal," recalled O'Rear. "We just kind of ripped the proposal off the printer and dashed for the airport, then reviewed it on the flight down." The report proposed that Microsoft supply four high-level languages—BASIC, FORTRAN, COBOL, and Pascal—for IBM's new microcomputer. More significantly, it proposed that Microsoft develop the computer's disk operating system, or DOS.

Their plane landed at Miami International Airport about eight o'clock in the morning. After picking up their luggage, Gates, Ballmer, and O'Rear ducked into an airport restroom and quickly changed into suits. It was then that Gates discovered he had forgotten to bring a tie. But they barely had enough time to make the meeting up the coast, let alone go shopping beforehand.

Normally, Gates was not big on appropriate dress. But after all, this was IBM. Gates knew he would be pelted with questions by the executives waiting for him in Boca Raton, and that he would be judged not only on his answers, but how he appeared and how he handled himself. He simply *had* to have a tie, even if it meant arriving late for the meeting. He could always say the plane was late. But to those men in white shirts and blue suits, there could be no excuse for showing up without a tie.

As their rental car sped north along Interstate 94 from the Miami airport toward Boca Raton, a worried Gates stopped at a small department store and waited for it to open so he could buy a tie. The store doors were unlocked at ten o'clock, and minutes later Gates was standing at the counter in the men's clothing department, buying a conservative-looking tie. Then he was back in the car, speeding toward Boca Raton and the meeting that was supposed to have already started.

In the back seat, Bob O'Rear watched the Florida landscape rush by. As the technical person in charge of designing Microsoft's proposed operating system for IBM's new computer, his stomach was tied up in knots from the strain of the last few hectic hours on the plane. How quickly everything was happening, like the blur of scenery outside the car window, he thought to himself. It had been only a year and a half since he had moved his family from Albuquerque to Seattle. Now Microsoft, a company with seven million dollars in annual sales and fewer than 40 employees, was about to go into business with IBM, an international giant with revenues approaching thirty billion dollars a year and a work force more than half as large as the population of Seattle.

That Bill Gates should be speeding along the south Florida coast toward a rendezvous with destiny on a fall morning in 1980 was a matter of luck rather than brilliant maneuvering, many industry pundits would later argue. Even Gates acknowledged that had it not been for a break or two, things might have turned out very differently. But there was more to it than just luck. He and Paul Allen had strategically positioned Microsoft so that it was in the right place at the right time when IBM broke with tradition and went looking for a software vendor for its entry into the personal computer market.

They made one of these strategic moves early in 1979, soon after Microsoft set up shop on the eighth floor of the Old National Bank building in Bellevue. Intel had recently released a new chip called the 8086, and although some in the trade press suggested it would never become an industry standard like the 8080 chip, Gates and Allen believed otherwise. They were certain this new chip would become the engine for the next generation of personal computers. As a result, they asked Bob O'Rear to begin work immediately on a BASIC for the 8086.

It had been four years since the Altair appeared on the cover of *Popular Electronics*. The 8080 chip had indeed become a standard, and the industry had invested heavily in programs that ran only on that chip. But it was never intended to supply the brain power for the advanced needs of microcomputers. Its makers at Intel had envisioned the 8080 chip going into such things as traffic light controllers. With the 8086, however, Intel's engineers had designed a microprocessor especially for the personal computer. Technically speaking, the 8086 chip represented 16-bit architecture, rather than the 8-bit architecture of the 8080 chip. This meant it could process packages of information of up to a million characters at a time, while the 8080 chip was limited to 64,000 characters. Intel's new chip could run rings around the old chip. Not only was the new chip many times faster, but it could run much more sophisticated software programs.

When O'Rear began developing 8086 BASIC for Microsoft, no one in the industry had built a microcomputer using the new chip. O'Rear borrowed a page from the work of Gates and Allen in the Aiken computer lab at Harvard when they developed 8080 BASIC without an Altair. O'Rear simulated the 8086 chip on a DEC computer. A couple months later in the spring of 1979, O'Rear had his simulated BASIC running. However, he still didn't have an 8086 computer.

Just down the freeway in Tukwila, Washington, at a mom-and-pop computer business called Seattle Computer Products, was a man who did have an 8086 computer—Tim Paterson. An electronic hobbyist since high school, Paterson was a thin, fast-talking, bearded programming whiz with a fondness for faded jeans. He had hacked away on his first microcomputer at the University of Washington in 1976, when his roommate bought an IMSAI 8080 with a 4K memory board. Like the Altair that it imitated, the IMSAI was mostly good for fun and games. That same year, Paterson saw a notice posted in the university computer lab that the Retail Computer Store in Seattle was looking for a salesperson. Paterson applied for and got the job. He soon became friends with Rod Brock, a frequent customer who owned Seattle Computer Products. When Paterson graduated from the university in early 1978, he went to work for Brock as his chief technician and programmer. At the time, Seattle Computer Products built memory boards for microcomputers, but after Paterson attended a local seminar on Intel's just-released 8086 chip in late summer of 1978, he convinced Brock that his company should design a central processing unit, or CPU, around the new chip. The CPU is the heart of a computer. Paterson had a prototype 8086 CPU board working by May 1979, and he took his "computer" over to Microsoft. "We were helping them because Seattle Computer needed an 8086 BASIC and Microsoft was working on one," Paterson recalled. "It was a remarkable coincidence that we got our hardware working about the same time they had a BASIC simulator. But they didn't know if their

BASIC would work, so we brought over the real computer and gave it a go."

Unlike the 8080 BASIC which ran the first time Allen fed it into the Altair at MITS in Albuquerque, the 8086 BASIC did not work the first time it was loaded into Paterson's machine. But a few minor bugs were soon eliminated, and before the end of May Microsoft had a working 8086 BASIC—just in time to show it off at the upcoming National Computer Conference in New York City, the computer industry's yearly fair. A software distribution company known as Lifeboat Associates had invited Microsoft to share its ten-by-ten foot booth at the fair, and Paul Allen had invited Paterson to come along and show Microsoft's 8086 BASIC running on Seattle Computer's machine.

"Our boards looked great sitting up there on display," said Paterson. "We had a terminal with 8086 BASIC running and you could type on it and make it do anything you wanted."

As usual when it came to industry shindigs like the NCC, Microsoft was well represented. Gates and Allen were there, as well as O'Rear, Kay Nishi, Steve Wood, and his wife Marla. Chris Larson also made the trip. He was still enrolled at Princeton, but worked summers at Microsoft.

Paterson had a cheap hotel room on the other side of town, but Gates checked his team into the plush Park Plaza, where kings and presidents usually stayed when they came to the Big Apple. Gates and Allen had adjoining rooms, which they quickly turned into the company's first "hospitality suite."

"It wasn't something a lot of industry people did back then," recalled Wood. "We decided to have a cocktail party in the suite."

Later that night around two o'clock, when, as Wood put it, "none of us were feeling any pain and the guests had cleared out," the Microkids got a bag of bottle rockets that Larson had brought along, found an empty booze bottle, opened a window in the suite, and set up a launch pad. For the next hour or so, they shot rockets out over neighboring Central Park.

While Gates and Allen were entertaining guests in the hospitality suite during the conference, Kay Nishi was out rounding up more business from Japan. One night during the conference, Nishi showed up at the Plaza Hotel with about a dozen executives from Japanese hardware companies who were interested in doing business with Microsoft. "They didn't have a place to stay, so we told them they could spend the night in the suite," said Wood. "We called housekeeping and told them to send up about ten roll-away beds."

———————

Microsoft's 8086 BASIC drew a lot of attention at the National Computer Conference in New York City that June of 1979, but not nearly as much as a slick electronic spread sheet program that was unveiled on an Apple II computer. The brainchild of 26-year-old Dan Bricklin, VisiCalc was demonstrated for the first time at the conference, although it would not be sold commercially for several more months.

VisiCalc, short for "visible calculator," was a software program that solved complex "what if" financial-planning problems by establishing mathematical relationships between numbers. When the value of one number changed, the program calculated the effect, if any, on other numbers. The possibilities of such an applications program were limitless. You could use VisiCalc to determine, for example, how the profits of your small business might be affected if labor costs rose or more product was produced, or how a tiny change in the price of stock could affect the value of your portfolio.

Bricklin had conceived the idea of an electronic spread sheet in 1978 during his first year at Harvard Business School. When Bricklin approached one of his Harvard professors for advice on his idea for a spread sheet program, the professor suggested he talk with one of his former students, Dan Fylstra, who had recently started a small software-marketing company called Personal Software. Fylstra liked Bricklin's idea, and loaned him an Apple II computer for the project. Bricklin then enlisted the help of Bob Frankston, a programmer he had become friends with while at MIT. They spent the winter of 1978 developing what would become known as VisiCalc, and in January of 1979 Bricklin started his own firm, Software Arts, in a refurbished chocolate factory in the Boston suburb of Wellesley. He and Frankston then signed a contract with Personal Software to market VisiCalc. Although sales were sluggish at first, VisiCalc eventually took off and became one of the hottest-selling software products in the personal computer industry.

About the same time VisiCalc hit the market in the fall of 1979, a company called MicroPro began selling a word processing program called WordStar. Application products such as VisiCalc and WordStar represented a potentially vast and lucrative new market for software developers, a fact not lost on Bill Gates. Microsoft was only in the language business when Gates got his first peek at VisiCalc during the New York City computer fair. Useful applications, he knew, could turn the public on to computers the way the Altair had turned on hobbyists. Applications represented a product for the consumer, the so-called end user of the rapidly growing personal computer industry.

A few months after Gates and other Microsoft employees were shooting off bottle rockets from a window of the Plaza Hotel, Microsoft announced it was establishing a consumer products division. Gates hand-picked a friend, Vern Raburn, to head the new division.

Gates and Raburn had first met when Microsoft was located in Albuquerque. In 1978, Raburn and a partner started a small software company and began selling a version of BASIC for microcomputers, until one day they got a letter from a lawyer representing Microsoft. Microsoft claimed that Raburn and his partner were illegally selling BASIC. "The letter said cease and desist or we will sue your ass," said Raburn, who got on a plane and flew out to Albuquerque for a face-to-face showdown with Gates. "I met with Bill and said 'What is the meaning of this!?' He proceeded to explain it to me. I said, 'You know, you're right.' " So Raburn went back and dissolved the partnership. Raburn then went to work for a company called GRT in Sunnyvale, in the heart of the Silicon Valley.

"My impression [upon first meeting Gates]," recalled Raburn, "was he was just another one of those computer guys. But we had some things in common. We enjoyed driving fast cars."

They soon became friends. When Gates had business in California, he and Raburn got together to race go-carts at the Malibu Grand Prix. Raburn quickly learned about Gates' competitive fires, which burned white hot in or out of a go-cart. "Bill is competitive-plus," said Raburn. "Race car drivers have a phrase for it: Red mist. They get so pumped up they get blood in their eyes. Bill gets red mist."

Raburn joined Microsoft shortly before VisiCalc came out. In hiring Raburn to head the company's consumer products division, Gates had picked the man he wanted to help orchestrate Microsoft's move into applications software like VisiCalc. Gates had laid the second foundation for his company's future growth.

Up to this point, Microsoft had been producing only languages. In the consumer products division, Raburn presided over the introduction into the market of best-selling Microsoft software applications such as Typing Tutor and a game called Adventure.

"We really tried to win, and when you have multiple products, you have a better chance of winning," said Steve Smith, Microsoft's first marketing director and genuine business manager. Smith had joined Microsoft in July of 1979, shortly before Raburn. "Let me tell you what I think occurred to Bill: We were out there with multiple products (languages) and we'd sell them, and we just weren't able to become a much bigger company than Digital Research or MicroPro. . . . What we realized at that time was we had a lot of products, we dominated the languages business, but the only product that really made a lot of money for us was BASIC. That's because you had to have a copy of BASIC on every computer to make the applications run. And then we saw WordStar, and realized that MicroPro was a one product company. And then we saw VisiCalc. Now we had no intention of being a one product company. What we realized was we needed to be in those markets.

Smith had a bachelor of science degree in marketing and an M.B.A. in finance. While in the service he had taught electronics in Colorado for roughly ten years. In January of 1977, Smith went to work for Tektronix, a $1.2 billion Oregon company that made engineering equipment. Smith was hired to help the company start a microcomputer development group. When the Tektronix group needed computer software languages, consultant Adam Osborne recommended Gates and Microsoft. Smith flew to Albuquerque to negotiate a license for FORTRAN, which Steve Wood was developing. Later, Smith negotiated with Microsoft to supply Tektronix with Pascal. (Named for the seventeenth century mathematician and philosopher Blaise Pascal, Pascal handles complex programs faster than BASIC and is often the computer language of choice for business programmers.)

Around Tektronix, Smith was regarded as something of a maverick. In late 1978, Smith told Wood that in another six months he would be ready to leave Tektronix. Microsoft, Smith said, was the kind of company he wanted to work for.

"It became apparent to me," Smith explained, ". . . that the guys at Microsoft really had their act together, but may not have really known it themselves. It wasn't obvious to me that they understood how to leverage the business. They had the contracts with Apple, with Radio Shack, but it wasn't clear they were turning it into an actual business. . . . I was amazed at how successful they were without what appeared to be any real business management."

Smith recognized that Microsoft was a company oozing with entrepreneurial talent. He decided that if a business expert such as himself joined the company, Microsoft could be even more successful. "From my point of view," he said, "they were just lucky, and if I got involved, we could probably add some discipline on the business side. It didn't take me very long to realize they really weren't lucky. Gates really understood what he was doing."

That realization came to Smith not long after he started working for Microsoft, when Gates came into Smith's office one day and shouted at him, "How can you possibly take this much time working on this contract? Just get it done!"

Recalled Smith of that short but educational meeting with his much younger boss: "I think what I realized was that I needed to focus, that the money and the opportunities were simply there, [and I needed] to close contracts with customers. So I focused on personal performance over management. Initially, I was dealing more with management issues, as a guy with an academic background coming out of a large company. But it only took me a couple of meetings to realize that personal performance was what mattered."

In hiring Smith, Gates was hoping to bring more credibility for Microsoft to the negotiating table. At 34 years old, Smith was ten years older than most of the people working for the company, with the exception of Bob O'Rear. Gates was only 23 and looked more like 17, which he recognized was a liability in many business circumstances. Gates told Smith during the job interview that he was seeking someone who *looked* older.

Smith was the first nontechnical person with the company to do OEM sales, which mostly had been handled by Gates. Smith had only been on the job a few weeks when he checked Microsoft's bank balance and discovered ten certificates of deposit for a hundred thousand dollars each. After that, he never worried about his marketing budget.

When it came to making deals for Microsoft, what Gates may have lacked in age and experience he made up for in self-confidence and business acumen. Usually, when OEM customers came to Microsoft, they were ushered into Smith's office. Gates would come in a short while later. Smith would be dressed in a suit; Gates would often be wearing whatever he had on from the day before after pulling an all-nighter in the office. "They always thought he was one of my tech support guys, until I introduced him," Smith said. "I think they were impressed by his youthfulness and his technical knowledge, and frankly, as soon as he started talking the credibility was there. The credibility wasn't there until he started discussing what Microsoft could do, and what BASIC could do."

In the fall of 1979, Gates and Smith made a trip to a division of the Xerox Corp. in Dallas, Texas, to negotiate a licensing agreement for Stand-alone Disk BASIC. This BASIC performed many of the functions normally handled by the computer's operating system, and that's what Xerox was looking for. At the time, Xerox was working on Project Surf, a joint venture with a company called Convergent Technologies, to develop a personal computer. It was a big deal, the biggest deal Microsoft had taken a shot at. When Gates walked into the Xerox conference room, he was taken aback by the august surroundings. Seated around a huge table were more than a dozen of the company's executives and technical people, dressed in expensive suits and ties. Gates leaned over to Smith and whispered, "This is the biggest conference table I've ever seen." Smith whispered back that there was an even bigger table at Tektronix.

The meeting was a bit of a revelation for Gates. Prior to this time, many of the computer companies he had dealt with were little start-up operations, manned by pie-eyed visionaries like Gates himself. They related. Now, Gates was dealing with some of the biggest corporations in America.

But if that caused his heart to race, no one around the table could tell. Within seconds of launching into his presentation,

Gates had the attention of the room, charming the room with his knowledge of the product and complete grasp of the work at hand. Years later, a person who had attended the meeting as a Xerox executive said Gates was "cool as a cucumber. I thought he did this every day for a living."

It turned out to be one of the easier deals to cut, although Project Surf never produced a marketable computer. Before the day was out, Microsoft and Xerox had signed a $150,000 contract—roughly double the size of Microsoft's previously largest contract.

Gates hated to lose business deals. He told Smith that when you lost a deal, you lost it twice—you didn't get the money, and the other company did. If the deal were worth $50,000, then you essentially lost $100,000 because that was the difference between what you could have had and what someone else walked away with. "We had one rule that we both agreed on," recalled Smith. "We would never lose the deal."

For all his native acumen, Gates was also rough-edged and inexperienced in the art of the deal. Gates' style was to browbeat customers until they wilted and acquiesced. But he often was so intense in negotiating sessions that he would push too hard and actually jeopardize the deal. A former top Microsoft executive said there was "almost a viciousness" to the intensity Gates displayed when trying to secure a deal with another customer. "I've seen Gates lose a deal in negotiations because of it," the executive said. "Most sales guys get more gentle. He gets mad at a customer."

After working together for a while, Gates and Smith developed a negotiating strategy to offset their shortcomings. Gates was cast as the bad cop, the one with final authority to agree to a deal. The more experienced Smith was the good cop, the one who handled the actual negotiations. He would try to coax every last dime out of customers, and if talks stalled over a penny, he would plead helplessness, claim he could do no better than the offer on the table—Gates, after all, was the guy calling the shots.

The tactic, and the fact that Gates was loath to let any contract get away, was productive. But there were potential pitfalls. Gates and Smith once blew an important deal with an Intel subsidiary after Gates let his temper flare unchecked. Smith and Gates, in separate offices at Microsoft headquarters, had gotten Intel on the phone for a conference call. In the course of the conversation, Gates became upset over a bad reference Microsoft had received from another division within Intel—something about Microsoft being late with delivery. Normally Smith would break into the conversation and smooth things out before tempers got out of hand.

Smith, however, was called away from the phone without Gates' knowledge, and before he could intervene, the Intel representative had been chewed over by Gates pretty thoroughly. When the shouting was over, the company decided to buy software from other sources. It could have been a costly lesson, except that the Intel subsidiary eventually disbanded and after six months of rebuilding bridges, Microsoft won back the contract. Microsoft eventually licensed all its languages to Intel.

Despite his occasional temper tantrums, Gates was a great salesperson. Microsoft overcommitted itself and set unrealistic deadlines, but as far as Gates was concerned, it was more important to get the sale and worry about the consequences later. And Gates had supreme confidence that he could handle those consequences.

The performance of Microsoft's small cadre of programmers was ragged in the company's early years. Deadlines were often missed, products weren't always well designed, and contracts had to be revised due to unforeseen obstacles or delays. What sustained the company was not Gates' ability to write programs, to "crank code," despite his vaunted grasp of detail and of the nuances of communicating with slivers of silicon. Gates sustained Microsoft through tireless salesmanship. For several years, he alone made the cold calls and haggled, cajoled, browbeat, and harangued the hardware makers of the emerging personal computer industry, convincing them to buy Microsoft's services and products.

He was the best kind of salesman there is: he knew the product, and he believed in it. Moreover, he approached every client with the zealotry of a true believer, from the day he first articulated the Microsoft mantra: "A computer on every desktop, and Microsoft software in every computer."

Executives from Japanese or European computer manufacturers would visit Microsoft's unprepossessing offices in Bellevue, Washington, often intending to strike fear into Gates because his programmers were dangerously behind in delivering on one contract or another. Silver-haired men of weight arrived in their power suits with their pencil-packing entourage ready to lay down the law. There to greet them would be Gates, looking 17-years-old, wearing whatever pizza-stained T-shirt he had had on the day before, dirt clouding the lenses of his glasses, unshaven after an all-nighter at the office.

Before they could fully digest the appearance of the boy whom they had not long ago entrusted with a part of the company's future, before the subject of breach of contract could be suggested, Gates would launch a counteroffensive.

"Bill would sort of paint the picture of where Microsoft was and what the important issues were at the moment and what was driving him, and then somehow go from there into how that was going to lead into new developments," said a former Microsoft programmer. "He'd say, 'We feel real bad about what's late and what hasn't been done, and here's what we can do for you,' and then he'd paint a grandiose picture about what Microsoft could do, the Gatesian vision."

"What it would amount to was selling them more stuff. 'We're sorry we haven't come through on this smaller delivery, but look, we'll get you in on this huge part of our vision, and that will put you in an even better position.' What started out as a complaint about a smaller deal would turn into the sale of a much bigger contract." He was confident, sometimes brazen. He could be impressed. He just couldn't be fazed.

As Microsoft headed into the Eighties, software development tools such as BASIC were the company's bread-and-butter products. Every few weeks or so, Kay Nishi flew first class between Tokyo and Seattle, bringing in more business. Gates, who always flew business or coach, didn't particularly like the high air fares Nishi was charging to Microsoft, but Nishi was more than making up for his lavish spending habits.

"We were selling BASIC to the Japanese like crazy," said Marc McDonald. "We were selling Disk BASIC for Japanese machines, and that typically would bring us anywhere from $150,000 to $200,000 a pop."

Microsoft had ended 1979 with about $4 million in annual sales, with much of the money coming from BASIC. But BASIC represented only one layer of the essential software needed on every personal computer. At the top end are application programs such as word processing, which turn the computer into a useful machine for the public. Languages such as BASIC are the middle layer, providing programmers with the tools they need to develop software. The bottom layer of software, without which the computer is virtually useless, is known as the operating system. This is a low-level language that actually runs the computer, performing the most elementary tasks required of the microprocessor in the arcane world of machine language. If the user wants to record data onto the computer's disk, for example, the operating system finds free disk space.

During the early years of the personal computer revolution, there was no standard operating system. Almost every new machine that came on the market used a different system to control the microprocessor. But gradually one operating system known as Control Program for Microcomputers, or CP/M, became something of an industry standard by 1979. It was developed by Gary Kildall of Digital Research.

In February 1980, Microsoft entered the operating systems market, too. Gates negotiated with AT&T and acquired the license for a standard version of its UNIX operating system, to be sold under the Microsoft name of XENIX. This multi-user operating system had became popular in the 1960s when Bell Labs made it available on university computer systems. Microsoft adapted its version for the new 16-bit microcomputers. "We were actually introducing XENIX while we were still negotiating the contract with AT&T," recalled a Microsoft manager. "But we had a lot of confidence that we had the contract."

Every personal computer needed applications, a high-level language like BASIC, and an operating system. Microsoft now had its fingers in all three layers of the personal computer software cake. Only the company's languages had become an industry standard, but Gates had high hopes for XENIX. As things turned out, Microsoft's operating system *would* become the industry standard, but this system would not be XENIX.

In acquiring a license to distribute UNIX, Microsoft had gotten its hands on an operating system that someone else had already spent the money to develop. Any computer company could license UNIX from AT&T, and a lot had already done just that. But Microsoft was the first to focus on microcomputers and did so through a master distribution agreement. Gates received a sliding-scale discount from AT&T so Microsoft could aggregate all the royalties coming in from the other companies it sublicensed XENIX to. Microsoft did not even spend a lot of time or money "porting", or adapting, XENIX to other computers. It hired a small California company known as Santa Cruz Operation to do that. They performed much of the technical work, and all Microsoft did was pass down part of the royalty money. It was a good deal for Santa Cruz, a better one for AT&T, and a great one for Microsoft, which now had an operating system and was making money with very little investment of capital.

One of Microsoft's first customers for XENIX was a software company known as 3Com Corporation, which had been founded in 1979 by Bob Metcalfe in Santa Clara, California. Metcalfe wanted to use XENIX for his company's initial product, networking software called TCP/IP that linked together personal computers.

Gates and Metcalfe had met each other for the first time in Chicago in late 1979, a short while before they did business together, when they appeared at an industry soiree to talk about the future of personal computers before executives of Sears Roebuck & Co. The function was organized by a crusading industry visionary named Blair Newman, whom Gates knew from Harvard.

During his talk that day in Chicago, Newman suggested that Sears establish high-tech stores across the land to sell computerized home appliances, which could all be controlled electronically by what he called a "Home Bus." (In this case "bus" referred to the path along which digital information was transmitted between a computer's microprocessor and hardware.) Newman continued to pitch his Home Bus idea at the Consumer Electronics Show in Las Vegas in January of 1980.

Newman was brilliant but impatient and unstable. He led a tragic, troubled, drug-addicted life until killing himself in 1990. He had entered Harvard Business School in 1975 at age 28, with the highest test score of anyone ever admitted. When Gates wasn't monopolizing the school's PDP-10 to further enhance BASIC for the Altair, Newman was using the computer to study a Las Vegas hotel owned by Hughes, a project which later landed him a job with Hughes' holding company, the Summa Corporation. In 1979, after working briefly as a consultant for Apple Computer, Newman formed Microtype, a company that planned to produce computerized typewriters. Newman persuaded Gates and others to invest about a quarter of a million dollars in the business. Gates and Steve Ballmer joined the board, as did Metcalfe, as a favor to Gates. But Microtype, which was operating right down the road from Metcalfe's 3Com, soon went defunct. Shortly before the company went under,

Ballmer phoned Metcalfe and told him they should resign from the board, immediately. Why?, asked Metcalfe. Because, Ballmer explained, Newman had just told him that the purchase of cocaine was a justifiable business expense. "We got out, before it blew up in our faces, and the company went away," recalled Metcalfe.

After Microsoft licensed XENIX to 3Com, Metcalfe became a consultant for General Electric and arranged a secret meeting between Gates and one of the company's senior executives to discuss General Electric's possible entry into the personal computer market. Although GE had licensed Microsoft's BASIC in 1976, it did not have a personal computer but planned to use the language on a minicomputer. The meeting between Gates and the GE executive took place in a room Metcalfe reserved in the San Francisco Airport. Gates flew down from Bellevue. General Electric's well-heeled representative flew in from Stamford, Connecticut. They met for less than two hours before each got back on a plane and headed home.

"Gates didn't really feel GE had the mentality for personal computers, and he was right," said Metcalfe. "GE found Bill to be flaky. He looked like he was 17 years old, and he didn't wear pin-striped suits like they did. It was oil and water."

While Gates was off selling Microsoft to AT&T, Xerox, and the like, as well as making a few public speeches, Paul Allen was quietly recruiting programmers and directing the company's technical work. In early 1980, Allen jumped in with a contribution that would prove to be as big a financial boost to Microsoft as the deals being hammered out by Gates. Sales of the Apple II had taken off, especially since it was the only computer licensed to run the extremely popular VisiCalc application program. The Apple II, however, had its own unique chip, the 6502, and a proprietary operating system. Apple didn't want anyone else to "clone" its computer. Microsoft faced a dilemma. Most of its programs and languages, comprising more than a quarter of a million bytes of code, had been developed for Intel's 8080 chip and the CP/M operating system of Digital Research. Programs and applications written for CP/M, which had become an industry standard, would not work on the Apple operating system. Other software companies with CP/M products were in the same fix as Microsoft.

Gates badly wanted a slice of the rapidly growing Apple software market. But it would be a major effort to translate all of Microsoft's 8080 code into 6502 code. One day, while sitting in the back of a pickup truck in the company's parking lot, Allen, brainstorming with Gates about the Apple problem, came up with an idea. Why not try a hardware solution to the software problem? His ingenious suggestion was to design an expansion card that could be plugged into the Apple to run programs and applications written for CP/M. With this card, Apple II users could run any of Microsoft's programs written for the 8080 chip and Gary Kildall's operating system.

Allen asked Tim Paterson of Seattle Computer Products to take a crack at developing what Microsoft decided to call the SoftCard. Paterson produced a prototype, but he could not get it to work properly. Allen brought in another programmer and put him on Microsoft's payroll to help finish the project. The SoftCard was released in the summer of 1980. Allen had hoped Microsoft could sell 5,000 of the cards. It sold that many in a couple of months. By the end of the year, more than 25,000 had been snatched up by Apple II owners. In all, more than 100,000 were sold. The SoftCard, with Zilog's Z80 microprocessor (a faster clone of the 8080), was teamed with CP/M, which Microsoft licensed from Digital Research, and came with a copy of Microsoft BASIC.

The SoftCard was Microsoft's first piece of hardware, produced in the company's new consumer products division headed by Vern Raburn.

"It was not until the Apple II came along that everyone realized just how huge a marketplace software could be," said Allen.

While Gates played the more visible and exciting public role of wheeling, dealing, and managing Microsoft, Allen was content to stay behind the scenes, working on technical innovations like the SoftCard. But their abilities and personalities tended to complement one another and thus the company.

Steve Wood, who would leave Microsoft for another job about the time the SoftCard came out, explained the differences and similarities he found in working with the two: "Bill was extremely driven, very intense, very impatient, and in terms of personal relationships, he was very challenging. He could be very confrontational, extremely so. A lot of people found him difficult to work with over long periods of time because of that. You had to have a lot of self-confidence. But what a lot of people don't understand is that Paul, to some extent, had some of those same traits. They just manifested themselves in different ways. He, too, was very ambitious and very competitive. But Paul tended to be a lot more patient about things than Bill. That was always a very nice counter."

Allen also had a diverse set of interests outside of work. He loved going to Seattle SuperSonics basketball games with his father, mother, and sister, or jamming with other Microsoft musicians at his home. He and a few of the company's new programmers had even formed a band. Gates, on the other hand, was much more focused on work. He had little in the way of a social life outside of Microsoft. "Bill was much less one of the guys than Paul," said a programmer who went to work at Microsoft in early 1980. "He was much more into working. If you wanted to be around him, you worked with him."

But Gates did unwind occasionally at Microsoft parties, which were thrown fairly often, usually at someone's home or apartment on a weekend night. These parties were a welcome break. Another programmer described the Microsoft party scene in 1980, before the company's project with IBM pretty much put everything outside of work on hold for about a year, this way: "There was drinking, some pot smoking. The parties were for the most part limited to people from the company staff. The number of males was pretty lopsided, just like at the company. It was fairly typical stuff for that age group at that time. It occasionally got out of hand, but usually not too much. I do remember one time Bill stumbling and falling down a staircase, and when somebody made a remark about that, he said something to the effect that he liked stair-diving, and he went up to the top of the stairs and did it again."

These parties were also a time for competitive game playing, in keeping with the character of the people who worked at Microsoft and their stair-diving boss. One game in particular, "spoons," was played at nearly every company party back then. Players sat in a circle, in the center of which a small circle of spoons were arranged with handles facing out. There was one less spoon than the number of players. Cards were then dealt as in poker, and when a player got a predetermined hand, he or she could reach for a spoon. Everyone else immediately grabbed for a spoon, too. The player who didn't react quickly enough was out of the game. But just like in poker, bluffing was a big part of the game, and anyone touching a spoon on a bluff was out.

"Of all the times that I played that game, and there was something like a couple of times a month at least, I don't think I ever saw a game that Bill didn't win," said Michael Orr, a manager on Microsoft's COBOL language development project who was hired in late 1979. "You can believe that a lot of pretty energetic and talented people were saying to themselves, 'God damn it, I'm going to get this guy this time, no matter what!' But I don't think I ever saw him lose."

This intense competitive spirit had been woven into the fabric of the company, and it was as much a part of the work scene as the party scene. Gates and his senior programmers, who often had out-of-town business with OEM customers, had a running contest to see who could leave the downtown Bellevue office closest to flight time and still catch their plane at Seattle-Tacoma International Airport, about 18 miles way. Gates held the record at something like 12 minutes, which would have been astounding even with no other cars on the road. And the freeways around Seattle, especially heading to the airport, were always congested.

Pushing things to the edge was the Gates way. The work ethic at Microsoft, if anything, had intensified since the move to Bellevue. There was, in fact, a mystique about the long hours employees worked at Microsoft. There was an unstated job requirement that employees had to be at the office late into the night and on the weekends, regardless of how much work they had on a given day. No one wanted to be the first to leave.

"We were being driven to the edge all the time," said one programmer.

The long hours and demanding personality of Gates finally got to Marla Wood, who kept the company's books and helped with other office chores after the move from Albuquerque. She often had to fetch hamburgers and milk shakes from across the street each day for the programmers, who never left the office for lunch.

For a while, Marla had been *the* office staff, but gradually the company hired a secretary, a receptionist, and several other people for clerical duties. Then Gates started dating Microsoft's secretary, which created hard feelings in the office. The young woman would show up late and leave early—not exactly the regimen expected of someone who worked for Microsoft.

Gates was often condescending to the five or six other women who worked in the office, none of whom had any technical background. Gates would often lose his temper, which was upsetting to staff workers unfamiliar with his confrontational style.

"Paul was much easier to work for," said Marla. "He would blow up, but five minutes later it would be as if nothing happened. . . . Of the two, I'd rather work for Paul than Bill any day. They are very different personalities. . . . [We] were always relieved when he was out of town."

In 1980, Steve and Marla Wood had bought a new home and were trying to landscape the yard and fix the place up. But because of the long hours they put in at Microsoft, they never got home until well after dark. They would typically sleep for a few hours, get up the next day, and head back to the office. They could only spend time working on their home from weekend to weekend, and even then, Steve was often unavailable.

"I was getting very frustrated with things," recalled Marla. "It was getting extremely hectic."

The last straw came for her one day at work when she went to see Steve, who was not only her husband but her boss, to tell him the women in the office wanted to be paid for all the hours of overtime they had been putting in. In addition, they wanted all the back pay they were entitled to. Unlike the men, who were paid a straight salary, the women were hourly workers.

Steve Wood took their grievance to Gates, who agreed to start paying overtime, but refused to pay any back pay.

Marla had warned Steve that the women might file a wage complaint with the state Department of Labor and Industries if their demands were not met. "Let them," Gates told Steve. "I don't care." So the women did just that.

"Bill came storming into my office, absolutely purple he was screaming so much," recalled Marla. "He said we had ruined the reputation of his company." She went in tears to Steve's office, saying she couldn't take it anymore. At that point, Steve told her that he himself had an appointment the next day with a corporate headhunter. It was the first time Marla realized her husband, Microsoft's general manager, wanted out, too.

Gates' fit over the overtime pay seemed excessive given that it amounted to only a couple hundred dollars. In the end, the women got their way.

When Marla Wood left, Microsoft hired a professional bookkeeper. The bookkeeper was appalled that a company approaching eight million dollars in annual revenues was keeping track of its money by handwritten ledgers. Microsoft soon computerized its bookkeeping, though even then it used only a small Radio Shack TRS-80.

Steve Wood left the company to join a young Texas outfit called Datapoint. Unlike his wife, it was not the work load that had driven him out. Microsoft was a partnership between Gates and Allen, and there was no equity participation for anyone else, no employee stock plan. For him there was little financial incentive to stay and work so hard. Also, Wood believed that Datapoint was on the cutting edge of computer technology, making state-of-the-art developments in office automation, word processing, networking, and electronic mail.

With Wood about to leave, Gates again turned to a friend for a key management job in the company. In June 1980, he brought in Steve Ballmer as assistant to the president.

Gates said later in an interview: "When we got up to 30 (employees), it was still just me, a secretary, and 28 programmers. I wrote all the checks, answered the mail, took the phone calls—it was a great research and development group, nothing more. Then I brought in Steve Ballmer, who knew a lot about business and not much about computers."

The son of Swiss immigrants, Ballmer grew up in Detroit, where his father worked for the Ford Motor Company. After getting his applied mathematics degree from Harvard, Ballmer worked for a couple years as assistant products manager at Procter & Gamble before heading off to Stanford's business school. He had been there about a year when Gates called.

At Procter & Gamble, Ballmer had become known for redesigning the company's Duncan Hines cake mix box so that it sat on store shelves horizontally rather than vertically to grab more shelf space. Ballmer would later say that's what he wanted to do at Microsoft—help Gates squeeze out the competition.

In time, Ballmer would be called everything from Gates' alter ego and Microsoft's No. 1 cheerleader, to the world's ultimate marketing expert. Regardless of the accuracy of those descriptions, his importance to the company—and to Gates— cannot be overstated.

"If you are going to write about Bill," said one of Microsoft's most senior executives, "you must give substantial attention to Steve Ballmer. He is a much more important player than he's chosen to let people know. He's so bright, so intense. He's much more than just a lieutenant for Bill. There's such a high level of trust and high bandwidth communication between the two. They trust in each other's IQ. They are equivalently intense."

It took time for Ballmer to find his place at Microsoft. Until then, he did just what his job title said, assist the president. And he was well prepared to serve. During his senior year at Harvard, Ballmer was head equipment manager for the football team.

"Steve would talk about how important that experience with the football team had been," recalled that same senior Microsoft executive. "I think he saw himself as not one of the players, but someone who loved making sure the bucket of water was there so the team could win. Bill was going to be the quarterback, and Steve was going to be the guy who would do any damn thing it took to make this work."

Ballmer did not have long to wait after joining Microsoft before he made himself very useful to Gates. In July of 1980, Gates was busy helping develop a BASIC for Atari. The video game company was entering the personal computer sweepstakes, and Gates had met several times already with chairman Ray Kassar.

One morning in late July, while Gates was preparing for a meeting with Kassar, he took a call from a man who identified himself as Jack Sams of IBM. Sams told Gates he wanted to fly out to Seattle for a talk. He was not specific about a time. Gates looked at his desk calendar. "What about next week?" he asked. Replied Sams, "What about tomorrow?" When Gates got off the phone with Sams, he called Kassar in California and canceled their meeting for the next day. Gates then walked in to Ballmer's office. IBM was coming, he told his friend. Better get out the suits, said Ballmer.

They were the corporate odd couple, on opposite sides of the country. The thought of free-spirited Microsoft climbing into bed with a stuffed-shirt outfit like IBM was about as incongruous as the fact that the greatest computer company in the world was shut out of the desk top computer market in 1980.

In the five years since the Altair had shined briefly in the night sky above Albuquerque, guiding the way for young entrepreneurs with genius and vision, nearly 200 different brands of microcomputers had been brought to the high-tech market place, and those with the IBM nameplate had been quietly withdrawn out of embarrassment. Thomas J. Watson, Sr., would have rolled over in his grave had he known that in July of 1980 high-level executives in the company were suggesting IBM go out and buy a personal computer from someone like Atari and stick Big Blue's name on it.

It was 1924 when Watson changed the name of Computing-Tabulating-Recording Co. to International Business Machines and created an accounting machine monopoly. Since then, the company had enjoyed a long history of success. In the 1950s, even though Sperry-Rand's UNIVAC I was the first commercial computer, IBM quickly captured more than ninety percent of the market with its punch-card "Giant Brain" machines. Its 360 series mainframe computer that debuted in 1964 took seventy percent of the market and set a standard that is still a model today. The initials IBM became synonymous with computers. IBM was one of the world's most successful and admired companies, the bluest of the blue chips, its stock a favorite of Wall Street. But the giant corporation was also straightlaced and stuffy, a bureaucratic institution that tended to stifle individuality, smother creativity, and paralyze action. For years, it had an unwritten dress code that executives wore only white shirts and conservative blue suits, hence the nickname Big Blue. Employees posted "THINK" signs in their offices and sang a company song, "Hail to IBM," which ended with a promise to "toast the name that lives forever"—IBM.

But the federal government didn't want IBM to live forever, at least in its present form. In January 1969, the Johnson administration, on its last working day in office, filed suit accusing IBM of monopolizing the U.S. computer industry. Three administrations would subsequently argue that IBM's market dominance should be diminished, that Big Blue be dismembered into Baby Blues, much the same way that Ma Bell was later chopped up into so many Baby Bells. The very life of the company was at stake. When the Reagan administration finally dropped the antitrust suit in January of 1982, the court proceedings had run over 200,000 pages and an entire law firm had been created to try to save IBM.

The suit hung over the company's head like the Sword of Damocles in 1975 when Paul Allen fed BASIC into the Altair and the machine typed out "Ready," signaling the start of the microcomputer revolution. In part because of an internal circle-the-wagons mentality that resulted from the suit, IBM had been steadily losing ground in the computer market. By 1980, its market share was down to about forty percent, and that came entirely from sales of mainframes and minicomputers. IBM had nearly drowned in its first attempt to test the waters of the small computer market with its 5100 series in the late 1970s. The machines were taken off the market.

The company's efforts to produce a low-end commercial product were centered at its plant in Boca Raton, Florida, known as the Entry Level Systems unit. There, several projects were underway. An engineering team headed by Bill Sydnes was working on the System 23 Datamaster, which was a follow-up to the ill-fated 5100 series. The System 23 machine used a mix of IBM and non-IBM parts. A competing group in Boca was considering a small computer sourced *entirely* from outside IBM—in other words, buying a machine from another company.

Most of those working in Boca Raton did not believe it possible for IBM to develop its own successful personal computer, given the existing structure and culture of the company. The personal computer had been created out of an entrepreneurial spirit that didn't exist at IBM. The personal computers' designers were hackers and hobbyists, young radicals with long hair who wore faded jeans and listened to loud rock 'n' roll music. The birthplace of the leading personal computer of the day, the Apple, was a garage, not a huge corporation that could not overcome its own bureaucratic inertia.

This was the message, anyway, that Bill Lowe delivered in early July of 1980 to his bosses at IBM corporate headquarters in Armonk, New York, about an hour's drive north of New York City in the Hudson Valley. In his meeting with the Corporate Management Committee (CMC), Lowe proposed that IBM go out and buy a computer from Atari.

Lowe, director of the Boca Raton lab, was told this was blasphemy, "the dumbest thing we've ever heard of." He was sent back to Florida with orders to do what ever had to be done to develop IBM's *own* personal computer. He was to assemble a task force and bring back a prototype of IBM's "Apple" in 30 days!

In the book *Blue Magic*, a fascinating, inside look at the development of the IBM PC, authors James Chposky and Ted Leonsis said Lowe had carefully planned this strategy, knowing the CMC would never accept his proposal and that they would tell him to come up with the company's own product, free of the current corporate structure.

Lowe went back to Boca Raton and picked his team, 13 engineers not cut from the traditional blue cloth of IBM—a baker's dozen of free spirits.

"If you're competing against people who started in a garage, you have to start in a garage," said Don Estridge, the man Lowe eventually selected as the day-to-day project manager and team leader. Of all those involved in the PC project, Estridge would become the most visible and the best known.

The task force agreed the new computer should be an "open architecture" system. In other words, critical components of the machine, such as the microprocessor, would come from existing technology in the market place and would not be proprietary, like components in the Apple. Industry guru Adam Osborne said he was one of two outside consultants advising IBM to make their architecture open. The other was Portia Isaacson. "I didn't realize at the time," said Osborne, "that both of us were telling IBM, 'Don't build your own hardware and software.' "

This radical break from Big Blue's tradition would turn out to be the key decision that made the IBM PC an industry standard. But it was done out of necessity, to save time.

It was decided that the machine's software, including the vital operating system, would also come from an outside vendor. Responsibility for securing the software fell to task-force member Jack Sams, and in late July of 1980 he placed a call to Microsoft out in Bellevue, Washington, and asked to speak with Bill Gates.

Sams was not altogether unfamiliar with Microsoft. A veteran of the IBM development team that produced its famous 360 series of mainframe computers, Sams was a software and operating system expert. Most recently, he had been involved with Bill Sydnes on the System 23 project in Boca Raton. In fact, Sams had recommended to Lowe that IBM contract with Microsoft to develop a BASIC for that project, but his recommendation was rejected. IBM came up with its own software for the System 23 machine. "It just took longer and cost us more," said Sams.

In July, when Sams phoned Gates, the task force had less than a month remaining to come up with a prototype machine and gather information that Lowe would need in making his report to the CMC in August. The corporate brass had not yet approved the PC project. Sams' mission in visiting Microsoft was merely to look the company over and report back to the task force. Gates would not be told of IBM's plans. He would only be asked very general questions. But he would have to sign IBM's famous nondisclosure agreement. The project was hush-hush even within IBM, and anything discussed at the meeting had to remain confidential.

"In that first meeting, we were just prospecting. We wanted to determine whether they had the capability to deliver on a schedule we knew we would have to meet," said Sams. "If we had gotten out there and found out they were only three guys, we'd have to take a hard look at whether they would be able to do the work or not."

Sams made the trip to Microsoft with two others from IBM, an executive from purchasing and someone from corporate relations. They were along more or less as "witnesses," Sams said. IBM was paranoid about security. When they got off the elevator on the eighth floor of the Old National Bank building in Bellevue, the receptionist notified Gates, who was in his office.

"I knew Bill was young, but I had never seen him before," said Sams. "When someone came out to take us back to his office, I thought the guy who came out was the office boy. It was Bill. Well, I'll tell you or anybody else, and I told IBM executives this the next week, that by the time you were with Bill for fifteen minutes, you no longer thought about how old he was or what he looked like. He had the most brilliant mind that I had ever dealt with."

Gates would later say that the IBM team asked him "a lot of crazy questions" at that first meeting. The next day, Steve Ballmer typed up a letter for Gates to sign, thanking IBM for the visit.

When Sams got back to Boca Raton, he gave a favorable report about Microsoft and its young president. "I recommended that we base our plan on using their firm," Sams said. "We left after the first meeting feeling they could respond to what we wanted them to do. I felt their answers were open, and I thought they were correct."

A few weeks later, in the dog days of August, Bill Lowe flew back to Armonk. With him were Bill Sydnes, Lewis Eggebrecht, and the prototype machine that would become known as the IBM PC. Sydnes was engineering manager for the project. Eggebrecht, an engineer, had worked with him on the prototype. After seeing a demonstration of the machine and hearing the report from Lowe, the CMC gave the go ahead. The project would be code named "Chess," and Lowe would have exactly one year to get the new machine to market.

The engineering team was to be cloistered in Boca Raton and would work as an Independent Business Unit, or IBU. Former IBM Chairman Frank Cary, in an oft-quoted remark, said the IBU was "IBM's answer to the question, 'How do you make an elephant tap dance?' "

This was an outfit of technological Green Berets, a Dirty Dozen who would soon grow into hundreds.

A second meeting between Microsoft and IBM was held in late August, not long after Project Chess had received corporate blessing from headquarters in Armonk. Sams told Gates on the phone that he was bringing along four others from IBM, including an attorney. When the five "suits" arrived at Microsoft, they were met by an equal number of representatives from Microsoft. Gates was joined by Allen, Ballmer, Nishi, and an attorney from his father's law firm.

Once again, Gates and his team were asked to sign the nondisclosure agreement, and after this formality they were then told what they already suspected: IBM had a top secret project underway to develop a personal computer.

Numerous published accounts over the years have said that it was Gates who, after hearing about the project, told the IBM group their microcomputer should be built around the 16-bit Intel chip and not the old 8-bit 8080 chip. Gates knew the more advanced chip would allow Microsoft to write much more powerful software for the new computer. The preface to Microsoft's own MS-DOS Encyclopedia states that Gates and Microsoft convinced IBM to base its machine on the newer and faster chip. "IBM was, however, unsure of microcomputing technology and the microcomputing market . . . ," the preface says. "One of IBM's solutions—the one outlined by Sams' group—was to base the new machine on products from other manufacturers. All the necessary hardware was available, but the same could not be said of the software. Hence the visit to Microsoft with the question: Given the specifications for an 8-bit computer, could Microsoft write a ROM BASIC for [IBM] by the following April? Microsoft responded positively, but added questions of its own: Why introduce an 8-bit computer? Why not release a 16-bit machine based on Intel's 8086 chip instead? At the end of this meeting—the first of many—Sams and his group returned to Boca Raton with a proposal for the development of a low-end, 16-bit business workstation. The venture was named Project Chess."

Microsoft's official version of history is exaggerated, however, according to key members of the Project Chess task force. All affirmed that IBM engineers in Boca Raton had decided to use 16-bit architecture long before Gates was ever told about the machine. Bill Sydnes, engineering manager for Project Chess and the first man to be hand-picked by Lowe for the 13-member task force, had this to say about Microsoft's claim:

"That's a crock of bull. Absolutely a crock of bull. We had already done the System 23 with an 8-bit architecture and the hardware was completely done and ready to ship and the operating system was about a year or year and a half away when we started the PC program. So I moved over to do that and we had firmly settled on the fact that it had to be a 16-bit architecture because of where we thought the machine was going to go over time."

Several chips were considered for the IBM personal computer, according to Sydnes, including Motorola's 68000. But this 32-bit chip had some technical flaws. "Basically, Motorola wasn't ready," Sydnes said. "They were still six to nine months off from where we needed them to be." The task force eventually decided to use Intel's 8088 chip rather than the 8086. The 8088 was a 16-bit chip with some characteristics of 8-bit technology. The main reason for going with this chip was that it was not as fast as the 8086, which Sydnes said had a little too much horsepower for the machine they envisioned. By using the 8088 chip, engineers could easily upgrade to the 8086 in time.

Sams confirmed that the Boca Raton group had already decided to use a 16-bit chip before Gates was contacted. But he said Gates was not told this at the second meeting, because of the IBM secrecy protocol, so Gates may well have believed he was making a recommendation that IBM acted on.

"We had selected the 8088 for reasons of our own, but we did not tell that to Bill," Sams said. "We essentially asked for his recommendations and among his recommendations was that we use the 16-bit architecture. I'm sure he believes he suggested it to us. But we clearly never intended to use the 8-bit CPU again."

Gates also recommended that the IBM computer have color capability, Sams said, and he made several suggestions about the keyboard.

IBM wanted Microsoft to supply software development tools such as BASIC for its personal computer, and Gates agreed to do so when he met with Sams for the second time in late August of 1980. Don Estridge, the leader of the Project Chess team, would later explain to *Byte* magazine why IBM did not go with its own BASIC: "IBM has an excellent BASIC—it's well received, runs fast on mainframe computers and it's a lot more functional than microcomputer BASICs were in 1980. But the number of users was infinitesimal compared to the number of Microsoft BASIC users. Microsoft BASIC had hundreds of thousands of users around the world. How are you going to argue with that?"

As far back as Albuquerque, Microsoft's slogan had been "We Set the Standard." That vision and commitment was now about to pay off.

Since there was not enough time to develop its own software for Project Chess, IBM not only needed to buy BASIC, but more importantly a microcomputer operating system from an outside source. And the most popular one at the time was CP/M, the operating system developed by Gary Kildall of Digital Research. Sams said he was under the assumption that Microsoft had the rights to the CP/M source code when he first contacted Gates in July. Microsoft had just released the SoftCard, which allowed products written for CP/M to run on the Apple II. "Our target market was the Apple software," said Sams. "People were buying the Apple for business purposes and we knew the products would sell. Many of these products were based on CP/M, so it was clear to us that we needed a CP/M or compatible machine. Our proposal, the one we originally talked to Microsoft about, was to use the source code for the SoftCard they were then marketing for the Apple. . . . I presumed they were able to offer us a 16-bit version of the operating system. But we really didn't discover until the second or third meeting that was not true, because we weren't able at the first meeting to ask the sort of detailed questions we wanted to ask."

Microsoft not only did not have the rights to sell or license the CP/M source code to IBM, but Digital Research, which owned CP/M, had not yet developed a 16-bit version of the software. Obviously, Sams and the IBM team were a little out of touch with what was happening in this new industry.

Sams flew to Bellevue to meet with Gates several more times during September. At what would have been their third or fourth meeting since the first contact, they talked at length about the operating system for the new PC. IBM wanted Microsoft to supply it with not only BASIC but also languages such as FOR-TRAN, COBOL, and Pascal. Stand-alone BASIC could function without an operating system, but Microsoft's other languages could not. IBM needed to make up its mind about what it wanted to do for an operating system, Gates said. Time was short. "Bill told us if we wanted a 16-bit CP/M, we would have to deal with Kildall," said Sams. "We said 'oops.' We had really only wanted to deal with one person. But now we had to talk with Kildall. I asked Bill if he would make an appointment for us."

Gates picked up the phone in his office and called Kildall at Digital Research. Gates told Kildall he was sending him some important customers, "so treat them right." He then handed the phone to Sams, who made an appointment for his team to visit Kildall the next day.

Gary Kildall and Bill Gates went back a long way, to Computer Center Corporation when Gates was one of the bunch of crazy kids from Lakeside hired to try to crash the C-Cubed computer.

Little did Gates know how often in the coming years his path would cross that of Kildall, who had occasionally paid night-time visits to the young programmers at C-Cubed, or how profound the consequences would be. A Seattle native whose father owned a navigation school, Kildall had enrolled as an under-graduate at the University of Washington with thoughts of becoming a high school math teacher until a friend showed him a computer program written in FORTRAN. He was immediately hooked. He later designed a program to help his father calculate tide tables, a job previously done by hand for a local publishing company.

After getting his graduate degree in computer science in 1972, Kildall moved to the California coastal town of Pacific Grove on the Monterey Peninsula, where he taught computer science at the nearby U.S. Naval Postgraduate School. Kildall bought one of Intel's first 4004 microprocessor chips and wrote a simple programming language for it, which landed him a one-day-a-week consulting job at Intel up the coast in the Silicon Valley. When Intel released its 8-bit 8008 chip, the same microprocessor that Gates and Allen were working with in Seattle to build their Traf-O-Data machine, Kildall developed a programming language for it, too. In return for his consulting work, Intel gave Kildall a small computer that he set up in his classroom at the Naval Postgraduate School. Kildall, who did not have the necessary hardware expertise, brought in John Torode, a friend from the University of Washington, to develop a disk drive for the computer, which had since been upgraded with Intel's 8080 chip. Kildall, meanwhile, worked on a simple operating system called Control Program for Micros to store information on Torode's computer disk. By 1974, they had a crude microcomputer with an operating system, and they sold two of the machines to a computer company in the Bay Area. This was several months before the Altair appeared on the cover of *Popular Electronics*. In time, Kildall began selling his software and the CP/M operating system to computer makers through Intergalactic Digital Research, a company he had formed with his wife, Dorothy McEwen. They quickly shortened the name to Digital Research. In 1977 Seymour Rubinstein, marketing director of IMSAI Manufacturing in San Leandro, California, paid Kildall $25,000 for the right to run CP/M on IMSAI 8080 microcomputers. IMSAI had been started soon after the Altair debuted in 1975, and quickly seized the lead in microcomputer sales.

Meanwhile in Albuquerque, Gates was doing everything he could to help make CP/M an industry standard.

For a language company like Microsoft, supporting different microcomputer operating systems was a business nightmare. Each operating system had its own way of doing things, such as managing memory and file systems. If Microsoft's programmers could write software for the same operating system on each computer, all they would have to do was modify their code slightly for whatever specific devices a customer's computer might have.

"When we were talking to another OEM, a hardware customer who wanted to run BASIC or any of our products, we got to a point by 1977 or '78 where we were always trying to get them to go to Digital first and get CP/M running because it made our job a whole lot easier," recalled Steve Wood. "When we were doing custom things like the General Electric version or NCR version, it got to be a real headache. It made our lives a lot easier if someone would just go license CP/M and get that up on their machines and then our stuff would pretty much run as is. And Gary would do likewise. If someone went to him to license CP/M and they were looking for languages, he would refer people to Microsoft. It was a very synergistic kind of thing."

In fact, there was an unwritten agreement between Gates and Kildall that Microsoft would stay out of the operating system end of the business, and Kildall would not get into microcomputer languages, according to industry sources.

Not that Microsoft did not want to get into this market, too. "Early on in New Mexico we talked about developing an operating system," said Wood. "We asked ourselves if we should really be referring all this business to Gary. We always came back with the same answer: We have all this other stuff to do."

At one point, probably in late 1978, Gates considered a merger with Digital, which certainly would have changed the face of the industry. Gates flew to Monterey and talked about a possible deal over dinner at the Kildall home. "It was a fairly serious discussion," said Kildall. "At the time, Microsoft was thinking about moving but they couldn't decide where, either back to Seattle or to the West Coast. . . . I thought it was an okay idea [a merger], but we weren't able to come to any final agreement. I don't know how our personalities would have mixed. I got along fine with him, but we would have had to explore it more. . . ."

Microsoft was not the only company trying to promote CP/M as an industry standard. LifeBoat Associates, a New York software distributor that had started out as a club for CP/M users, pushed it as well, publishing a catalog of Digital's software. Microsoft also sold its CP/M-based languages such as FORTRAN through the catalog. Later, LifeBoat Associates did CP/M implementations. OEM customers would license the operating system from Digital, then ask LifeBoat to have it ported to their computer. Microsoft worked closely with LifeBoat in trying to make CP/M a standard. "There was this vigorous effort to get all the computer makers to support that operating system, and Microsoft's languages too," said one Microsoft programmer. "There was intense lobbying from Bill and from Tony Gold of LifeBoat Associates. What really created the microcomputer industry more than any other thing was that all these hardware manufactures didn't really have a clue what the industry as a whole was going to be doing, and they all got lobbied real hard to support a consistent operating system so there would be a market for applications."

But in late 1979, the synergistic relationship between Microsoft and Digital began to unravel after Kildall packaged his operating system with a BASIC that had been developed by Gordon Eubanks, one of his students at the Naval Postgraduate School. Eubanks' CBASIC had been on the market for about two years, and it represented the only real alternative to the BASIC offered by Microsoft.

"It wasn't a real strong competitor but it was a competitor," said Wood of CBASIC. "When Digital started marketing that, it upset things a little bit. What it did was add a little more fuel to our internal discussions whether we should be in the operating systems. There was a big market there. CP/M wasn't all that sophisticated. Should we try and do something on our own?"

Kildall said there was never any promise on his part to keep out of languages. Digital Research, in fact, had developed several languages, such as BASIC and FORTRAN, which it had introduced in the business market. "There was an agreement in principal that Microsoft would do languages and we would do operating systems. But that was only because at the time, we were doing operating systems and they were doing languages. It wasn't like we had divvied up the market place. My own personal expertise was in languages, so I certainly wasn't going to give that up."

CBASIC posed no market threat to Microsoft, Kildall said. Regardless of whether it was a real or perceived threat, it was at that time that Gates, in reaction, went to AT&T and licensed its UNIX operating system, which Microsoft sold at a discount under the name XENIX. "Bill was not happy," recalled Steve Smith, Microsoft's marketing manager who had joined the company in 1979. "Digital was now in our languages, and it couldn't have been more than a month or two before we were introducing XENIX. It was as simple as that. When they came into our market, we went after their market . . . . We knew that eventually we would be competing with all the software companies. But when they were the ones that were aggressively moving into our markets, we tended to react aggressively."

Kildall said he did not lose any sleep when he learned Gates had licensed an operating system. "XENIX was not significant," Kildall said. "It was not any bother to me at all. It didn't make any difference. It was like, so what. UNIX was not in the market place we were into. It was mostly for scientific work stations, as it is now. It was never a threat to us in our business markets."

Such was the state of affairs between Microsoft and Digital Research in September of 1980 when Gates picked up the phone and called Kildall. Once again, he was sending business to someone he now considered a competitor, but now he had no choice. IBM wanted CP/M as an operating system for its first personal computer.

What happened the day IBM came courting Digital Research in Pacific Grove, California, just off scenic Highway 1, has become part of the folklore of the personal computer industry, a story that is told over and over whenever the talk at an industry convention or dinner party turns to Microsoft and its money-making monopoly, DOS. Gary Kildall blew the opportunity of the century, someone will say. The tale is told how Kildall was out flying his twin-engine plane while the men in blue suits from IBM were waiting for him on the ground.

In the dozen years since that fateful day, many different versions have appeared in books, magazines, newspapers, and trade journals. Few of the accounts are exactly the same. The details usually differ in small ways and in large.

The two central players in the story, Gary Kildall and Jack Sams, remember the day's events much differently. Sams said his group, which consisted of himself and two or three others from IBM, flew down from Seattle to talk with Kildall as planned the day after Gates made the call from his office. They were met by Kildall's wife, Dorothy McEwen, who was actually running the business at the time while Gary handled the technical work. Also present was a lawyer from Digital Research. But Gary was not around.

"The meeting was a fiasco," recalled Sams.

Before Sams could talk about why he was there, McEwen and the lawyer first had to agree to sign IBM's standard non-disclosure agreement, the same one Gates had signed. They would not do so. To outsiders unaware of IBM's policy with vendors, the agreement was somewhat intimidating, but it helped protect IBM from lawsuits. It stipulated that a vendor, in this case Digital, could not tell IBM anything confidential in the meeting, and if something confidential were revealed, IBM could not be sued if it acted on the information. On the other hand, if Digital revealed or acted on anything confidential it heard from IBM at the meeting, it could be sued.

"We tried to get past the point of signing this nondisclosure agreement so we could talk about what we came down to talk about," said Sams. "It was three o'clock in the afternoon before they finally got around to the point of signing an agreement that [said] we had been there and they would not disclose it. I was completely frustrated. We went back to Seattle the next day and I told Bill we had been unsuccessful in trying to deal with Gary and would he see what he could do about getting a commitment from him for a 16-bit operating system."

Sams said Gary Kildall never did show up before he and his group left Digital Research. Bill Sydnes, engineering manager for Project Chess, confirmed that Sams later told the task force Kildall would not meet with him.

An industry friend of Kildall's, who did not want to be quoted by name because of their friendship, said he once talked with a member of Sams' team who visited with Dorothy McEwen and Digital's lawyer that day. "The IBM guy told me they had never seen anyone [McEwen and the lawyer] quite as rude and arrogant in their lives."

Kildall acknowledged he was flying his plane at the time of the meeting, but he said he was on a business trip in the Bay Area. "The stories make it sound like I was doing loops or something. But I was out flying on business, just like someone else would be driving a car. I knew the IBM people were coming in." Kildall claimed he was back at Digital by early afternoon, in plenty of time for the meeting with the IBM group.

"My wife had some concerns before I arrived, sure. If you sign this agreement, it says they can take any of your ideas and use them anyway they want. It's pretty scary. My wife had never seen anything like that before. I explained that these were not bad guys, they just had to protect themselves from future suits. I had no problem with the nondisclosure agreement."

Kildall said that when the meeting ended, he felt there was an understanding that Digital would supply IBM with its CP/M operating system. That night, Kildall continued, he and his wife happened to be on the same commercial flight from San Francisco to Miami as the IBM group, and they all talked some more. The Kildalls were headed for a long-awaited Caribbean vacation. Kildall said he was told to contact Sams when he returned from vacation, "but I couldn't get through. He had apparently been moved from IBM. It was like he had moved off the planet." The next thing he knew, Kildall said, Microsoft and IBM were doing business together on an operating system.

Sams said it's possible a member of his team who visited Digital Research that day flew back to Boca Raton, rather than returning with him to Seattle. He said he just can't remember. But Sams said he is absolutely, positively sure he never met with Gary Kildall. "Not unless he was there pretending to be someone else."

Sams *was* later taken off Project Chess and given another assignment. But this was toward the end of October, over a month later.

Kildall said it was Gates, in an interview with the *London Times* after the IBM PC was unveiled to the world in August of 1981, who first told the story that Kildall was off flying in his plane when IBM wanted to do business with him. "That's Microsoft's version," Kildall said. "It became legend. The winner of the battle, not the loser, gets their version recorded as history." And Kildall has had his nose rubbed in that story for a dozen years. He's clearly sensitive to the criticism that his bad business judgment allowed Gates to walk away with the agreement to produce an operating system for IBM.

"It would certainly bother me if I had made that dumb a move, or if others had made it on my behalf," said John Torode,

Kildall's friend who designed the disk system for their micro-computer. He now runs a computer business in Seattle. "But how much preparation did Digital have? Did they know it was IBM that was coming? Did they have time to develop a strategy? Had they already concluded it was smart to tell IBM to go jump in the lake, or did it just happen because of the personalities of the folks who were there at the time? I've never discussed that with Gary. I never wanted to rub his nose in it."

Regardless of what really happened that day, most of those in the computer industry believe Kildall's actions helped make Microsoft the software giant it is today.

Sams said he subsequently telephoned Kildall after the ill-fated trek to Digital Research. "I told him we were serious, we really did want to talk with him. I had to assume we had gotten off to a bad start and that he wouldn't arbitrarily refuse to do business with us, you know, did he have some religious opposition to us. He said 'No, no, no, we really do want to talk with you.' " But Sams said he and others at IBM could not get Kildall to agree to spend the money to develop a 16-bit version of CP/M in the tight schedule IBM required. "We tried very hard to get a commitment from Gary," Sams said. "When we couldn't, I finally told him, 'Look, we just can't go with you. We've got to have a schedule and a commitment. We can get one from Gates.' "

In a series of meetings with Microsoft after the initial rebuff from Digital Research, Sams threw the operating systems problem in Gates' lap. "This was the negotiating tactic we took with them," said Sams. "We wanted this to be their problem, to find us the right operating system, one that we could integrate successfully on our schedule."

Luck once again would shine on Bill Gates. An operating system for the 16-bit Intel chips had just been developed by Tim Paterson at Seattle Computer Products, not more than a twenty-minute drive from Microsoft.

Tim Paterson had always wanted to design an operating system for a microcomputer. But had the "Father of DOS" realized he was going to stir up so much controversy, he might have stuck with racing cars, which he enjoyed almost as much as programming.

After showing off Seattle Computer's 8086 CPU boards at the National Computer Conference in the spring of 1979, Paterson had returned to Seattle to perfect the boards so they could be sold commercially. During this time, he was contacted by Digital Research, which wanted one of the CPU boards in order to develop a 16-bit version of CP/M. But Seattle Computer did not have any boards to spare. Paterson asked when Digital expected to have its new version of CP/M ready. By December, he was told.

Seattle Computer began shipping its first 8086 CPU boards to customers in November of 1979. Microsoft's Stand-alone BASIC was offered as an option. These first customers were mostly software developers. By April of 1980, Digital Research had still not designed CP/M-86. Paterson decided to wait no longer; he would develop his own operating system.

"Here we had something that would work, but we were waiting and waiting for Digital to come out with their version of the operating system for the 8086," said Rod Brock, owner of Seattle Computer Products. "They kept telling us any day now we will have it. This delay was really costing us sales. It's hard to sell a product without an operating system. We were probably selling five to ten boards a month, but figured there were a lot more sales out there than that. We needed an operating system to get them."

Five months later in September, around the time Jack Sams was being stonewalled by Dorothy McEwen and the lawyer at Digital Research, Paterson had his operating system up and running for the first time. He called it 86-QDOS, which stood for quick and dirty operating system.

Seattle Computer began shipping Paterson's 86-QDOS to customers. "This was a real product," said Paterson. "Everyone always thinks IBM was the first to have it. That's crap. We shipped it a year before they did. It was used on our computer. We were selling a computer that was more than twice as fast as the one IBM was going to come out with." (The reason for the difference in speed was that the IBM PC used the slower 8088 chip.)

Just as Gary Kildall has had to read over the years how he lost the IBM deal because he was off flying in the clouds, Paterson has had to read how he ripped off CP/M in developing an operating system that became the industry standard. Typical is this comment from an unidentified Digital employee who was quoted in a 1990 *Business Month* article that depicted Gates as a silicon bully: "We never tried to patent CP/M. Nobody was patenting software then; it was almost unethical. But if we had, Microsoft probably couldn't have developed MS DOS because parts of the original source code looked a lot like CP/M's. How else did Paterson and Gates come up with that nice new operating system overnight?"

At one point, Kildall telephoned Paterson and accused him of "ripping off" CP/M.

"At the time," said Paterson, "I told him I didn't copy anything. I just took his printed documentation and did something that did the same thing. That's not by any stretch violating any kind of intellectual property laws. Making the recipe in the book does not violate the copyright on the recipe. I'd be happy to debate this in front of anybody, any judge."

Although Paterson's operating system mimicked some CP/M functions, there were significant improvements. QDOS stored data on disk in a completely different way than CP/M did, and it also organized files differently. Paterson's goal was to make it as easy as possible for software developers to be able to translate what had become a huge body of 8080 programs that ran on the popular CP/M so they could run on his operating system. He first obtained Intel's manual for its 8086 chip, which had detailed rules for translating 8080 instructions into 8086 instructions. Paterson wrote a translator that followed Intel's guide. He then got Digital's CP/M manual, and for each 8080 function he wrote a corresponding 8086 function.

"Once you translated these programs, my operating system would take the CP/M function after translation and it would respond in the same way," said Paterson. "To do this did not require ever having CP/M. It only required taking Digital's manual and writing my operating system. And that's exactly what I did. I never looked at Kildall's code, just his manual."

Once Paterson had 86-QDOS working, he contacted Paul Allen and asked him if Microsoft wanted to adapt any of its software for Seattle Computer's new operating system. "That's when they found out we had it," said Paterson.

Up until then, Microsoft had been unsure what it was going to do about obtaining an operating system. Digital Research was out of the picture. IBM did not have time to develop an operating system within the 12-month deadline set by its corporate brass. Neither did Microsoft, at least not if it had to start from scratch. Without an operating system, the entire PC project appeared to be in jeopardy. "The feeling was if we couldn't solve it, the project couldn't go forward," said Bob O'Rear, the Microsoft programmer who would soon be given technical responsibility for the operating system. "We'd have no languages to sell on the IBM PC. It was of paramount importance that we engineer a solution to the operating system equation. . . . We had to do something so that this project could go forward."

In late September, Allen contacted Rod Brock and told him that Microsoft had a potential OEM customer who might be interested in Seattle Computer's new operating system. Allen, who could not reveal the identity of the customer, wanted to know if Microsoft could act as the licensing agent. Brock said yes.

Gates would later say that obtaining Seattle Computer's operating system saved Microsoft about one year of work.

IBM had told Gates it wanted a final proposal from Microsoft in October, and time was running out. Gates faced a critical decision. Could Microsoft deliver languages *and* an operating system and still meet the demanding schedule IBM had set to have a computer ready for market within a year? The software would have to be finished before that, probably in about six or seven months. The four languages IBM wanted—BASIC, COBOL, FORTRAN, and Pascal—would require writing about 40,000 bytes of code. An operating system would likely mean another 2,000 bytes of code. According to Microsoft, on September 28, 1980, a Sunday night, Gates, Allen, and Nishi were in Gates' eighth-floor corner office in the downtown bank building, brainstorming about the operating system. Should they commit to it? Suddenly, Nishi jumped to his feet, waved his short little arms in the air and shouted, "Gotta do it! Gotta do it!"

That's when it became obvious to Gates that 2,000 more bytes of code for an operating system was no big deal. Of course they had to do it. "Kay's kind of a flamboyant guy, and when he believes in something, he believes in it very strongly," Gates would say later. "He stood up, made his case and we just said 'Yeah!' "

Not long after this, Gates was pacing nervously in his office late at night, waiting impatiently for the last pages of a lengthy computer printout. When the machine was finally silent, he grabbed the pile of paper it had been spitting out, stuck it in his briefcase, and dashed out of the building with Ballmer and O'Rear for the airport. Microsoft's final report to IBM was ready. It was now time to get down to hard-core negotiations with the guys in blue suits in Boca Raton.

Previously published accounts of this crucial meeting between Microsoft and IBM, including the books *Blue Magic, Fire in the Valley,* and *The Making of Microsoft,* reported that Paul Allen made the trip to Boca Raton with Gates and Ballmer. This was not so. "It was Bill and Steve and myself," said O'Rear. "I'm not sure why Paul didn't make it, because he was certainly heavily involved. Maybe he was off on some other project that evening. It was a situation where we kind of finished the proposal to IBM, tore it off the computer, raced out to the airport, barely made the flight, flew all night, got there, bought a tie for Bill and made the pitch."

The report Gates carried with him covered hundreds of technical issues, involving both hardware and software recommendations for the PC. But it also detailed financial matters. Early on, Sams had talked to Gates about a fixed price for an unlimited number of copies of any software Microsoft licensed to IBM. The longer Gates thought about this proposal, the more he became convinced it was bad business. Microsoft would be making a huge financial investment in this project, and a lump sum payment from IBM would not give the young company much of a return on its investment over time. When Gates boarded the nonstop Delta flight for Miami, he had decided to insist on a royalty arrangement with IBM.

Sams had made it clear from the first of his meetings with Gates that Microsoft would retain ownership of whatever software it developed. In fact, IBM wanted nothing to do with helping Microsoft, other than making suggestions from afar. "There has been a lot of speculation about why we ever let Microsoft have the proprietorship and all that," said Sams. "The reasons were internal. We had had a terrible problem being sued by people claiming we had stolen their stuff. It could be horribly expensive for us to have our programmers look at code that belonged to someone else because they would then come back and say we stole it and made all this money. We had lost a series of suits on this, and so we didn't want to have a product which was clearly someone else's product worked on by IBM people. We went to Microsoft on the proposition that we wanted this to be their product. . . . I've always thought it was the right decision."

When the rental car carrying Gates, Ballmer, and O'Rear pulled up in front of IBM's Entry Level System unit in Boca Raton, it was half past ten in the morning. They were 30 minutes late. But Gates had a new tie dangling from his neck, and he walked confidently into the large conference room where about seven or eight IBM employees were waiting for him, including a couple of lawyers.

Gates planned to make the presentation himself. Ballmer and O'Rear were there to make points if necessary and to answer questions. "Bill was on the firing line," Ballmer said later.

If Gates was nervous, he didn't show it. As usual, he was in complete command of his material and his audience. The much older executives asked question after question, making notes on yellow, legal-sized writing tablets as they went around the table taking turns. Many of the questions concerned the operating system that Microsoft proposed to supply IBM. Gates answered with confidence and maturity, often rocking back and forth with characteristic intensity. Everyone in the room wanted the joint venture to work. It was in the interest of both parties to resolve any differences here at this meeting. IBM was about to forge an alliance with an outside supplier unlike any in the company's history. Microsoft would not be supplying nuts and bolts for the new PC but rather the vital operating system, the very soul of the machine.

"We had a lot of coaching from the IBM people, they really wanted to do the thing," said O'Rear. "We'd talk to them about what we wanted to do and how we wanted to do it, and they'd say things like, well, it'll be more acceptable if you do this, that or the other. . . . Everybody was searching for a solution. Everybody in that room wanted to do the project. They just wanted to explore all the issues."

That evening, Gates, Ballmer, and O'Rear had dinner with Jack Sams, who had been part of the IBM team quizzing them throughout the morning and afternoon. Over dinner, Sams coached Gates on how he should modify parts of his proposal to make it more acceptable. Later, the three exhausted Microsoft employees went to their rooms at a nearby Holiday Inn. It had been two days since any of them had slept.

When the meetings ended the next day, Gates and Ballmer immediately flew back to Seattle. O'Rear remained in Miami for two days visiting friends. It would be his last consecutive days off for the next ten months.

The talks had gone well in Boca Raton. Gates and his team had made a good impression. During the two-day meeting, Gates had gotten to know Don Estridge, the brilliant, maverick leader of the Project Chess team. Although Estridge was almost 20 years older than Gates, they would develop a close friendship. When it came to computers, they were kindred souls sharing the same vision. Estridge told Gates that IBM chief executive John Opel, who was known around the company as "The Brain," had mentioned to him that he knew Mary Gates, having served with her on the national board of United Way. (Before joining the national board, whose members, like Opel, were for the most part chief executives of Fortune 500 companies, Mary Gates was the first woman president of United Way in Seattle.) Whether this United Way connection helped Microsoft get the IBM deal is not clear. Opel, now retired, won't talk. Sams said Estridge made the same comment to him about Opel and Mary Gates. Sams believed Opel may have been reassured about Gates because he knew his mother. After all, Gates was only 24 years old, and IBM was betting the reputation of the company on Gates, and Microsoft, coming through.

It was shortly after the Florida meeting between Microsoft and IBM that Estridge replaced Sams on the Project Chess team. But Sams, who would continue to see Gates off and on during the coming years, had formed a lasting impression of the young cofounder of Microsoft. "He was an extraordinarily competent person," said Sams. "More than anyone I've ever known, Bill had committed himself to the idea of being ready for what was coming before it happened. He was willing to make investments on the strength of what he saw happening two or three years ahead of time. . . . I've never dealt with anyone since who was such a force."

In early November of 1980, the corporate odd couple officially signed the paperwork. Microsoft would develop the software for IBM's first personal computer and supply the vital disk operating system, or DOS. Deadlines had been set, numerous timetables established, commitments and promises made. The schedule would be brutal. IBM wanted an initial working version of the operating system and BASIC by mid-January. "They showed us we were three months behind schedule before we started," recalled Gates.

On Sunday nights, Gates usually took time off from work and went to his parents' home for dinner. But he now told his mother that she probably wouldn't see him again for six months.

A few days after Thanksgiving, two prototypes of the top secret Acorn arrived at Microsoft, hand delivered by Dave Bradley, an IBM engineer on the PC project in Boca Raton. "Acorn" was the codename that the corporate brass in Armonk had given to what they hoped would be the newest and smallest member of the IBM computer family. The overall project was still known as "Chess." Big Blue was big on codenames and secrecy. When Bradley landed with the Acorns early one morning at Seattle-Tacoma International Airport, he rented a station wagon for the drive to Bellevue. It was the only way he could get all nine boxes of parts to Microsoft.

He was met at Microsoft's offices by Steve Ballmer, who took him to a back supply room used by the shipping department. Large plastic bags and boxes littered the floor. IBM's prized prototype computers would be kept here, Ballmer said, along with all documentation regarding the secret project.

IBM executives had made it clear to Gates at the two-day meeting in Boca Raton that they considered security a matter of the highest priority. The outside world was to know nothing about the Acorn. The cloak of secrecy would not be lifted until the official announcement when the computer was unveiled to the press and public—an event tentatively set for sometime in the summer of 1981. Any breach of security could jeopardize the project, they emphasized. The computer was to remain in the room at all times, with the door locked even when Microsoft programmers were in the room. All manuals and documents also were to stay in the room, secured in filing cabinets and a safe. IBM sent Microsoft special file locks. They also sent someone to install the locks. But when IBM insisted that Microsoft install chicken wire above the ceiling tiles to protect the room from an assault from above, Gates finally said enough is enough and nixed it.

All work on the computer had to be done in this unventilated, windowless room, which measured only ten feet by six feet. Heat generated by the computer and other electronics equipment quickly built up in the tiny, enclosed room. The temperature, which often reached 100 degrees Fahrenheit, not only made for an uncomfortable work environment, but further contributed to numerous hardware problems. Programmers would spend hours running down what they thought was a software glitch, only to discover the problem was with the unstable hardware.

Occasionally, IBM would send inspectors out to Microsoft just to nose around and check on security precautions. On one visit, an IBM security man found part of the company's computer in the hallway *outside* The Room. And the door had been left ajar to allow a little fresh air for the sweaty programmer inside. Ballmer was called on the carpet by IBM. "After that, we got hard core," said Gates.

One Microsoft programmer remembered Ballmer running down the hallway one day, shouting, "Close the door and lock the safe! They're here!'' Ballmer, it turned out, had gotten a call from an IBM executive, and when he asked how the weather was in Boca Raton, the IBM guy said he didn't know. He was in Bellevue and would be there shortly.

An elaborate communication system was established between Microsoft and the Entry Level Systems unit in Boca Raton. Electronic mail allowed messages to be immediately transmitted between computers at the two companies. Packages and hardware were shipped back and forth via Delta Dash, an express service provided by Delta Air Lines. Gates made frequent trips to Boca Raton on the red-eye flight for quick business meetings, returning to Seattle the same day.

No two U.S. cities in the contiguous 48 states are further apart than Seattle and Miami, kitty-corner across the country, and probably no one from either IBM or Microsoft made that 4,000 mile trip more often than Bradley, who had brought the first PC prototypes out to Microsoft. His role in the project was to develop what is known as the BIOS, the basic input and output of the computer system, which Microsoft was helping IBM write. Every time Bradley made the trip to Seattle, it rained. Gates, who had a corner office with a view of the Cascades, would tell Bradley on each of his visits that if it weren't so cloudy he'd be able to look out the window and see majestic Mount Rainier. But Bradley never did see the mountain. A few years later, Bradley took a vacation to Seattle just to see for himself that there really was a Mount Rainier.

About the time the Acorns arrived at Microsoft, Miriam Lubow did as well. The company's secretary and den mother from its Albuquerque days had moved with her family to Bellevue so she could go back to work for Microsoft and continue looking after its youthful president. One morning, not long after Lubow had returned to work, she was surprised to see Gates arrive at the office dressed in a suit. Later that morning, three strangers arrived carrying briefcases and wearing jeans, tennis shoes, and casual shirts. The men amazed Lubow by saying they were from IBM. Shaking her head, she showed them into Gates' office. The IBM men took one look at the spiffy-looking Gates, and he took one look at them, and everyone burst out laughing.

The hardware and software engineers in Boca Raton had much more in common with the Microsoft employees than they did with some of the executives they were used to dealing with at IBM. "A lot of people on the team were not cut of the IBM cloth," said Bill Sydnes, engineering manager for Project Chess. "We did not recruit what you might call typical IBM blue for work on the PC program. They were all unusual characters."

A special camaraderie developed between the IBM and Microsoft teams working on the project. Personal, nontechnical E-mail was sent daily, and the two groups gave each other a good-natured hard time when one group fell behind schedule, which was often. In an interview with *PC Magazine* after the project was finished, Gates talked about that camaraderie:

"This IBM project was a super-exciting, fun project. We were given, even for a small company, an incredible amount of latitude in changing how things got done as the project progressed. . . . And we had a really great interface with the people from the customer (IBM), even though they were as far away as they could be. . . . We loved to kid them about all the security—how we had to have locks, and sign things in, and use code names and stuff like that. . . . I was very, very impressed with the team they put together. . . . We were the only vendor that understood what the project was about. Even up to the announcement, most vendors were kept in the dark about the general scope and the general push of things. So we enjoyed a really unique relationship."

Gates went on to describe the scene at Microsoft during the year-long project as very much like that which Tracy Kidder captured in his book, *The Soul of a New Machine*, about a group of computer whiz kids at Data General who pushed themselves to the limits of endurance to build a new kind of computer.

Microsoft's first priority was getting the operating system up and running on the Acorn. This responsibility fell to Bob O'Rear. Other software being developed for the PC had to run on top of the operating system, and if O'Rear couldn't adapt Seattle Computer's 86-DOS to the prototype, the entire project was doomed.

"If I was awake, I was thinking about the project," said O'Rear, who worked throughout December without even taking Christmas or New Year's Day off just like many of the others at Microsoft who were on the project.

Though Seattle Computer had furnished Microsoft a copy of 86-DOS back in September, when Microsoft informed the company it had a possible OEM customer for the operating system, no licensing agreement had been signed by the end of 1980. That didn't seem to worry anyone. "We had no hesitation to let them try it out," said Tim Paterson. Six days into the new year, Microsoft and Seattle Computer finally signed an agreement giving Microsoft a nonexclusive right to market 86-DOS. This meant Seattle Computer could continue to license its operating system to other customers. The negotiations were handled by Paul Allen and Rod Brock, the owner of Seattle Computer. Although the agreement was signed by Gates, he and Brock never met or even talked. For each sublicense of 86-DOS, Microsoft agreed to pay Seattle Computer $10,000, plus an additional $5,000 if the source code were part of the sublicense. Seattle Computer also received $10,000 for signing the agreement.

"We came to an agreement fairly easily," said Paterson, vice-president of Seattle Computer. "We even called Digital Research to see what they sold their stuff for. We got a feel for what the prices were like."

Of course, no one at Seattle Computer knew that Microsoft's unnamed customer for the operating system was IBM, with revenues approaching nearly thirty billion dollars.

One important clause in the contract stated: "Nothing in this licensing agreement shall require Microsoft to identify its customer to Seattle Computer Products."

Recalled Brock: "That seemed strange to us, but we agreed to go along."

Microsoft ended up paying Seattle Computer a total of $25,000 under terms of the agreement, because it turned around and sublicensed 86-DOS and the source code to only one customer, IBM.

A source at Microsoft who was privy to the negotiations with IBM for the operating system said Microsoft licensed the first version of DOS to Big Blue for only $15,000. Microsoft also received royalties as part of the license, although the royalty arrangement has always been a closely guarded secret at IBM and Microsoft. "We were an aggressive company," the Microsoft employee said. "Our strategy was, we would make our money on the languages. Remember, we already had the deal for all the languages, and Digital Research was supposed to have the deal for CP/M. And when it looked like we might lose the language deal because IBM didn't have an operating system, we simply were going to solve the problem. And we solved that problem for about $15,000. But I can assure you it cost us more than that to make the delivery. And I can also assure you we made money on the BASIC. We made money on the licenses we already had, and we made sure that we got the operating system deal. Not so much to make money, and not so much to set the world standard, but simply because we couldn't close our language deals without it."

For a while, O'Rear wondered if he would ever get 86-DOS running on the hardware he was using in the small, stuffy, windowless room at Microsoft. The technical problems with both the software and hardware seemed endless. The prototype machines delivered to Microsoft just after Thanksgiving were just that—rough drafts. They didn't work very well. O'Rear continuously fired off memos to his contacts in Boca Raton about equipment problems, complaining about the difficulty of meeting the January 12 date for the delivery of DOS and the BASIC due to breakdowns in the hardware IBM had provided.

Microsoft didn't make the January 12 deadline. It was not until February that O'Rear finally got 86-DOS to run on the prototype. He still vividly remembers the moment. "It was like the middle of the night. It was one of the most joyous moments of my life, to finally after all the preparation and work, and back and forth, to have that operating system boot up and tell you that it's ready to accept a command. That was an exciting moment."

The IBM team in Boca Raton wanted several changes in the operating system, and Allen asked Paterson to help with these. The changes were all fairly minor. For example, IBM wanted one feature that remains on DOS today—the date and time stamp. Another change involved the so-called prompt that DOS left on the screen when the system came up. The prompt that Paterson had designed for 86-DOS was the drive letter followed by a colon. Neat and simple. But IBM wanted the CP/M prompt, which was the drive letter followed by a colon followed by the "greater than" sign used in mathematics.

"It made me want to throw up," said Paterson of the request for CP/M prompts. But he obliged. Paterson was working blind as he made the requested changes in his operating system. He did not have a prototype computer. He did not even know one existed.

Seattle Computer picked up an occasional hint that Microsoft's unnamed customer might be IBM. One day in early spring of 1981, Brock received a call from someone who said he was with IBM, and he had a question about the operating system. Brock knew his company had not licensed 86-DOS to IBM, so he asked the caller where he was located. The caller immediately hung up. Brock later mentioned to a sales rep who called on Seattle Computer from time to time that Microsoft was dealing with an OEM who did not want to be identified. The computer sales rep told Brock he had heard a similar story from a friend at Intel. The chip maker also had an agreement with an OEM who wanted to remain anonymous.

Given the scope of the PC project and the number of people at IBM who were either working on the computer or knew about it, word probably *should* have leaked out about what was going on at Microsoft and at the Entry Level Systems facility in Boca Raton. But other than rumors, specific details didn't get out, at least not until near the end.

The original group of 13 engineers assigned to Project Chess grew to several hundred. Programmers at Microsoft joked that this was IBM's smallest project and Microsoft's biggest, yet IBM had more people writing requirements for the computer than Microsoft had writing code. O'Rear often felt overwhelmed by the number of people he had to deal with in Boca Raton. He had the authority to say "yes" to anything requested of him by the IBM team. But only Gates could say "no."

"If they said we have to have this or we have to have that, I could immediately give approval," O'Rear said. "Otherwise, it had to go through Bill. I was dealing with a lot of people. IBM had this mainframe program where they outlined every little point and conversation that we would have, and I would get calls from people doing all different kinds of things, from contract administration to looking at the technical details to deciding where we were in the schedule to writing documentation. All these calls would be from different people. And I'm trying to write all this stuff and make it work on the PC. Just to take two or three or four phone calls a day, and do all this stuff, and follow up on several of these phone calls, looking into each little aspect, or trying to educate them towards the project, it was a lot of work, it was a lot of stress."

Everyone involved in the project at Microsoft was under incredible strain. One by one, deadlines for various stages of the project slipped by because of technical problems. Most programmers writing code for the PC worked seven-day weeks, frequently pulling all-nighters. Gates did not leave the office for days at a time, unless he had business in Boca Raton to talk about the design of the computer with Estridge or others.

Although he didn't write much code himself, Gates reviewed most of the software code being written by his programmers for the PC. And he also helped with technical problems, as did Allen. Both suggested or ordered changes in the code when they found something they didn't like or thought could be improved.

Bradley, the IBM software engineer, recalled a trip he made to Microsoft to bring a new power supply for one of the broken-down prototypes. The problem was fixed on a Saturday, but Bradley was told by his office to remain in Bellevue until Monday so he could pick up a new version of BASIC that Microsoft was supposed to have finished by then. But on Monday, Gates told Bradley it was not yet ready and to come back Tuesday. Around five the next morning, Bradley got off the elevator at Microsoft's offices, walked down the hallway, and found Gates sprawled on the floor of a back office, going over a huge computer printout with a red pen, marking changes he wanted. He had been up all night debugging the BASIC.

Although the pace of work was unrelenting during the spring of 1981, Allen and a couple programmers took a quick break and flew to Florida in mid-April for the maiden launch of the Space Shuttle. "This was the first mission, and it was a big deal," said Charles Simonyi, who had to talk an exhausted Allen into making the trip. But they almost didn't get to go. Gates had scheduled a company meeting for Friday, April 11, the day Columbia was supposed to blast off. But a computer software glitch at NASA postponed the flight until Sunday, so Simonyi, Allen, and Marc McDonald flew down on Saturday. They rented a car in Miami and drove all night up the Florida coast to Cape Kennedy. The Columbia, carrying astronauts John Young and Robert Crippen, blasted into orbit at seven o'clock in the morning, Eastern Daylight Time. The three space enthusiasts from Microsoft then drove back to Miami and flew home.

Simonyi was not working on Project Chess. He had recently been hired to take over development of Microsoft's applications. Although much of the company's attention was focused on the IBM project, Microsoft could not neglect its other business. Deals with OEM customers in this country and in Japan continued. Programmers like Simonyi worked on various applications. In dealing with these other customers, Microsoft took advantage of its inside knowledge that IBM was going to introduce its own personal computer based on Intel's 8088 chip, according to a manager who was working for Microsoft at that time. "We would highly advise some of our customers to chose the 16-bit processor," he said. "Nobody really knew that we were working on the IBM contract."

On May 1, Tim Paterson went to work for Microsoft, where he learned for the first time who the customer for his operating system was. He had asked Allen about a job a few weeks earlier. Paterson decided to leave Seattle Computer because Brock could not make up his mind whether to sell the company's products by mail order or through dealers. Brock was thinking of going back to a mail-order business, and Paterson did not want to work for what he figured would soon be a mom-and-pop operation. At Microsoft, Paterson joined O'Rear on the operating system. By the end of June, DOS was pretty much finished.

The company was growing rapidly, in part because of so many new employees hired to help with the IBM project. By June, the number of Microsoft employees had more than doubled from the previous year, to about 70.

One programmer hired in June, Richard Leeds, thought he was joining Microsoft to work on something else until he came to work the first morning, signed the nondisclosure agreement, and was told he would be helping with Project Chess. Each Microsoft employee on the project had to sign the document. Leeds was surprised when he got his first look at the PC. It had a clear plastic keyboard, and he could see right through the keys into the workings underneath. "We called IBM the typewriter company," he said. "But the joke was, here was a typewriter company that couldn't come up with a usable keyboard."

Leeds was made project manager for COBOL, one of the languages that Microsoft was supposed to deliver to IBM. His job was to convert Microsoft's 8-bit version of COBOL to a version that could run on the 16-bit chip.

"It was very hectic around there," Leeds recalled. "Everybody was real driven, real proud to be kids working on the next machine from IBM. . . . It was nonstop work. I was working 65-plus hours a week and I had a girlfriend, and there were complaints that I wasn't working hard enough. They wanted 80. There *were* times that I worked 80."

When the COBOL work was done, Leeds received only a fourteen percent bonus instead of the promised fifteen percent.

Leeds had a habit of collecting pens that had been chewed obsessively by Gates. In only a couple of months, its grew to be a very large collection. Gates worried incessantly about the project. He knew that IBM had a habit of spending vast amounts of money on research projects that never saw the light of day. IBM would conclude a product could not be marketed, and then put the lid on it, buried forever in its giant bureaucracy. Up until the final days before the PC was announced, Gates was haunted by the thought that IBM would cancel the project. Had his nightmare scenario come true, Microsoft would have been hurt significantly because Gates had thrown so much of the company's resources into the project.

"There was always the fear that IBM would decide not to announce this, that someone would say, 'Nice effort guys, but we don't want to go into this personal computer business,' " said O'Rear.

Gates got a particularly bad case of the jitters when the industry journal *InfoWorld*, in its June 8 issue, reported in alarming detail about the top secret PC project in Boca Raton. Gates worried that such stories would blow IBM's cover and cause it to abandon the effort.

The *InfoWorld* article was entitled "IBM to Pounce on Micro Market." It was datelined Boca Raton. "A reliable source within IBM's Entry Level Systems group in Boca Raton has provided *InfoWorld* with exclusive details on IBM's new personal computer," the article said. "The system is scheduled to be announced in New York in mid July 1981. The central processor for this new system will be the 16-bit Intel 8088."

It went on to describe the computer's memory size, monitor, and keyboard. The article even talked about the operating system. "IBM gave some thought to using CP/M as the disk operating system for the personal computer, but this would have been an incredible departure from normal IBM product development strategies," *InfoWorld* reported. "Instead, the operating system for this new computer will be similar to CP/M in many respects. The designers didn't strive for compatibility, just similarity."

The article ended with a strong denial from an IBM spokesperson. "We asked Harry Smith of the Entry Level Systems group if he could tell us about the application software planned for the machine. He responded, 'To my knowledge we are not introducing any such product.'"

Gates was so upset by the *InfoWorld* story that he called the editors as an industry spokesperson and scolded them for printing rumors. In fact, about the only thing the article got wrong was the date of the official announcement. IBM did announce a new computer in July, but it was the System 23 Datamaster that Bill Sydnes and others from the Project Chess team had been working on when they were pulled off to develop the PC. The Datamaster was a $9,830 small business computer designed to compete with similar models by Data General and DEC.

The announcement of the System 23 machine obviously caught the business press off guard. They believed the rumors that IBM was working on a personal computer. *Business Week* magazine ran a short story regarding the July 28 announcement of the Datamaster. "The capacity of International Business Machines Corp. to surprise competitors and other IBM watchers remains unimpaired," the magazine said. "IBM was expected to introduce a low-cost personal computer to compete with popular models made by Apple Computer Inc., and Tandy Corp.'s Radio Shack Division."

The day before IBM cleverly threw the press off the scent of its new PC by announcing the Datamaster, Gates signed what would prove to be the key financial agreement that made him a billionaire and many of those working for him millionaires.

For only $50,000, Gates bought all rights to 86-DOS previously owned by Seattle Computer Products. It was the bargain of the century. Once again, Gates had proved he was a master businessman.

How Gates came by the deal begins with an old friend from Gates' days at MITS, Eddie Curry.

After Pertec bought out MITS in 1977, Curry worked at Pertec for nearly four years, waiting to be fully vested with generous stock options he had received from the company. In June 1981, he joined LifeBoat Associates, the software distributor. LifeBoat had recently been approached by Datapoint (the company that Steve Wood was now working for), which wanted to know if LifeBoat could get CP/M working on its new 16-bit computer. Curry's first assignment at LifeBoat was to go to Digital Research and negotiate a license for the 16-bit version of CP/M that could be used on Datapoint's machine. When he was unable to get an agreement, Curry headed up the West Coast to Seattle Computer, which he knew was marketing a 16-bit operating system known as 86-DOS. Curry offered Brock a quarter of a million dollars for the rights to DOS.

While he was in Seattle, Curry made one other visit, to Microsoft. He told Gates why he was in town.

"There was no reason not to tell him because I couldn't, in good faith, do the deal with Brock and have Bill find out about it," Curry said. "LifeBoat had business relationships with Bill and I would have had to tell him something that wasn't true. Plus, I had a personal relationship with Bill. So I told him about the offer."

Allen, who had dealt with Seattle Computer in the past, wrote Brock a letter asking that Microsoft be given an exclusive license to sell 86-DOS. Allen said Microsoft wanted to compete directly against Digital Research.

"I felt Paul out on the phone and we arrived at a halfway decent agreement, I thought," said Brock. "They would come up with fifty grand and give us beneficial terms on buying all the high-level languages Microsoft offered."

But when Brock received the agreement drawn up by Microsoft's lawyer, it had changed from what Allen had told him over the phone. It was now a sales agreement. Microsoft wanted to buy the operating system outright. It would then relicense DOS back to Seattle Computer.

An attorney who saw the original agreement said Gates personally went through the document and in his own handwriting changed key language to specify a sale of DOS instead of an exclusive license. "That was just a brilliant master stroke on his part," the lawyer said. "Microsoft, not Seattle Computer, would have ownership of DOS."

Said Brock: "I called Paul on it. He said Microsoft's attorney thought it would work out better this way. Well, I wasn't fully convinced, but I could see the fifty thousand bucks on the other hand and we certainly needed capital at that point."

Brock didn't take Curry's offer of five times that much because Microsoft agreed to provide Seattle Computer with updated versions of DOS. Brock figured this would be of great benefit to Seattle Computer since Tim Paterson was no longer around to work on the operating system.

"Microsoft must have been getting antsy," said Brock, "because they sent Steve Ballmer over. He tried to get us to hurry up and agree to the thing and sign it. I met with him personally. He basically told me how it was a good deal, how it would not change anything whether or not they owned it or we owned it, since we would have unlimited rights to use it. I guess he convinced me, because Paul called a few days later and said come on over to Bellevue and let's sign the papers."

When Brock showed up at Microsoft on July 27, Allen called in Paterson to read over the agreement. Paterson told Brock he thought the offer was a fair one.

"We had no idea IBM was going to sell many of these computers," Paterson said. "They were a stranger to this business. Somehow, people seem to think we had an inkling it was going to be this big success. I certainly didn't. So buying DOS for fifty thousand dollars was a massive gamble on Microsoft's part, a 50/50 chance."

Before Brock signed the agreement, Allen took it into Gates, who was in another office. Brock could hear Gates and Allen talking. But Gates never came in to greet him. A few minutes later, Allen came back with the agreement and Brock signed over ownership of 86-DOS to Microsoft.

Brock met Gates by chance for the first time a couple of years later, at a popular Bellevue restaurant called "Jonah and the Whale." The name was appropriate. The big fish had eaten the little fish. The operating system that once belonged to Seattle Computer had by then become an industry standard; by 1991 Microsoft was making more than $200 million a year just from sales of MS-DOS.

On August 12, 1981, two weeks and two days after Microsoft acquired ownership of the operating system from Seattle Computer, IBM triumphantly introduced its new personal computer to the press at the Waldorf-Astoria Hotel in New York City.

The industry would never be the same again. Neither would Microsoft. The IBM announcement came almost one year to the day after the corporate brass in Armonk, New York, had given Bill Lowe the go ahead for Project Chess, with orders to have a machine ready for market in 12 months.

"International Business Machines Corp. has made its bold entry into the personal-computer market, and experts believe the computer giant could capture the lead in the youthful industry within two years," wrote a reporter for the *Wall Street Journal* who covered the coming-out party for the PC.

The basic machine introduced that day had one disk drive, sixteen kilobytes of random access memory, and came with a $1,565 price tag. With options, the price quickly rose as high as $6,000. IBM, which teamed with Sears Roebuck & Co. and ComputerLand Corp. to sell the PC, offered customers a mix of software and application products that would run on its machine. None of the software had been developed by IBM.

Microsoft's software for the PC included BASIC and the game Adventure, the company's first product that was not a language or operating system. "Microsoft Adventure brings players into a fantasy world of caves and treasures," said the IBM press release. It was a microcomputer version of a game played for years by computer hobbyists and hackers on larger minicomputers. Adventure, which was in the public domain, was originally written on a mainframe computer at the Massachusetts Institute of Technology. The player was a participant in the game, typing in commands like WALK NORTH or OPEN THE DOOR. Along the way, the traveler solved puzzles, outfoxed opponents, and found buried treasure.

IBM offered several application programs for the PC, including the popular spread sheet program, VisiCalc, and a word processing program called Easy Writer from Information Unlimited Software. Unbeknown to IBM, the infamous phone phreak Captain Crunch wrote Easy Writer, reportedly while serving a jail sentence after the feds caught him making free long-distance phone calls with his blue box. (Captain Crunch got his name when he discovered that a toy whistle included in boxes of the breakfast cereal of the same name emitted a tone that caused Ma Bell's circuitry to release a long-distance trunk line to the caller.)

Although DOS was the only operating system available on the PC when it was introduced in New York City, IBM had finally been able to reach an agreement with Gary Kildall for a 16-bit version of CP/M. But Digital's operating system would not be ready for another six months, and when it did come out, CP/M was priced much higher than DOS. Also, IBM had indicated it would only provide further support for DOS.

There was little celebrating back at Microsoft when the big day came and the shroud of secrecy was finally lifted. Steve Ballmer tore off the telex from the Dow Jones newswire and posted it on the front door. There were smiles, hand shakes, and pats on the back. But no wild partying; no champagne corks popping. There was still a lot of work to do. A new version of DOS was already in the works.

No one really knew what to expect. "We thought it was going to be important because it was IBM," said O'Rear. "But I don't think I had a sense for the scale. I'm thinking more in terms of the hardware itself. I didn't give much thought at all at that time to the ramifications of the operating system and what an impact that would have. I still had a lot of ideas that 86-CP/M was going to be extremely important, and the IBM DOS was just going to be for the PC."

The word "clone" had not yet entered the industry vocabulary.

About a week or so after the official PC announcement, Microsoft received a form letter from IBM. "Dear vendor," the letter said. "You've done a fine job." It wasn't a very warm way to affirm a marriage. Although IBM apologized an appropriate number of times to Gates for the letter, it was a sign of things to come. When a company climbed into bed with IBM, it usually got kicked out once the honeymoon was over.

CHAPTER 5

Growing Pains

As was common for that time of the year in the Pacific Northwest, a gentle rain fell steadily throughout the Seattle area on Friday, November 13, 1981. But neither the cold drizzle nor the inauspicious date could dampen the spirits of the boisterous group who had gathered in the Seahawks Room of the Ramada Inn just off Interstate 520, across Lake Washington from Seattle. At times, the roar coming from the room sounded like a crowd of college kids holding a pep rally before a big football game. The occasion was Microsoft's second company-wide meeting.

The atmosphere was intoxicating. Bill Gates and sidekick Steve Ballmer acted more like cheerleaders than executives, whipping up the emotions of the more than 100 employees into a frenzy as they talked enthusiastically about the company's future.

Gates and Ballmer established a company tradition that rainy November day: Microsoft's employee meetings would always be lively and entertaining affairs. Each year, Gates and other executives would try to top what had been done previously to rouse the faithful who gathered to hear reports of record profits and sales. In 1991, for example, Gates would ride into the annual meeting on a Harley Davidson motorcycle, leading a gang of bikers. More than 7,000 of the faithful went wild.

Gates made no such dramatic entrance in 1981. In fact, he was upstaged by one of Microsoft's newer programmers, Charles Simonyi, who delivered what would go down in company folklore as the "Simonyi Revenue Bomb."

"Charles was the hit of the meeting," recalled Jeff Raikes, who had been with Microsoft only a few days, hired away from Apple Computer to market Microsoft's software application products that were then under development.

The Hungarian-born Simonyi was the hot-shot programmer in charge of developing Microsoft's applications. As he stood in front of the employees that rainy November day, he explained that the company was about to invest heavily in applications. The market place for personal computers was still very fragmented; the IBM PC with Microsoft's new operating system had not yet become an industry standard. Simonyi said that his goal was to have as many different Microsoft applications running on as many different computer platforms as possible. He pointed to a large chart showing the results of this strategy. Every line on the chart, from revenue to labor force, started fairly flat and then exploded upwards off the scale. In 15 years or so, according to Simonyi's chart, everyone in the state of Washington would be working for Microsoft.

When they saw the numbers on the chart, the 100 or so employees in the Seahawks Room went wild.

Microsoft's revenues had at least doubled every year since Gates and Allen had founded the company in 1975. By 1981, revenues had grown to nearly $16 million. But the company's real growth was just beginning.

"It was exciting to be in a place that was growing so quickly," said programmer Bob Wallace. "I can't remember if we were doubling employees and tripling sales or the other way every year for awhile. . . ."

Shortly after Microsoft's move to the Seattle area, Gates had told one of his programmers at a party that he had two objectives—to design software that would make a computer easy enough for his mother to use and to build a company bigger than his dad's law firm. By November of 1981, one of those objectives had been realized. Microsoft had more employees and was making more money than the law firm of Shidler McBroom Gates & Lucas. In fact, Microsoft had been growing so fast that at the time of the second employee meeting in November, the company was completing a move from the downtown Bellevue bank tower into new, spacious offices in the Northup building, a few hundred feet from the Ramada Inn off Interstate 520.

One side of the Northup building faced a fast food restaurant called The Burgermaster, and Gates' secretary soon had the restaurant's number on her telephone speed-dial so she could quickly order Gates' favorite meal: hamburger, fries, and a chocolate shake. Not long after the move to the Northup building, Miriam Lubow went to lunch with Gates and others at one of Bellevue's more fashionable restaurants. Gates ordered an expensive wine for the table and the usual hamburger for himself.

Not only did growing pains force Microsoft in 1981 to move into new offices, but the company was reorganized from a partnership into a privately held corporation. Gates became chairman of the board, with Allen serving as a director. Then, in a carefully planned move that had been under discussion for some time, Chairman Bill sold five percent of Microsoft for a million dollars to Technology Venture Investors, a venture capital firm in Menlo Park, California, the heart of the Silicon Valley. David Marquardt, a general partner in TVI, was made a director of Microsoft's new board. Gates had been introduced to TVI officials a year earlier by Blair Newman, the computer whiz who later killed himself.

Microsoft did not need the venture capital; Gates was essentially hiring the firm's expertise in incorporation procedures. He was also positioning the company should it eventually go public, as Apple Computer had done the year before, in December 1980. It was Ballmer who convinced Gates to sell off a small part of the company as a long-term investment in the future.

"We just threw that million dollars into the bank with all our other millions," said Steve Smith, Microsoft's first business manager.

As a private corporation, Microsoft could now offer stock incentives to its employees. Although there had been some grumbling about the lack of a company stock plan, most of the technical people working for Gates would probably have remained with Microsoft even without one. But stock participation in the company made it easier to attract good people. Employees could buy stock for about $1 a share. Owning stock in the company made up for a lot of hard work at low pay. Microsoft did not pay very well in comparison with the rest of the industry, but it was very generous with its stock options. (When the company went public in 1986, a number of long-time employees became millionaires on paper).

"The pay was always okay, but never much more than okay," said one programmer who was working for Microsoft in 1981 when the stock plan was first announced following incorporation. "Nobody ever did real well at Microsoft until the stock started coming. They didn't pay well at all, especially when you considered the hours involved. The big compensation for most people was being in a place where you were going to know more about what was happening in the industry than you could anywhere else. Although it took a long time for the rest of the world to realize it, everybody at Microsoft understood the company's significance from early on. There was never any doubt in my mind, practically from the time I hired on, that Microsoft was going to be the most important company in the personal computer industry."

Gates underscored that message to his programmers whenever he got the chance.

One day in late 1981, Gates approached Richard Leeds, project manager for COBOL, one of the languages that Microsoft delivered to IBM for the PC, in the hallway of the Northup building outside of Leeds' office. Gates was trying to get the word out about what he considered Microsoft's top priority. And what was on his mind was Microsoft's operating systems strategy. "We're going to put Digital Research out of business," he told Leeds, slamming his fist into the palm of his other hand.

He would issue a similar vow twice more during the next year, according to Leeds, promising to put MicroPro and Lotus out of business, each time emphasizing his promise by smashing his fist into his hand.

At the time, MicroPro had the best-selling word processing program, entitled WordStar. Lotus announced a spreadsheet program known as 1-2-3 toward the end of 1982 that quickly overtook the popular VisiCalc.

It was clearly not enough for Microsoft to beat the competition; Gates wanted to eliminate his opponents from the playing field. "Bill learned early on that killing the competition is the name of the game," said a Microsoft executive who was with the company in the early 1980s. "There just aren't as many people later to take you on. In game theory, you improve the probability you are going to win if you have fewer competitors."

At the time Gates issued his threats, Digital Research was working on a 16-bit version of its CP/M operating system for the personal computer. When CP/M was finally released for the PC in the spring of 1982, it was priced at $240, or four times as much as DOS. Eventually Digital slashed its price to be more competitive with Microsoft.

Gates wanted to eliminate Digital Research before CP/M was available for the IBM PC and could compete directly with MS-DOS. Soon after IBM's PC made its debut, Gates suggested to his friend Eddie Curry of LifeBoat Associates that perhaps Microsoft should put DOS in the public domain as a way of getting rid of CP/M once and for all. Gates may have been only half serious, said Curry, but the remark showed how badly Gates wanted to eliminate what he thought could be a serious competitor for the PC operating system.

"There was absolute determination on Bill's part to take Digital Research out of the market," said Curry. "It's part of Bill's strategy. You smash people. You either make them line up or you smash them."

Gates surrounded himself with trusted lieutenants who shared his predatory nature. Two of these people, Kay Nishi and Steve Ballmer, were involved in every strategic move Gates made in the early 1980s, according to one former Microsoft executive. "Kay was as driven as Bill to beat Digital," he said. "And you have to include Ballmer, too. Those three were intense guys. Digital was a very important target for us all."

Part of Gates' strategy was to get so much industry momentum built up in support of DOS that CP/M would become an also-ran. To this end, he tried to convince manufacturers to use DOS on their machines. Sometimes, he used strong-arm tactics bordering on the unethical. One such case involved the Rainbow computer introduced by Digital Equipment Corporation in 1982. At the time, DEC dominated the minicomputer market with its famous PDP series of machines. The Rainbow was the company's first attempt at a personal computer. The Rainbow was unique in that it had dual processors enabling it to run 8-bit and 16-bit software. According to a knowledgeable industry source, the Rainbow was originally intended to run only on CP/M. But Gates "persuaded" DEC to eventually include DOS as an option. According to this source, DEC wanted to be able to offer Microsoft Word with the Rainbow. This word processing application was under development at Microsoft in 1982, but was not officially released until the following year. Although versions of Word were designed to work on computers that ran on either CP/M or DOS, Gates insisted that Digital Equipment's deal for Word also include his DOS operating system.

"I remember them [DEC officials] telling me they were not going to follow in IBM's wake with DOS," the industry source said. "And that was a thorn in Bill's side because his gambit was to get all the OEMs signed up with DOS so Digital Research would get bumped off, and more importantly, so that DOS would be secure. The fact that DEC had picked up a different operating system was sort of an embarrassment to Bill. . . . But when the smoke cleared, DEC was offering MS-DOS as an option. There's no question in my mind that Bill told them if they wanted Microsoft Word, they had to at least offer MS-DOS."

Curry, for one, believed it was good for the industry in the long run that Microsoft beat out Digital Research for control of the operating system that became the standard in personal computers.

"You could not have relied on people like Gary Kildall," said Curry. "He didn't have the vision, the understanding of the problems. . . . If you talk to Bill about any software company or any hardware company, there's a very high probability that he will be able to tell you who the CEO is, what their revenues were last year, what they are currently working on, what the problems are with their products. He's very, very knowledgeable and he prides himself on knowing what's going on in the industry. Kildall never had that."

As things turned out, Microsoft didn't have to worry about CP/M, although it would take a while before a majority of computer makers lined up solidly in support of DOS. The IBM PC was an instant hit, and with DOS being the only operating system available on the machine for the first six months, Microsoft jumped out to an early lead, and CP/M was virtually shut out of the IBM PC market.

Arguably, MS-DOS became an industry standard as much from the momentum generated by the huge success of the PC as anything Microsoft's brash, competitive chairman did. As the IBM PC gained in popularity, more and more programmers wrote software for that machine and for the operating system Gates had acquired.

Before the PC announcement in August of 1981, Commodore, Apple, and Tandy's Radio Shack had been the Big Three of the personal computer industry, with a 75 percent market share. None of them seemed to take IBM's PC seriously, because there was nothing innovative about it. The computer used existing technology and software.

But that was just what the Boca Raton team had intended. "When we first conceived the idea for the personal computer in 1980, we talked about IBM being in a special position to establish standards, but we decided we didn't want to introduce standards," explained Project Chess leader Don Estridge in an interview with *Byte* magazine two years after the PC was announced. "We firmly believed that being different was the most incorrect thing we could do. We reached that conclusion because we thought personal computer usage would grow far beyond any bounds anybody could see back in 1980. Our judgment was that no single software supplier or single hardware add-on manufacturer could provide the totality of function that customers would want. We didn't think we were introducing standards. We were trying to discover what was there and then build a machine, a marketing strategy, and distribution plan that fit what had been pioneered and established by others in machines, software and marketing channels."

Not long after the official unveiling of the PC in New York City, Apple Computer, with great arrogance, ran what would become a famous full-page ad in the *Wall Street Journal*. "Welcome IBM," the ad proclaimed. "Welcome to the most exciting and important marketplace since the computer revolution began 35 years ago. We look forward to responsible competition in the massive effort to distribute this American technology to the world."

Apple Chairman John Sculley later told *Playboy* magazine that running such an ad was like Little Red Ridinghood welcoming the big bad wolf into her grandmother's home. "There is a very fine line between being self-confident and getting cocky about it," Sculley told his interviewer. "We have all learned a lot."

The IBM PC soon eclipsed the Apple II and every other machine on the market, thanks in part to a clever television ad campaign featuring Charlie Chaplin's adorable "Little Tramp" typing away on one of the ivory-colored machines. The Tramp, with his ever-present red rose, made the PC seem like a friendly and easy-to-use machine. The market targeted for the PC was not the home but the work place, where IBM had long established its reputation. As it turned out, the company underestimated preliminary sales by as much as 800 percent. Its Boca Raton facility could not turn out PCs fast enough to meet the market demand, and this resulted in a huge backlog of orders. From August through December of 1981, IBM sold 13,533 personal computers, which accounted for $43 million in revenues. By the end of 1983, it had sold more than a half million PCs.

Toward the end of 1981, Microsoft went to work on an updated version of its new operating system. Tim Paterson did all the coding for this first upgrade, which was called DOS 1.1. It allowed information to be written on both sides of a diskette, thus doubling the disk capacity of the IBM machine from 160K to 320K.

When the DOS 1.1 upgrade was finished in March of 1982, Gates and Paterson went on the road to show off Microsoft's operating system running on the PC. Presentations to hardware companies and individuals on both coasts were usually made in hotel rooms. It was reminiscent of the song-and-dance trip Gates made in the MITS-mobile back in 1975 to demonstrate BASIC running on the Altair.

Although the road show was a success, Paterson quit Microsoft at the end of March and went back to work for Rod Brock at Seattle Computer Products. Thanks to the deal with Gates that allowed Brock to package DOS and Microsoft's programming languages with Seattle Computer's hardware, Seattle Computer would have its best year in 1982, reaping more than a million dollars in profit on about $4 million in revenues.

Later, Microsoft began work on DOS 2.0, the next version of Microsoft's operating system for the IBM PC/XT ("XT" stood for Extended Technology), the first personal computer to store data on a hard disk instead of floppy diskettes. DOS 2.0 was to be a much more sophisticated program than DOS 1.0. It had 20,000 lines of code, compared to about 4,000 lines for the first version of the operating system.

The PC/XT was officially announced by IBM in New York City in March of 1983. Priced at $4,995, it featured a 10-megabyte hard disk as well as a 360K floppy disk drive. The computer also had 128K of random access memory, or twice as much as the original PC.

Joe Sarubbi, who had been put in charge of the IBM XT team in Boca Raton, worked closely with Gates and Microsoft on the project for much of 1982. "Bill was arrogant but technically astute," said Sarubbi, now retired and living in Florida. "He liked to test your technical knowledge. He also would take exception to me because I was kind of hard on his team about making the fixes. He would say, 'Well, I'm going to be with Don Estridge on Friday,' and I'd say, 'Bill, I don't give a shit who you are going to be with or where you are going to be. I'm the program manager and you are going to get the job done through me or you are not going to get it done at all.' " More than 500 fixes had to be made in DOS 2.0 before it was ready to work on the PC/XT.

In his relentless drive to dominate the personal computer software industry, Gates' battle plan was always to try to establish the industry standard.

"We Set the Standard" had long been the Microsoft motto, and it was preached by Gates as gospel until it had been burned into his company's psyche. Microsoft won control of the market in languages and operating systems by using this standard-setting strategy. But BASIC and MS-DOS didn't only become industry standards. They became cash cows that provided a steady flow of money to finance the company's breakneck growth. When Gates finally turned his attention to the growing retail market for application software in 1982, he wanted Microsoft to become the standard setter there, too. He intended to take the lucrative consumer market by storm, but it would prove a more formidable battle than he ever imagined.

As a newcomer in applications, Microsoft faced stiff competition, going up against entrenched industry veterans like MicroPro and VisiCorp. Gates would later acknowledge that he "blundered" by not getting into applications sooner.

In 1982, VisiCorp's old warhorse, VisiCalc, was still the best-selling spreadsheet on the market. It had been running at the head of the pack, pretty much unchallenged since being introduced three years earlier at the National Computer Conference in New York City. Gates decided that VisiCorp would be Microsoft's first target. Gates had had his eyes on VisiCorp ever since he and Vern Raburn had tried unsuccessfully to buy half the company from Dan Fylstra in 1979.

Gates planned to overtake VisiCorp with Microsoft's first application product, a spreadsheet called Multiplan. In the spring of 1982, while one group of programmers at Microsoft worked on DOS 2.0, another group, led by Charles Simonyi, was putting the final touches on Multiplan. In development for a couple of years, Multiplan was to be the first of perhaps a dozen so-called Multi-Tool applications that Gates wanted Simonyi and his team to develop over the next two years.

Simonyi had quit his job at Xerox PARC, one of the top computer research centers in the country, to work for Gates. They shared the same vision of creating software that would make computers easier to use than ever before. Gates wanted applications to become more important to Microsoft than its operating system and Simonyi was the programming genius he picked to make that happen. He would become one of Gates' most loyal and trusted lieutenants, a member of Microsoft's inner power circle who always had the chairman's ear. They were very much alike, except for their backgrounds. Charles Simonyi was the kind of character who could have come from the pages of a Horatio Alger story, a boy who started with nothing and ended up with his own Lear jet.

Born in Budapest, Hungary, three years after the end of World War II, Simonyi had been a teenager when he saw his first computer, a room-sized, Russian-made machine with a couple thousand vacuum tubes called the Ural II. At the time, it was one of the few computers in Hungary. Simonyi's father, a professor of electrical engineering, had arranged for his son to assist an engineer who was working with the computer. The Ural II had 4K of memory, about as much as the Altair.

"The excitement I experienced with the Ural II in 1964 was the same kind of excitement that Bill Gates experienced with the Altair in 1974," Simonyi would tell author Susan Lammers. (It was actually 1975 when Gates developed BASIC for the Altair.)

His first professional program was a high-level language that he sold to the state. During a trade fair in Budapest, Simonyi presented a Danish computer trade delegation with a demonstration program he had written and told them to take his program back to Denmark and show it to someone "in charge." They did, and Simonyi was contacted about a job. At age 16, he said goodbye to his family and defected to the West and the wide-open, high-tech frontier of computers.

Simonyi worked for a year as a programmer in Denmark, saving enough money to enroll at the University of California at Berkeley. In 1972 he was recruited to work at PARC, Xerox's computer research center which had opened in Palo Alto, California, near Stanford University. Simonyi worked at PARC while getting his doctorate from Stanford, and wrote his doctoral thesis on his own method of writing code. (When Simonyi went to work for Microsoft, his programming style would come to be known as the "Hungarian method.")

With financial backing from Xerox, PARC quickly became one of the top research and development facilities in the country. It was PARC that designed the experimental Alto computer—several times more powerful than the Altair. Its visionary work would inspire Steve Jobs to develop the Macintosh for Apple Computer and Bill Gates to develop Windows. Research scientists at PARC, expanding on work done at the Stanford Research Center, also pioneered a technology known as GUI, or graphical user interface, developing a revolutionary advanced language program for the Alto called Smalltalk, which worked like an early version of Windows. Smalltalk displayed menus on a screen and used point-and-click technology known as a "mouse," which had been developed by the Stanford Research Institute.

In 1981, Xerox introduced the Star, a computer developed at PARC that took GUI software technology a step further. To accomplish a specific task, the user pointed to icons, small symbols on the computer screen, instead of typing complicated commands. To erase a file, for example, the mouse was used to place a pointer on the icon representing a trash can. With a simple click of the mouse, the file disappeared.

The Star could have been released much sooner, but either Xerox was uninterested in the commercial potential of the work being done at PARC, or it was too slow to react in the market place. As a result, PARC began to lose some of its best people to less sluggish companies like Apple and Microsoft.

"I lost faith in Xerox's ability to do anything," recalled Simonyi.

Shortly after he decided to start looking for a new job in late 1980, Simonyi had lunch with a former PARC colleague, Bob Metcalfe, who had recently founded his own software company, 3Com. Metcalfe gave Simonyi a list of industry people to contact about a job. At the top of the list was the name Bill Gates.

"I called Bill and Steve Ballmer and told 'em they should jump at the chance to get Simonyi," said Metcalfe. "And of course they did."

"We had a fantastic meeting," Simonyi said of his initial visit to Microsoft for the interview with Gates and Ballmer. I was incredibly impressed. . . . Bill had an incredible grasp of the future. It was not something I expected from an operation that, compared to Xerox, was a fly-by-night outfit. We were kind of snobbish at Xerox. We thought the Apple II was kind of a joke."

Simonyi was also impressed that Gates knew so much about programming. "People talk about how lucky Bill is, or how nice his parents are. But when I came here I wasn't betting on his nice family. I was betting on his ability to understand the business and his vision of the future, which has turned out to be right."

After hiring Simonyi, Gates spent $100,000 on a Xerox Star and laser printer, making Microsoft one of the first companies to buy the computer. Gates was laying the foundation for Microsoft's development of Windows, as well as applications for Apple's Macintosh computer, which would incorporate a graphical user interface in its design.

"The Star wasn't a real popular machine, but it was there to play with if you wanted to learn something about the user interface principals," recalled programmer Bob Wallace.

Although Apple's Macintosh was not publicly announced until early 1984, its secret development was already underway in Cupertino by 1981. In fact, Gates had been given a sneak peek at the first prototype and when additional prototypes were available in early 1982, Apple quietly delivered them to Microsoft. Apple wanted Microsoft to develop software for the Macintosh and to have it ready to ship with the first computers. Microsoft had as many people working on Macintosh software as Steve Jobs had on the project at Apple.

There were prototype machines from other companies strewn about Microsoft as well, most of them in rooms with paper covering the glass walls so no one could look inside. Computer manufacturers often furnished Microsoft with a prototype months before their computer was due to be released so systems software could be installed. Although the corporate atmosphere around Microsoft was still very informal, with programmers working in jeans and T-shirts, there was a lot more security than in the early days in Albuquerque.

"Before the serious work started with IBM, everything was out in the open, on tables," said Wallace, who left Microsoft to start his own software company in early 1983. "In Albuquerque, we had a large table and you could see maybe twenty different personal computers on that table that were due out the next year. Everything that was going to happen in the personal computer world was on that table. There was no real secrecy and nobody thought much about that. But then IBM imposed a lot of secrecy. And that was true of the Macintosh work. It got to the point where you knew there was going to be an industry announcement about a new computer. . . . Some of the offices were covered with computer paper on the inside, so you couldn't look in them, and you knew there was a private project in there. Then you would read in the newspaper that a new computer had been announced, and you would walk down the corridor and all the paper had come down on one of the offices, and there was the new machine."

Virtually the only programmers at Microsoft not working under strict secrecy requirements imposed by either Apple, IBM, or other computer manufacturers were those developing Multiplan.

With Multiplan, Charles Simonyi had inherited a project that had been underway for more than a year. In 1980, when work began on the project, Gates hired an outside consultant to thoroughly examine VisiCalc and make a report on how it could be improved. Gates did not like the way the VisiCalc spreadsheet worked, and he intended to improve not only on its performance but its looks. A spreadsheet is made of many different "cells," and in VisiCalc these cells were referred to by a coordinate, such as "A10." Gates wanted to use English names for Multiplan's cells, such as "Sales. June." Simonyi made further enhancements to Multiplan. Drawing from his work at PARC, he incorporated user-friendly menus into the product.

Multiplan was finished in 1981, but extensive beta testing delayed its release. (In a beta test, the product is given free of charge to selected customers who use it for a period of time. In this way, bugs not found during the development stage can be discovered and eliminated before the product is officially marketed.) The release of Multiplan was also held up while Microsoft perfected software tools allowing easy adaption of its spreadsheet to other computer platforms. Though Microsoft had developed the operating system for the IBM personal computer, not even Gates believed the machine or his DOS would become as successful as they did, eventually dominating the market. So a key Microsoft goal for Multiplan was portability. Multiplan was to be an application that could be run on different machines and different operating systems; it was eventually tailored to run on more than 80 different computer platforms.

"Everybody was guessing about how the personal computer market would develop," said Jeff Raikes. "To be honest we guessed wrong. We thought there would be dozens and dozens of platforms, maybe even hundreds."

Multiplan was officially introduced in the summer of 1982 to general praise throughout the industry. *Software Review* said Multiplan was easy to use and rated it "excellent" in every category tested, adding that "Multiplan seems to have been designed with the sole objective of taking VisiCalc's place as market leader." At the time, VisiCalc had sold nearly 400,000 copies since its introduction in 1979.

Gates believed Microsoft now had the spreadsheet that would become the industry standard. As it turned out, he was wrong. VisiCalc would eventually be knocked down for the count, but it would not be Microsoft that threw the punch.

The first versions of Multiplan were released for the Apple II and the IBM PC. A version for machines that ran on the CP/M operating system followed. Multiplan was soon running on dozens of different computers, from the PDP-11 minicomputer made by DEC to the Osborne I, the industry's smallest computer.

The $1,795 Osborne I was the brainchild of industry gadfly Adam Osborne. It was the world's first commercially successful portable business computer.

When Osborne had first developed his new computer, he licensed the CP/M operating system from Gary Kildall and made deals with Gordon Eubanks and Gates for their BASIC languages. He offered Gates and Kildall stock in his company, which incorporated in early 1981. Osborne had a high regard for Gates, and he wanted the young CEO on his board of directors. Gates took the stock offer but turned down the board position.

"He's one of the few in the industry who has an enormous technical acumen," said Osborne of Gates. "He's the only entrepreneur in the industry who will pick up the code and comment on how good it is. He has the ability to look at it and tell what the programmer is doing right or wrong."

But Osborne, a very proper fellow who speaks with a very precise British accent, did come to question Gates' judgment in one nontechnical area—women. In 1982, Gates reportedly had an affair with the wife of one of Osborne Computer's overseas executives. The woman was about 40 years old and had been married several times.

"Bill had a real fondness for older women then," said another Osborne Computer executive who knew about the affair. The woman made the first move, according to the executive. "She decided she was going to sleep with Bill Gates." When Osborne found out about the affair, he talked to Gates and told him to stop playing around; he was ruining a marriage. Gates told Osborne to mind his own business.

The tryst did not last long. Neither did Osborne Computer. In 1983, with a public stock offering in the works, the company declared bankruptcy. In two years, its revenues had soared from nothing to more than $100 million. But the growth was uncontrolled. The company collapsed under mounting debt as a result of questionable strategy.

Osborne had tapped into a vast and lucrative market with the Osborne I. Microsoft saw the possibilities for a small computer, too. Throughout 1982, it helped to develop what would become known as the Radio Shack Model 100, a portable computer small enough to sit on a person's lap. The Model 100 laptop was the brainchild of Kay Nishi, Microsoft's high-flying, globe-trotting representative for the Far East. The genesis for the project was the first-class cabin of a Boeing 747 Jumbo jet, 38,000 feet above the Pacific Ocean.

Nishi was flying back to Tokyo after one of his frequent business meetings with Gates when he found himself seated next to Kazuo Inamori, the president of the big Japanese industrial ceramics firm Kyocera Corporation. Nishi, who could turn a roomful of skeptics into believers, began describing to Inamori a portable computer with a liquid-crystal display screen. Nishi said the computer could be made small enough to fit into a briefcase.

The intense, long-haired, disheveled, baby-faced Nishi, dressed in sweat pants and sneakers, must have been a surprising sight. Obviously, he was not the typical Japanese businessman. But Nishi was convincing. Kyocera Corporation, Inamori said, would be honored to manufacture the computer.

Before long, Nishi had lined up others for the project. Hitachi agreed to produce in volume the 8-line liquid-crystal display.

A few months later, Nishi was on a plane heading for Fort Worth, Texas, to demonstrate a plastic mockup to Radio Shack.

Gates wanted Radio Shack to market the computer in the United States, and he had arranged for Nishi to meet with Jon Shirley, who was then vice-president of computer marketing for the Tandy Corporation. Nishi delivered one of his patented presentations, and the marketing ball was rolling. NEC later signed on to sell the computer in Japan.

The Radio Shack Model 100 represented his concept of the ideal computer.

"I remember Nishi running around with this calculator-sized computer, showing it to everybody and saying "This is the future, everything is going little," said Raymond Bily, who had joined Microsoft as a software developer in 1982.

Although the Model 100 did not sell as well as Tandy expected, it was still considered a marketing and technological success and was used by thousands of travelling sales representatives and journalists.

Coupled with Microsoft's push into applications and retail sales, Gates wanted to expand the company's marketing base outside of the United States. He had moved into Japan before his competitors and, with Kay Nishi's aggressive salesmanship, bagged the lion's share of the language market there. The reward was millions of dollars in revenue for Microsoft's coffers, almost as much as that pouring into the company from all its U.S. sales. But Europe and other overseas markets for the most part remained untapped.

In early 1982 Gates decided Microsoft needed an International Division. He handed the assignment to Scott Oki, a recent recruit from the Sequoia Group, which built turn-key computer systems for physicians.

Oki was taken by surprise when Gates asked him to organize the International Division. He had only been to Europe once in his life. Not long afterward, Oki informed Gates that he had prepared a business plan for the International Division.

"What's a business plan?" Gates asked. The Microsoft CEO had never heard of one of the most basic business planning tools.

Oki's plan called for the formal launch of the International Division in April of 1982. Microsoft would set up subsidiaries in Europe and elsewhere, finding local agents to handle its business interests. For Oki, it was the start of several years of off-and-on 20-hour days. "I went weeks at a time at that pace," he said.

At first, success in penetrating the foreign markets came slowly. Until 1983, Digital Research dominated the operating systems market in Europe. It took a while before the IBM PC and compatible machines that ran on MS-DOS became as popular there as in the United States. Within a few years, however, Microsoft had wholly owned subsidiaries in Italy, Sweden, Australia, Canada, Japan, Mexico, and the Netherlands.

It was a heady time for Microsoft on both sides of the Atlantic. One of the company's executives, recalling the pace of activity in late summer of 1982, said: "We were introducing products into several market places. We were setting up offices in Europe. We were pumping DOS, trying to beat CP/M. We were trying to expand Multiplan's position. We were starting to talk about Word. We were still pushing XENIX. We were doing a new COBOL. It was crazy."

Gates was still pretty much running Microsoft single-handedly. But a lot of his time was being taken up with technical matters—he wanted the final say in everything. Allen, on the other hand, was becoming more involved in management. He had taken over responsibility for operating systems and the Multi-Tool line of application products. Steve Ballmer, in the two years he had been with Microsoft, had bounced all over the company, serving as a roving troubleshooter for Gates, general manager of the Consumer Products Division, vice-president of corporate staff, and finally chief financial officer. He also handled recruiting and hiring.

In recruiting people like Raikes, Oki, and Simonyi for key management positions in the company, Microsoft went after highly competent technical people rather than skilled managers with an MBA. The recruiting emphasis was on finding exceptionally bright young employees with intensity, technical ability, and almost rabid enthusiasm. Knowing how to write code was more important than knowing how to write a business plan.

But Ballmer recognized that Microsoft needed a professional manager. The company was in the throes of diversification and faced the inevitable management problems brought on by rapid growth and expansion. There was serious concern over whether Microsoft had the key management talent, as well as the management structure and control, to move into all these highly competitive arenas at once. In the summer of 1982, Ballmer convinced Gates to allow him to initiate a search for the company's first outside president, someone who could take some of the load off Gates.

Although Microsoft had established a considerable reputation in the industry, it was still a relatively small company, with fewer than 200 employees. Most of the explosive growth in the personal computer industry was taking place in the Silicon Valley of California, and it was difficult to induce top industry managers to move to Oregon and Washington. Several possible candidates who were approached did not want to relocate there. Frustrated, the headhunter hired by Microsoft called James Towne, an old friend from Stanford Business School who worked for Tektronix, a $1.2 billion maker of engineering equipment.

At Tektronix, Towne had worked his way up the management ladder, rising in 12 years from a low-level employee to a vice-president in charge of the company's largest division, with annual revenues of about $700 million and some 7,000 employees worldwide. But Towne was ready for a change. And Towne was a Portland native—Tektronix was located in Beaverton, just 180 miles south of Seattle.

After a brief courtship, Towne agreed to take the job at Microsoft.

Towne hardly fit the profile of the typical Microkid. About to turn 40, with a wife and two kids, he was 15 years older than the average Microsoft employee, and he did not have a technical background. What he did have was a brilliant mind and a lot of energy, qualities that Ballmer and Gates demanded of key people who worked for the company. Towne was a personable man who believed in delegating authority and managing through subtleties. He would prove quite a contrast to Gates and Ballmer, whose styles were anything but subtle. Despite its overwhelming financial success, Microsoft was in dire need of sound management practices, as Towne quickly discovered. Bookkeeping for the multimillion-dollar company was still being done on a small Radio Shack computer. The marketing people had no idea how much of a product they thought they could sell. There was no budgeting system or salary structure. For example, huge differences existed in the stock options granted to programmers who did equivalent work. It seemed to Towne there was a philosophy at Microsoft that to be creative, one had to be out of control.

"This is a critical time for the company," Towne said in an interview with *Softalk*, the industry magazine for the IBM personal computer user. "It's my job to shepherd it through the stage from twenty to sixty million dollars in sales. . . . I'm not a software guy, but I enjoy this company . . . helping solve their industrial problems. All the structures get different in bigger companies, but we have to recognize that to bright people, big is not beautiful."

One of Gates' managers would not survive the company's explosive growth. Vern Raburn, president of the Consumer Products Division, was responsible for developing retail markets where Microsoft's new software application products would be sold. Microsoft had little experience in the risky retail end of the business. It was used to dealing with computer manufacturers who needed languages or an operating system. Penetrating the consumer retail market required more than technical ability. It required a strong marketing and sales department as well.

Raburn's great strength lay in his relationships with the early pioneers in the industry. He knew everyone, and he did business by simply picking up the phone and calling on a friend. Early on at Microsoft, he had achieved terrific results based on these friendships. But his way of doing business could not sustain Microsoft as the company grew. A more formal and professional marketing approach was required.

"We needed to move to the next level of distribution sophistication," said one Microsoft executive. "We needed broader and more aggressive merchandising tactics that an IBM would use rather than a small company."

Gates made the painful decision that Raburn, although a good friend, wasn't the right person to take Microsoft to that next level. Raburn denied he was fired or asked to resign. "There were a series of blowups. If I hadn't quit, Bill probably would have fired me," Raburn said. "It was the wrong place for me to be. . . . I left Microsoft because it wasn't an enjoyable place for me to work. It was an environment I didn't perform well in. I was hurting the company."

His friendship with Gates remained intact, despite the difficult parting. In fact, Gates was best man at Raburn's wedding several years later.

When he left Microsoft in late 1982, Raburn ironically landed a position as general manager for Lotus Development Corporation. At Microsoft, Raburn had been trying to open up new markets for the spreadsheet Multiplan, the company's first application software. When he joined Lotus, the company was just about to come out with its own electronic spreadsheet, and it proved so successful that sales would eventually catapult Lotus ahead of Microsoft as the industry's top revenue-producing software company. It would take several years of aggressive battling before Microsoft reclaimed its place at the top of the heap.

Lotus introduced its 1-2-3 spreadsheet in November 1982 at the fall computer trade show, Comdex, held in the cavernous

Las Vegas Convention Center. More than 1,000 computer companies, including Microsoft, were in attendance, showing off their latest products to more than 50,000 eager buyers. Microsoft had expected to have a successful convention. But when Charles Simonyi took one look at Lotus's 1-2-3 crunching numbers lickety split on an IBM PC, he knew Microsoft's much slower Multiplan was in serious trouble.

By the end of 1982, revenues at Microsoft had more than doubled to $34 million, and employment had topped the 200 figure. But Microsoft wasn't the only computer company experiencing explosive growth. In fact, the personal computer industry as a whole had taken off.

In January of 1983, the editors of *Time* magazine broke with 55 years of tradition and chose the personal computer as its "Machine of the Year."

Wrote Otto Friedrich in the cover story: "There are some occasions . . . when the most significant force in a year's news is not a single individual but a process, and a widespread recognition by a whole society that this process is changing the course of all other processes. This is why, after weighing the ebb and flow of events around the world . . . *Time*'s Man of the Year for 1982 . . . is not a man at all. It is a machine: the computer."

The information revolution long predicted had arrived, and neither America nor the world would ever be the same again. A nationwide poll commissioned by the magazine indicated that nearly 80 percent of Americans expected that in the very near future the personal computer would be as commonplace in the home as the television set. By the end of the century it was estimated that as many as 80 million personal computers would be in use around the world. That prediction would fall remarkably short of the mark. By the end of 1991, Microsoft's operating system alone was being used on nearly 80 million IBM and compatible computers worldwide.

The article talked about the lack of good software that had so far made its way into retail stores. Alan Kay, chief scientist for Atari, was quoted as saying, "Software is getting to be embarrassing."

Gates had said much the same thing a couple months earlier in a cover story in the November 1982 issue of *Money* magazine. It was the first time his picture had appeared on the cover of a major national publication, and Gates complained to Miriam Lubow that the picture made him look too young. The 27-year-old CEO still looked barely 19.

"Technology is out of control," Gates told *Money*. "There are tons of software out there. Much of it is pathetic. I've bought programs that don't work, and with some I can't even get past the manual." But Gates said he expected software to get better. "Over the next two years, we'll come up with software that will actually meet people's needs all the way. . . . Right now much of the software is either bad or too hard to use. But these barriers are coming down."

Microsoft's Multiplan certainly met the needs of consumers who wanted a better spreadsheet to computerize the drudgery of bookkeeping. At the end of 1982, *InfoWorld* magazine had named Multiplan "software of the year." Unfortunately for Microsoft, Lotus 1-2-3 was even better. Only a few months into the new year, it had completely overtaken both Multiplan and VisiCalc in the all-important retail market.

"When Lotus came out with 1-2-3, Bill was furious," recalled Jonathan Prusky, a software developer who came to work for Microsoft in 1983. "Bill knew that applications was where the money was."

Gates admired what Lotus founder Mitch Kapor had been able to do with Lotus 1-2-3, though losing to a competitor drove him up the wall. The 32-year-old Kapor, a former disk jockey with a fondness for psychedelic rock music and transcendental meditation, had founded Lotus in 1982 with several million dollars in venture capital, as well as a couple million dollars of his own money. He had made his fortune by writing two financial software packages for VisiCorp (then known as Personal Software) and later selling the rights to the programs.

Kapor's strategy in developing his spreadsheet was just the opposite of that taken by Microsoft. Lotus 1-2-3 only ran on one machine: the IBM PC. It took full advantage of newer versions of the PC with 256K of memory. Multiplan, by comparison, had been designed at IBM's request to fit into the 64K memory of the first version of the PC. The result, of course, was that 1-2-3 easily outperformed Multiplan. Lotus, and not Microsoft, had created the spreadsheet standard.

What helped to kill Multiplan was that it was built to go on every computer platform. During its development, Gates had made deals with dozens of computer makers. Although Microsoft owned the operating system for the IBM PC, it didn't realize the PC was going to become the only computer platform of significance. Kapor, on the other hand, gambled that there would be a big enough market if he focused solely on the IBM PC; and he was right. Multiplan was better than Lotus in many ways, but it was slow. Lotus 1-2-3 ran ten times faster than any other spreadsheet on the market.

"This was a big, big loss," said one industry executive, talking about the beating Microsoft took from Lotus. "It derailed a lot more than just Multiplan. It derailed all of Bill's ideas [the Multi-Tool products Microsoft planned as a follow-up to Multiplan]. They were all going to be built around the same kind of architecture that Multiplan was, and it was no longer a reasonable way of approaching applications. Lotus definitely derailed and sidetracked Microsoft."

But no one, including Lotus, knew in 1982 (when 1-2-3 was developed) that the IBM PC would become the standard. According to Multiplan marketing manager Jeff Raikes, Kapor just happened to guess right. "I don't even think they [Lotus] understood the key elements of their success."

Still, for a very brief time in early 1983, Multiplan *did* enjoy an advantage over 1-2-3. Microsoft released its DOS 2.0 upgrade for the IBM PC/XT, causing problems for 1-2-3 on the updated operating system.

According to one Microsoft programmer, the problems encountered by Lotus were not unexpected. A few of the key people working on DOS 2.0, he claimed, had a saying at the time that "DOS isn't done until Lotus won't run." They managed to code a few hidden bugs into DOS 2.0 that caused Lotus 1-2-3 to break down when it was loaded. "There were as few as three or four people who knew this was being done," he said. He felt the highly competitive Gates was the ringleader.

In time, Lotus 1-2-3 did for the IBM PC what VisiCalc did for the Apple II. Earlier, many consumers had bought Apple's computer because they wanted a good spreadsheet, and initially VisiCalc only ran on the Apple II. When Lotus came out with 1-2-3, consumers who might have decided on another computer bought the IBM PC to get the Lotus spreadsheet.

What helped to reinforce the IBM PC as an industry standard were the ubiquitous PC clones that began appearing on the market in early 1983. IBM had never intended to make a computer that would be particularly easy to copy, but that's exactly what happened when it used off-the-shelf parts from other manufacturers for more than 80 percent of the computer's hardware. IBM decided to use "open architecture" because it did not have time to design its own proprietary parts and get the PC out in a year. Also, Big Blue's corporate management simply did not believe the baby of its computer family would be significant enough to warrant investment in a proprietary system.

Compaq Computer Corporation, based in Houston, Texas, was first out of the gate with a PC-compatible machine in January of 1983. The company did more than $100 million in sales its first year. Within three years of the company's founding, Compaq had cracked the Fortune 500 list of the top American companies, smashing the previous record of five years held by Apple Computer.

The clones hurt IBM, but helped Microsoft. "IBM compatibility" meant manufacturers had to license DOS from Microsoft. In addition, any application developed to run on the PC could also run on these much cheaper machines. By the end of 1983, Microsoft had made more than $10 million from sales of MS-DOS alone.

"With the Compaq computer, we saw the real power of IBM compatibility," said Microsoft's Raikes. "Everybody else had been building computers saying 'We are different from the rest.' Compaq came out and said 'We are not different. We can run any software right off the shelf written for an IBM compatible computer.' That was the beginning of PC compatibility."

It was also the beginning of a change in strategy by Microsoft, whose programmers had been working hard to adapt software to a number of machines that were not compatible.

"We wound up doing a lot of work for nothing when the IBM PC emerged as a standard and compatible clones began showing up," said Bily, the software developer who had joined Microsoft in 1982 after graduating from MIT.

Bily had been assigned to work with Paul Allen on developing a BASIC that could be quickly adapted for any computer platform with only a few hours of work. Microsoft felt that this project had the potential to bring the company enormous amounts of money with little investment of resources. The project was in beta testing in 1983 when it was suddenly canceled. A lot of other projects around Microsoft were also shelved because of the shift in strategy away from multiple computer platforms.

"You put your heart into a project and the world changes underneath you," said Bily. "Software engineering was not a job with us, it was an obsession. . . . A lot of resources got lost because the industry changed and the engineers weren't told about it."

Bill Gates in his office on Microsoft's sprawling, collegelike campus in Redmond, Washington. (Courtesy of the Seattle Post-Intelligencer)

Gates as an eighth-grader at Lakeside School.

Mary Gates with her 3½-year-old son during one of her volunteer lectures to Seattle-area schools. (Courtesy of the Seattle Post-Intelligencer)

Above: Bill Gates in the computer room at Lakeside School. This photo of Gates appeared in the Lakeside yearbook of Gates' senior year with the caption "Who is this man?"

Below: The famous "Poker Room" at Currier House on the Harvard campus. (Courtesy of the Seattle Post-Intelligencer)

Ed Roberts, designer of the world's first personal computer, the Altair. He is now a country doctor in a small town in Georgia. (Courtesy of the Seattle Post-Intelligencer)

Microsoft was a company of fewer than a dozen employees in 1978 when this photo was taken. Top row, left to right: Steve Wood, Bob Wallace and Jim Lane. Middle row, left to right: Bob O'Rear, Bob Greenburg, Marc McDonald, and Gordon Letwin. Bottom row, left to right: Bill Gates, Andrea Lewis, Marla Wood, and Paul Allen. (Courtesy of Bob O'Rear)

Above, Left: Gary Kildall, chairman of the board of Digital Research. (Courtesy of the Seattle Post-Intelligencer)

Above, Right: Tim Paterson, who designed what became known as DOS, or Disk Operating System. (Courtesy of the Seattle Post-Intelligencer)

Below, Left: Bill Gates and Paul Allen in Microsoft offices in July 1981, a month before IBM announced its first personal computer. (Courtesy of the Seattle Post-Intelligencer)

Charles Simonyi, one of the key programmers at Microsoft today, and chief architect of several of Microsoft's best-selling applications. (Courtesy of the Seattle Post-Intelligencer)

Jon Shirley, president of Microsoft from 1983 until 1990. He helped guide the company from a small software business of fewer than 100 employees to a global empire of more than 6,000. (Courtesy of the Seattle Post-Intelligencer)

Microsoft president Mike Hallman, who took over when Jon Shirley retired in 1990. Hallman left Microsoft in March 1992. (Courtesy of the Seattle Post-Intelligencer)

Bill Gates and former girlfriend Jill Bennett in 1984. Gates was dating Bennett when he appeared on the cover of *Time* magazine that year.

Ann Winblad, a respected venture capitalist in the software industry, dated Gates in the mid-1980s. (Courtesy of the Seattle Post-Intelligencer)

Bill Gates in his office at Microsoft in early 1984. (Courtesy of the Seattle Post-Intelligencer)

The Microsoft chairman's father, Bill Gates Jr., a highly respected Seattle lawyer. (Courtesy of the Seattle Post-Intelligencer)

Mary Gates, at a board of regents meeting at the University of Washington in 1991. (Courtesy of the Seattle Post-Intelligencer)

Paul Allen left Microsoft in 1983 after he was diagnosed with Hodgkin's disease. He is now one of the richest men in America, with assets of more than two billion dollars. (Courtesy of the Seattle Post-Intelligencer)

Bill Gates during a relaxed moment in his office in March 1991. His favorite attire is an open-neck shirt, slacks, and loafers. (Courtesy of the Seattle Post-Intelligencer)

It was not surprising that software developers around Microsoft didn't see what was happening in the industry. They were usually sequestered in their offices like monks in a monastery, leaving only to sleep or have a late-night beer at the Mustard Seed Tavern in Bellevue. Sometimes, they just slept in the office. Bily described what it was like in 1982 and '83 when he was working on the BASIC project with Allen: "It was all guys. . . . I started at age 21, and about a year later I was one of the oldest guys in the group. Everyone had moved here from out of state, and didn't know anyone. . . . So you buried yourself in your work and got a lot of work done."

Every Thursday night, many of these young programmers would go out for a beer, play foosball on the tavern machines, and talk science fiction before going home or back to work. Although Paul Allen would often join them for a beer, Gates did not.

Gates was so busy running Microsoft that he no longer even had time for his boyhood friend Carl Edmark. In early 1983 their friendship was inexplicably damaged by a seemingly minor incident. They had planned to see the just-released movie "Star 80," based on the true story of Dorothy Stratton, a *Playboy* model and rising young movie actress who was killed by her jealous boyfriend. But Edmark showed up late at Gates' house to go to the movie. "From then on, our relationship was strained," Edmark recalled. "It's something I never fully understood. We eventually grew apart completely. After that night, he simply didn't have time for the friendship." Edmark felt that Gates had rebuffed him because he was not rigorous enough in scheduling his time with Gates. The Microsoft CEO's time had grown too limited.

The BASIC project Paul Allen had been working on with Raymond Bily would turn out to be one of his last at Microsoft.

Allen had discovered he was seriously ill in late 1982. While on a business trip in Paris with James Towne, Scott Oki, and a couple of others from Microsoft, he had to excuse himself during a meeting to return to his hotel room because he was feverish. Allen told the others he feared this was something more serious than just the flu. When he didn't feel better after a couple of days, he went to consult a French doctor. But he felt uncomfortable so far from home in a country whose language he didn't understand. Still running a high fever, Allen left the others in Paris, boarded the supersonic Concord jetliner at Orly Airport, and headed back to Seattle. The diagnosis took some time, but after extensive tests doctors determined Allen had Hodgkin's disease, a form of lymph cancer. To save his life, they said, he needed to undergo a combination of radiation treatments and chemotherapy—immediately.

Colleagues said the relationship between Gates and Allen had become strained even before Allen became sick; this may have played a part in his decision to leave Microsoft. There were bound to be problems between the two after so many years working together. They pointed out that being around someone as intense as Gates was difficult even for short periods of times.

"It's almost inevitable when people work so close together," said David Bunnell, the former technical writer for MITS who knew Gates and Allen back in Albuquerque, "It's like a marriage." As a publisher of a national computer magazine, Bunnell stayed in touch with the two after Microsoft moved to Bellevue.

"They have very different personalities," Bunnell said of Gates and Allen. "Paul was always much more laid back. All along, I thought Paul wanted to enjoy the fruits of his success a lot more than Bill. Bill wanted to drive on and on. I think Paul really wanted to not work so hard. I know he had a rock 'n' roll band. He had a lot more interest in just enjoying life."

One Microsoft manager said it was clear to him in mid-1982 that Allen and Gates were having problems. "They were not getting along. . . . There was a confrontation of some kind. It happened before I got there. Paul would much rather read science fiction novels, play his guitar and listen to music than be around the company after a while." He would also occasionally take days off, something Gates would never do and which went against the hardcore work ethic at Microsoft, especially at a time when everyone was putting in 14-hour days.

Rather than discussing their differences with each other directly, Gates and Allen communicated primarily through electronic messages, or E-Mail, according to another company manager. Employees would almost never see Allen in Gates' office, although Steve Ballmer was in there a lot.

When asked about speculation that he and Gates had had a falling out, Allen replied, "That's bullshit." A deeply sensitive man, Allen seemed genuinely hurt that anyone at Microsoft would think he didn't want to work as hard as everyone else. He was receiving radiation and chemotherapy treatments, he pointed out, while continuing to work, and this was why he wasn't around at times. In fact, Allen used to joke with friends at Microsoft about his hair falling out. Some in the company did not even know he was sick. Allen, although a captivating conversationalist, was a very private man and never one to explain his feelings.

Of his relationship with Gates at the time, Allen said: "There certainly were times when Bill and I had our differences. Sure, it was intense. We didn't always see eye to eye. But what always came out in the end was productive."

Allen did acknowledge that the illness changed his outlook on life, and that's why he decided to leave the company. "For a while, I just needed to get away from work. . . . You have to strike a balance between work and enjoying the other things in life." Microsoft's other co-founder could never make such a statement. For Gates, work *was* his life.

In early 1983, after eight years of grueling 80-hour weeks and few vacations, Allen left the company he had helped found to recover from his bout with cancer and to enjoy a life that now seemed much more precious. Although he resigned as executive vice-president of Microsoft, Allen remained on the board of directors with Gates.

After leaving Microsoft, Allen toured Europe and spent time with family and friends. His cancer went into remission, and it remains so today. It would turn out to be a difficult year for Allen. In November his father died unexpectedly after routine surgery on his knee. Five days after the operation, while walking around his Seattle home on crutches, he collapsed and died from a blood clot. Only 62 years old, he had just recently retired as associate director of libraries at the University of Washington. Allen and his father were very close, and he took his father's death hard.

At the spring Comdex show in Atlanta in 1983, six months after Lotus had announced its 1-2-3 spreadsheet at the fall Comdex show in Las Vegas, Microsoft took its second swing at a hit in the retail market. On an IBM PC in the Microsoft booth the company displayed a new word processing application called Microsoft Word. Charles Simonyi, like a proud father, demonstrated to curious customers the new features of the program.

Microsoft Word had been under development for about a year, and it incorporated many of the cutting-edge graphical user interface (GUI) concepts Simonyi had toyed with at Xerox PARC. The most unusual attention getter was a "mouse" that allowed the user to position a pointer on the computer screen by moving the small device around on a flat surface. Most of those who watched the demonstration at Comdex had never heard of a mouse. In addition, as many as eight different documents could be viewed and edited at the same time in so-called windows, which divided the screen up into sections. Word also included features such as multiple fonts and italics and was designed to work with the latest laser printer technology.

Simonyi and his team had developed Microsoft Word specifically for the IBM PC and compatible machines. But it could also work on other computer platforms. As far as Gates and Simonyi were concerned, the GUI concepts used in Microsoft's first word processing application represented the next generation of personal computer software, concepts that would soon become the foundation of a new product to be announced later in the year—Windows.

When he had launched Multiplan, Gates wanted to overtake and eliminate VisiCorp, which at the time marketed the best-selling VisiCalc spreadsheet. With Microsoft Word, Gates was now taking aim at MicroPro. Only a few months earlier, he had told programmer Richard Leeds that Microsoft was going to put MicroPro out of business.

MicroPro was riding high with its best-selling WordStar, which had captured 50 percent of the word processing market. WordStar had been comfortably on top since its introduction in 1979. Sales in 1983 hit $25 million. Seymour Rubinstein, MicroPro's founder, was well acquainted with Gates. They had first done business together in 1978 when Rubinstein was working for IMSAI Manufacturing, which produced a personal computer that was a rival to the Altair. Rubinstein negotiated with Gates for Microsoft's FORTRAN language as well as something called an "overlay editor," which allowed the language to be broken into modules that could be placed into memory as needed—a very useful program given the limited memory capacity of the early microcomputers. Typically, Gates had been eager to close the deal with Rubinstein, although Microsoft had never made an overlay editor before. Skeptical that Gates could deliver the software in the agreed-upon time, Rubinstein insisted the contract provide for penalties in case Microsoft was late. It was. "Bill never did deliver it," said Rubinstein. But IMSAI soon went bankrupt and was unable to collect on the penalties from Microsoft.

After the release of his new company's WordStar, Rubinstein occasionally ran into Gates at industry trade shows and in Europe. By this time, Gates was helping establish the company's International Division and pushing MS-DOS. Rubinstein hardly held Gates in awe. In fact, he felt Gates was lucky to have ended up with the operating system on the IBM PC.

"He was able to maximize a series of good fortune and lucky breaks," Rubinstein said. "He was able to make a lot of mistakes and recover. He was not in operating systems when he started, but through foulups from Gary Kildall, Gary lost that position and IBM chose Bill Gates. That was pure luck. There was no foresight, no imagination, no brilliant maneuvers, just a lucky break caused by a combination of Digital Research screwing up and Seattle Computer Products having something which wasn't very good that could be modified for IBM."

But Rubinstein respected Gates. He knew it was just a matter of time before Microsoft came out with its own word processing program to compete with WordStar. "I'd talked to Bill many times," Rubinstein said. "He was a very ambitious guy."

Their companies traded products back and forth. Microsoft needed the program editors made by MicroPro, and MicroPro needed Microsoft's languages. Not long before Microsoft introduced Word in 1983, Rubinstein visited Gates in what turned out to be one of the most unusual business meetings Rubinstein can remember. Gates had a date in traffic court and if he didn't go, the police had threatened to jail him, according to Rubinstein. Gates asked Rubinstein to come along with him, which he did.

Gates had been getting a lot of speeding tickets of late. He had traded in his green Porsche 911 for a much faster, high-performance Porsche 930. Gates had good lawyers who had been able to get some of his speeding tickets dismissed on technicalities, but his driving record was poor. He was in danger of losing his license.

On the way to traffic court with Rubinstein, Gates explained that he had a radar detector in his Porsche. He felt the police officer had given him a speeding ticket because he saw the device. Gates was going to argue with the judge that he was within his rights to have the radar detector. Rubinstein gave the combative Gates some friendly advice:

"I told Bill, 'You may very well be within your rights to have a radar detector in your fast Porsche. But the fact is they won't like it because they'll think the principal reason that you have it is to escape the law. The best thing for you to do is to tell them that you are going to throw away your radar detector, that you are really sorry about what you did, and that you are not going to speed anymore. Otherwise they are going to crush your nuts.' "

In court Gates did as Rubinstein suggested and as a result, he got off with only a fine.

Not long after his day in traffic court Gates, worried he would lose his license if he didn't slow down, bought a sluggish Mercedes diesel sedan. He said the car was a good test of his mental discipline because it was so slow. And there was no radio to distract his thinking. Actually, the Mercedes just took a bit longer to get up to high speed. Gates pushed it hard, too, and racked up several more speeding tickets, but he never did lose his license. The brown Mercedes, however, was a topic of conversation at Gates' tenth anniversary high school reunion. Apparently, Gates had forgotten to put oil in the Mercedes and had burned up the engine.

The Mercedes was soon repaired. Nonetheless, Gates continued to use the Porsche 930 for late-night drives when he needed to do some serious thinking. Jonathan Prusky, who was hired by Microsoft in 1983 to work on Word, recalled Gates telling him that he would go out late at night and drive the legal speed limit down the express lanes of Interstate 5 (the main interstate through Seattle), checking for police, and then would roar back through the stretch at 150 miles per hour if the coast was clear.

No doubt Gates wished Microsoft Word could run as fast as the Porsche. Word was in beta testing when the company decided the program ran far too slowly.

Richard Brodie, chief coder for Word along with Simonyi, worked for weeks to make it faster, but Gates pointedly told him it wasn't good enough. Somehow, over the next weekend, Brodie was able to make it two to three times faster, according to Prusky. But it still wasn't particularly fast.

"Bill wasn't really involved in the design of the product, contrary to some stuff that I've read," said Brodie. "I did almost all the coding initially. Bill saw it after it was pretty much done and tried it out, as he likes to do. He sent E-Mail back with about 17 things he didn't like about it. So I took the E-Mail and not knowing any better I started working on what he wanted. The next time I saw Bill he was really surprised because evidently it was the first time anyone had ever responded like that to a piece of E-Mail. People got E-Mail from him all the time, but this was the first time anyone had ever done anything about it."

When Microsoft Word was released several months after the Comdex show in Atlanta, Microsoft used a glitzy $3.5 million campaign to market the software that included a diskette-in-a-magazine promotional gimmick. Microsoft planned to distribute 450,000 demonstration diskettes of Word. The company made a $350,000 deal with publisher David Bunnell to include 100,000 free diskettes in a special subscriber edition of *PC World* magazine. Other copies of the magazine sold on newsstands contained a subscription offer for 14 weeks along with a free demonstration diskette of Microsoft Word. The remaining diskettes were distributed through the subscription offer.

The promotional campaign for Word was part of an aggressive sales approach by Rowland Hanson, the newest member of the Microsoft management team. Before he arrived at Microsoft in early 1983, Hanson was vice-president of marketing for Neutrogena Corporation, which made soap and other products. He had also been marketing manager for General Mills. Why not market software like the cosmetics industry marketed soap, he suggested, and provide some free samples? Hanson knew nothing about computers, but he *did* know a thing or two about soap and marketing.

Gates' decision to bring in an outsider to the computer industry reflected the growing emphasis he placed on marketing. Microsoft was in the midst of its transition from being a language and operating system company to one selling applications into the retail market. It was not enough just to develop good software—Microsoft had to make customers want to buy it, too.

"If you think about it," said Hanson, "who understands brands better than the cosmetics industry? Look at the halo around Clinique or Neutrogena. These companies are brand dominated. If their brand isn't strong, then nothing else matters, because there isn't reality to cosmetics. Soap is soap."

At Microsoft, Hanson's job title was vice-president of corporate communications, which involved all advertising, public relations, and production services—anything and everything pertaining to packaging, merchandising, and marketing Microsoft's products.

Word was originally going to be released as Multi-Tool Word, a continuation of the Multi-Tool application product line that was to follow Multiplan. Hanson suggested a different product-naming strategy. It was important for a product to be identified by its brand name, he pointed out. Microsoft had to get its name associated with its products, just like Neutrogena.

Hanson later elaborated on the concept in this way: "If you look back at some of the old articles that were written in the industry, you'll see the word 'Multiplan' but no 'Microsoft' associated with it. That was because Multiplan was a stand-alone name. It started to take on its own meaning, beyond Microsoft, just like WordStar. People who wanted a word processing program knew the name 'WordStar,' but they could not have told you MicroPro was the company that made it."

Hanson wanted to make Microsoft the Sara Lee of the software industry. Everyone knew the Sara Lee brand, regardless of whether they were shopping for apple pie or pound cake.

"The brand is the hero," Hanson said. "People start to associate certain images with the brand, and that becomes much more important than any single product. What the consumer goods companies realized years ago was that products come and go. You are going to have a product and it's going to rise and fall. But if you can create a halo around a brand name and create equity in a brand, when you introduce new products under that brand halo it becomes much easier to create synergy, momentum. . . . We decided that we needed to make Microsoft the hero."

Gates immediately saw the logic of Hanson's argument. As a result of Hanson's efforts, the Multi-Tool names were thrown out. Taking their place were Microsoft Word, Microsoft Plan, Microsoft Chart, and Microsoft File.

The strategy worked as Hanson had hoped. Word became known as a Microsoft product. Unfortunately, the first version of Word for the PC was a fairly mediocre program, and reviews were mixed. Word was widely criticized for being too technical and difficult to learn. Sales, while healthy enough to put Word into the top 100 of the best-selling software products on the market, were below expectations.

According to Simonyi, Word was too far ahead of its time. Some of the concepts, such as the mouse, were intimidating to users. And Simonyi took the blame for incorrectly insisting that Word use publishing industry jargon such as "folio," which he later believed contributed to the slow start.

"There is no question that version one of Word or version one of Multiplan weren't the incredible successes other programs in their category were," Simonyi said. "They were tactical disappointments, but I think they were fantastic strategic successes."

Microsoft would eventually get Word right, but it took several major revisions. This would become a pattern with most of the company's initial application products for the IBM PC and compatible computers. Vern Raburn, former president of Microsoft's Consumer Products Division, discussed this aspect of Microsoft in *Fortune* magazine: "With few exceptions, they've never shipped a good product in its first version. But they never give up and eventually get it right. Bill is too willing to compromise just to get going in a business."

In a sense, it was all part of Gates' master plan. As that master of military combat tactics, General George S. Patton, liked to say, a good plan, violently executed now, is better than a perfect plan next week.

In hiring Roland Hanson, an industry outsider, for a key executive position at Microsoft, Gates was taking something of a risk at a critical juncture in the company's development. Gates had gambled similarily on his new president, James Towne, and the gamble had not paid off.

In an interview with *Business Week* in May of 1983, Towne dismissed reports of serious tension between him and Gates: "We are going through a transition process from a centrally organized outfit to something where others have more responsibility." But not long after that interview, Towne was gone. Microsoft's first president had lasted just 11 months. Gates would later say that Towne was "sort of random"—a favorite "techie" expression used at Microsoft, meaning confused or haphazard behavior, and usually used to describe someone you didn't like. Towne has declined comment on why he left Microsoft. Gates, too, has said very little. But based on interviews with other managers at Microsoft during Towne's tenure, a revealing picture emerges of two people who came to dislike each other intensely. The parting was far less amicable than it was portrayed in the press and by both parties.

The crux of the matter was that Towne never gained Gates' respect. He just wasn't technically proficient enough to talk bytes and bits with Gates, who lived in the strange, rarefied language of computers.

"I came aboard about the time Towne did," said Raymond Bily. "Jim came in from a corporate environment at Tektronix to help Microsoft through some of the growth stages, and he felt very strongly that professionally trained managers needed to be in management positions. And Bill felt strongly that technologists needed to be managing technical people. It was a question of whether this company was going to be technology driven or management driven."

Others said Towne only wanted to bring traditional management practices into the business side of the company, not into the more creative software development area that Gates handled. "The part of the company that needed creative organization was software development," one manager said. "They have always been difficult to manage. That was always under Bill. He could motivate those guys. But the other side of the company, the financial organization, really didn't require all that much creativity."

There were deeper problems, however, than just differences in management philosophy. Towne was never invited into Microsoft's inner sanctum of power, which at the time included only Gates and Ballmer. Although Ballmer officially reported to Towne on the management chart, Towne was often left out of the decision making. He would learn weeks later of something that had been decided by Gates and Ballmer at 3:00 in the morning. Part of the problem was that their lifestyles didn't mesh.

Towne was 40 years old and, with a wife and two kids at home, he understandably wanted to spend time with them. Gates had no such desires or obligations. He would get increasingly intense late at night, about the time Towne was heading out the door for his home.

"Bill would say that some of his best times were sitting in his office at 2:00 A.M.," said one Microsoft manager who worked with Towne. "Bill felt better then than any other time, knowing his company was working. And Towne wasn't around a lot of those hours. He was with his family."

After staying up most of the night, Gates would often be late for important morning meetings, which irritated Towne. He once complained to a colleague that Gates was immature. At times he felt more like a babysitter than a company president. Once, as Gates and Towne were leaving an industry trade show, Gates told Towne he had left his bags in his room and asked Towne to fetch them. When Towne entered the room, he found Gates' dirty underwear on the floor and his clothes scattered helter-skelter. He had to pick up the underwear and clothes and put them in Gates' suitcase. This was not, Towne told a friend, what a company president should have to do.

"Bill admitted lots of times he needed to grow up, but he didn't know how," said one Microsoft executive who was with the company when Towne left. "Frankly, he needed a big brother more than he needed a president."

After a while, the two avoided each other whenever possible. Towne felt his meetings with others in the company went much better when Gates was not around. But it was clearly not a healthy situation. Both men knew it wasn't working out. One Friday morning Gates called Towne into his office and informed him he had nine months to find another job. Towne had a job in Portland by the following Monday. He would later be named Oregon's "executive of the year."

Gates assumed the role of company president once again after Towne departed. But he understood the mistake he had made in hiring Towne. From the start, there had never been any rapport between the two. Gates needed to find someone he already knew, someone he liked and felt comfortable with. That was as important as a candidate's managerial and technical acumen. In Jon Shirley, a vice-president of the Tandy Corporation in Texas, Gates found both a friend and someone knowledgeable about the industry.

Unlike a lot of corporate executives, Gates was able to put his ego aside, look at himself honestly, and to learn from his mistakes. He knew he had made a mistake in hiring Towne. In hiring Shirley, he would not make that mistake a second time.

"As you watch how Microsoft has developed, what you see is Gates realizing well in advance what he's not good at and going out and finding exactly the right person to do the job," said Stewart Alsop, a respected industry observer and longtime Gates admirer who writes a national computer newsletter. "This is so rare. I've been following startup companies for years. I can't tell you how rare this is. Look at what happened with James Towne. Gates was told that as the founder of the company what he needed was a management guy, someone to organize the company. So he found Towne. But Gates realized quickly that Towne was not taking into account the history and culture of Microsoft. He was organizing Microsoft in a classical way rather than as it should have been run. He realized Towne was not bad, but that he, Gates, had made a mistake and Towne was the wrong guy for the job. So Gates went out and hired Jon Shirley. And he was absolutely the right guy. . . . The process of identifying the mistake, figuring out the problem and fixing it is what makes Bill Gates different. I've watched him do it over and over again."

Shirley arrived at Microsoft in August of 1983, after 25 years with the Tandy Corporation, where he had earned a reputation as a tremendous organizer known for his toughness and efficiency. He had most recently been a vice-president of computer merchandising at Tandy. He had also worked in sales, international operations, and manufacturing. At 45, Shirley was five years older than Towne, but he and Gates had known each other for years and had negotiated many times across the table. The two had worked closely during the previous year on the Model 100 portable computer. They liked each other, despite the fact that Shirley, in an interview a couple months before he joined Microsoft, had said of Gates: "He can be difficult to work with." Gates knew and respected Shirley enough that he trusted him to run parts of Microsoft without Gates' direct supervision. This freed Gates to concentrate more on the development side of Microsoft and less on day-to-day administrative matters.

The two men had very different personalities. Gates was intense and energetic, like a shark always on the move. The dour, pipe-smoking Shirley, on the other hand, was quiet and contained, preferring cold logic to hot emotion. He had a no-nonsense approach to business.

"If you presented something to Jon, the emotion would stay out of it," said one of the first managers Shirley hired. "A lot of people found that very cold and were put off by it. I liked it."

Shirley brought a calmer, more mature management style to Microsoft. He was the perfect complement to the combative Gates when diplomatic skills were needed. He had a "tempering" role with others in the industry when relationships with Gates became too tense.

"Shirley was a very easy guy to work with, easy guy to talk to," said Raymond Bily. "He helped round out the team. He wasn't like Bill or Steve Ballmer. He had kid gloves. He was more able to make you feel good about a bad decision and re-direct your efforts."

When he joined Microsoft, Shirley went to work immediately on the company's numerous organizational and managerial weaknesses. He restructured the retail sales force, tapping Ballmer as a vice-president of marketing. Shirley wanted to better utilize Ballmer's brand-management experience from his days at Procter & Gamble.

Shirley found new suppliers and cut Microsoft's manufacturing costs by 20 percent. As Towne had discovered during his tenure, the marketing people had little idea how much product they could sell. Shirley ordered production based on 90-day projections instead of annual projections. This soon eliminated a huge backlog of unfilled orders. And Shirley finally did something about the stone-age computer system used by accounting.

Secure with his new president in place, Gates could now turn his attention to what would prove to be Microsoft's most ambitious and difficult undertaking—the development of Windows, a software program that Gates hoped would make computers easier to use than ever before. Easy enough, in fact, for his mother to use.

What Gates couldn't foresee in 1983 was that his vision would consume the labors of as many as 30 of his best programmers for the next two years while they worked around the clock on making Gates' vision a reality. Before the first version of Windows was finished, those programmers would spend some 80 work-years designing, writing, and testing Windows, in contrast to the 6 work-year investment originally approved by Ballmer. Gates' ability to manage complicated development programs would be severely tested, as would his relationships with his closest advisers. Several of his hand-picked managers would quit, unable to tolerate the screaming fits he and Ballmer threw as the project slipped embarrassingly behind schedule. Microsoft would be reorganized a year into the project to improve efficiency, but it would nonetheless suffer its first significant loss of credibility with the press and the public. A few computer writers would even venture that Gates had badly blundered when he chose to champion graphical user interfaces. In time, Gates would prove them wrong. But a new decade would have dawned before Windows finally lived up to its promise.

With Windows, Gates intended to draw on technology developed in the early 1970s at the Palo Alto Research Center, that fountainhead of creativity that gave birth to the Alto and Star computers.

In the summer of 1981, Steve Jobs had given Gates a peek at the prototype of a new computer Apple was developing—the Macintosh—which used GUI concepts developed at the Xerox research center. Later that year Microsoft formally began a GUI project of its own called Interface Manager. Gates had his own vision of what the program should do. Popular software application programs each had a unique way of working on a computer. Users could not easily switch from WordStar to VisiCalc, for example, because the commands to print a file or move text were different. Gates wanted Interface Manager to be sandwiched between MS-DOS and applications. By acting as an interpreter for users, Interface Manager would make different application programs look the same, and users could operate them in nearly the same way. The display screen would be divided up into individual "windows" so several different applications could be viewed simultaneously.

Development of Interface Manager proceeded in secret at Microsoft along those lines throughout 1982. By the middle of the year, however, it was becoming clear that other software companies were developing GUI programs of their own for the IBM personal computer. At the fall Comdex trade show in 1982, VisiCorp announced it was working on something called VisiOn. This represented a double whammy for Microsoft. Charles Simonyi had already seen the swift new Lotus 1-2-3 spreadsheet at the show. When he got a look at VisiOn, it appeared very similar to Microsoft's own efforts to develop Interface Manager. Not long afterwards, in the early days of 1983, Apple introduced Lisa, the first personal computer with a graphical interface and mouse. It had been under development since 1979. Jobs had hired away one of PARC's top scientists to work on the Lisa. The machine generated quite a buzz in the trade publications, notwithstanding its $10,000 price tag.

Unwilling to let VisiCorp steal a march on Microsoft, Gates hinted to the press in January 1983 that Microsoft would ship a product before VisiCorp could bring VisiOn to market. The promise was made weeks before a prototype of Interface Manager had even run on an IBM PC. It was the first of several pronouncements that would later embarrass Microsoft.

A graphical user interface was the linchpin in Gates' strategy to overtake Lotus in the applications business. The plan was twofold. By writing programs for the Macintosh, which was still under secret development, Microsoft would get the jump on other software developers in creating applications for the graphical environment. And if Gates could make Microsoft's Interface Manager the industry standard for the IBM PC, he could shift millions of DOS users over to his applications, rather than those developed by Lotus. To establish an interface standard, Gates had to get other software publishers to agree to write application programs that would support Microsoft in the graphical environment. He also needed to convince the big personal computer manufacturers to sell Microsoft's Interface Manager with their machines.

With characteristic zeal, Gates spent months selling computer manufacturers and software developers on his vision of GUI. One software company executive recalled that in early 1983, Gates paid to fly him and a colleague to Microsoft. Gates wanted to convince them to write program development tools for Interface Manager rather than to work with Lotus on developing tools for 1-2-3. "He walked us all around Seattle and told us about this grand scheme," the executive said. "He was doing Multiplan, Multifile, and right in the middle of it was this graphical user interface. He said it was going to be done in a year."

It was Rowland Hanson who came up with the name Windows in place of Interface Manager. At the time, trade articles about graphical user interfaces described the concept as a "windowing" system. Even VisiOn was described in that manner. "It appeared there were going to be multiple systems like this on the market," Hanson said. "Well, we wanted to have our name basically define the generic."

But a catchy name by itself wouldn't make Windows a winner. Microsoft was being outflanked on several fronts by competitors that were further along in the development of their own GUI system. Worse, Gates was having a tough time selling IBM on the product. More than 20 other computer makers, including Compaq and Radio Shack, had indicated their willingness to endorse Windows. But there was one name conspicuously absent from the Windows alliance—IBM. Gates wanted Big Blue to endorse Windows, but it refused to do so. IBM executives, never particularly happy about sharing revenues with another company, wanted to bring software development in-house. IBM decided to design its own graphical user interface, called TopView.

Clearly, Microsoft needed more firepower to counter the growing threat. As Steve Jobs had done before him, Gates looked to Xerox PARC for software developers experienced in GUI who could put the spurs to Windows development. Charles Simonyi had been the first from PARC to join Microsoft. Now, in the summer of 1983, Gates went after Scott MacGregor.

"Microsoft was looking for somebody who had done this thing before," recalled MacGregor. "They didn't want to reinvent the wheel. That's why they went shopping at Xerox."

The belly dancer who undulated her way around Bill Gates wasn't doing much to distract him from his quest.

Earlier this August day he had flown from Seattle to San Francisco to personally handle the recruitment of MacGregor for the Windows team. Now he was sitting in a Moroccan restaurant in Palo Alto, listening to the surreal background drone and twang of Middle Eastern music, sizing up the man sitting across the table from him.

MacGregor, 26, was a friend of Charles Simonyi. Weeks before, Simonyi had suggested to Gates that MacGregor might be induced to leave Xerox PARC for more amiable surroundings. MacGregor, prematurely bald with a scholarly air about him, headed a small software engineering team that helped create the windowing system for the Xerox Star. When Simonyi called, MacGregor agreed to an interview after talking by phone with Gates. Although he was only vaguely aware of Microsoft, his curiosity was piqued when Gates hinted he wanted to talk to him about a graphical user interface for personal computers.

Their dinner conversation that night came easily, despite the distraction of the belly dancer. Recalled MacGregor: "There are a relatively small number of people in the industry who understand ideas very quickly, and one of the things I like is if somebody is really smart and understands what you're saying, you can complete each other's sentences. You start speaking in an abbreviated way. . . . Bill and I hit it off right away. I think he concluded I knew something about Windows, and I think I concluded he knew something about the PC industry and had some visions and goals he wanted to get done."

Both found they shared an enthusiasm for the possibilities of a windowing system that could make personal computers far more accessible to the average office worker and home user. The Star had incorporated all the features necessary for an electronic replica of a typical office setting: icons, menus, multiple windows symbolizing the desktop, file cabinet, telephone, in-and-out boxes, and wastepaper basket. Data could be coaxed in and out of the computer with a mouse. Software combined text and graphics into one document, and the system was designed so that what the user saw on the screen was what came out in hard copy when the "print" command was given. It all sounded very much like what Gates envisioned for Windows.

"We talked about Windows and how we were going to change the world while watching a belly dancer do her thing," said MacGregor. "I think Bill in a sense realized GUI was something that was important that he really didn't know enough about. He figured he better get something in place fast because all his competitors were doing it. Apple was driving forward on the Macintosh, as were some of the other competitors like VisiCorp and Digital Research. I think he didn't quite understand it, but he didn't want to be blindsided by this one."

MacGregor visited Microsoft a couple of times before he agreed to sign on to head the new Windows engineering team. On MacGregor's first day at work, he and Gates talked about a name for the development team. They finally settled on the Interactive Systems Group.

Around the same time Gates was wooing MacGregor, he hired two more people from Xerox: a talented programmer named Dan Lipkie, and Leo Nikora, a management veteran of the Star project with 17 years of software programming experience.

Finding Xerox defectors wasn't difficult. MacGregor and Nikora, like Simonyi before them, had grown disillusioned with the fact that so many good ideas developed by PARC never got to market or failed when they did so.

"Xerox was the epitome of corporate culture," said Nikora. "Everything was run by committee, and there was not too much individuality—and I'm talking about the creative side of Xerox. Microsoft, on the other hand, was a bunch of individualists, with the whole show run minute-to-minute by Bill Gates. He was in on every decision, from top to bottom."

Nikora decided to leave Xerox when he watched the Star crash and burn after years of painstaking evolution. He felt the fault lay not in product design but in marketing, and decided it was time for a career move. The first person he called was Gates, who he remembered from the presentation Gates had made to Xerox with Steve Smith years before. He had been particularly impressed with Gates' chutzpah. Gates, he'd discovered, was not just a brilliant programmer and technical person, but also a terrific salesman and marketer.

When Nikora contacted Gates in August of 1983 and told him of his interest to switch to marketing, Gates reacted enthusiastically. "I'd much rather teach a technician marketing than teach a marketer the technology." Gates offered to make Nikora marketing manager for Windows and to teach him the marketing end of the business.

After a formal job offer with generous stock options, Nikora made the jump to Microsoft. He wasn't quite expecting the run-and-gun style that characterized Microsoft, however. On his first day at work, he was ordered to hop on a plane and report to IBM in Boca Raton. Gates and Ballmer were already there for a scheduled conference. Upon reaching IBM's offices, Nikora linked up with Gates and Ballmer and walked into the meeting without a hint of what it was about.

"I was introduced as the marketing manager for Windows," Nikora recalled, "and we started talking with IBM. I wasn't told what was going on, why I was there, what I was supposed to do, and I have no idea what happened that day. It was totally over my head."

That feeling continued throughout the day. During the plane ride back, Gates and Ballmer launched into an involved conversation about DOS, leaving Nikora without a clue about what they were discussing. The two executives were debating a point about the command-line prompt in DOS—"A:>"—that tells the user which disk drive is operating. Nikora had no idea what Gates and Ballmer meant when they referred to the "greater than" prompt. "I had never used DOS in my life. I was at Xerox. We were in the Ivory Tower. We built everything ourselves. So I had never even seen DOS."

In October of 1983, VisiCorp announced that it planned to start shipping VisiOn. Gates' boast nine months before—that Microsoft would be the first to market with a graphical user interface—evaporated like so much hot air. VisiCorp's bomb-shell was followed by one from Quarterdeck, a startup software publisher that announced it, too, would build a graphical user interface, named DESQ. The market was becoming more crowded, and Microsoft began to take on the look of an also-ran.

Gates was furious. To steal some of the spotlight from VisiCorp and Quarterdeck, he ordered that Windows be formally announced. Within two weeks, MacGregor was airborne with Gates, headed for New York.

Gates felt he couldn't afford to keep Windows under wraps any longer. He had learned that one way to prevent potential customers from flocking to a competitor's product was to announce that your company was working on something even better. It was a tried-and-true IBM gambit that worked well when customers looked to your firm to set standards; they usually would gladly wait for the market leader's product to come out.

InfoWorld magazine would later coin a term for such a product—"vaporware."

"There seemed to be this notion that since all of our competitors were announcing products that were vaporware, we had to have one too," recalled one Microsoft manager of the decision to announce Windows.

Gates had other motives, as well. He knew the still-secret Macintosh with its graphical user interface and mouse was going to shake up the industry when it was released early in 1984, and by announcing Windows now Microsoft could make a preemptive strike. Gates wanted the industry to know Microsoft was surfing the curl of the breaking GUI groundswell, not languishing in the backwash. The announcement would also help to neutralize not just competing software publishers but also IBM. Big Blue had recently moved away from Microsoft with its decision to publish TopView. Gates had fought back like a Chinese warlord by forging alliances with 24 computer makers who agreed to support Windows, including Compaq, Texas Instruments, Hewlett-Packard, Zenith, Burroughs, and Digital Equipment Corporation. Clone manufacturers didn't want IBM to shut them out of the market by setting the standard for Windows environments, and they were only too happy to rally behind Microsoft. The wrath of mighty IBM was evident—the company signed an agreement with VisiCorp making IBM a distributor for VisiOn.

The morning of November 10, at the Helmsley Palace Hotel in New York City, Microsoft staged what was up to then the most elaborate product introduction ever witnessed in the industry, one that made Lotus Corporation's introduction of 1-2-3 look like "cold cuts," in the words of a writer who attended the event. For most of the morning, one Microsoft technician after another trooped to the stage, putting on a detailed demonstration of a Windows prototype and showing what the finished product would be able to do, at least in theory. It wasn't an unprecedented display of the power of GUI. But the idea that you could get a clunky IBM PC to use graphics was considered reasonably amazing.

Taking his place at the podium, Gates explained to the press that Windows would end the problem of compatibility of applications once and for all, and that it would be able to run most software written for MS-DOS. The statement was an attempt to head off growing industry enthusiasm for software that included several functions, such as a word processor and spreadsheet. Lotus had an integrated program, Symphony, in the works, and there were no similar integrated applications on the horizon at Microsoft. Gates wanted people to believe that Windows would make integrated software obsolete.

By the end of 1984 Gates boldly predicted, as he stood center stage pushing up his boxy glasses, Windows would be used on more than 90 percent of all IBM compatible computers. It was a brash prophecy that Microsoft, and particularly the fledgling Windows development team, would come to greatly regret.

The day before the Windows announcement in New York City, Steve Ballmer and Scott MacGregor made a brief recruiting trip to Carnegie Mellon University in Pittsburgh.

Ballmer had been Microsoft's recruiting coordinator almost from the day he was hired as Gates' assistant, and it was an assignment he relished. In some ways it was similar to his days as the equipment manager for the Harvard football team. Once again, he was helping his team win.

Crisp thinking and a high IQ were essential to landing a technical job at Microsoft. Except in very rare cases, Gates wanted young people right out of college with a background in science, math, or computers. Usually, candidates were interviewed on campus and later flown out to Microsoft for a brief visit. Though the company did not pay well, Microsoft usually was able to hire anyone it really wanted by promising generous stock options and a chance to work in a free-spirited environment.

"We initially tried to recruit people from other companies," recalled Ingrid Rasch, Microsoft's first human resources director who was part of a wave of new managers hired in 1983. "But we could never find the type of experience we wanted. We wound up having to go back to universities and recruiting new kids."

In addition to a high IQ, the recruiters looked for candidates with drive and initiative. During a phone screening, Microsoft personnel would ask a series of open-ended questions: "We'd have them describe a typical work week, or their typical day. We wanted to know how many hours they were awake, what they did in those hours. We'd ask how they felt about projects that didn't get done. The kind of person we wanted was the one who responded, 'God, I just hate that!'. . . . We were looking for what people did with their time, and the amount of energy in their voice would tell us what we wanted to know. We wanted to know if they were driven enough, so we could drop them into our atmosphere and have them thrive."

Microsoft's favorite recruiting grounds were Harvard, Yale, Massachusetts Institute of Technology, Carnegie Mellon, and a little college near Toronto named the University of Waterloo, which specialized in mathematics. Eventually, 15 universities in the United States, four in Canada, and six in Japan were targeted. Microsoft recruiters made personal visits to each of these schools in search of brilliant students, diligent and driven, who were cut from a cloth different than their peers. In short, Microsoft hired clones of its leader, over and over again.

"There's a standing policy here," Ballmer told *InfoWorld* magazine in a 1983 interview. "Whenever you meet a kick-ass guy, get him. Do we have a head-count budget? No way. There are some guys you meet only once in a lifetime. So why screw around?"

Job candidates were often asked difficult questions that had nothing to do with programming. Ballmer liked to find out quickly how smart someone was, and in the middle of an interview he would fire a logic problem at the prospective employee, trying to throw the person off balance. "You don't have to be a programmer to tell if someone is smart," said Ballmer.

Ballmer sometimes asked game-theory questions. He would ask the job candidate a basic question, and once that was answered he would take them through harder and harder variations of the question.

"What we were interested in was not just if someone knew the answer, but could they *think*," said one senior Microsoft programmer who made recruiting trips to college campuses in 1983. "A lot of bright people don't always do well in Microsoft interviews because they can't handle the pressure . . . the first person you interview with has the first say on whether you get the job. If you don't do well, that's the end of the road."

Microsoft recruiters had to change their questions from time to time because students who didn't get a job would tell their friends what questions had been asked. And the word spread quickly, from campus to campus.

Although Ballmer interviewed all software developers hired at Microsoft, Gates and other senior technical people from the company would often accompany him on recruiting trips and ask the tough technical questions.

"We would rip people to pieces," said McGregor. "We would ask them very difficult technical questions, hand them a piece of paper and pen and say solve this problem. We probably lost some people but the people we did hire were good at solving very difficult problems under pressure."

With the stopover at Carnegie Mellon University on November 9, Ballmer and MacGregor were following up on a planned recruiting visit that had been announced weeks before at the school. Students who were interested in a job at Microsoft had signed up for an interview and submitted a resume. One student who did not sign up for an interview was Neal Friedman. He didn't think much of personal computers. He had decided the future was in big computers, like the one he was working on at the university.

"I figured this PC stuff was just some mom and pop thing, that there was no future in it," said Friedman. "When I saw this notice that Microsoft was going to be on campus, I thought, 'This is just some garage-type operation, and I'm not interested.' "

But Microsoft had sent away for the university's resume book on graduating students. A few days before the company's recruiters were to arrive on campus, Friedman received a mailgram from Steve Ballmer, saying Microsoft was impressed by his resume and an interview spot had been reserved for him. Having never received a personal mailgram before, Friedman, too, was impressed. He decided he'd go to the interview.

Ballmer handled one group of students, MacGregor another. Each interview lasted about 30 minutes. Friedman was interviewed by MacGregor, who was wearing a sweater and jeans. Friedman was able to handle MacGregor's first tough question, the high-low number puzzle. This is a game theory question in which the candidate has to guess a number from 1 to 100 that the interviewer has selected. The candidate is told if the guess is high or low and continues until guessing the correct number. There is a mathematical strategy for getting the number in the fewest possible guesses, which is about seven.

Friedman was also asked a more difficult technical question: How would he represent numbers in base negative one? (The binary language of computers is a base two numbering system.) He handled that mind twister, as well.

When the interview was successfully finished, MacGregor threw out a hook to reel in his catch. He told Friedman he was headed for New York City where Microsoft planned to announce a big new project called Windows.

"I got a 24-hour scoop on the world," said Friedman, who was hooked and agreed to fly out to Microsoft for a visit. He had previously interviewed at IBM.

"The difference in attitude was actually visible when you visited Microsoft and compared it to other companies," he said. "There was no dress code. At other companies you didn't see people in tennis shoes and sneakers. I was told at IBM that men are expected to wear ties at least two times a week. At IBM I encountered one guy wearing a neon multicolored tie. That was the limit at IBM. At Microsoft you didn't wear a tie."

Friedman eventually narrowed his choice of jobs to Microsoft and Tektronix, the engineering company where James Towne had worked before joining Microsoft as its first outside president. Tektronix had also offered Friedman a job. A few weeks after he had narrowed his choice, while in his Portland hotel room waiting for a breakfast interview with someone from Tektronix, Friedman flipped on the television and saw Jane Pauley doing a segment of the NBC Today show on Microsoft. Friedman saw a camera shot of two programmers in a hallway, fencing with rubber swords.

"I said to myself when I saw the thing on TV, 'Oh wow! That's my company!' "

When he was hired, Friedman was specifically told not to discuss with colleagues the stock options he had been given. Each new employee got the same lecture but not the same options. The option to buy stock in the company was a powerful recruiting tool, and the prospect of getting rich convinced more than one programming whiz kid just out of college to come to work for Microsoft. These options were dangled in their faces like strings of pearls.

His first day on the job, Friedman got a window office. A week later he had his first major project—connecting Microsoft's foreign offices to corporate headquarters in Bellevue by E-Mail. When he had visited IBM, Friedman had been told more than a hundred people usually worked on the same project. At Microsoft, he had the E-Mail job pretty much to himself. He was soon in Paris, hooking up the system at that end.

"Everyone put in long hours," Friedman said. "The people were just as bright as I thought when I first interviewed with them. The environment was friendly and open. I had a lot of intellectual freedom, or creative freedom. There weren't any constraints on how I did things. E-Mail to Europe had to work, and they didn't much care how I did it."

Friedman found a feel-good spirit in the hallways of the Northup building where programmers not only conducted sword fights but rolled tennis balls filled with pennies into empty pop cans arranged like bowling pins. Pranks were perpetrated any hour of the day or night. Ballmer was the victim of one such prank when upon his return from a business trip, he found his office filled from floor to ceiling with small, rubber "bouncy balls." At least it appeared that way from outside the office, looking through the glass partition. In his absence, employees had built a plywood sleeve behind the glass and filled it with the balls, making the office appear to be packed with them.

Bouncy balls had become a fixture at the company before the Ballmer incident, although it's unclear how the tradition started. Some workers bought them by the gross, and it wasn't unusual for programmers to arrive in the morning and find them on their keyboards, in coffee cups, in their desks—they seemed to multiply like Tribbles in a well-known episode of "Star Trek." There were pick-up bouncy ball games outside, and bouncy ball hockey games in the hallways. Somebody once introduced an orange to a bouncy ball fight in the hallway. It made quite a mess. At one point, a memo was sent out banning juggling in the hallway during daylight hours, so a group of programmers set aside a special room just for juggling.

Microsoft's programmers, who by late 1983 numbered more than 100 of the nearly 450 company employees, worked hard and played hard, just as a handful of their brethren had done years earlier in Albuquerque. They had all been hand-picked by Gates and Ballmer. They were special, and everyone in the company knew it.

"The software engineers got the best of everything," said one programmer who was hired from MIT about the same time as Friedman. "From the day you started you got your own office. That was really nice, really a motivating thing. It was about the only company where you could get your own office at that stage in your career . . . . There was a lot of respect for a young kid right out of college. The software engineers are the lifeblood of the company. If you want to surround yourself with world class engineers, give them the respect that they need."

Friedman was particularly impressed that Gates not only knew the name and face of every programmer but also their telephone extension number. Gates also knew the license number of the programmer's car. A former Microsoft manager recalled walking through the parking lot of the Northup building with Gates one morning in 1983. Gates would glance at each license plate and name the employee—he had memorized every tag. The manager didn't think that Gates had tried to memorize them—"he just noticed them and remembered."

Friedman's office was only five doors down from Gates, who was very visible and often talked shop with programmers in the hallways late at night about projects they were working on. The management structure on the "creative" side of the company was purposefully very flat. There were no middle managers getting in the way of access to "Bill," as everyone called him. Just being able to see Gates in the hallway was important to many of the young programmers who had joined Microsoft's crusade.

Gates was becoming a cult figure in the industry. At Microsoft, he was a hero. It was little wonder that, as they idolized him, the programmers also emulated him. Within the industry, stories abounded of Microsoft programmers and executives who became Gates clones, adopting his speech patterns, his mannerisms, even his trademark quirk, that oddball rocking tic.

"I know people who came back from working at Microsoft," said an executive with a rival software company, "and they had this expression to describe the influence Gates had there. And their expression was, 'If Bill said drink Kool-Aid, they would do it'." This was not flattery. The description alluded to the infamous Jonestown Massacre, where the Reverend Jim Jones killed himself and hundreds of his fanatic religious followers by ordering them to drink poisoned Kool-Aid.

The Microsoft work force of young programmers was nothing if not motivated. Gates expected his programmers to work as hard as he did, which meant 60- to 80-hour weeks. Bonuses were awarded only for working overtime, along with Saturdays, Sundays, and holidays.

"You are surrounded with people who are very much the same, and the people who run the company are the same, so you just go and go and go," said Rasch, the company's human resources director. "There would be times when people would work more than we wanted them to, and we would try to get them to slow down. But sometimes you couldn't get them to stop. When they collapsed you covered them with a blanket and turned off the computer. Sometimes we would try to lock them out of their offices, temporarily."

Added a former Microsoft vice-president: "I saw kids, you know, who worked at Microsoft for a few years and truly, I wondered if they would ever be able to work again."

There is a story that circulates in the industry that Gates at one time required his managers to park in the order they arrived for work in the morning. No one wanted to leave until the person who had arrived earlier and parked in the space next to them had slumped exhausted behind the wheel and driven home.

Microsoft officials insist the story is apocryphal. But Mark Eisner, president of Softbridge Microsystems, a Massachusetts software company, remembered visiting Gates in 1983. "We were walking out of the building about 8:00 o'clock at night, and a programmer was just signing out for the day. He said, 'Hey Bill, I've been here for 12 hours.'

"And Bill looked at him and said, 'Ahhhhh, working half-days again?' It was funny, but you could tell Bill was half-serious."

Gates often wore his people down not just by his own personal tenacity but also by his sometimes shocking lack of diplomacy. In discussions, he wielded his formidable intellect like a blunt instrument. He could be rude and sarcastic, even insulting, when he wanted to make a point. If angered, said one ex-employee, he became "apoplectic."

For many programmers, attending a technical staff meeting with Gates was like going through an oral examination with a verbal executioner. He had the uncanny ability to spot the weak link in even the most logical argument. Show him the Mona Lisa, and he would see the errant brush stroke. Once the flaw was pinpointed, he would rip the person to shreds, hurling favorite insults such as "stupid" and "random."

"In those days," said a Microsoft product manager, "when you would attend a meeting with him, he'd be rocking and his knee would be jerking up and down, and there's all this idiosyncratic motion which I guess is a channel for some of his internal energy. You just knew there was a dynamo moving inside. He was a very clear thinker. But he would get emotional. . . . He would browbeat people. Just imposing your intellectual prowess on somebody doesn't win the battle, and he didn't know that. It may not be the right thing to do to bash your point across, but he didn't know that then. He was very rich and very immature. He had never matured emotionally."

The commercial ran only once, on January 22, 1984, while millions of people were watching the Oakland Raiders destroy the Washington Redskins, 38–9, in Super Bowl XVIII.

Apple Computer was about to introduce its Macintosh computer to the world, and the commercial was intended to stir up anticipation for the big event. It showed a roomful of gaunt, zombie-like workers with shaved heads, dressed in pajamas like those worn by concentration camp prisoners, watching a huge viewing screen as Big Brother intoned about the great accomplishments of the computer age. The scene was stark, in dull, gray tones. Suddenly, a tanned and beautiful young woman wearing bright red track clothes sprinted into the room and hurled a sledgehammer into the screen, which exploded into blackness. Then a message appeared: "On January 24, Apple Computer will introduce the Macintosh. And you'll see why 1984 won't be like 1984."

If the $400,000 commercial did not get across the notion that IBM was an Orwellian despot, Steve Jobs certainly did when he took the stage of a packed auditorium at Apple's headquarters in Cupertino in the Silicon Valley for the official unveiling of the Macintosh.

"IBM wants it all and is aiming its guns on its last obstacle to industry control, Apple. Will Big Blue dominate the entire industry?" Jobs exhorted the crowd.

"No!" they shouted.

"Was George Orwell right?"

"No!" they shouted again.

The Mac, as the $2,500 stylish computer would be fondly called, was advertised as "the computer for the rest of us." It featured a mouse and splashy, easy-to-use graphics that set it apart from the IBM PC. Apple was bucking the "compatibility" trend. It was hoping the Macintosh could challenge IBM in the corporate marketplace, where Big Blue dominated.

Bill Gates led a delegation from Microsoft for the coming-out party for the Macintosh. Despite his strategic relationship with IBM, Gates had bet half the farm on the success of Apple's new computer and its innovative technology. The Mac's desk top utilities, such as the alarm clock and calculator, had been developed by Microsoft. A team of Microsoft programmers, under the direction of Charles Simonyi, had been working in secret on applications for the Macintosh since Gates and Jobs signed an agreement to do business together on January 22, 1982. Now, two years later, Multiplan for the Macintosh was ready to ship with the Mac, as was BASIC. And the Microsoft team was still working on Word and a couple other applications for the Macintosh.

Gates predicted to a group of software developers at the Macintosh announcement that Microsoft eventually expected half its revenues to come from the sale of software for the new computer.

In an interview with *Rolling Stone* magazine shortly after the announcement, Gates told author Steven Levy the Apple engineers who developed the Macintosh had "worked miracles." Gates had been smitten by the simplicity of the Mac ever since he saw a prototype back in the summer of 1981, shortly before IBM announced the PC. Andy Hertzfeld, one of Apple's software engineers on the Macintosh project, had given Gates the first demonstration. Gates was unfamiliar with the mouse technology used in the Macintosh, and the first question he asked Hertzfeld was what kind of hardware was used to make the pointer move around the screen in response to the movement of the mouse. Actually, Apple had solved the problem with software, not hardware.

"I had gotten a similar type of mouse system going on the Apple II about two weeks earlier," Hertzfeld recalled, "and just as Gates asked that question I was about to say, 'Of course we don't have any hardware for it. We even can do it on an Apple II.' But Steve Jobs yelled at me, 'Shut up!' "

Jobs wanted Gates to know as little as possible about graphical user interface software.

Microsoft received the first prototypes of the Macintosh in late January of 1982. Programmers needed a machine before they could design applications for it.

In creating the Macintosh, Steve Jobs had gone shopping at PARC, too. He had met with officials of the Xerox Corporation in 1978 and proposed a venture capital deal whereby Xerox could own part of Apple if Jobs could get a peek at the technology under development at its Palo Alto Research Center. Jobs was quoted as saying, "I will let you invest a million dollars in Apple if you will sort of open the kimono at Xerox PARC."

Both Gates and Jobs obviously knew a good thing when they saw it and appropriated everything they could from PARC, including its best minds. When he was later asked about the similarities between Windows and the graphics used in the Macintosh, Gates kidded that he and Jobs had lived next to a rich neighbor named Xerox and when he (Gates) broke in to steal the television set, he discovered Jobs had already taken it. His point was that Windows came from technology developed at PARC, not Apple.

The development of the Macintosh was something of a pirate operation from the start, kept separate from the rest of the company in a building that was known as Texaco Towers because it was right next to a Texaco station. The engineers, almost all of them in their twenties, kept a pirate flag on the wall, although the rainbow-colored Apple logo had replaced one of the eyes in the pirate skull. Jobs considered the Mac his baby and later neglected other parts of the company to run the show, but he had at first opposed the project, according to Mac team leader Jeff Raskin.

Raskin complained in a memo to Apple Chairman Mike Markkula that Jobs was a "dreadful manager" and that Apple should "see that he gets management training before being allowed to manage other company projects that involve creative work." When Jobs got a copy of the confidential memo, Raskin was fired.

Publicly, at least, Gates had only nice things to say about Jobs when the Macintosh was released. He told *Rolling Stone* that "people concentrate on finding Jobs' flaws, but there's no way this group could have done any of this stuff without Jobs."

Privately though, Gates had a different opinion, according to colleagues at Microsoft. They said Gates didn't have respect for Jobs' technical abilities.

"Gates looked with disdain on Steve Jobs," said one Microsoft manager who was part of the team working on applications for the Macintosh. "I think he thought Jobs was a fake, that he was all bluster and no go. I don't think he thought Jobs knew how to design anything himself."

———

Like Steve Jobs before him, Bill Gates was starting to make a name for himself in the national press. He was being hailed as the next wunderkind of the personal computer revolution, the *new* Steve Jobs. Journalists who trekked to Seattle to write about Microsoft's brilliant young leader found a skinny kid with a high-pitched voice, oversized glasses, dandruff, and uncombed hair whose techie talk was liberally sprinkled with words such as "cool" and "super." Gates' unassuming manner was a welcome contrast to what writers often referred to as the "darker side" of Steve Jobs.

"There is a hint of Andy Hardy in his boyish grin and unruly cowlick," wrote *People* magazine. The magazine had named Gates as one of the 25 most "intriguing" people of 1983. "Now 28, Gates is to software what Edison was to the light bulb—part innovator, part entrepreneur, part salesman and full-time genius."

The comparison to Thomas Alva Edison was appropriate. Although he is remembered for inventing the electric light bulb,

Edison spent most of his life as an entrepreneur, selling the public on his vision of the future.

Many of these early national stories about Gates focused on his obsessive work habits, his Midas touch, and competitive personality. An article in *Fortune* magazine that appeared shortly after the *People* piece was headlined "Microsoft's Drive to Dominate Software." The article described Gates as "a remarkable piece of software in his own right. He is childishly awkward at times, throws things when angry, and fidgets uncontrollably when he speaks. But he is an extraordinarily intelligent master programmer steeped in technical knowledge about his complicated business. At the same time, he is monstrously competitive."

The national press usually portrayed Gates as a computer whiz kid and hardcore technoid, a peculiar egg who liked to spend his Saturday nights watching physics lectures on his VCR. The *Wall Street Journal* described him as a nerd on its front page—not once, but twice. Gates took exception to the tag. A nerd, he said, could not manage people or run a multimillion-dollar business. But if people wanted to call him a nerd because he enjoyed watching physics lectures, that was all right with him. Gates did occasionally watch a videotaped series of Cornell University lectures given by Richard Feynman, the brilliant, iconoclastic, and influential postwar theoretical physicist with whom Gates later corresponded.

Reporters for newspapers and magazines who flocked to Bellevue to do stories about Gates and Microsoft tried to outdo each other in finding colorful tidbits that helped build the Gatesian legend, like the time in the early 1980s he turned a $40,000 ante into a million-dollar windfall by investing in undervalued stock, including Apple. But the common thread that ran through each of their stories was Gates' youthful appearance. He did not fit the mold of the typical CEO. In fact, he didn't look old enough to drive a car, much less run the fastest-growing software company on the planet.

Even *Time* magazine got into the act with a cover story on Gates in its April 16, 1984 issue. "He looks like an undernourished graduate student as he waits for a plane at Seattle-Tacoma International Airport," *Time* wrote of Gates. "His gray sweater has patches on the elbows, his shoes are scuffed; his ginger hair flops over a pair of steel-framed glasses. . . ." The *Time* cover photo of a nervous-looking, bespectacled Gates balancing a floppy computer disk on the index finger of his left hand was not especially flattering. The article described Gates as America's software tycoon, having amassed a personal fortune estimated at $100 million. It noted that in 1978 Microsoft had 15 employees and now had 510, with projected 1984 revenues of $100 million.

The *Time* magazine article was the first to mention that Gates had a girlfriend, Jill Bennett, a 27-year-old computer sales representative for Digital Equipment Corporation. Gates had first started dating Bennett in 1983. Although he had occasionally gone out with women since high school, it was his first serious relationship. They had met at a party thrown by a college friend of Bennett's who worked at Microsoft. "One of the first questions I asked him was why the company didn't develop software for a 32-bit microcomputer," said Bennett, who now lives in the Boston area. "He laughed pretty hard and nicknamed me '32-bit.' " (Only recently has Microsoft started to get into the 32-bit software market.)

She described Gates as a combination of Albert Einstein, Woody Allen, and John Cougar Mellancamp, the popular rock singer. Mellancamp, she explained, is rebellious and sensitive, with tremendous sex appeal. Gates, for her money, has all of those qualities. But dating him was no picnic because he was so thoroughly consumed with his work. "There was a fair share of pain and challenge involved for both of us," she said. "He often showed up on my doorstep dead on arrival. Girlfriends are clearly peripheral in the whole scheme of things."

While they had similar backgrounds and interests, there were also clear differences. Gates was introverted while Bennett was much more outgoing. Gates was extremely focused, she said, and did not tolerate distractions. As a result, he didn't own a television and had disconnected the radio in his car. "Bill is a . . . person with a high level of intensity and competitiveness. He is also a man of sensitivity and compassion." Few people, however, are able to get close enough to Gates to see that sensitivity, she said.

"Although he hides it well . . . and certainly will not admit to it, Bill's feelings get hurt easily," she said. "He has a particularly difficult time when key employees leave Microsoft. Bill has always been a bit of a loner. The age-old adage is true: it *is* very lonely at the top." She found a vulnerability in Gates that was very appealing. "It made me want to protect him." Gates had felt very lonely growing up, she believed, and felt just as lonely as an adult.

Having a close-knit family, however, helped Gates deal with his loneliness, according to Bennett, who was particularly fond of the Gates family. For example, on Christmas Eve Gates and his two sisters always returned home to be with their parents, and would sleep in their childhood beds. New pajamas were laid out for them. In the morning, the family would get up and open gifts together. This kind of closeness, in Bennett's eyes, helped to provide Gates with the emotional stability and love that he needed. "He derives major strength and support from them, and loves each of them intensely, more than they'll ever know. . . . He would not be the man he is today . . . without them. . . . His family is one of his greatest assets."

Gates and Bennett stopped dating in 1984, not long after the *Time* article appeared. "In the end it was difficult to sustain a relationship with someone who could boast a 'seven-hour' turnaround—meaning that from the time he left Microsoft to the time he returned in the morning was a mere seven hours." At one point in their relationship, when Gates felt particularly overloaded from work, he told Bennett that he wished she and Steve Ballmer would get together. That way she could still be close to him, but he could remain more focused on work. It wasn't exactly what Bennett hoped to hear from Gates.

"He was, and is, very hung-up on setting a hardcore work example in his company," Bennett said. "I think this . . . is unrealistic and inhuman and will eventually break him."

Gates remains a loyal friend, says Bennett. "I know he is there and would do anything for me if I asked him." Gates could not have been too heartbroken over his breakup with Bennett, however. Before long, he was seeing another woman, Ann Winblad, a software venture capitalist with Hummer/Winblad in San Francisco.

What not many people realize is that in many ways, Bill Gates is something of a mama's boy. When he socialized with customers, Gates often invited his mother along. Mary Gates called her son several times a day and even wrote letters to him, as well as cards, according to a former Microsoft executive. Gates used to keep his mother's letters stacked on his desk. "I always thought it was weird," the executive recalled, "because, gee, they had just talked. . . ."

He found Mary Gates to be warm, nurturing, and very different from her son, who was structured and "not a warm guy." "She worried about him and would talk to key managers about him."

Mary Gates liked having her son close by her. When Microsoft moved to Bellevue in 1979, Gates had rented an apartment for several years. In 1983 his mother located a home for him in Laurelhurst, less than a mile from the Gates' family home. One family acquaintance remembered Mary feeling that she had to take care of her son. For example, Gates' parents and grandmother moved his things out of his apartment into the new house while he was out of town on a business trip. Bill took care of himself in his own world, but the world of needs and desires is one they took care of.

The house, a three-bedroom, $889,000 affair on the shores of Lake Washington, was Gates' first home. Over the years, various articles on Gates described his home as "modest," and it is, considering some of the more fashionable homes in the area. But it does have a 30-foot indoor swimming pool and a boathouse. From his backyard, Gates has a commanding view of Mount Rainier to the southeast and the University of Washington to the west. Curiously, it was Gates' father who actually bought the house. The previous owner, Joe Diamond, had built a fortune as Seattle's parking-lot czar. Diamond negotiated directly with the elder Gates over the property, and court records show that Bill Gates, Jr., is still legal owner and taxpayer on the property, although the reason for this is not clear. Neither son nor father will comment.

Early visitors to Chairman Bill's home were surprised to find that he not only made do without a television but also with little living room furniture. A computer was set up in the den, and it was there that Gates spent most his time when he was home, which was not that often. A giant map of the world was pasted on the ceiling of his study, so he could look up at the map whenever he took a break from the computer. The mind has a lot of "unused bandwidth," Gates explained, that can be filled in while the eyes are just wandering around. He put up a map of Africa on the wall of his garage so his eyes could sweep over it while getting in and out of his car.

Microsoft's offices in the Northup building on the other side of Lake Washington were only about a ten-minute drive from Gates' home. Typically, he would arrive at work mid-morning and not return home until well after midnight. He would then spend at least a couple of hours answering or writing E-Mail to his employees. His home computer was connected to computers at Microsoft. Mary Gates was also on the E-Mail system and could send messages to her son either at work or at home.

As Microsoft grew, Gates relied on E-mail more and more to communicate with his employees. And he encouraged them to communicate with him the same way. He tried to respond to each personal message. "Most people liked electronic mail," said Ingrid Rasch, Microsoft's human resources director in 1984. "I thought it was the best thing since sliced bread. Electronic mail was the hardest thing for me to give up when I left Microsoft [in 1987]. Everyone was connected to everyone else. . . ."

But the system had a darker, "Big Brother" side to it as well. Beginning in 1984, Microsoft managers secretly began using the E-Mail system to determine which hourly employees were working on weekends, according to a knowledgeable management source at Microsoft. Whenever an employee logged into E-Mail, it left a trail of electronic footprints in the computers' memory banks. This information was retrieved and then used by the company to determine employee bonuses. Bonuses were tied not to how effectively one worked, how much was accomplished, or on the importance of a specific project, but rather on how many hours of overtime an employee put in late at night or on the weekends. In time, word got out that Big Brother was watching, and some employees began logging into their E-Mail on weekends with a modem from home so it would appear they had come in. But Microsoft management found a way to detect this, too, according to the source.

Although the bonus system had its pluses, it also provoked hard feelings. Since most employees worked strange hours, and no one punched in or out on a time clock, it was difficult for management to know how much overtime a person worked. Many employees complained the system was not equitable.

E-Mail had another downside—an information explosion. Employees would sometimes have to spend the first two hours of their day answering what might be as many as 100 electronic messages. Each message was tagged in military time so it was clear what time it had been sent, and many of the messages were sent long after "quitting time." "It was a big macho thing to send E-Mail late at night," said a young woman who was hired in early 1984 as a technical writer for applications. "I'd send a message to my supervisor and look at my watch and say, 'Oh yea! This is great! He will see that I was here late. . . .' Not that you were afraid to go home, but it looked bad. Actually, you were so caught up in the work that you didn't want to go home."

Gates himself fired off E-Mail at all hours of the night and early morning. It was not unusual for programmers to come to work and find an electronic message from Gates that had been written in the early hours of the morning, commenting on code they had written. His messages were blunt and often sarcastic, what Microsoft employees would eventually term flame mail. Raymond Bily said most of his communication with Gates was by E-Mail after he moved from software development to marketing in late 1983. "I would get these huge E-mail letters from him that had been written at 2:00 in the morning. They would be this kind of stream of consciousness," said Bily. Many of the messages sent to Bily had to do with Borland International and its colorful CEO, Philippe Kahn.

At the time, Borland had successfully launched a series of computer languages called Turbo Pascal, which were much faster than anything Microsoft had. Turbo Pascal made it possible for software developers to write application programs for the IBM PC and compatible machines faster than ever before. Gates was angry that Microsoft, the original microcomputer language company, was being beaten so badly by a mail-order startup company only a year old.

Scott MacGregor, the developer in charge of the Windows project, said Gates "couldn't understand why our stuff was so slow. He was incredibly upset. He would bring in poor Greg Whitten [programming director of Microsoft languages] and yell at him for half an hour."

Gates saw Kahn's success in very personal terms, according to Bily. He couldn't understand why Kahn had been able to beat an established competitor like Microsoft.

"That's just how he looked at things," said Bily. "When Turbo Pascal was successful, it wasn't something that Borland did, it was something Philippe did. It was very personal to him. . . . That was just his way of personalizing or focussing. It was Bill versus Philippe rather than Microsoft versus Borland." Gates' competitive fires were once again fully stoked.

During the first few months of 1984, Gates was also fired up about another of his competitors, Mitch Kapor of Lotus Development Corporation. It had been more than a year and a half since the chairman had vowed to put Lotus out of business. Nonetheless, Lotus still dominated the spreadsheet market.

Kapor was himself upset. The issue of *Time* magazine that featured Gates on the cover had touted Microsoft as the number one software company. Yet Lotus' revenues just from the sale of 1-2-3 were more than that generated by all of Microsoft's products combined. (For the 12 months ending in June 1985, Lotus would report revenues of $200 million to Microsoft's $140 million.)

Although Lotus had established the spreadsheet standard for the PC, Gates hoped to counterattack with Odyssey, the codename for a souped-up new spreadsheet under development at Microsoft. The genesis for the project had been a three-day retreat in late 1983 at which Gates, Jeff Raikes, Charles Simonyi, and several programmers discussed what to do about the formidable threat from Lotus 1-2-3. Simply improving Multiplan would not be enough. They had to come up with a new product. The project they came up with, Odyssey, would incorporate many of the features used in 1-2-3 but would run faster and offer several improvements. Doug Klunder was given the job of chief coder. Gates wanted Odyssey delivered before the end of the year.

"This was to be a very strategic product for Bill," said one of the managers working on Odyssey. "He knew all along he was going to take on Mitch Kapor with it. This was to be the real Mitch-beater."

With Gates devoting much of his time to the development of Windows and Odyssey, Jon Shirley focused his efforts on problems in the company's retail division. Microsoft was now selling applications for the Macintosh as well as the PC and the PC clones, and it was critical that the retail side get up to speed. The manager brought in to run the department in 1983 after Vern Raburn left had not worked out. In March of 1984, after an exhaustive search, Microsoft hired Jerry Ruttenbur to be vice-president of retail sales.

Ruttenbur had spent 13 years in the candy business, managing sales and marketing for M&M Mars. He had also served a stint as national sales director for Atari and as vice-president of sales for Koala Technologies Corporation, a producer of hardware and software for microcomputers. Ruttenbur was one of a series of more experienced managers that Shirley was bringing in to the company to fix some long-neglected problems.

"Microsoft's applications products were beginning to come on stream," Ruttenbur said, "and they really didn't have anybody in the company who understood the retail side of the business, the different types of selling that had to be done, all of the distribution issues, the channel conflicts, how to put a sales force together and keep them motivated. There were lots of problems at that time. But the biggest challenge at that point in their evolution was their customer service area. It was a total disaster. . . . They didn't realize how important it was until somebody got in there and started making them aware of the impact it had on their overall business."

His first week on the job, Ruttenbur walked into the customer service office and found it staffed by two women who were on the phone returning calls to customers wanting an updated version of one of the company's products or having complaints or questions. Ruttenbur was shocked to see two stacks of hundreds of unreturned phone messages on each of their desks. That's nothing, the two women told him, pointing to another table filled with hundreds of other as-yet unreturned messages.

"That's when I knew that I had a major challenge on my hands," Ruttenbur said.

Ruttenbur was given complete authority to make any changes he felt were necessary. Customer service would soon grow to more than 30 employees, while the technical support staff tripled to about 60 employees. Ruttenbur also greatly expanded the company's retail sales force. Only major changes involving corporate strategy had to be cleared by Shirley.

"Shirley watched the day-to-day stuff at Microsoft, he was good at that, a good detail guy," Ruttenbur said. "He paid attention to the details so that Bill could think product and do the strategic stuff. Although that's how a lot of people described Bill in those days, he was also very much involved in everything that happened in that company. Bill wanted to know everything that was going on. He didn't require approval, he just wanted to know what you were doing and he wanted you to explain and justify it. . . ."

By his second or third product management meeting, Ruttenbur realized that it was vital that he stand up and speak his mind if he felt strongly about something. Some managers seemed intimidated by Gates, who would often rock back and forth in his chair, staring off into space as if he were not paying attention. Then suddenly, when he heard something he didn't like or didn't agree with, he would stop rocking, sit up straight, and become visibly angry, sometimes throwing his pencil. He often yelled or pounded his fist on the table to make a point. At first, Ruttenbur thought Gates was just putting on an act. It was hard for him to believe a CEO could react so emotionally to every issue. But he soon realized this was no show; Gates simply reacted to things on an intense emotional level.

"He would get upset if we were behind the competition in any way," said Ruttenbur, "and that meant in terms of the product, in terms of the distribution, the accounts, in terms of shelf space, all of those things. It was made very clear that our job was to make sure we were number one. . . . But I learned after awhile that he respected people who disagreed with him. He didn't expect people to always agree with him, and I think sometimes he disagreed just to see if someone was that strong in their beliefs to really support and fight for their opinion. With the right people it really works well, but with some people it suppresses their creativity." He felt that if Gates could have learned to use his intensity and anger with strong employees who responded well to that kind of motivation and to temper it with people who became intimidated by it, he would have become a more effective manager.

Ruttenbur was part of the group that came up with the name for the Odyssey spreadsheet project—Excel. But the project had taken a strange turn. In mid-1984, Gates completely changed his strategy and decided Excel would be developed for the Macintosh, rather than the IBM PC and its clones. Lotus was designing a new spreadsheet called Jazz for Apple, and Microsoft simply could not allow Lotus to establish an applications foothold with the Mac as it had with the PC. Gates desperately wanted Microsoft to become the standard bearer for graphical user interface applications. That was the future, as he saw it. Jazz was clearly a new threat, and he could not allow it to catch on.

With Jazz, Lotus planned to offer customers much more than just a spreadsheet like 1-2-3. The hot new trend in application development was so-called integrated software that combined several different applications into one easy-to-use program. The user could switch, say, from a spreadsheet to word processing without having to load another application. Jazz would combine several functions, including a database, word processing, and graphics, as well as a spreadsheet.

Apple was enthusiastically supporting Jazz. The initial excitement over the Macintosh had died down and sales were sluggish. What the company needed was a hit application that would make people line up to buy the Mac just as they had bought thousands of Apple II computers because they wanted VisiCalc.

"Apple was in a lot of trouble then. They really thought Jazz was going to be their savior," said Ida Cole, who in 1984 was director of new product development at Apple.

When Lotus demonstrated a prototype of Jazz at a trade show, Gates dispatched two of his programmers to check it out. The two furiously scribbled notes as Mitch Kapor talked about Jazz and gave a demonstration. Some Jazz features later turned up in Excel.

Microsoft was experiencing internal squabbling over the Excel project. Although Gates had decided to develop Excel for the Mac after talking with his marketing managers, he had never discussed the change in strategy with Doug Klunder, the programmer in charge of coding Excel for the PC machines. Because the coding for Excel up to that point had been done for the PC, the switch meant basically starting over after months of hard work. Klunder was furious and threatened to quit, which he ended up doing a few months later.

"Bill just screwed up from a human management point of view. I was killing myself on Excel," Klunder would later say.

Gates brought in a new programmer from Wang to head the project, Philip Florence. Before working for Wang, Florence had created the research and development group at Leading Edge, one of the PC clone makers.

"It was a pressure cooker," Florence said of Microsoft. "I was working directly under Bill and he took a special interest in Excel."

Florence thought he was being brought in to manage the project. But before long Gates told Florence to write code and check for bugs in the program as well. The project fell further and further behind schedule. When Florence told Gates he couldn't manage the project and write code at the same time, Gates exploded, slamming his fist down on the table to get his point across and carrying on in a rage. Said one of the managers who worked with Florence, "Imagine an extremely smart, millionaire genius who's 14 years old and spoiled and subject to temper tantrums."

It was clear that Florence was not cut out to work in an emotionally charged, pressured environment like Microsoft on a project that Gates himself took such an intense interest in. A few months after he arrived, Florence, who had been putting in 100-hour weeks, had a heart attack. As a result, he had to have bypass surgery.

During this time, Steve Jobs had been trying to convince Gates to incorporate integrated software features in Excel similar to those in Jazz. But Gates refused. He was convinced Lotus was taking the wrong approach. And this time, unlike his strategy with Multiplan, Gates would be proved right.

Because Microsoft did not have any integrated programs, it needed a way to respond directly to this bonus feature of the Jazz software. Gates was savvy enough to realize that if Microsoft could develop a quick way of switching between smaller programs on the Mac, it would be more effective than having one huge integrated program like Jazz. Thus was born the idea behind the "switcher."

Andy Hertzfeld, who had left Apple to strike out on his own, was in the midst of designing his own switcher when he got a call from a friend at Microsoft. His friend asked him to come in and talk about a hot new project that Microsoft was working on for the Mac. It was Hertzfeld who several years earlier had given Gates the first demonstration of the Macintosh prototype at Apple's offices. When Hertzfeld sat down with the folks at Microsoft, he discovered the company wanted him to write a switcher program very much like the one he had started a couple weeks earlier.

Hertzfeld was convinced his design was better. At the end of his meeting with several of the Microsoft managers, he was ushered in to see Gates for a one-on-one meeting. Hertzfeld was about to get a first-hand demonstration in the art of The Deal from the young master himself.

According to Hertzfeld, Gates treated him as if he were a naive technical person who had little business sense, whom Gates tried to manipulate into an unfavorable business arrangement.

The negotiating, according to Hertzfeld, went like this:

"You're a really great programmer, right?" asked Gates.

"Yeah . . . I don't know. Sure, I guess so," said Hertzfeld, caught off guard and unsure where Gates was heading.

"Well," said Gates, "a *really* great programmer should be able to write this program pretty quick, right?"

"Yeah, I guess so . . . I don't know, sure," said Hertzfeld.

"So how long do you think it should take you?" asked Gates.

"Gee, I don't really know."

"Well," said Gates, "if you are *really* good, and you *are* really good, right, then it shouldn't take you too long."

Gates' strategy soon became clear to Hertzfeld. Gates was attempting to appeal to Hertzfeld's ego, his vanity, to get him to vastly underestimate the time it would take to write the program. Like a chess master, Gates was planning his negotiating strategy for the sale price several moves ahead. They finally agreed that Hertzfeld could write the program in about eight weeks.

Gates then asked Hertzfeld how much money he made a week. Hertzfeld told him about $5,000.

"Well," said Gates, "you can't expect to make more than that, right? So eight times $5,000—that's $40,000."

Realizing his program was strategically important to Apple and to Microsoft, Hertzfeld resisted Gates' maneuvering and rejected his offer of $40,000. But they left on friendly terms. "Bill said even if I didn't sell it to Microsoft, they wanted to support it."

Hertzfeld turned around and sold the switcher program to Apple for $150,000. It was packaged with the Mac for free and also was sold separately. The switcher enabled the user to run as many as four different applications on the Mac at the same time, keeping each in memory while moving between them with the flick of the mouse.

When Gates received a prototype of the switcher, he sent Hertzfeld a note telling him how "great" he thought the program was. "I have been demoing it to everyone who walks in my office." He added that it was important enough to Microsoft that the switcher worked well that he was adding sections to the manuals of Microsoft software describing how to use the switcher. "You are really the only person who knows all the system insides well enough to get it done," he added. "Keep up the good work."

Lotus officially announced Jazz in November 1984. Kapor said it would be ready to ship to customers in a few months. Both Jobs and new Apple Chairman John Sculley couldn't praise the program enough. But in March 1985, Lotus admitted that Jazz would be a couple months late. By this time Apple was hurting. The personal computer industry was going through a rough time. Business was down, and Apple had laid off hundreds of workers. Sales of the Macintosh had slowed to a trickle. Only sales of the still popular Apple II were keeping the situation at Apple from becoming much worse.

Microsoft decided to officially announce Excel in New York City on May 2, 1985, several weeks before Lotus shipped the first copies of Jazz. An elaborate launch was planned, with a press conference and demonstration of the program's capabilities. Gates talked Steve Jobs into attending, even though Apple was still backing Jazz.

Microsoft's public relations agency booked Gates and his party into the Pierre, an elegant hotel next to Central Park. The Excel announcement was to take place at the Tavern on the Green near Central Park. But when Gates arrived in New York on May 1 and saw the accommodations, he was furious. The Pierre, he told his people, was much too expensive.

"I thought the Pierre was wonderful," said one member of the Microsoft group who arrived with Gates. "But Bill couldn't believe that we would do anything that extravagant. . . ."

There was no time to book rooms elsewhere. Gates, his feathers already ruffled, immediately went to work with several of his programmers on setting up the Excel demonstration at the Tavern on the Green. A large television screen was wired to a computer terminal, displaying what was shown on the computer screen. Everything had worked flawlessly at Microsoft. But suddenly Gates and his programmers could no longer get the demo to work. When Excel was brought up on the computer, the computer immediately crashed. Gates became hysterical, screaming at his programmers, who began shouting back at him. For a time the situation threatened to degenerate into chaos. Finally, hours later, they got the program to work twice in a row and they called it a night.

The next morning a limousine came by the Pierre to pick up Gates and a couple of his senior managers for the official Excel announcement. Gates, his face creased with worry, was a mess. He had neither shaved nor showered, and he had obviously not had much sleep. His hair was matted and oily, and he was badly in need of deodorant.

At least one of his managers was appalled. "It was obvious Bill had not bathed in some time. I just couldn't believe it. This was the most important announcement that we'd ever made. And Steve Jobs was there to endorse the product, as well as a lot of other important people. We'd really pulled out all the stops with the press, and here Bill was. . . . I just couldn't imagine, you know, it only takes five minutes to shower."

If the press noticed, however, no one wrote anything about Gates' appearance. Perhaps they were used to seeing him that way.

To Gates' relief, the announcement went off without a hitch. Despite his fears, Excel worked perfectly. Jon Shirley spoke, as did Jobs, who for the first time publicly endorsed Excel as well.

Excel was on the market by September, and the reviews were excellent. Lotus spent about $7.5 million on a marketing campaign for Jazz. Microsoft spent less than $1 million to promote Excel, yet the Microsoft program blew Jazz away. Some trade publications said Excel on the Mac worked even better than 1-2-3 on the PC. The Mac now had a winner of an applications program, and Apple could rest easier. And Gates once again had set the standard. In time, Microsoft would become the top seller of software applications for the Mac. Lotus, as it turned out, had badly miscalculated with Jazz and its integrated software strategy.

Jeff Raikes, director of Microsoft's applications marketing, told the *New York Times*: "They [Lotus] thought all Mac owners are yuppies who drive BMWs. They said, 'Let's boogie with Jazz.' But we gave the market a product that proved you could do more with a Mac than with an IBM PC."

The euphoria over Excel, however, was tempered by Microsoft's disappointment with Windows. After many delays, Windows had still not been officially released at the time of the Excel unveiling, even though the project was well into its second year.

The ragged appearance of Gates when he left the Pierre Hotel for the Excel announcement would not have surprised most people who worked closely with him at Microsoft. Although he was about to celebrate his 29th birthday, Gates had not changed much from his hacker days in the computer room at Lakeside when he would forget to clip his fingernails.

It wasn't so much that Gates didn't care about his appearance; he just couldn't bring himself to allocate the time to clean up on a regular basis. There always seemed to be more pressing matters that needed his attention. When he could find the time, he did shave, shower, and change his shirts. But that part of his life just wasn't a high priority.

"When you saw Bill, it always made you wonder, where did he sleep last night, in his office?" said one young woman who worked at Microsoft from 1983 through 1986. "You always wanted to go up and ask him, 'Gee Bill, I don't know if you shower every day, but if you do you should also wash your hair.' "

Of course, no one would ever have *said* such a thing to Gates, even though many employees probably thought it. He was legendary around Microsoft for never cleaning his glasses; they always had a coating of oil and dirt on the lenses.

When Gates began appearing on the cover of national magazines, beginning with *Money* in late 1982, Microsoft's public relations department trusted his secretary to make sure he looked his best. "She would actually go out to his house and pick up some stuff, bring him a clean shirt," said another Microsoft employee.

A few weeks after the Excel announcement, the *Wall Street Journal* called Microsoft about arranging a photo shoot with Gates. The paper was running a series of promotional ads featuring various CEOs around the country. One of the ads showed Eddie Bauer holding up a *Wall Street Journal* with the tag line, "Next to the *Wall Street Journal*, nothing keeps you warmer on a winter night." It was good publicity for the paper and good advertising for Bauer's clothing stores. The *Wall Street Journal* told Microsoft it would like a shot of Gates holding up the paper, with the tag line, "Next to my software, nothing is more user friendly than the *Wall Street Journal*." Gates reluctantly agreed to the shoot, as long as it didn't take more than one hour of his time.

When the *Wall Street Journal* group came out to Microsoft, they brought along a hair stylist. Microsoft had never hired a hair stylist to work with Gates when national magazines wanted pictures. "We finally figured out that if we wanted his hair washed we might have his secretary set up an appointment to get his hair cut the day we needed him to do something because at least then we knew it would be washed," said one Microsoft manager who sometimes "handled" Gates.

The *Wall Street Journal* people figured Gates would be thrilled to have his picture taken for a national ad campaign. In fact, Gates hated having his picture taken. "He thought it was a waste of time and he was just sort of obliging them because someone had said it would be good for Microsoft," the Microsoft manager said.

On the day of the shoot, Gates was wearing a green sweater with the Microsoft logo. He had been told specifically to wear something casual for the photo session, which was to be done in his office. While his office was being set up, Gates left, telling one of his employees that he couldn't stand to see so many people standing around with so little to do with their time. An hour or so later, when everything had been properly arranged, Gates was brought back in. He got into position and held up the newspaper as directed. But there was a very visible hole under the armpit of his sweater. Rather than telling Gates he had a hole in his sweater, the *Wall Street Journal* people said the shot wasn't going to work from that angle and they needed him to hold up the paper with the other hand. They explained that it would take a few minutes to rearrange the lighting.

"By this time, Bill was very, very irritated. But he came back in and held up the paper with his other arm, and lo and behold there was an even bigger hole in his sweater under that armpit. So they said, 'Bill, Bill, look, this sweater is just too dark on the film.'" The shot had to be done without the sweater, Gates was told. So he took off the sweater and held up the paper and there was a huge, ugly stain under the armpit of his shirt.

"The people from the paper told Bill there was something wrong with the camera and they needed to have a meeting outside. By this time, Bill was really hacked off," recalled the Microsoft manager. "Everybody went out into the hallway and this one woman told me, 'We just had to get some ventilation in that office! It smells so bad I thought I was going to be sick.' Well, for us that was pretty much par for the course."

Having done something like this once before, the handler from Microsoft went down the hall to find someone about the same size as Gates. The employee was brought back to Gates' office, and Gates was told the color of his shirt was wrong. He and the employee were asked to exchange shirts. Finally, everything was set, and the shooting commenced. But after only a couple of shots Gates had had enough, and he angrily told everyone in the room to clear out. "Why don't you people go make a better living and leave me to make mine," he said. The session was over.

The professional hair stylist later explained to the Microsoft people that an airbrush would be used on the photo to get rid of the grease streaks in Gates' hair.

This public relations fiasco was described as "typical" of Gates. But also typically, everyone was afraid to say anything that would offend the Microsoft chairman.

The growing number of older and more experienced executives who had been hired during 1983 and 1984 to help manage Microsoft's tremendous growth had one noticeable trait in common—they were all males. Although there were a few female programmers, for the most part women working at Microsoft were relegated to nontechnical positions. It was the men who called the corporate shots at Microsoft.

In February of 1985, however, the company seemed to reverse that trend when it hired its first two female executives, Ida Cole and Jean Richardson. Both had considerable management experience. Cole, 37, had spent four years with Apple, most recently as director of new product development; she had previously been director of applications software and manager of applications software development at Apple. Richardson, 48, also came from Apple and had built the company's communications division from scratch.

Cole was recruited as part of Microsoft's reorganization of applications and operating systems into separate divisions. Steve Ballmer was made a vice-president in charge of operating systems, which included the Windows project. Cole was named a vice-president in charge of applications. Jean Richardson was made vice-president of corporate communications. (Rowland Hanson, the previous head, had recently left the company.)

Had Gates developed an enlightened attitude regarding women? Not according to one well-placed source at Microsoft who was involved in the hiring process. In essence, both were hired as a result of Microsoft's attempt to win a lucrative government contract to provide the Air Force with computer software. The company had been told it did not have enough women in top management roles to qualify for the contract under government affirmative action guidelines. (Microsoft had hired a consultant in Washington, D.C., just to stay on top of government contracts for computer-related products.)

Gates and several of his managers would discuss from time to time whether to hire a man or a women for a particular job, according to the source. "They would say, 'Well, let's hire two women because we can pay them half as much as we will have to pay a man, and we can give them all this other 'crap' work to do because they are women.' That's directly out of Bill's mouth. . . . I thought it was surprising that he wasn't more sensitive to the issue. His parents were pillars of the community."

On paper, Ida Cole seemed the perfect choice to head Microsoft's new applications division. She knew how to program, and she had experience managing large groups of people from her days at Apple. She even understood the marketing side— her resume included a stint as chief marketer for the Apple II.

Gates had met Cole in 1983 at the wedding of Jeff Raikes, who had previously worked with Cole at Apple. She and Gates continued to run into each other at industry functions and seemed to get along together.

Less than a month after her arrival at Microsoft, Cole was asked to speak at Microsoft's companywide meeting. Four years earlier, Charles Simonyi had galvanized nearly 100 employees with his famous revenue bomb speech at the Ramada Inn. In early 1985, nearly 900 employees crowded into a Bellevue theater to cheer glowing reports about the company's future. These gatherings had grown into fairly elaborate productions. Gifts were handed out to employees, ranging over the last few years from name-brand tennis shoes, to director's chairs. Employees were free to ask questions of Gates and the other officers of the company.

Cole wasn't sure what to talk to the Microsoft troops about, having only been with Microsoft for a few weeks. After a few general comments, she outwardly thanked people for doing such a great job, for working overtime and putting out so many good products.

"I talked to them about how much I appreciated the warm welcome I had been given, and that I was looking forward to meeting all of them, and I was looking forward to a great career at Microsoft," Cole said. "It was very personal, and again nobody had ever gotten personal with them before. They had Ballmer up there being the cheerleader, but it was so impersonal."

Cole left the stage to great applause.

Some of the more experienced technical managers listening to her remarks were not sure what to make of it all. Praise was not something Microsoft employees were accustomed to hearing from their managers.

"It was very weird," said a manager on the Windows development team. "It was this very mushy, person-to-person, I'm going to make it a better place, very non-technical, and very non-marketing. It was very touchy feely. And of course, here are all these guys and nobody had ever encouraged them to take an interest in each other personally, and here's Ida talking about personal values and all this stuff. It was real obvious she was a square peg in a round hole. We had no idea why Bill would have chosen this person. . . ."

Not long after the company meeting, Cole gave an employee two weeks of paternity leave so he could take care of his small children while his wife recuperated from delivering her third child. There was no company policy on paternity leave, and Gates told Cole the decision was "unwise."

By September of 1985, Cole's relationship with Gates was becoming strained. Cole, who had worked with another of the industry's wunderkinds, Steve Jobs, had great admiration for Gates, but she had trouble dealing with his confrontational personality.

"Steve Jobs, who is probably the most charismatic person I've ever met, can't hold a candle to Bill on substance," she said. "Bill knows what he's doing. He's thought it out. He demands excellence in people. I don't mind that because I do, too. But Bill's whole modus operandi was railing at the Gods. Bill was constantly in this confrontational state, whether or not it made sense to be there. I'd just wait for him to get finished ranting and raving and when he got tired we would talk. He would on occasion send me just rabid E-Mail. I would write him back and say, 'Look I didn't come here to take this stuff.' "

At the beginning of September, Cole learned she needed major surgery. But because her division was due to begin shipping Excel by the end of the month, she postponed the surgery and instead finished a series of press tours and other tasks related to the product release. Three weeks after she finally had the surgery she returned to work—much too soon, she realized later—to finish off nearly 200 staff performance reviews that were due out by the end of October. On her third day back, Cole met with Gates to talk about firing Philip Florence, the Excel manager who had had a heart attack. He had since returned to work but wasn't getting the job done. In the middle of the discussion, Gates suddenly began shouting at Cole that she was not up to speed about a product scheduling change.

"I was hurting from surgery. . . . I had a fairly life threatening situation. They thought I had ovarian cancer when they did the surgery. I had a benign mass removed. It was really scary and not a great thing to go through. I didn't really want to have a hysterectomy. I was 37 at the time. So Bill's screaming at me [made me decide] 'I'm not doing it anymore.' "

Cole got up and went in to talk with Jon Shirley, whom she told "I can't come in to work everyday thinking it's never going to get any better than this."

Eventually, Cole was moved into the International Division, far removed from the day-to-day meetings and tirades with Gates. Gates took over as head of applications; it would be two years before he found a replacement.

No Microsoft manager, man or woman, escaped the emotional tirades and verbal abuse of Bill Gates, but none took more of it than those working on Windows.

The project, which had been announced with such fanfare, had slipped so far behind schedule that Gates had reorganized the company and put Steve Ballmer in charge of the development team. If possible, Ballmer was throwing even more tantrums than Gates.

The first weeks after the announcement of Windows in New York in November 1983 had been hectic. There was a tremendous sense of urgency to the project. The first meetings, however, had more to do with explaining the project in more detail to the press than actually designing code.

"It was sort of ironic," Scott MacGregor, the manager hired away from Xerox to guide the development of Windows, said, "because here we were talking to the press about what was going to be in the first version of Windows and we hadn't even designed the product yet."

Following the company's New York announcement, Windows was demonstrated a second time a couple weeks later at the fall Comdex in Las Vegas. Gates, the keynote speaker for the show, devoted little of his valuable time preparing. He worked on his remarks less than an hour, showed up only ten minutes before he was to go on stage, and appeared disheveled in his rumpled suit. His father ran the slide projector for the presentation.

Having promised a software system to two dozen computer manufacturers as well as hundreds of application publishers, Gates had raised enormous expectations. But within Microsoft, there were doubters.

"I don't think Bill understood the magnitude of doing a project such as Windows," MacGregor said later, reflecting back on it all. "All the projects Bill had ever worked on could be done in a week or a weekend by one or two different people. That's a very different kind of project than one which takes multiple people more than a year to do. There were 30 some odd people in the Windows group by the time we were fully staffed, which for Microsoft was the largest project they'd ever done."

The technical challenges were formidable. As became evident later, to operate most efficiently the program required more memory than available on the most widely used IBM-compatible computers of the day. Those machines, based on Intel's 8088 chip, had only 256K of memory. The goal for Windows was to create a system that could accommodate very different applications and allow them to run at the same time, with just the click of a mouse. But most application programs written at the time were "incredibly rude," according to MacGregor. "When they'd start up, they'd grab as much memory as they could lock down, on the assumption that they were the only important thing running. So typically, the conversation something like Lotus 1-2-3 would have with the operating system when it started up would be, 'How much memory do you have?'

And the system would say, 'This much,' and Lotus would say, 'Fine I'll take that'."

Windows, then, had to make better use of the limited memory capacity of the computers available on the commercial market. One of the major challenges was writing code containing very advanced features that could run fast on the 8088 chip and be crowded into so little available memory. Programmers on the Windows team had to find a way to provide the application only some of the memory it thought it needed to run, at precisely the time it needed it.

During the first several months of the project, there was little to suggest such an undertaking was impossible. In fact, nothing seemed impossible. The atmosphere was electric.

"It was exhilarating, exciting, fun. We were competing with the world and winning," said one of the programmers. "Other companies already had announced windowing products, but we were able to persuade the OEMs to wait for ours. There was a great deal of interest in the press, a great deal of excitement around Windows. That first year or so was really exciting."

But there were difficult times just ahead. The Windows project would soon reveal some serious organizational and managerial problems within the company. *Fortune* magazine, in an article on Microsoft that ran at the end of January 1984, made what would turn out to be a very accurate assessment of the company's inexperienced management structure:

". . . a lot is riding on Windows. If it fails to become an industry standard, Microsoft may not get another chance to take the consumer market by storm. Momentum is an ephemeral quality in any business, and in an industry evolving as fast as microcomputer software, it can be lost in the blink of an eye. . . . Like other fast-growing companies racing to seize transient opportunities, Microsoft has devoted little time to develop the kind of management depth that will be needed to turn temporary victories into long-term dominance."

The arrival of MacGregor and Nikora in late 1983 had represented an attempt to bring more experienced management into the organization. Microsoft had to have more officers and sergeants to keep the soldiers marching in semi-orderly columns. At that time, there was little corporate hierarchy at Microsoft. Individual product development teams were small, usually no more than three people. Simonyi was in charge of applications development. MacGregor headed the brand new Interactive Systems Group, with a staff of three. There was a development group for languages and one for operating systems. Each group had its own guru, its resident genius. With Paul Allen gone, software creation was very much under the direct, day-to-day control of Gates.

"I don't think of Bill as having a lot of formal management skills, not in those days," said MacGregor. "He was kind of weak on managing people, so there was a certain kind of person who would do well in the environment. There were a lot of people at that time with no people skills whatsoever, people who were absolutely incompetent at managing people. It was the Peter Principle: very successful technical people would get promoted to management roles. You'd get 30 people reporting to one guy who was not on speaking terms with two-thirds of the group, which is inconceivable."

MacGregor tried to interest the company in sending its managers to a short but intensive management training program offered by Xerox. He met with resistance and in one case outright hostility from Gordon Letwin, who was in charge of operating systems. Letwin had been the last of the original programmers hired while Microsoft was still in Albuquerque.

The Microsoft work environment for programmers was deliberately chaotic, and Letwin liked it that way. The feeling was that with less structure you could be more creative and produce innovative products. A rival software programmer who had toured the company in 1983 found little formal managing going on at all, at least in software development.

"They had a model where they just totally forgot about being efficient," he said. "That blew our minds. We came out of a mainframe world, and there we were at Microsoft watching all of these software tools that were supposed to work together being built by totally independent units, and nobody was talking to each other. They didn't use any of each other's code and they didn't share anything. But over the years, that's turned out to be, probably in the PC world, one of the most effective models."

With his experience at Xerox, MacGregor seemed the perfect choice to guide the creative process. One year younger than Gates, he was thoughtful, intellectual, and selfcontained. The two of them spent a lot of time together in the first weeks of 1984, often sitting around each other's offices on Saturday or Sunday debating the proper course of Windows development.

"I was pretty much handed off the ball, but Bill and I would meet frequently to talk about the design, and various needs," MacGregor recalled. "I'll give credit to Bill, he came up to speed pretty fast on understanding the issues. But if you wanted to see Bill, you never tried to reach him during the weekdays. His schedule was packed. If you really wanted to have a longer conversation you went in on Saturday or Sunday. Then you could get a couple hours and just talk about something."

They did a lot of talking. How should memory management work? Should the windows on the screen be overlapped, like on the Macintosh, or should they butt up against each other like tiles on the kitchen sink? Should Windows require a mouse?

MacGregor understood Gates' pushy, pugnacious way of making a point, and he respected his quick, sure grasp of all the ramifications of various solutions to a given problem.

"A lot of people don't like their jobs because they don't get any feedback," MacGregor said. "There was no problem there. You would know exactly what Bill thought about what you were doing. The goal, the motivational force for a lot of programmers, was to get Bill to like your product."

MacGregor also liked the fact that Gates did not let his ego get in the way.

"If he really believed in something, he would have this intense zeal and support it and push it through the organization and talk it up, and whenever he met with people talk about how great it was," MacGregor said. "But if that particular thing was no longer great, he'd walk away from it and it was forgotten. A lot of people have a hard time doing that. It made him incredibly agile in a business sense. . . . People usually fight to the death long beyond when it is the right thing to do."

In late February of 1984, four months after the announcement of Windows in New York, about 300 representatives from various software publishers and computer manufacturers paid $500 each to attend a Windows conference sponsored by Microsoft. Most of the companies that had publicly pledged their support were represented. If Windows was to become the industry standard that Gates sought, these software developers would have to write applications for it. So it was essential that Gates be able to keep the alliance together.

Before the conference, the word out of the Microsoft headquarters was that Windows would be available by the end of March. But those who attended the Microsoft conference got bad news. Microsoft was still unable to provide them with the development tools to write those applications. The Windows deadline had been pushed back to at least May.

Inside the company, there were growing problems between MacGregor's Interactive Systems Group and the Operating Systems Group run by Letwin.

At the outset of Windows development, it was the Operating Systems Group, at work on a new version of MS-DOS, that was supposed to take the lead writing some of the most advanced code, which would be delivered to the Interactive Systems Group and adapted for Windows. But as the months dragged on, the code wasn't being cranked out fast enough. So MacGregor had his team do some of the coding. Letwin was furious.

For the skilled and ambitious programmers, the place to be at Microsoft was Interactive Systems. Windows was getting all the press, generating all the excitement. MacGregor was approached often by programmers in other groups, wanting to be taken aboard. This only increased Letwin's resentment. The bushy-bearded Letwin was a programming prodigy and one of Microsoft's older hands. He had gained his position as head of the operating group in the way most people got promoted at Microsoft, because of technical prowess and not because of his management skills. He would get into fights with programmers who worked under him and would go for days or weeks giving them the silent treatment.

"It's one of those things that happens when a little company that's highly technically focused, with a highly technical CEO, grows up," said a programmer."All of the CEO's coding friends become his senior managers."

Gates didn't intervene, nor did he play favorites. The operating system clearly remained an important product. After IBM announced its decision to distribute VisiOn while development of TopView continued, Gates said Microsoft would counterpunch with a multitasking version of MS-DOS, complete with graphics, the ability to be commanded by mouse, and a windows management function. These GUI features have yet to make it into DOS. But Windows had them.

"We pretty much decided that Windows was supposed to be the first one out the door, so that was the one you didn't want to hold up," MacGregor said.

As Windows development proceeded, the program stopped being seen as a thin veneer over the operating system. It became far more complex and technologically advanced. But as the complexity of the code increased, so did the time needed to write it. Windows developers were falling further behind. The May target date was missed, and the end of August was established as the new date. OEM customers were getting nervous. Jon Shirley, in interviews with the trade press, insisted that Microsoft remained firmly committed to the project. In the summer of 1984 company officials were dispatched to the most important computer makers and software publishers to apologize in person for the latest slip in the schedule.

Microsoft officially blamed the setback on a change in the way images appeared on the screen, a decision based on feedback from testing of the still-evolving program. But it was becoming obvious that the problems went deeper.

For one thing, Gates kept changing his mind about the graphics presentation of Windows—whether individual windows should appear tiled or overlapped on the monitor. He decided to add features to the product or insisted on other midcourse corrections. And, although he hired MacGregor and Nikora to oversee the project, Gates paid no heed to his chain-of-command. Delegating decision making on such an important project was anathema to him, and he interceded in every decision, no matter how small.

"He was down there micro-managing everything, everyday, and it happened all the time," said one former member of the Interactive Systems Group. "People would be going along and we would find out, behind our backs, that Bill had totally reversed the direction we were going and never even bothered to tell us."

It was more than a minor annoyance. Whenever a change was made or a glitch uncovered, it cost the company time. Changes made by Gates generally improved the product, but the delays were having a cumulative effect that was hurting morale. MacGregor would argue for more programmers and more time. He and Gates had loud, fierce disagreements about how long the project was taking.

"There were shouting matches all the time," Nikora said. "If he didn't like the way Scott was doing something or anybody else was doing something, he'd say 'OK I'll take this weekend, and I'll code it, and I'll show you how it's done!' and he'd pound his fist on the desk."

When MacGregor would produce the latest development schedule, he included extra time for sickness among employees, fixing unexpected bugs, field testing of the product, and other routine contingencies. Gates would go through the schedule and

knock out all of the contingency times, saying he didn't understand why it was necessary.

"I think Bill thought I was blackmailing him," MacGregor
said. "He had this notion that, gee, it was easy to make changes.
He had typically worked on projects that were fairly small, and
Microsoft then did almost no field testing. What Bill didn't understand was that when you have large and complicated projects
with a lot of documentation and a lot of people, the trivial change
takes a long time. You have to factor it through, change the
code, change the documentation and retest it, make sure the
change works with all the other pieces of the program. If you
made a change once every three months, you'd never ship the
product. . . . There was this very real conflict between Bill's
desire to make Windows better, and the need to have a plan to
execute, to actually get the product out."

One of the most costly reversals came about a year into the
project. At the outset, Windows had been designed to operate
only with a mouse, like Apple's Macintosh. But most PC users
were only familiar with typing commands on a keyboard. There
was a growing sense of consumer resistance to additional hardware. Also, Microsoft didn't want to jeopardize its chance at
retaining lucrative military contracts.

As MacGregor put it: "There was concern about trying to
use a mouse while driving a tank."

Despite growing pressure from Digital Equipment Corporation, Tandy, and Intel to deliver Windows, Gates and Mac-
Gregor reluctantly decided that Windows should also be able
to operate with a keyboard. It was a decision that cost three to
six months of development effort.

"It was frustrating in a sense, because, shoot, if we had
known that in the beginning, we would have designed it that
way," MacGregor said.

So why did he go along with Gates?

"He just wore me down."

As the deadline slipped further into 1984, and the pressure
mounted to get a product out, there were constant arguments

in Gates' office. "It went on all the time," said Nikora, whose office was next to that of Gates'. "He would spot the fatal flaw [in his opponent's argument], and he would just tear into the person."

Some, like MacGregor, thought the obnoxious streak in Gates was his way of testing his own ideas, as well as those of others.

"His style is to yell a lot. I think people who get along best with Bill are those who can yell back, and make him feel they might be right," MacGregor said. "Bill doesn't surround himself with yes men."

It was also important not to take the arguments personally. Gates doesn't rant so much at people, but at situations.

'It's not like he's trying to vent his spleen on them," said his friend Vern Raburn, who had resigned under pressure in 1982 as president of the company's Consumer Products Division. "Because of his competitiveness he gets so upset with a situation, it's like a stray cruise missile—anything in the blast range gets in trouble."

MacGregor said he had frequent and intense arguments with Gates. "Bill could be just apoplectic over things. . . . that was just the emotional level he reacted to things on. We'd be yelling at each other, but at the end of the argument, we could say 'so, what are you doing for dinner?' "

This challenging, confrontational style is inherently part of Gates' personality. His father described it as "hard-nosed conversation engagement." Gates dismissed it as "high bandwidth communication."

"If I am trying to get a point across efficiently and I am with people I worked with for a long time or we are talking about something we're really excited about, then if an outsider listened in it would sound awfully hardcore," Gates said. "To characterize it as just aggressive is inaccurate."

But Ruthann Quindlen, who specializes in software deals for investment banker Alex Brown and has known Gates since the early 1980s, said he is basically insensitive to other people. "Because of his position and his fame, people are willing to put up with what he wants to dish out," she said. "But he can't distinguish between those who can't take it and those who can. He pays no attention at all to social niceties. You and I might put our criticism of someone in guarded tones. He can't do that in any fashion."

On the Windows project, this confrontational style was wearing down Nikora. So were the long hours.

"Bill required everyone to devote their entire life to Microsoft, like he did, and that was another sticking point between myself and him," said Nikora, who was then in his early 40s. "I had another life. I had a family. I was willing to put in 60 hours a week. But the weekends were mine, for my family. . . . I was right on the edge of being considered someone who didn't put in enough time. I really felt he was stepping on my toes and he felt I was insubordinate."

Gates didn't want to hear excuses. Despite their management responsibilities, he wanted MacGregor and Nikora to really pitch in. It was at that point that he decided they should start writing Windows code.

MacGregor was incredulous. "Bill," he argued, "it's not my job. I'm supposed to be building a team, hiring people, dividing up the tasks. . . . I'm not supposed to be down there cranking code."

Nikora didn't agree either, but he dutifully went along.

A former Microsoft manager described the atmosphere under Gates in 1984 as management by crisis. "Everything was a crisis."

In August, Microsoft and Gates faced up to the reality that at least part of that haphazard style, which had helped power a remarkable if sometimes inefficient software incubator for nearly ten years, was creating too many management problems. The crash program to develop Windows had stretched into nearly a year, and still there was no marketable product in sight. Gates, under the firm prodding of Jon Shirley, agreed to take himself out of the day-to-day decision making. He was trying to oversee five product lines, and key planning decisions were often delayed or were never made at all.

"It was a strange structure," Gates admitted in an interview with *Business Week* after the company's reorganization. "We could never focus enough on the different parts of the business."

After Microsoft was reorganized into separate systems software and business applications divisions, each with a corporate vice-president, Gates' responsibilities became somewhat less defined. He no longer had anyone reporting directly to him. He was supposed to think about the future, something he had been brilliant at all along. He also had more time to become a more visible spokesperson for Microsoft.

But there was another reason for the split into separate divisions not disclosed to the press. There were complaints from software developers that Microsoft had a competitive advantage because its application group got inside information from the operating systems group, including the group developing Windows. Programmers working on applications at Microsoft to run under Windows, for example, knew a lot more about Windows than outside competitors who were developing applications to work with Windows. With this inside knowledge, Microsoft's products would naturally be better. Also, each small change in the software forced these companies to meet with Microsoft to make sure the change would also work with MS-DOS. This gave Microsoft, which has its own application programs, an inside look at a competitor's best products. It was an advantage enjoyed by no other company in the software industry.

Gates insisted that Microsoft kept the playing field level by erecting an imaginary barrier between the company's Operating Systems Group and its application division. This barrier became known in the industry as the "Chinese Wall."

MacGregor said that at the time of the reorganization, information flowed freely between applications developers and Windows developers. Dan Lipkie, the former Xerox programmer, worked on Microsoft Word before transferring to Windows. And Neil Konzen, a top Microsoft software engineer, switched from the applications group to Windows in August 1984.

"All of Konzen's friends were in the applications group, and they'd talk at lunch all the time, so it really was true," MacGregor said. "The application developers at Microsoft had better knowledge of Windows than programmers outside the company."

Two months after the August reorganization, Leo Nikora found himself on the phone to the press, explaining yet another delay. Windows was supposed to be finished in October. But after a year of development, Microsoft officials had reached the conclusion that the program took up too much memory and was too slow to run on the 8088 microchip effectively. Major parts of the program would have to be redesigned. A flashy product rollout slated for the fall Comdex was canceled, and the release was rescheduled for spring, 1985.

The situation was frustrating. Each time Gates told his Windows marketing crew the schedule was being moved back, he would also tell them that this time the release date would be met. And each time, Nikora found himself going back out to the independent software vendors to tell them that the target had been missed again. "I just felt like an idiot after two or three of those," Nikora said.

Things weren't easier for Gates, who in early October 1984 wrote a letter to one impatient software publisher explaining the latest glitch: "Windows is the most strategic product that Microsoft is working on," Gates wrote. "We want it to be the environment of choice for the next generation of graphical applications. To achieve this goal, it must have the functionality and performance required by this new generation of graphical applications. This will not be easy; it will be a significant advancement of the state of the art."

He went on to explain how he felt there had not been enough progress on improving the product's performance, and he told the developer that Windows would be delayed until April 15. The press, he said, would be told that Windows would be available in June. This was an attempt by Gates to make it appear the already embarrassed company had actually beaten its self-imposed deadline with the April release. Gates also wrote that the company intended to pull out all the stops promoting Windows at the spring Comdex. Microsoft, he said, would make a "big splash."

"We hope that you too can beat this date with your Windows application before June," Gates wrote. "We will be talking to the press between now and October 15th. Should you receive any inquiries from the press before then, please refer them to Microsoft; after then, please support us in keeping expectations to the June time frame."

By this time, however, no amount of spin control could undo the damage to Microsoft's reputation. Word of the latest delay prompted numerous questions in computer publications of the need and utility of graphical user interfaces. *Forbes* magazine noted that VisiCorp and Quarterdeck were on their deathbeds because of expensive and futile gambles that PC users would flock to these windowing products. One trade publication predicted all the excitement over GUI was a flash in the pan and would burn off. *InfoWorld* used the term "vaporware" to describe Windows and all other software that was hyped ad nauseum but never made it to dealers' shelves.

In the past, Gates' strategy was to always get out first with a product and grab a share of the market and fix the problems later. With Windows, he inexplicably took just the opposite approach. He couldn't bring himself to turn it lose until everything was perfect.

"Most of the reason Windows didn't get out was because Bill kept adding functionality [features] and changing the rules," Nikora said. "All these other products were on the market. I was saying, 'Look, Bill, you've got to be out there, take what you've got and get it out there. You can always make it better, you can always improve it later, but get out there.' Bill's feeling was, 'No, we've got to go out there with something that's just head and shoulders above everybody else. It's gotta be the right product.' "

Gates was increasingly under fire from the industry. For the first time, his judgment and business acumen were being questioned.

The numerous delays of Windows provided little encouragement for software publishers to develop applications for the graphical PC environment. VisiOn had been on the market for more than a year and had won few converts, despite VisiCorp's three-year, $10 million investment. VisiCorp was going broke and would soon be gone. Quarterdeck introduced its DESQ windowing product, but it too suffered disappointing sales. Digital Research had a graphical user interface product called GEM due for release soon. But the battle, as the industry press saw it, was going to be between Windows and TopView, which IBM planned to market in early 1985.

In the opening days of 1985, Microsoft was forced into a key strategic marketing shift. After months of testing and tinkering, Gates had to admit Windows just didn't work fast enough or well enough on existing hardware. That ended plans to bundle Windows as part of a package with new PCs made by Compaq, Tandy, and the rest of the OEMs who had originally supported the program.

With IBM pushing TopView instead of Windows, Microsoft had only one move left if it wanted the program to become a standard. It would have to sell Windows separately on the retail market and hope consumers bought it in sufficient numbers.

In-house, meanwhile, there was more trouble on the project. Ballmer was not getting along with Nikora. He would storm into Nikora's office almost daily, pound his fist on the table, call Nikora an "idiot," and dismiss his ideas as "complete jokes."

"They didn't like what I was doing in marketing," Nikora said. "They didn't think I was a very good marketer. And you know what, they were right." Nikora had, after all, arrived at the company as an accomplished programmer and manager. "I'd never marketed a day in my life—and they never did anything to teach me."

Nikora soon quit. "I was burned out," he said. "I also left because Microsoft wasn't quite ready for middle management. They thought they were ready, but they weren't."

MacGregor was also having his problems with Ballmer. The former equipment manager of the Harvard football team had become something of a wild man. He was a Gates' clone, but without Gates' charm or technical know-how.

Said one member of the Windows team: "None of the developers admired Ballmer, because Bill had established this ethos that development managers coded. Then he appoints Steve Ballmer, who had never written a line of code in his life."

Gates and Ballmer had very different styles. Ballmer was more of a cheerleader. Instead of working with the programming team through MacGregor, Ballmer was always intervening personally, exhorting the engineers to work faster. He would get the software engineers psyched to really go all out and push the outside of the envelope. But this caused monumental problems for MacGregor. By their nature, software engineers, when excited about a project, would always underestimate how long something would take. Then Ballmer would get in meetings with the engineers, look at their development schedules, and give 'em hell. "You can do better than that!" he would shout while beating his fist on the table.

"These guys were pretty young, just out of school," said MacGregor, "and they'd try to take some time off their schedules which were already unmakeable. This was incredibly frustrating for me, because you'd get a quote to do a particular function in four weeks, and I knew they didn't have a prayer of doing it in less than six, and here Ballmer is pushing to do it in two or three. It's set up for failure. He knew people were going to bust their butts, but there was a lot of stress in the group, marriages were strained. My philosophy is, you want to build a team for the long term. Its okay to sprint, you need to sprint to get products out the door. But you can't sprint all the time."

Ballmer believed that scheduling was something to be "negotiated" rather than an attempt to accurately project how much time something would take. "It meant that we'd quote dates [to software publishers writing Windows applications] that were totally unrealistic," said MacGregor.

But there were fewer and fewer customers to worry about. According to the president of a software publishing firm that supported Windows, the repeated delays had caused a crisis of confidence in the industry: "What was interesting was everybody from Lotus to Ashton-Tate, everybody that was anybody, was at that Windows developers conference in early 1984 and they were all up on the stage saying 'Yeah, we're going to do Windows and Windows is great, blah, blah, blah. But by mid-1985 they'd all dropped what they were doing and walked off. Part of it was they just got disgusted with Microsoft. Halfway through it they changed the design, and we had to throw away what we'd done and start over."

One of the biggest disappointments for Microsoft was that Lotus decided not to follow through on a pledge to support Windows. Mitch Kapor knew he couldn't afford to have Microsoft set the graphical user interface standard for the PC. Allowing Windows to run 1-2-3, the best-selling spreadsheet on the market, would have given Microsoft too much leverage. "If Mitch had put the seal of approval on Windows, it would have been a big deal, and he didn't want to do that," said one of Microsoft's managers. Both Gates and Ballmer did a lot of arm twisting with Kapor, but he refused to come around.

By the spring of 1985 MacGregor, too, had decided to leave. "There was some frustration, a sense of wanting to do some other things," he said. "The team was pretty stressed out. It had been a long haul. I didn't agree with some of the strategy. . . . I wasn't having fun. I think its very important, if you have the luxury of choosing jobs, to choose one that's fun. But I have positive feelings toward the company. I'm glad to have worked there, glad to have known the people. But sometimes you just want to do other things."

Differences with Ballmer helped MacGregor make up his mind that it was time to move on.

"The fact that Steve and I had our differences was probably one of the reasons I didn't stay. I think his style of directly interacting with the programmers and beating them up is just not a good management technique. He probably felt I was dragging the project out, and that could have been his rationale."

Gates did his best to persuade MacGregor to stay on. In the weeks before MacGregor left, they often went out to dinner and talked about the company. Gates would drive over to his apartment in his brown Mercedes, the back seat filled with empty milk cartons. Gates drank a lot of milk and he would toss the empty carton over his shoulder and continue driving. The car smelled like sour milk.

Gates took it personally when MacGregor finally left. He couldn't understand why the relationship couldn't be repaired, according to MacGregor. The day after MacGregor left, Ballmer moved into his vacated office.

Some time later that spring, with another deadline approaching, Gates called Ballmer himself into his office on a rain-sodden weekday morning. The night before, Gates had uncovered a bug in the latest version of the Windows program. He had had enough. Fixing Ballmer with a cold blue stare, Gates began shouting at him. If Windows was not on the shelves by the end of the year, Gates threatened, Ballmer would be looking for another job.

The ultimatum galvanized Ballmer. He gathered his engineering staff together to pass along the message. "Kids," Ballmer said, "we must ship this product before the snow falls."

Dedication quickly turned into fanaticism. Gabe Newell, one of the Windows testers who went on to enjoy a long and successful career at Microsoft, showed up at the office with a sleeping bag. For a solid month, he camped in his office, working around the clock and catching a few catnaps when he could no longer stay awake. He became known as "Madman" Newell from that point on.

The unrelenting push, however, required an occasional diversion. While waiting for code to be compiled in the early morning hours, several programmers took to creating bombs and rockets out of sugar and saltpeter. The makeshift explosives were carted outside and set off in the night air of the quiet suburb. The games ended when the police arrived with bomb-sniffing dogs, though no one was caught.

In an attempt to amp up the power of the homemade explosives, one young programmer came up with a plan to melt the sugar in the cafeteria's microwave oven to give the mixture more kick. The fuel ignited while it was brewing, blowing up the oven and sending a plume of smoke throughout the building.

The police were alerted on one other occasion. This time, the more musically inclined, after growing bored with full-volume jam sessions in the hallways, lifted their amplifiers to the roof and serenaded the surrounding community with electric guitars. The cops weren't fast enough; by the time they arrived, the programmers were snickering over their computer terminals.

One ex-Microsoft employee summed up the programmers feelings under such terrible pressure: "You felt you were at the center of the universe. That was the motivation, that and just trying to get clean code out there. It was an invigorating feeling to be working for Microsoft. And all this pounding by Steve Ballmer, and yanking by Bill, was the price you paid to be there."

When Comdex rolled around that May, Microsoft demonstrated an advanced version of Windows. But there was no "big splash" as Gates had promised in his letter to software publishers seven months before. The company's Comdex profile was uncharacteristically subdued. Windows wasn't ready. The new target had been set for June. June came and went.

In the end, Windows wasn't ready until November, at the fall Comdex. Fortunately for Ballmer, it rarely snowed in Seattle before Christmas (when it snowed at all). Ballmer kept his job.

"We will never have another delay like Windows," vowed Ballmer to a writer for *Business Week*.

There was an anticlimactic atmosphere to the final product announcement Microsoft made the evening of Nov. 21, 1985 at the fall Comdex. The major PC magazine writers and editors were in attendance, as were representatives of the software and computer distribution chains. The event was marked by a roast for Microsoft, a chance for Gates and Ballmer to be served a generous helping of crow.

After more than two years of delays, disappointments, public embarrassment, and overblown promises made by Gates and other top company officials, Windows was "officially" finished. During that time, Gates and Ballmer had ridden and prodded the team working on Windows to the limits of their endurance. They had yelled, screamed and verbally whipped the team mercilessly as one deadline after another slipped by. Now it was time for the industry to indulge in a little payback.

Stewart Alsop from *InfoWorld* fired the opening salvo when he presented Gates with the Golden Vaporware Award, the derisive term coined by the magazine to describe software products that existed mainly in the words and vapor of grandiose and overreaching marketing plans. Another guest speaker, John Dvorak of *PC Magazine*, wisecracked that when Windows was announced in late 1983, the balding Ballmer still had some of his hair. What he didn't realize was that Ballmer was lucky to have a job.

At the end of the roasting, Ballmer led the audience in a song to which Gates joined in as a giant shopping cart filled with

500 packaged Windows programs was rolled out on stage. On this night, as laughter and singing filled the room, all seemed forgiven. But a long trail of human carnage left behind at Microsoft marked the frenzied forced march to develop Windows.

The shipment of the first Windows products was a watershed in the evolution of the PC, as well as the fruition of a vision Gates had been nursing for years. But the first version of Windows was not the success Gates had hoped for and promised. In fact, it was a flop. It would take two major revisions before Windows was made right. Not until the release of Windows 3.0 in 1990 would it deliver as promised.

"Windows was a pig," acknowledged one of the programmers who had labored almost two years to develop it. The program was too ambitious to run efficiently on most of the personal computers then in use. The machines lacked the memory and speed to take advantage of the best features the software had to offer. In addition, because of all the delays at Microsoft, there were few application programs available to run under Windows. The graphical environment, for all of Gates' efforts to boost it, looked dead. Fortunately for Microsoft, IBM's TopView had also been unsuccessful, despite the marketing clout of Big Blue. Windows was seemingly a product whose time had not yet come.

In some ways Bill Gates, the CEO *Time* magazine described as looking like an undernourished graduate student, had became something of a Silicon bully by 1985, kicking sand in the face of competitors who got in his way. Apple Computer, for one, found itself picking sand from its eyes for years after tangling with Gates over the development of Windows.

On November 22, one day after the Comdex roast, Microsoft and Apple signed a confidential agreement that three years later would become the crux of the most significant lawsuit in the history of the personal computer industry. Gates had dragged Apple to the negotiating table kicking and screaming. Apple claimed that Windows was a rip-off of Macintosh technology. As the *Wall Street Journal* would write later, Gates used "high pressure tactics . . . to extract a virtual blank check to borrow many Macintosh ideas for Microsoft's own products. These ideas included mouse-activated pull-down command menus and overlapping windows of on-screen text."

Throughout 1985, Apple officials had become increasingly concerned that Microsoft was borrowing ideas from the Macintosh to use in Windows and other products in violation of a 1982 agreement signed by Gates and Jobs. Under terms of that agreement, Microsoft was to develop application programs for the Macintosh. By providing Microsoft with prototypes of the Mac, as well as software tools to write those applications, Apple believed Microsoft was developing graphical user interface programs only for the Mac. Instead, Microsoft turned around and developed Windows for competing IBM clone machines.

When Apple threatened to sue Microsoft in 1985 over Windows for copyright violations, Gates said he would stop development of Excel and Word for the Mac, which at the time were desperately needed software applications which Apple hoped would spur sagging sales of the Macintosh. Apple had no choice but to back down on its threat to take legal action. Instead, it signed a licensing agreement giving Microsoft royalty-free rights to use the graphical display technology developed for the Macintosh.

"The parties have a long history of cooperation and trust and wish to maintain that mutual beneficial relationship," the agreement stated. "However, a dispute has arisen concerning the ownership of and possible copyright infringement as to certain visual displays generated by several Microsoft software products." Those products included Excel, Windows, Multiplan, and Word.

"For purposes of resolving this dispute and in consideration of the license grant from Apple . . . ," the agreement went on,

"Microsoft acknowledges that the visual displays in [Excel, Windows, Word, and Multiplan] are derivative works of the visual displays generated by Apple's Lisa and Macintosh graphic user interface programs."

The agreement was signed by Gates and John Sculley, Apple's new chairman. In a reorganization of Apple, Sculley had recently forced out his friend Steve Jobs in a much publicized showdown. Sculley and others on the Apple board felt Jobs was not an effective enough corporate manager to take the company through the tough times Sculley foresaw.

Apple received little in return for granting Microsoft an exclusive license to use Macintosh graphics technology. But Microsoft did promise to fix problems in Word, which had been released for the Macintosh in late 1984 with numerous bugs. (Gates later admitted Microsoft took too many shortcuts in trying to get the product out quickly.)

At the same time Gates was brow-beating Sculley to the negotiating table in 1985, he was also using his muscle to force Apple to stop work on a Macintosh program of its own. Apple was planning to bring out its version of MacBASIC, even though Microsoft had a similar product that was already being sold with the computer. Apple engineers believed their BASIC was better. When Gates heard of Apple's plans, he was beside himself. He felt betrayed, since Microsoft had thrown so much of its resources into developing applications for the Macintosh. Arguably, Microsoft saved the Mac with the introduction of Excel. Gates demanded that Sculley cancel the project and sign over to Microsoft rights to the MacBASIC name. As a lever, Gates told Sculley he would not renegotiate the license for Apple to use Microsoft's BASIC on the best-selling Apple II. At the time, sales for the Macintosh were down to nothing and the Apple II was the company's bread and butter product.

"Essentially, since Microsoft started their company with BASIC, they felt proprietary towards it," said Andy Hertzfeld, the Apple software engineer who had worked on the Macintosh project. "They felt threatened by Apple's BASIC, which was a considerably better implementation than theirs. And Bill Gates felt compelled to convince Apple not to ship the one Donn Denman had developed. And he succeeded."

Denman had been working on MacBASIC for two years at Apple. When Sculley suddenly scuttled the project, it broke Denman's heart. "I felt like my two-year-old child had been taken from me," he recalled. Beside himself after two years of work, Denman climbed on his motorcycle and went racing wildly through the foothills above Cupertino. As he was rounding a sharp curve he lost control and crashed. Although he scraped several layers of skin off his arms and legs, he escaped serious injury. "I felt like I didn't have too much to live for at that point," he said. Denman would end up taking a six-month leave from Apple before coming back.

The decision to cancel MacBASIC came at a time of very low morale around Apple. The Mac was not doing particularly well, the industry was in a slump, employees had been laid off, and Steve Jobs had been kicked out of the company. But caving in to Microsoft hurt the most.

"Everyone was somewhat disgusted over it," Denman said. "I know the issue came up several times in public meetings. People would ask John Sculley, 'Whatever happened to BASIC? I'm working away on this project and how do I know it's not going to get canceled like BASIC. . . ?' Sculley's answer was, 'We did some horse trading there. It was the right decision for the company. It was a business decision.' Ultimately, I came to accept that point of view. I wanted to create something for people to use, and it didn't get used. To me that was a big tragedy. But it was an ace that Apple traded with Microsoft for something, and I'm not in a position to evaluate whether that was a good deal or not."

There were others around Apple more outspoken about Microsoft's hard-ball tactics. Bill Atkinson, one of the company's top software developers, said of Gates: "'He insisted that Apple withdraw what was an exceptional product. He held the gun to our head."

Other companies would soon have similar things to say about the way Gates and Microsoft did business. What particularly frightened industry insiders was that Microsoft was still a fairly small, privately held company in 1985. But even as he was arm-twisting Apple, Microsoft's boyish-looking leader had set in motion a series of events to take his company public. The Microsoft juggernaut was just starting to gather momentum.

CHAPTER 6

King of the Hill

Weaving in and out among the other skaters as he picked up speed, Bill Gates was riding the fine edge between being in and out of control, one misguided step from disaster, pushing himself, as usual, to the limit. On the hardwood floor of the roller skating rink, many of the more than 100 Microsoft employees who had turned out for Gates' 30th birthday party marveled at his skating abilities. Rock 'n' roll music from Paul Allen's band blared in the background. The more intense the music, the faster Gates seemed to skate, gliding backwards and forwards with equal ease.

There had not been much time for roller skating in the last ten years since Gates and Allen had formed Microsoft, but Gates, who learned to skate at an early age, quickly found his childhood form.

Although Microsoft's leader appeared to be in good spirits as he spun through lap after lap this October day in 1985, he had a lot on his mind. The company's board of directors was due to meet in less than 24 hours to hear his decision about taking Microsoft public. Gates had avoided the unavoidable as long as possible, and he was not looking forward to the next few months. A legal prospectus would have to be prepared, and then he would have to tour the country selling investors on the company's stock, which would consume much of his valuable time. And Gates knew that in the end, along with the fantastic personal riches, would come the inevitable distractions to his employees as programmers wrote code with one eye on the price of their stock.

In the last few years, several computer startup companies had gone public, the most celebrated of which was Apple. When its stock was traded publicly for the first time in December of 1980, Apple's value was estimated at $1.8 billion, which was more than Ford Motor Company. The fortunes that had been made were mind boggling. On paper, Steve Jobs was suddenly worth more than $250 million. In 1983, two of Microsoft's fiercest competitors, Lotus Development Corporation and Ashton-Tate, also went public, to enormous financial success. But Gates was in no hurry for Microsoft to take this same rite of passage. He did not want to open Microsoft's corporate doors to the public. For one thing, the company did not need the instant infusion of cash that a public offering would provide. It was making a great deal of money. Pretax profits were running as high as thirty-four percent of revenues. And remaining private had definite advantages. There were no stockholders to please, no onerous filings with the Securities and Exchange Commission. The only disadvantage was that Microsoft's key employees and managers who had been getting stock options over the years had no tradable security. Until Gates decided to take the company public, there was no liquid market for Microsoft stock.

Regardless of what Gates' wanted, however, his hand was about to be forced. It was only a question of time until the day arrived when Microsoft would have to offer its stock to the public. The 1934 Securities Exchange Act required all companies to register and file public reports as soon as stock had been distributed to 500 or more employees. As far back as 1983, Gates had projected that Microsoft would reach that figure by 1986 or 1987. It now made a lot more sense for Microsoft to take charge of its own future.

"We decided to do it when we wanted to, not when we had to," Jon Shirley, Microsoft's president, told *Fortune* magazine.

In early 1985, Shirley, Gates, and David Marquardt, the sole venture capitalist in Microsoft, had started serious discussions about an initial public offering. But Gates wanted to wait until two major products, Excel and Windows, had been released. He told the board he would have a recommendation by the end of October.

The roller skating party was held on Sunday, October 27, the day before Gates' birthday. When he met with the board the next day, he had made up his mind to go ahead with the selection of underwriters, even though he still had serious reservations about the entire process. With this decision finally out of the way, Gates hurried off to the elegant Four Seasons Hotel in downtown Seattle, where his mother was throwing him a much more private birthday party.

Microsoft's point man in dealing with Wall Street would be 50-year-old Frank Gaudette, the company's chief financial officer who had arrived the year before. He had previously managed the public offerings of three software companies. But those companies did not have Microsoft's leverage, and Gaudette couldn't wait to start negotiating with underwriters who had been tripping over themselves for years as they called on Microsoft, trying to get close to Gates for the day Gates decided to take the company public. This time, Gaudette and not the investment bankers would be setting the terms. Gaudette recommended that Microsoft select two underwriters to co-manage the public offering. One would be a leading Wall Street investment firm, which would act as lead underwriter, putting together a syndicate of underwriters and allocating stock among them. The second co-managing firm needed to be one that specialized in technology stocks. Choosing this specialty, or "boutique," firm would be simpler, as only four firms with the kind of expertise Microsoft was looking for existed. Choosing the Wall Street firm, however, would be more difficult. Eventually, Gaudette narrowed the field to eight firms, telling each of them they would have half a day to pitch their firm to him. In the end Gaudette was particularly impressed with Goldman Sachs. As a result of his recommendations to Gates and Shirley, Microsoft invited representatives of Goldman Sachs to meet with Microsoft officials over dinner at Seattle's Rainier Club the night of December 11.

The conversation at dinner was awkward. Gates, who wasn't thrilled at the notion of going public in the first place, had heard horror stories about investment bankers from Lotus leader Mitch Kapor. Gates was tired and prepared to be bored during dinner. Shirley was caustic, despite Goldman's attempts to establish a rapport. At the end of the evening, Eff Martin, a vice-president of Goldman Sachs, told Gates that Microsoft could have the "most visible initial public offering of 1986—or ever." In the parking lot of the Rainier Club after dinner, Gates told Shirley, "Well, they didn't spill their food and they seemed like nice guys. I guess we should go with them."

A few days later, the firm of Alex. Brown & Sons of Baltimore, which had been courting Microsoft for years, was picked as the specialty investment banker.

There was one sticky problem left to resolve.

Gates had signed an agreement with the managing editor of *Fortune* magazine to allow one of its writers to tag along throughout the public offering process. Gates, in fact, was enthusiastic about the idea. He felt other entrepreneurs might learn from Microsoft's experience. The publicity wouldn't hurt, either. A year or so earlier, Fred Gibbons of Software Publishing Corporation had wanted *Fortune* to write a similar article when his company went public, but the underwriters and lawyers balked. A public offering is a sensitive matter to investment bankers and lawyers; any information disclosed in such an article that is not contained in the company's prospectus could be used by disgruntled shareholders as the basis for a suit should the stock not do well.

Negotiations between Microsoft and *Fortune* took more than a month. The agreement that was finally signed allowed lawyers for Microsoft and the underwriters to read the story and suggest—not approve—changes before publication. The story would not be published until well after the public offering, when the stock had a chance to stabilize. *Fortune* writer Bro Uttal, chief of the magazine's West Coast bureau in Menlo Park, California, was handed the assignment.

When they found out about the *Fortune* deal, the two principal underwriters Microsoft had picked wanted nothing to do with the article. But Gates held his ground—if they wouldn't agree, he told them, Microsoft would select other underwriters to manage its public offering. As Gates pointed out, firms were lined up at the door to underwrite the offering, smelling millions of dollars in fees. The two underwriters quickly backed down.

By the end of the year, the national press began writing stories of a possible public offering by Microsoft in the near future. Although the negotiations to select the underwriters had been done in secret, there were tell-tale signs of the company's plans. Microsoft had recently announced that William Neukom, formerly a senior partner with Shidler McBroom Gates & Lucas, had become Microsoft's vice-president of law and corporate affairs, a newly created position. Microsoft had also announced that Portia Isaacson, 43, founder of Future Computing and a respected industry forecaster, had been named to Microsoft's board of directors. Fleshing out a board of directors and bringing in legal counsel is usually a sure sign that a private company like Microsoft is preparing for a public stock offering.

Throughout January of 1986, Neukom worked on drafting the critical prospectus. By law, Microsoft's stock could only be offered on the basis of information contained in the prospectus. If the company's stock fell after it was publicly traded, angry investors could sue Microsoft if pertinent information about the company's affairs was left out of the prospectus.

"Like all such documents, it had to be a discrete sales tool, soft-pedaling weaknesses and stressing strengths, all the while concealing as much as possible from competitors," wrote *Fortune*'s Bro Uttal in his article.

Ruthann Quindlen, a security analyst for underwriter Alex. Brown, said Gates was very concerned about some of the problems Microsoft was having at the time the prospectus was being prepared. The company had invested heavily in writing applications for Apple's Macintosh computer, which had failed to do as well as expected. And Microsoft Windows was getting very bad reviews from the trade press. Quindlen was part of the "due diligence" examination that the lawyers and underwriters conducted with Gates and other Microsoft executives, looking for potential skeletons in the closet. While Alex. Brown & Sons was used to dealing with software companies and the unusual personalities of people who spent their lives in front of a computer screen, Goldman Sachs was not.

"Steve Ballmer was pretty wild during the due diligence," recalled Quindlen. "He was his normal, ebullient self. Once, he was right behind one of the minions from Goldman Sachs and he clapped his hands together to make a point and the guy jumped about five feet out of his chair. They'd never seen anything like it. They just weren't used to this kind of company."

Ballmer, even more than the other Microsoft executives, came up with so many potential developments that could result in Microsoft's demise during due diligence that one of the investment bankers quipped, "I'd hate to hear you on a bad day."

The final step before filing with the SEC was to set the price range of the stock to be sold to investors. The underwriters suggested a range of $17 to $20 a share. At first Gates insisted on a range of $16 to $19. It was highly unusual for a CEO to argue for a *lower* price. But Gates felt uncomfortable. A price of $16 would give Microsoft's stock a price-earnings multiple of more than ten times estimated earnings, which was comfortably between the multiples of personal computer software companies and mainframe companies. At $20 per share, Microsoft's market value would shoot up to more than half a billion dollars.

"Bill had a sense of proportion," said one of those involved in pricing the stock. "It seemed ridiculous that a company would have that kind of price earnings ratio. He just felt uncomfortable with that kind of prominence, and with the expectations that would be raised in the minds of people who bought the stock. He just didn't have any way to predict how well the company would do."

Microsoft was considering what amounted to about a $40 million deal. Of that, $30 million would come from the sale of roughly two million shares at an assumed price of about $16 a share. The remaining $10 million would be collected through the sale of stock by existing shareholders in the company, who had agreed beforehand not to sell more than ten percent of their holdings. If the underwriters exercised options for an additional 300,000 shares, about twelve percent of Microsoft's stock would be traded publicly.

By the end of January the prospectus was ready. On February 3 Microsoft registered with the SEC, and the underwriters sent out 38,000 copies of the prospectus. For the first time, the media got an inside look at the internal operations of Microsoft. The prospectus was a journalistic gold mine, rich in detail, with nuggets scattered throughout its 50 pages.

Microsoft's co-founders, Gates and Allen, were about to become millionaires many times over. Gates owned 11,222,000 shares of Microsoft stock, or slightly over forty-nine percent. He planned to sell 80,000 shares. Allen owned 6,390,000 shares, or twenty-eight percent. He planned to sell 200,000 shares.

Steve Ballmer, who owned 1,710,000 shares, would also do very well. Jon Shirley owned 400,000 shares. Other major stockholders included Charles Simonyi, with 305,667 shares; Gordon Letwin, with 293,850 shares; and Gates' parents, who together owned 114,000 shares. After Gates, Allen, and Ballmer, the largest stockholder was Technology Venture Investors, with 1,378,901 shares.

The prospectus also revealed that Microsoft's senior managers had been able to take out large company loans to purchase stock options in the company. Shirley had borrowed $810,751, of which he still owed more than $600,000. Steve Ballmer had borrowed $533,711 and had not paid back any of the loan. Scott Oki owed $56,211 on his loan of $198,711. And Frank Gaudette, the chief financial officer in charge of Microsoft's public offering, had borrowed $143,888 from Microsoft.

For the first time, Gates' annual salary, as well as that of his top managers, was public record. Shirley was Microsoft's highest paid manager, with a salary in 1985 of $228,000. Gates received only $133,000 in salary, far below what most CEOs of American corporations made. Ballmer received $88,000 in compensation in 1985.

The prospectus listed three board members in addition to Gates: Marquardt, Shirley and Portia Isaacson.

Allen was no longer on the board. Although he had not played an active role in the company since 1983, he had recently resigned from the board to start his own Bellevue software company, Asymetrix. Two of Microsoft's first programmers, Steve Wood and Marc McDonald, had joined him in founding Asymetrix.

". . . I had pushed him pretty hard," Gates would later say of Allen. "He wanted to go out and prove he could do his own thing. I tried to convince him to do that within the context of Microsoft, but he decided to do it himself."

The prospectus showed that Microsoft had been doing even better than most outsiders had thought. For the year that ended June 30, 1985, Microsoft had revenues of $140 million. Its profits had totalled $31.2 million, or nineteen percent of revenue. That was better than its two chief public rivals, Ashton-Tate and Lotus. Of its total revenues, $75 million came from its operating systems division and $54 million from applications. The remaining revenue came from the sale of hardware, such as the Microsoft Mouse, and from the sale of computer-related books published by Microsoft Press, which the company had founded in 1983. Microsoft's International Division accounted for a whopping thirty-four percent of total revenues as of June 30, 1985. Of that, fully twelve percent came from Japan. No single customer accounted for more than ten percent of Microsoft's total business.

Once the prospectus was out, Gates and other Microsoft executives were besieged with calls from friends, relatives, and acquaintances wanting to buy shares of stock in the company. Gates even got a call from his doctor. According to *Fortune*, except for about a dozen people, including Gates' grandmother and his former housekeeper, Gates turned down most of the requests.

"I won't grant any of these goofy requests," he said. "I hate the whole thing. All I'm thinking and dreaming about is selling software, not stock."

But Gates still had one more obligation to fulfill before he could get back to managing his company. A road show had been organized to promote the company's stock with institutional investors. It was set to kick off in Phoenix on February 18. At a February 7 rehearsal, Gates spoke in a flat monotone to the assembled investment bankers, going over the company's vital statistics. When one banker criticized Gates' delivery, Gates snapped, "You mean I'm supposed to say boring things in an exciting way?" Once the tour kicked off, Gates and company would make stops in eight cities, including London, over the next ten days.

There was a great deal of excitement and anticipation surrounding Microsoft's public offering, and Gates and Gaudette spoke to packed audiences in each city. Institutional investors said they would take as much stock as they could get their hands on, and the show quickly took on a festive mood. Even Gates relaxed, when he found he could use the tour to push Microsoft products as well as Microsoft stock. In London, everyone celebrated by going to dinner at Annabel's, a popular club that

British gentlemen supposedly took their mistresses to. After dinner, Gates and Ruthann Quindlen, the security analyst from Alex. Brown & Sons, danced long into the night.

"Bill loves to dance," said Quindlen, who had known Gates since the early 1980s. "When he's on the floor, he's in his own world."

During the road show, Quindlen discovered a side of Gates that few have seen. Microsoft's youthful chairman was being publicly measured, and he was afraid to fail.

"He's never failed at anything. He has picked things he will win at," she said. "In every situation Bill gets into, private and public, he sets himself up not to fail. It's what drives him so much. . . . I'm not sure he's equipped to deal with failure."

Because Gates has never known failure, according to Quindlen, he lacks a certain humaneness, and until he fails miserably at something that means a lot to him, he will never be a great man, despite all his accomplishments.

When Gates returned from the promotional trip, he suddenly had a change of heart regarding the offering price of the stock. He now felt driven to get the best price he could for Microsoft's stock. These were heady days on Wall Street, where a bull market was raging. The underwriters thought the stock would trade publicly as high as $25 a share. Gates now wanted to set the price range for institutional investors at $21 to $22 a share. Why, he felt, should he give Goldman Sachs' institutional clients millions of Microsoft's dollars—the difference between the offering price and the price investors thought the stock would publicly trade at? After several days of intense negotiations with Goldman Sachs, with several major investors threatening to pull out of the deal if the price were too high, everyone agreed on a final price of $21 a share.

By March 12, the only remaining issue on the table was the management fee charged by the underwriters. Initially, Microsoft had said it would pay the underwriters no more than 6.5 percent of the selling price of the stock. But in the last few days, another computer company, Sun Microsystems, had managed to get a 6.13 percent fee on its $64 million public offering, far lower than usual. Gates had told Gaudette that Microsoft should be able to get at least as good a deal.

Goldman Sachs refused to go that low. At the stock price they were discussing, each penny a share was worth $31,000 in management fees. After a full day of haggling with Frank Gaudette in New York, Goldman Sachs' best offer was $1.33 per share. The situation was tense. Gaudette was under orders from Gates—who, showing utter disdain for the excitement of the offering, had left the country for a few days of vacation—not to go above 6.13 percent, which amounted to about $1.29 a share. They were down to quibbling over pennies.

On the evening of March 12, a frantic Gaudette, unable to reach Gates, caught up with Shirley as he was about to leave a restaurant to buy his daughter a car for her 16th birthday. Gaudette had been able to get the underwriters down to $1.31. That was as low as they would go, he said. Shirley approved, and the deal was done.

The tight-fisted Gates later told Microsoft managers that he would have called off the public offering had he been around and the underwriters refused to meet his price. And he was dead serious.

At 9:35 A.M., March 13, 1986, Microsoft's stock was traded publicly on the New York Stock Exchange for the first time. It opened at $25.75 a share. By the end of the first day, some 3.6 million shares had changed hands. It peaked at $29.25 before closing for the day at $27.75.

According to *Fortune* magazine, Gaudette called Shirley from the floor of the exchange during the morning free-for-all. "It's wild!" he shouted into the phone. "I've never seen anything like it—every last person here is trading Microsoft and nothing else."

The frenzied over-the-counter trading surprised even the underwriters. By noon, the stock was changing hands at the rate of thousands of shares a minute. Had they sold at the peak, investors who had grabbed up the stock at $21 a share could have made a forty percent return in one afternoon.

Analysts said they could not recall when a stock traded more volume in its first day.

"I'm pretty happy," Paul Allen told the *Seattle Post-Intelligencer* newspaper as he watched the price of the stock climb throughout the morning. "Everybody involved in Microsoft since the beginning has been looking forward to this day."

Within weeks, the stock had hit $35.50 a share. Although Gates made only $1.6 million from the shares he sold, his remaining forty-five percent stake in the company was worth an estimated $350 million. A year after the public offering, in March of 1987, Microsoft's stock hit $90.75 a share and was still climbing. At age 31, Bill Gates was officially a billionaire. No one in American history, from the great industrial barons and financiers of the nineteenth century to the modern day corporate raiders, had ever made so much money at such a young age. The computer whiz kid who had once seemed to define the term "nerd" was now the youngest billionaire in the country.

And he could have cared less.

On the day Microsoft went public and company employees were celebrating their riches, Bill Gates was off the coast of Australia on a 56-foot sailing vessel reading books and getting a closeup look at the Great Barrier Reef. He had chartered the boat and its crew for five days. This was to be one of his so-called reading vacations, in which he spent time alone plowing through as many books as possible.

"I was sort of pampering myself," Gates said.

It would have been his longest vacation in years, except that Gates cut it short to meet with his old friend Kay Nishi the day after Microsoft's public offering.

Their partnership had been disintegrating for months, and Gates now had to decide between friendship and what was best for his company. Nishi had become too unpredictable, too impulsive, and Gates was convinced Nishi was not going to change his cowboy ways. He felt that Nishi was not pushing Microsoft's products, such as Multiplan, hard enough in Japan, but was instead running around promoting his own random high-tech projects. Nishi, for example, wanted to branch out into semiconductors. Gates wanted to stay with software. Nishi thought special chips should be designed to take over the duties of the operating system. Gates belittled the chip-development efforts of Nishi's company, ASCII. Microsoft's operating system was a standard, he said, and what Nishi proposed didn't make sense.

"If microcomputer software based on a standard is not a good thing," Gates told the *Los Angeles Times*, "then hey, we're not going to do much business. If that's wrong, then God bless Kay Nishi and I hope he finds a raft that floats, because I'm on this ship tied to the wheel."

Although the two computer whiz kids were much alike, Nishi had a wild streak that Gates never exhibited, especially when it came to business. "They were both very bright, intense, ambitious and driven," said one Microsoft executive who worked closely with the two. "But Kay was always wanting to go off and do something else. His attention span was not very long. He always wanted to start something new and he always tended to have a dozen things going at the same time, of which six were just great and the other six were just random. Who knew what he was going to try and do next? So he was pretty much uncontrollable."

Nishi had become something of a Japanese folk hero. He was featured in the Japanese edition of *Playboy* magazine. And he was spending money like crazy, which did not please the fiscally conservative Gates. Nishi lived out of the most expensive hotel rooms available. He traveled to appointments by helicopter. On one occasion, when he was trying to get an appointment with the president of Fujitsu Ltd., Nishi waited outside the executive's home and cornered him when he arrived. This kind of flamboyance did not engender the trust from business executives that is so important in Japan.

The final straw for Gates came when Nishi spent $1 million for a life-size replica of a dinosaur, complete with special effects, as a prop for a television show to teach school children about computers, as well as to promote Nishi's own computer company, ASCII. The brontosaurus was erected outside the Tokyo train station. Although the story line for the television show was about a boy who used Microsoft's software to recreate a dinosaur on his computer, Gates went ballistic when he found out how Nishi had spent the money. There were better ways to market Microsoft's software, he told his friend in a series of angry telegrams to Tokyo.

Shortly before Microsoft went public, according to the *Wall Street Journal*, Gates realized he had to get Nishi under control. Gates offered him a full-time job with Microsoft, as well as a very attractive stock package. Although Nishi was a director in the company and a vice-president, as Microsoft's Far East agent he was paid a thirty percent commission on OEM sales. He was not considered a regular employee.

Nishi refused Microsoft's offer. "Bill Gates demands 100 percent loyalty and demands being his subordinate," Nishi said. "I'd be very happy to work with him, but I don't want to sell my soul to him."

The day after Microsoft went public, with their relationship on the skids, Nishi and Gates met in Microsoft's office in Sydney, Australia. They then flew to Tokyo and spent three days trying to resolve their differences and save the partnership. "We'd talk about our vision, and then we'd get mad at each other and then we'd apologize," Gates said.

But they were unable to patch things up. The bitter breakup was especially painful for Gates. He and Nishi had been very close. "Kay's more like me than probably anybody I've ever met," Gates said. "But he just went overboard."

At the time the partnership ended in March 1986, Nishi owed Microsoft $509,850. Not wanting to file suit, Microsoft was unable to collect the debt. Nishi had borrowed the money as a result of a series of bad investments. For example, a couple of years earlier Gates was in the San Jose airport about to board a plane when he was paged by Nishi. Nishi had bought $275,000 of stock in an American company, and now his broker was demanding payment. Nishi didn't have the money to cover the debt. Gates loaned him the cash—at twelve percent annual interest. "What did I want, my best guy ever to go to jail for bad debts?" Gates said later, explaining why he bailed out his friend.

When the partnership with Nishi ended, Microsoft opened its own subsidiary in Japan in May of 1986 and hired away more than a dozen of Nishi's top people from ASCII, which infuriated Nishi. In various interviews, Nishi called Gates a series of names. Gates fired back some shots of his own.

"The guy's life is a mess," Gates said. "He's worth negative half a million and I'm worth X million—that's certainly seeds for bitterness."

Among the people Gates sent to Japan to help establish Microsoft's new subsidiary was his old Lakeside pal Chris Larson. Gates had finally been able to persuade Larson to come to work for Microsoft full-time, rather than go on to graduate school at Stanford. Gates kept promising Larson more and more stock in the company, until the offer was so good Larson couldn't refuse. Larson was one of many at Microsoft who became an instant multi-millionaire the day the company went public.

Microsoft's growth at the time of the public offering continued to explode off the company's planning charts, just as Charles Simonyi had predicted in his famous "revenue bomb" speech in 1981. Gates was worried that Microsoft would lose its competitive edge if it became too big, but there seemed to be nothing he could do.

Not long after the move from Albuquerque into the Old National Bank building in downtown Bellevue, Gates had told one of his programmers that he never wanted his company to have more than a couple hundred people. Several years later, at a pizza party with some of his managers in the Northup building, Gates once again emphasized his desire to keep Microsoft small. "People were starting to worry the growth was getting out of hand," recalled Leo Nikora, one of those munching on pizza that day as the chairman talked about the future. "Bill said he felt the same way. He agreed there had been a lot of growth, but he said it was going to slow down. He said that he never wanted the company to become larger than 1,000 people."

Not only did the growth not slow down, it accelerated. By March of 1986, Microsoft had nearly 1,200 employees. The company had outgrown the Northup complex and was about to move into new offices about eight miles away, on the outskirts of Redmond. Microsoft had purchased 29 acres of an undeveloped corporate park and hurriedly constructed four X-shaped buildings, specially designed so every employee had his or her own windowed office that looked out onto the woodsy surroundings. The software engineers were put in two buildings, and everyone else was put in the other two. Each building, designated by a number from one to four, had its own fast-food 7-Eleven store. All beverages were free. Employees were also given free memberships in a sports club less than a mile away. Sports fields were soon added to the campus so people could play baseball, soccer, and volleyball. In the middle of the four buildings was a small artificial lake that became known as Lake Bill.

The company's long-range capital improvement plans called for no more than three more office buildings to be built over the next 25 years. Within the year, however, construction was started on buildings five and six, which were full before they were finished. Building seven was skipped because it was to have been located in a spot occupied by a nice stand of trees. By the time buildings eight and nine had been completed, Microsoft occupied the equivalent of a 60-story skyscraper. Eventually, the company purchased the entire corporate park and changed the name of the perimeter street to Microsoft Way. Six years after the move from the Northup complex, the "campus" had grown to 22 buildings on 260 acres.

From the beginning, the new corporate headquarters had the genial informality of a campus. Such an atmosphere was no accident.

"The idea was to foster that sense of collegiality," said Ingrid Rasch, Microsoft's director of human resources at the time of the move. "We were basically taking a lot of young kids, who in many cases had never been away from home or only as far as wherever they went to college, and we were moving them halfway across the country. How do you make them comfortable? These are not necessarily people who would go out and immerse themselves in the social opportunities of the area. They weren't going to go out and make friends easily or quickly or participate in a lot of the things going on in the area, and besides, we needed them at work. So we wanted to keep the atmosphere at work one they were somewhat familiar with, and secondly, also make sure it gave them a sense of social belonging."

Employees were encouraged to decorate their offices however they wanted. "It was kind of like their dorm room," said Rasch. "They could have whatever they wanted in there with them and their computer. It was their space."

Shortly after the move, colleagues of a programmer who was out of town for a couple days moved all his office furniture into the hall, put down sod throughout the room, then brought the furniture back in, along with several potted flowers. When the programmer returned to work and walked into his new grass yard, a tape of environment music was playing on his stereo.

Given the long hours and fanatical pace, having a comfortable work environment was essential to morale and mental health.

There were no assigned parking places on the new campus, either, even for Chairman Bill. The best places went to those who arrived at work first. After Microsoft went public, these parking lots began to be sprinkled with Porsches, Mercedes, and even a Ferrari or two as a result of the number of employees who had been around long enough to buy stock at bargain prices who were suddenly paper millionaires, or at least financially well off. (It was not until 1991 that Gates finally got his own reserved underground parking spot. The reason, according to Microsoft, was that he was sometimes harassed as he walked to his car by people wanting to borrow money from him.)

As Gates had feared, the public offering diverted attention from people's work. Charts began showing up in offices, plotting the price of Microsoft's stock. "Is this a distraction?" a concerned Gates asked one programmer who posted a stock chart on his office door. Some long-time employees started coming to work wearing buttons inscribed with the letters FYIFV, which stood for "Fuck You. I'm Fully Vested."

Gates warned employees not to get carried away by their paper wealth. "It's stupid," he told *Fortune* magazine. "The company is a high-tech stock, and high-tech stocks are volatile."

For his part, Gates spent very little of his new fortune on himself. He and Paul Allen did give some money in August of 1986 to Lakeside School, where their dream of one day owning a computer company had originated, donating $2.2 million for a new science and math center to be named after them. Unable to decide whose name should go first, they flipped a coin. Allen won. The building was called Allen Gates Hall.

And Gates also bought a speedboat. But even then, he kept a cool head when it came to spending his money, according to Vern Raburn, who went shopping with Gates at a Seattle-area boat show.

"Bill had been saying for years, 'Gosh, I should get a boat,' but he just couldn't bring himself to spend the money," said Raburn. "At the boat show, we walked around all day, and he just wouldn't do it. Finally, a half hour before the show closed, he bought a ski boat. Not a terribly fancy one, something like $12,000. It was a nice one, but not the fastest or most expensive one around. He agonized over buying that thing like he was spending fifty million bucks."

True to form, Gates soon got a speeding ticket in his new boat.

"Bill is not an extravagant consumer," said Ann Winblad, who had also accompanied Gates on the boat-buying trip. "The local media, they focus on the silly things, like his Porsche. Everyone knows Bill bought a Porsche. How many times do the people have to know that? It's not 'Bill Gates: The life of the rich and famous.' Bill loves his work."

Gates and Winblad had been dating since 1984. They met when they were speaking at an industry conference. The two entrepreneurs had a lot in common. Winblad had just sold her Minneapolis startup software company, which she had founded with $500, for $15 million. Winblad would later team up with John Hummer, a former Seattle SuperSonic basketball player, to form Hummer/Winblad Venture Partners.

Winblad, who is about six years older than Gates, found Gates to be nothing like the nerdish character she had read about in many news stories. "I always learn something when I'm around Bill," Winblad said. "He's an adventurer, a risk taker who likes to live close to the edge. . . ."

Winblad recalled one trip with Gates to Mexico when she went to the restroom and came out to find that Gates had subleased their rental car to a couple of hippies for $10 for the afternoon. She was sure Bill would never see the car again. Four hours later they showed up, looking like they were tripping on acid, but with the car still in one piece.

Winblad had a beach house not far from Kitty Hawk, on the outer banks of North Carolina. Once, Gates arrived at her place for a short vacation without his suitcase; she had to take him shopping for clothes at a Ben Franklin store in Kitty Hawk. True to form, Gates color-coordinated his wardrobe, just as his mother used to do for him years before.

During another vacation, Winblad and Gates drove to a wind-swept dune called Jockey's Ridge not far from Kitty Hawk, where the Wright Brothers learned to fly. Chairman Bill decided he wanted to learn to fly there too, enrolling in hang-gliding lessons. On his first flight, Gates nosed his glider into the bank of the dune shortly after take off, like most first-time students. On the second flight, he followed the instructor's directions and made it to the bottom of the steep dune. By the third flight, Gates decided he had had enough instruction. He soared into the wind, disregarded orders not to turn the glider, and ended up hundreds of yards from the bottom of the hill, tangled in bramble bushes.

"Of course, he's going to take off and glide better than any other student," Winblad said. "It didn't bother him at all that he had no idea how to maneuver that glider, that there might actually be some danger leaving the area."

Gates and Winblad would assign motifs to their brief vacations together. One vacation, for example, had a physics theme—they read as many physics books as they could and listened to tapes of the Feynman lecture series Gates had brought with him. Winblad could not believe how much Gates read; the breadth of his knowledge sometimes overwhelmed her. For a simple lunch at Burger King, Gates once brought along four magazines to read, including *Scientific American* and his favorite, the *Economist.* Nonetheless, there were significant gaps in what Gates read. When a writer from the *New Yorker* approached him for an interview, a nonplussed Gates responded, "What's the *New Yorker*?"

The always competitive Gates loved to test his knowledge against others', especially when there was something to win or lose. The betting usually escalated into double or nothing, with a few side bets. One time, Gates bet with some friends about which year the MGM Hotel in Las Vegas burned down. To verify the date, the group had to call the MGM. The game went on throughout the evening, and by the end, Gates had lost about $1,200.

"Once Bill had been betting someone and it kept going double or nothing," said a friend of Winblad's. "Bill made a side deal that worked out to his advantage, and someone said, 'Isn't that typical of Bill; double or nothing just won't do for him.' But that's why Bill is Bill."

Winblad, who is fluent in "Gates-speak," once described Gates as "massively parallel" with "extraordinary bandwidth." The term "massively parallel" refers to a configuration of hundreds of thousands of independent microprocessors teaming up in parallel structure, functioning like a supercomputer to solve a problem. "Bandwidth" refers to one's intelligence, or the amount of information one can absorb.

This massively parallel man could also be very entertaining, according to Winblad. Gates was a fabulous story teller, often resorting to theatrics to make a point or tell a story over dinner.

"If he has a story to tell, it doesn't matter if there are four people in the restaurant or a thousand," she said. "Bill will jump up from the table, stand somewhere and start acting out the story. It's no longer, 'Let me recount to you what happened.' It's now *Hamlet*! It becomes more theater than story telling. Years ago, when no one knew who Bill was, he would do this kind of stuff and who would care? But now, he's totally, totally unconscious that half the people in that restaurant are probably mumbling to the other person, 'Is that Bill Gates over there, jumping up and down and waving his arms?' And this includes things like jumping up in the air, even jumping over the furniture in a restaurant to prove a point."

According to friends, Gates and Winblad talked of marriage at one point. Winblad reportedly wanted to get married, but Gates did not. He felt he didn't have time for a wife. Microsoft was his first love. After almost three years, the two broke up.

Before long, Gates was going out with other women. But he and Winblad would remain good friends, and her picture still hangs on the wall of his office at Microsoft.

In the winter of 1986, Bill Gates found himself in a Seattle courtroom, listening to an attorney compare MS-DOS to a dog named Spud. Seattle Computer Products, the mom-and-pop business that once owned exclusive rights to the operating system that had helped make Microsoft the second largest computer software company in the world, was suing Microsoft for $60 million. Kelly Corr, one of the attorneys for Rod Brock, owner of Seattle Computer, was trying to explain the suit to the jury in his opening remarks. It was a highly technical case that had grown to fill eight volumes and hundreds of pages in the months leading up to trial. As he began his opening statement, Corr placed a bronze statue of a dog on a table so everyone could see it.

"I bet you thought this was a case about computers," Corr said. "Well, it's really a case about dogs. Rod Brock used to have this mut named Spud and Bill Gates came to him one day and said, 'I'm really into dogs and I would like to raise and breed dogs and if you give me this dog Spud I'll turn him into a champ and as part of the deal I'll always give you the pick of the litter.' "

As he sat with his mother listening to the dog story, Gates started rocking back and forth, a sure sign of interest. A lot was riding on the outcome of what was a potentially crippling lawsuit for his company.

The dispute had started months before when Brock decided to sell Seattle Computer Products. The business had gone under. About the only asset Brock had left was the license he had received when he signed over ownership rights to DOS for $50,000 that day in Paul Allen's office back in 1981. The license allowed Seattle Computer to continue to sell DOS with its computer hardware. And Microsoft also had agreed to provide Seattle Computer with updated versions of the operating system. Since Brock did not have to pay any royalties to Microsoft for DOS, which was now an industry standard, the perpetual license could be worth millions to a company with computers to sell.

Brock planned to offer the license to the highest bidder. He had in mind someone like the Tandy Corporation. But first, he gave Microsoft an opportunity to buy back the license. In a letter to Gates, he wrote that he had decided to sell Seattle Computer, and that as Seattle Computer's agreement with Microsoft constituted its largest asset, it would likely have "significant value" to manufacturers of computers based on the MS-DOS operating system. "We believe the value of Seattle Computer to be approximately $20 million. Before making presentations to potential buyers, we want to see if you might have an interest in purchasing Seattle Computer."

Brock did not have to wait long for a response. Jon Shirley fired off a reply the day he received the letter, claiming to be shocked at Seattle Computer's "exaggerated interpretation" of the agreement.

When Shirley informed Brock his license to sell DOS was nontransferable, Brock sued. Brock was represented by the firm of Bogle & Gates (no relation), one of Seattle's largest and most prestigious law offices. Microsoft's legal counterattack was led by David McDonald, a fluent computer programmer and Harvard Law School graduate, and a partner in Shidler McBroom Gates & Lucas.

Seattle Computer was the only company left with a royalty-free license from Microsoft to sell its money-making DOS product. In a strategic move earlier in the year, Gates had reclaimed a similar license given to Tim Paterson, the author of DOS. After leaving Microsoft in 1982, Paterson had gone back to work for Seattle Computer for only a short while before forming his own computer company, Falcon Technology. As payment for some programming work Paterson did for Microsoft, Paul Allen gave him a license to package DOS with Falcon hardware products. By 1986, however, Falcon was failing, and Paterson was considering an offer from a group of foreign businessmen who wanted to buy Falcon just to get their hands on the invaluable DOS license. Paterson met with Gates, who was irate. After some tense negotiating, Microsoft bought Falcon's assets for $1 million, and Paterson returned to work for Microsoft, where he remains today.

The trial with Seattle Computer lasted three weeks. Gates was at the court room for much of the time, usually accompanied by his mother. Both he and Paul Allen had to testify. In the end, an out-of-court settlement was reached while the jury was deliberating. Microsoft paid Seattle Computer $925,000 and reclaimed the critical license for DOS. Brock's lawyers later took a straw poll of the jury and found it leaning 8–4 in his favor. Two jurors said their minds could have been changed by the majority had the deliberations lasted longer. All Brock needed was a 10–2 vote to win his suit.

As part of the settlement, attorneys for both sides agreed not to discuss details of their eleventh-hour negotiations to end the dispute. But Brock had been willing to settle all along for about a half-million dollars. Gates, however, refused. He told Microsoft's lawyer he had paid for DOS once; he was not going to pay for it again.

During the trial, Microsoft did offer Brock $50,000 to settle, an offer that was quickly rejected. Once the jury was sequestered for deliberations, the offer went up about $100,000 every couple of hours. Corr was surprised that Gates did not try to cut his losses and settle sooner before trial. "I used to sit there in court and say to myself, 'Why's this guy [Gates] in trial here wasting his time everyday? His time is so much more valuable. If he could buy Brock out for a half-million, it would be money well spent. . . .' I wasn't sure if he was just trying to squash Brock on the principal of the thing or what. . . . These guys [Microsoft] play hardball. They grind people. It almost doesn't make good business sense."

But after the trial, it made good business sense to Corr to go out and buy some of Microsoft's stock, which had nearly tripled in value since the company went public nine months earlier. "I thought, 'They are very hard-nosed businessmen, very tough. And they now have a lock on the market.'"

A number of people in the computer industry with complaints about the way Microsoft did business with them contacted the firm of Bogle & Gates when the trial was over and inquired about starting litigation of their own against Microsoft. No suits were ever filed as a result of those calls, but the complaints did show a deepening resentment of Microsoft's growing power and the way Chairman Bill exercised it.

Kelly Corr had occasion to square off against Microsoft's lawyers again not too long after the Seattle Computer settlement, this time in federal court in San Francisco over one of the first software piracy cases in the country. Authorities in the Bay Area had seized a boatload of pirated MS-DOS software. A group of Taiwanese entrepreneurs with an outfit called VCCP (Very Cheap Computer Products) claimed they had a legitimate license to sell copies of MS-DOS. Microsoft said they did not and sued. Although Corr had been hired to represent VCCP, he was not being paid as the case dragged on in pre-trial arguments. His Taiwanese clients would sometimes call him at home in the middle of the night, promising to pay up. They didn't. Finally, frustrated at doing so much expensive legal work for his firm for nothing, Corr decided to quit the case. But in federal court, an attorney must have the judge's permission to withdraw. Motions must be heard. Usually, opposing counsel is only too happy to agree to the withdrawal knowing their chance of winning the suit would strengthen considerably. But in this case, Microsoft opposed Corr's withdrawal. Seeing Corr's big Seattle law firm tied up in court, unable to make any money, was to their liking. It was payback time for the million-dollar judgment in the Seattle Computer case.

"Why did they do this?" Corr asked rhetorically. "You tell me. Like I said, they play hardball."

During negotiations of the million-dollar settlement with Seattle Computer, lawyers for Microsoft, in an attempt to get Rod Brock to settle the case cheaply, told him that even if he won the civil suit, he would lose in the end. Microsoft, they said, was working on a new operating system with IBM that would eventually make DOS look like the Model A Ford of the fast-moving personal computer industry.

"They kept saying, 'Even if you win everything, it's going to be worth squat two years from now because everyone is going to be in on this new operating system,'" said attorney Kelly Corr. "In hindsight, who was kidding who on that one?"

The operating system Microsoft was referring to, still under development in late 1986, was secretly known at the time as OS/2. It was designed to harness the power of a second generation of personal computers that were replacing the original PCs. When OS/2 was announced publicly in April of 1987, both Microsoft and IBM predicted it would become *the* operating system of the 1990s for personal computers. Instead, OS/2 turned out to be a huge flop. The joint venture between Microsoft and IBM produced not a Cadillac but an Edsel. The venture's failure would shake the computer industry to its very foundation.

The story of OS/2 is still being written. No one can say how it will end, or what surprising turns the plot will take. But the story begins in 1984, with a new personal computer called the PC/AT.

After the brilliant success of its PC, Big Blue had followed with several marketing disasters, the most notable of which was the $699 PC Junior, with a keyboard that one reporter described as resembling pieces of "Chiclets" chewing gum. Unfortunately for IBM, the tag stuck. But on August 14, 1984, two years and two days after the original PC had been unveiled in New York

City, IBM introduced the PC/AT ("AT" stood for Advanced Technology), a computer built around Intel's powerful new 80286 chip that ran on DOS 3.0. This computer, unlike the PC Junior, featured a streamlined keyboard based on IBM's popular Selectric typewriter. Don Estridge, the leader of the original Project Chess team, was counting on the PC/AT to make up for the disappointment of the PC Junior. IBM needed a hit, and even though the price for the PC/AT started at about $4,000, Estridge was convinced the new computer would attract customers who wanted to take advantage of the more powerful 286 chip.

The PC/AT had been developed with typical IBM secrecy, under the code name Salmon. This time, IBM even got Microsoft to install chicken wire in the ceiling of the room where about a dozen prototypes of the prized computer were kept. Microsoft programmers, busily perfecting the third version of DOS to run on the machine, jokingly called the room the Fish Tank.

Gates did not share IBM's enthusiasm for the 286 chip. He described the chip as "brain dead." He wanted IBM to wait and build its next computer around an even more advanced chip that Intel was working on, the 80386. The decision by IBM to go ahead with a personal computer strategy based on the 286 chip would prove to be a major blunder.

"Estridge ignored what Bill was telling him about the 386 and decided to introduce the 286 machine, and that was the key decision that created all the problems," said Stewart Alsop, editor and publisher of *PC Letter* and a respected authority on Gates and Microsoft. Estridge knew Gates was right about the 286 chip, but Estridge was under pressure from higher ups at IBM to market a successful PC after the failure of the PC Junior, according to Alsop. Estridge figured the 286 machine could keep the corporate dogs in Armonk off his heels until Intel's 386 chip was ready, probably by 1986.

Although the PC/AT was introduced with DOS 3.0, Gates realized the operating system was being pushed to the limits.

Something new was needed—a replacement for DOS. In 1985, Gates signed a long-term joint development agreement with IBM to create a new operating system from scratch, known at the time as Advanced DOS. Eventually, it took the name OS/2. IBM saw the new operating system as part of a grand strategy to link computers of all kinds, big and small. IBM wanted an operating system that would allow it to connect personal computers to its mainframes.

But the project soon ran into major technical problems because of the flawed 286 chip, which made it difficult for the chip to handle old software written for MS-DOS machines under the new operating system. Gates did not want to continue wasting time and money trying to develop the new operating system for the 286 chip. Unfortunately, the one person at IBM whom Gates might have been able to convince, Estridge, was killed on a stormy August evening in 1985 in the crash of Delta Air Lines Flight 191 at the Dallas-Forth Worth Airport. Though they often disagreed, Gates and Estridge had gotten along famously—probably because Estridge *would* argue with Gates. They had respected and trusted each other. Now Gates had to deal with Bill Lowe, who took over the Entry Level Division at Boca Raton. Although Lowe had convinced the corporate brass at IBM to approve Project Chess in 1980, he did not have Estridge's technical competence. Gates and Lowe professed mutual respect, but they had an arm's-length relationship.

"You now have a guy in charge who knows nothing about computers," Alsop said of Lowe.

Gates tried to make his case regarding the 286 chip, but Lowe would not listen. The new operating system, he said, had to work on the 286 chip. That chip represented the future. IBM had invested too much in the PC/AT and it could not abandon those customers.

In early 1986, during a retreat for Microsoft's application development team, Gates ranted at what he called IBM's "fucked up" strategy, according to one of the programmers who was there. "Bill said, 'Screw the people with the ATs; let's just make it [the new operating system] for the 386, so they can upgrade.' "

It was left to Compaq to do what IBM refused to do. In September of 1986, Compaq introduced a PC with Intel's 386 chip. The other clone computer makers had been waiting for IBM to make the move to the 386. After all, it was IBM that had always set the standard. When Compaq jumped in and took the lead, its gamble paid off handsomely. The Compaq Deskpro 386 was the most powerful personal computer on the market. By the time the fall Comdex rolled around that year, some of those other clone computer makers were showing off machines compatible with Compaq, but not IBM. According to Alsop, at the time Compaq introduced its new computer, IBM had not ordered a single 386 chip from Intel. IBM apparently had decided the chip was better suited from minicomputers. But once the Compaq Deskpro was out, IBM realized it had seriously miscalculated—and not only by ignoring the 386. Apple's Macintosh with its user-friendly graphics was finally starting to do well, and IBM did not have a graphical user interface in the works to go with the new operating system it was developing with Microsoft. Lowe finally realized IBM had to have a graphics system for OS/2—as Gates had been telling him all along.

Thus the stage was set for a fateful meeting between Gates and Lowe in Armonk, New York.

Gates would later tell Alsop that when he met with Lowe, he figured he had no chance of getting IBM to go along with developing Windows for OS/2.

"Gates walked in there thinking he had lost the account, when in fact he could have gotten anything he wanted," Alsop said. "He had been working so long and so hard to get IBM to buy into Windows and the 386 and he hadn't gotten anywhere. So he goes in and right off the bat offers to do whatever Lowe wants. Well, Bill Lowe, being a smart guy, takes advantage of it. . . . At that point Lowe drove a stake into the ground and said, 'Here are the things we are going to stand on.' "

Lowe told Gates IBM wanted OS/2 to run on the 386 chip, but he insisted it first work on the 286. He also agreed to license Windows for the new operating system but insisted the name be changed to Presentation Manager. More importantly, he convinced Gates to revise the graphical user interface and incorporate concepts of a graphics system used in IBM mainframe machines. What this meant, however, was that Microsoft's Windows for DOS would not be compatible with Windows for OS/2. Gates had wanted Windows to run with both systems.

Why would Gates, the ultimate tough-nosed negotiator, roll over so easily in dealing with Lowe? Gates was uncharacteristically deferential toward IBM executives, according to several Microsoft managers. Whenever he talked with someone from IBM, it was as if his mother was in the room with him. Gates was on his best behavior.

"Bill sort of had two modes," said Scott MacGregor, the Windows development manager Gates hired away from Xerox PARC. "For all the other OEMs he would be very confident and very self assured, and feel very comfortable telling them what the right thing to do was. But when he worked with IBM, he was always much more reserved, and quiet, and humble. It was really funny, because this was the only company he would be that way with. In meetings with IBM, this change in Bill was amazing."

MacGregor said he left Microsoft partly because he thought the company was making some strategic mistakes in the joint development work with IBM on OS/2. "IBM wanted to merge Presentation Manager and OS/2, and there were those of us [on the Windows team] who didn't feel like it was the right direction," MacGregor said.

Eventually, Windows began to take a back seat within the company in the push to develop Presentation Manager. At one point, after the meeting between Gates and Lowe in 1986, Steve Ballmer wanted to kill Windows entirely, arguing that Microsoft was splitting its resources by sticking with Windows. Ballmer was just being a good soldier. He had been responsible for maintaining good relations with IBM almost from the day Jack Sams first called on Microsoft from Boca Raton in the summer of 1980.

"I know from conversations with people at Microsoft in environments where they didn't have to bullshit me that they almost killed Windows," said Alsop. "It came down to Ballmer and Gates having it out. Ballmer wanted to kill Windows. Gates prevented him from doing it. Gates viewed it as a defensive strategy. Just look at Gates. Every time he does something, he tries to cover his bet. He tries to have more than one thing going at once. He didn't want to commit everything to OS/2, just on the off chance it didn't work. And in hindsight, he was right. Ballmer, because it was his job to keep the IBM account, wanted to go all the way. He wanted to make IBM happy."

Although Microsoft stuck with Windows, it soon had only a handful of people working on the project, a far cry from the more than 30 programmers who worked non-stop getting the first version of Windows out the door. The emphasis at Microsoft clearly had shifted to OS/2 and Presentation Manager.

For the programmers at Microsoft, working with IBM became a clash of very different cultures. Compared to free-spirited Microsoft, IBM was as stodgy as some of the command names it wanted to incorporate into Presentation Manager. IBM insisted that Microsoft change the name of some of the zippy commands Gates had used in Windows. For example, the "Zoom" and "Icon" commands, which shrank the size of the work space, were changed to "Maximize" and "Minimize" in Presentation Manager.

Big Blue managed the OS/2 project by committee, and it took a long time to get things done through such formal channels. While Microsoft programmers worked in small, tightly integrated teams, IBM took just the opposite approach. It had hundreds of people working on OS/2 in Boca Raton and at the IBM lab in Winchester, England. Programmers working on the OS/2 project at IBM were only too aware of the company's ineffective bureaucratic structure. The *Wall Street Journal* reported on an allegorical memo making the rounds among IBM programmers that told how IBM lost a rowing race to Microsoft. An IBM task force, appointed to look into the loss, found that Microsoft had eight people rowing and one steering, while IBM had eight people steering and one rowing. The task force recommended that the one rower should row harder.

Neal Friedman, the young programmer who had joined Microsoft after seeing the "Today" show feature on Gates, recalled spending a couple days in Boca Raton trying to work out some technical problems on OS/2. Wherever he went, an IBM chaperone followed, even to the restroom. An IBM manager had to sign for him just to get access to a computer.

"The project was extremely frustrating for people at Microsoft, and for people at IBM, too," Friedman said. "It was a clash of two companies at opposite ends of the spectrum. At IBM, things got done very formally. Nobody did anything on their own. You went high enough to find somebody who could make a decision. . . . You couldn't change things without getting approval of the joint design review committee. It took weeks even to fix a tiny little bug, to get approval for anything."

On the other hand, Microsoft ended up adopting some IBM methods. IBM was fanatical about testing a product during the development stages. Friedman said when he joined Microsoft, there were on average two testers for every 40 programmers. After a couple of years working with IBM on OS/2, Microsoft had nearly one tester for every programmer.

IBM publicly announced the joint OS/2 project with Microsoft in April 1987. At the same time, IBM also introduced what it said was its next generation of personal computers, the PS/2 (for Personal Systems). The new machines represented an aggressive effort by IBM to regain lost industry momentum. The clone makers had been trouncing IBM in the marketplace for several years, and IBM had lost control of the personal computer market. Clones were selling as much as 30 percent below the cost of similar IBM machines. IBM decided to go after the clone market with the PS/2. About half the technology in the PS/2 machines was developed by IBM, making it much harder to copy than the original PC. But of the four new PS/2 machines introduced by IBM, only one used the 386 chip. The others were based on the "brain dead" 286 microprocessor.

"The development of OS/2 will open up a whole new class of applications," Microsoft's Jon Shirley predicted confidently. The new operating system was designed to run on any IBM or IBM-compatible machine that used the 286 or 386 chip, including the PS/2 models. But OS/2 was not available to customers until late 1987. And Presentation Manager would not be shipped until nearly a year after that.

At the fall Comdex in 1987, IBM demonstrated OS/2 on its new line of computers. For most of the 90,000 people who jammed the show, this was what they most wanted to see—future industry trends. Although there was great enthusiasm for OS/2 among the crowd at Comdex, there were also skeptics. Pete Peterson, executive vice-president of WordPerfect Corporation, which made the best-selling word processing program of the same name, predicted that many computer users would not want to switch over to the new operating system. Why would they need to? DOS worked just fine. And he questioned Microsoft's commitment to OS/2. He suggested Microsoft went along on OS/2 in order to get IBM to endorse Windows in the form of Presentation Manager.

"Microsoft has a religious approach to the graphical user interface," Peterson told a reporter for the *San Jose Mercury News*. "If Microsoft could choose between improved earnings and growth and bringing the graphical user interface to the world, they'd pick the graphical user interface."

Microsoft's development of Presentation Manager and OS/2 with IBM had been making the folks at Apple Computer very nervous. Security analysts who followed Apple wondered how the company would respond to this new threat to the Macintosh. But Apple was planning its own surprise.

On March 17, 1988, Apple Computer, Microsoft's longtime business ally and competitor, one of its industry brethren, filed an 11-page copyright suit in federal court in San Jose, accusing Microsoft of stealing visual display features of the Macintosh computer in the latest version of Windows.

Just the day before, Gates had met with Apple Chairman John Sculley on other business. Sculley had said nothing about a lawsuit or even hinted at any unhappiness with Microsoft. When Gates learned of the suit, he was dumbfounded as well as angry that Apple had provided copies of the suit to the press before telling Microsoft.

"He never mentioned it to me . . . not one word," Gates told the *San Jose Mercury News* of his meeting with Sculley the day before Apple dropped its bombshell. "So I told people at first, when the rumors started, that it wasn't true. Then we found out they'd called all these reporters and sent them all a copy of the lawsuit. This was a massive [public relations] attack. . . . We're confused. I'm not kidding. I've been involved in a lot of lawsuits and every lawsuit I've been in, I've thought, 'I hope we're OK.' But not this one. You have to wonder—if they're rational people—what are they thinking. . . . Apple is using the press to send a message. The suit is supposed to strike fear into people's hearts and make them think that Apple invented this stuff and not Xerox."

What Apple wanted, industry insiders agreed, was to torpedo the plans of archrival IBM to develop a personal computer with the same easy-to-use graphics of the Macintosh. The suit, they said, was aimed as much at Presentation Manager as Windows. "Apple is saying between the lines, 'Watch out IBM, we'll come and get you if you use Windows,' " Stewart Alsop was quoted as saying the day the suit was filed.

Not only Gates but the entire personal computer industry was caught off guard by the suit. It hit like an earthquake in the

Silicon Valley, sending tremors not only up the West Coast to the Silicon Forest outside Seattle but across the country. No one had expected Apple to counter the latest IBM threat with a lawsuit. Although opinion was mixed on how successful Apple might be in court, there was general agreement in the industry that the suit could have a chilling effect on software development for Windows. Microsoft had been pushing to establish Windows as an industry standard and to get software companies to write Windows applications. It was now pushing equally hard for Presentation Manager.

"Although Apple has a right to protect the results of its development and marketing efforts, it should not try to thwart the obvious direction of the industry," said Lawrence Magid, a Silicon Valley computer industry analyst. He and others pointed out, as Gates had before, that Apple, when it developed the Macintosh displays, used technology perfected at Xerox PARC. Critics of the suit said Apple apparently had lost the entrepreneurial spirit that transformed it from a garage operation into the world's second biggest computer company.

"In general, it's a horrible thing," Andy Hertzfeld, the former Apple programmer who had worked on the Macintosh, said of the suit. "Apple could end up really hurting itself."

Dan Bricklin, who developed VisiCalc, the first spreadsheet program, had a similar reaction: "If Apple is trying to push this as far as they appear to be trying to push it, this is a sad day for the software industry in America." Writing software, Bricklin said, is not the same as writing a book. Software builds on what was there before.

In its suit, Apple said it had granted Microsoft in 1985 a limited license to use Macintosh-like features in Windows 1.0, but features in Windows 2.03 were not covered by the license. Apple said Windows 2.03 violated 13 different copyrights. Windows 2.03 was the basis for Presentation Manager, which had not been officially released at the time the suit was filed. In addition to Microsoft, the suit named Hewlett-Packard as a defendant and accused the Palo Alto company of copyright violations in New Wave, a Windows-based product for IBM compatible machines. Like Windows 2.03, New Wave had been announced but not yet shipped. Hewlett-Packard asked Apple if it could license Macintosh technology, but Apple refused, according to the suit. Since New Wave needed Windows 2.03 to operate, in essence the suit was really over Windows.

Apple argued in its suit that Windows 2.03 and New Wave had the distinctive "look and feel" of the visual displays of Macintosh. But there were differences between Macintosh displays and those in Windows. The Macintosh, for example, could display files as icons. In Windows, files were displayed only by a name. And the Macintosh erased a file by dragging the icon or file name into a "trash can." With Windows, a mouse was used to highlight a file name, and "erase" was selected from a menu.

This was not the first time Apple had accused a competitor of copying visual display features of the Macintosh. A few years earlier, Apple had threatened to haul Digital Research into court over its Macintosh-like product GEM. Digital changed GEM to Apple's liking and avoided a court battle.

There was legal precedent for Apple's suit. In 1987, a federal court in Atlanta had ruled that Softklone Corporation infringed on Digital Communications Associates' copyright of the visual display of one of its programs.

Less than a month after the Apple filing, Microsoft counterattacked with a suit of its own, accusing Apple of breaking the 1985 licensing agreement and deliberating trying to damage Microsoft's business with negative publicity. Microsoft said Windows 2.03 was "virtually identical" to Windows 1.0, which was covered in the license from Apple. According to Microsoft, Apple wrote the company in 1986, saying the 1985 agreement was limited to Windows 1.0. Apple gave no explanation for the letter, the Microsoft suit said. Microsoft said Windows 2.03 should be covered under that 1985 agreement. It also argued that the graphical interface used in the Macintosh was not original to Apple and thus should not be protected by copyright.

As Apple had done, Microsoft also took its case to the press, faxing copies of formerly confidential agreements with Apple to reporters, including the disputed 1985 licensing agreement.

Apple subsequently filed additional court papers accusing Microsoft of using lies and threats to extract the 1985 licensing agreement. Apple said Microsoft threatened to stop work on vital applications for the Macintosh. Sculley, Apple's leader, had said pretty much the same thing in his book *Odyssey*, which was published shortly before the Apple lawsuit.

Gates disputed Sculley's version of events. He said Apple officials in 1985 had requested a meeting at Microsoft to talk about Windows 1.0 and brought along a "hot shot" lawyer who made threats about a lawsuit. Sculley was unaware, Gates said, of agreements Steve Jobs had made with Microsoft in 1982 to develop applications for the Macintosh.

"I informed Sculley about the agreements," Gates said. "We said, 'Come on, this isn't productive for our two companies to be doing this.' There was no threat from Microsoft. We never went to them and asked for a license. They're the ones who started things off."

After the suit was filed, there were several important pre-trial rulings. Early on, a federal judge ruled that Microsoft had a legal license under the 1985 agreement for many of the displays used in Windows 2.03. Still at issue, however, even today, is whether Microsoft copied the concept of overlapping Windows used in the Macintosh. Having to change such a critical aspect of Microsoft's Windows would be a costly setback. The judge also ruled that Microsoft could attempt to prove at trial that elements of the visual displays used in the Macintosh were copied from Xerox and thus should not be the basis for a copyright suit.

The various rulings in the Apple lawsuit have occasionally sent Microsoft's stock tumbling or soaring, depending on how legal experts interpreted the overall outcome. In March of 1989, after the court ruled that the 1985 agreement between Microsoft and Apple "was not a complete defense" for Microsoft, its stock price dropped nearly twenty-seven percent.

Steve Ballmer decided to take advantage of the panic selling by Wall Street traders, telling colleagues at Microsoft he thought the stock had been unduly pummeled by the unfavorable court ruling. Ballmer went out and purchased 935,000 shares of Microsoft stock on the open market for $46.2 million—his first purchase since the company went public in 1986. Ballmer bought the stock at an average price of $48.91 a share. Within a month, the stock had climbed to $53.25 a share and was still going up.

"It's nice to have that kind of money to put where your mouth is," said one Wall Street analyst.

If the real target of Apple's copyright lawsuit against Microsoft was actually OS/2 as many industry insiders suspected at the time, the Cupertino computer maker could have saved itself a lot of money in legal fees by doing nothing. As it turned out, its fears were unfounded. After all the media hype and industry anticipation, the much-ballyhooed operating system was a failure.

In early 1988, shortly after OS/2 was first shipped, IBM and Microsoft predicted sales would overtake DOS within two years. "During the next 10 years, millions of programmers and users will utilize this system," wrote Bill Gates in the foreword to a 1988 technical book on OS/2 by Gordon Letwin, systems architect for Microsoft.

But once they got a look at OS/2, others in the industry soon had a different opinion. "The broad market will turn its back on OS/2," predicted Jeffrey Tarter, publisher of the industry newsletter *Softletter*, in September of 1988. He was right. While technically impressive, OS/2 did not catch on for several reasons. At $325 a copy, it was more than twice as expensive as DOS. In order to use the new system, some PC owners had to spend $2,000 or more to update their existing hardware. For big corporate customers, this meant millions of dollars. Even if customers decided to switch over to the new operating system, there were few applications available to use with it. But the biggest obstacle OS/2 faced was from DOS. At the time OS/2 was introduced, DOS was used on more than 20 million personal computers. It accounted for thirty-eight percent of Microsoft's sales and nearly half its profits during the year that ended in June 1987. Gates had established an entrenched industry standard with DOS, just as he had set out to do, and loyal customers would not give it up easily.

By 1989, Gates was a lonely voice in the crusade for OS/2. Wrote Sandra Reed in a *Personal Computing* column in July of that year: "Once gospel, Gates' word now has to compete with disparate voices in a world that won't give up the DOS standard easily."

Gates professed not to be concerned about the miserable performance of OS/2 in the market place. "We are patient people," he told a reporter for *Business Week.* "All the progress is in the right direction."

He knew better, however. Within Microsoft, Gates had already started shifting programmers away from OS/2 to work on Windows. In 1988, Microsoft had introduced a second version of Windows designed for computers with the powerful 386 chip. Windows finally was starting to show promise. Sales were picking up. Gates had finally convinced software developers to write applications for Windows 2.0. Yet another, more advanced version, Windows 3.0, was already under development.

But Microsoft's continued tinkering with Windows was straining its relationship with IBM, which supported Presentation Manager. There were industry rumors of a serious rift between the two companies over how Windows should be positioned in relation to OS/2. As it turned out, the rumors were true. The marriage between the two companies was having problems. Gates was no longer dealing with Bill Lowe at IBM. Lowe's star had fallen, and he left for a job with Xerox. Replacing him as vice-president of IBM's desktop computer division was Jim Cannavino, a veteran of the company's mainframe division who was considered something of a hot shot. Although Cannavino had no experience with personal computers, he was smart and understood the technology much better than Lowe. But Cannavino didn't trust Gates. He felt Gates had manipulated Lowe into making wrong decisions about OS/2 to the benefit of Microsoft. In fact, Lowe had *not* listened to Gates, which is what caused all the problems in the first place. But Cannavino knew none of the history of OS/2.

"Jim became very suspicious of Microsoft and the relationship started to fall apart," said Stewart Alsop. "Had Lowe listened to Gates, none of the problems would exist."

At the fall Comdex in November of 1989, Microsoft and IBM attempted to present a scene of reconciliation. At a Sunday night dinner meeting attended by Gates and Cannavino, the two companies announced to about 30 software dealers that they were "strengthening" their agreement on OS/2. A joint press release described OS/2 as the "platform of the 90s." Microsoft would limit capabilities of Windows and add features to OS/2, the statement said. It suggested Windows would be used on less powerful computers and OS/2 on more powerful ones.

Two days after the dinner meeting, during a press conference at Comdex, Cannavino gave half-hearted praise for Windows. Some software developers took this lack of enthusiasm to mean Windows was going to be sacrificed for OS/2. When Gates read some of the comments about the demise of Windows in the press, particularly one from Jim Manzi, chief executive of Lotus Development Corporation, he was furious. Gates now flip-flopped and did just the opposite of what Microsoft had promised in the press release. Instead of backing off from Windows, he aggressively pushed ahead with version three, shifting even more programmers off the OS/2 project and further angering IBM.

It made good business sense for Microsoft to go with Windows, even if it meant risking the lucrative marriage with IBM. By the end of 1989, OS/2 accounted for less than one percent of all operating systems sold worldwide. DOS, meanwhile, had sixty-six percent of the market. And Windows 3.0 was designed to run on top of DOS, not on OS/2. It represented the culmination of six years of work and more than $100 million in development costs. About three million copies of the two earlier versions had been shipped, and most were now gathering dust. But Gates had doggedly hung in with Windows, refusing to give up his vision of making the PC as easy to use as the Macintosh.

Gates hoped the third time would be the charm. Windows 3.0, in his mind, would be vindication for all the criticism he had taken over the first version released in 1985. It would be the "cool" product he had first envisioned. Gates staked his reputation and the company's future on the success of Windows 3.0. He planned the biggest coming-out party for a software product in industry history. And if it worked, Microsoft would take a big bite out of Apple.

A huge grin like the Cheshire Cat's spreading across his face, Bill Gates hitched up the pants of his new suit, pushed up the glasses that had slipped down his nose, and strolled out onto the stage in his penny loafers. He walked slowly, as if to enjoy every last decibel of the roar of approval from the hundreds who had gathered in New York's Center City at Columbus Circle to hear the industry's software guru spread the word about Windows 3.0.

His mother Mary had flown in from Seattle just to be with her son this day. May 22, 1990 would prove to be one of the most exciting and rewarding days of Gates' young career.

Watching the glitzy event simultaneously on closed-circuit television in a half-dozen cities in the United States and seven more around the world, were an estimated 6,000 journalists, industry analysts, software developers, and various high-tech professionals. In London, Paris, Madrid, Singapore, Stockholm, Milan, and Mexico City, they crowded around big-screen televisions to watch satellite pictures of what had become the most hyped media event ever in the personal computer industry.

Some, caught up in the hoopla, were starting to sound a little giddy from Windows fever. "This is probably the most anticipated product in the history of the world," gushed one analyst from the prestigious firm of Smith Barney to a reporter for USA Today.

"If you think technology has changed the world in the last few years, hold on to your seats," said Paul Grayson, head of a Texas software company and a long-time Windows booster.

Even many skeptics who had once ridiculed Windows had become supporters. "Believe me, I have not been a Windows fan in the past. But from what I've seen this is really slick," said Nancy McSharry, an industry analyst with International Data Corporation.

On the West Coast, about 400 people crowded into the San Francisco Concourse to watch the multimedia production, which included a combination of Hollywood-style endorsements by industry figures and an MTV-like video hyping the new product. Up the coast in Seattle, at the world headquarters of Microsoft, hundreds of the company's more than 5,000 employees jammed a large auditorium to watch Chairman Bill via satellite. They cheered wildly when Gates brought on stage the "Win 3" team of some two dozen programmers who had spent the last two years developing this latest version of Windows.

Unlike 1985, when Windows 1.0 was introduced with few applications because it was so late getting to market, this time Gates had lined up every major player in the software industry, including Lotus Development Corporation, which had steadfastly refused to endorse Windows as early as a month before the big rollout in New York. The video tape for the Windows

3.0 bash featured Frank King, software vice-president of Lotus, dressed up like a maintenance worker, wiping a large window with a rag. Lotus had committed to spending millions to finally bring a version of 1-2-3 out for Windows. In fact, it had little choice. Microsoft's Excel for Windows had been closing in on the competition in the PC spreadsheet market.

The one-day extravaganza cost Microsoft a cool $3 million and change. It was, Gates said, "The most extravagant, extensive and expensive software introduction ever." Microsoft, which in 1990 would become the first computer software company to make a billion dollars in revenues, would spend another $10 million in the coming weeks promoting Windows 3.0. It planned to distribute 400,000 free demonstration copies. The high-profile ad campaign was further helped when Gates appeared on several television shows, including "Good Morning America." As usual with Gates, it was money well spent. Windows 3.0 quickly became the hottest selling computer software product ever. The price of Microsoft's stock headed up into the stratosphere, and Gates headed toward the top of *Forbes'* list of the 400 richest people in America.

As the second largest Microsoft stockholder, Paul Allen was moving up the list, too. Allen had come to New York not only to be with Gates for the Windows announcement but also to make one of his own. The day before the big Windows show, Allen stood in an elegant room of the New York City Public Library to announce Asymetrix's first product, called ToolBook, an application for Windows that let hobbyists create customized software. That Allen should choose a library to announce his company's first piece of software was not surprising, given his father's former position as associate director of libraries at the University of Washington.

Only a couple weeks before the New York announcement, Allen had rejoined Microsoft's board of directors. "This is something that Bill and I have been talking about for a number of years," Allen said at the time. "Bill and I have worked together in the past and productive things have usually come of that relationship."

While they were in New York for their respective product introductions, the two old friends went to a downtown sports bar to have a few beers and watch the televised playoff game between Portland and Phoenix of the National Basketball Association. A basketball fanatic who keeps a basketball in the back seat of his Porsche, Allen had bought the Portland Trail Blazers for $70 million in 1988. He could easily afford to do so. In 1990, *Forbes* listed Allen's wealth at $1.2 billion. Allen not only bought the team; he also bought the team its own airplane, a plush 21-seat jet once owned by hotel magnate Leona Helmsley. Allen had the plane equipped with a host of high-tech gadgets, such as digital readouts in the cabin to show speed and altitude. He later bought his own jet and routinely flew to Portland from his home in Seattle to watch his team. Gates occasionally went with him.

"There was a lot of excitement working at Microsoft, but for pure joy, it didn't compare with this," Allen said of owning a professional basketball team.

Within four months of the New York coming-out party, Windows 3.0 had sold a million copies. "There is nothing that even compares or comes close to the success of this product," said Tim Bajarin, executive vice-president of Creative Strategies Inc., a research and consulting firm. "Microsoft is on a path to continue dominating everything in desktop computing when it comes to software. No one can touch them or slow them down." For the first time, computer users could spend $150 for a copy of Windows 3.0 and make a $2,500 PC clone as easy to operate as a $4,000 Macintosh.

Wrote *PC Computing:* "When the annals of the PC are written, May 22, 1990, will mark the first day of the second era of IBM-compatible PCs. On that day, Microsoft released Windows 3.0. And on that day, the IBM-compatible PC, a machine hobbled by an outmoded, character-based operating system and seventies style programs, was transformed into a computer that could soar in a decade of multitasking graphical operating environments and powerful new applications. Windows 3.0 gets right what its predecessors—VisiOn, GEM, earlier versions of Windows, and OS/2 Presentation Manager—got wrong. It delivers adequate performance, it accommodates existing DOS applications, and it makes you believe that it belongs on a PC."

About the only people who were not saying great things about Windows were at Apple. "Windows is simply an endorsement of what we've been doing all along," said Jim Davis, director of systems software marketing at Apple. Using Windows on a PC was like putting a Rolls Royce front on a Volkswagen Bug—a pretty face, but still a Bug, he said.

To Microsoft, that was just Apple's usual spin control. Chairman Bill had indeed taken a bite of the Apple. And it tasted good.

But he had also left some teeth marks on IBM, and that was not good for their continued relationship. While Gates was basking in the glow of the success of Windows, OS/2 was languishing in the shadows. And the folks in Armonk were as unhappy as those on the other side of the country in Cupertino.

"The success of Windows 3.0 has already caused OS/2 acceptance to go from dismal to cataclysmic," *InfoWorld* said three months after Windows 3.0 was introduced. "Analysts have now pushed back their estimates of when OS/2 will gain broad acceptance to late this decade, with some predicting that the so-called next generation operating system is all but dead."

In promoting Windows, Microsoft was plotting a strategy that was steering it further and further away from IBM. Microsoft had proved with Windows that it didn't need Big Blue's support to successfully launch a new product. Software, not hardware, was driving the industry, and IBM had to play to Gates' strength. And Gates knew it. By September of 1990, troubles between the two companies had become a growing source of industry gossip and speculation. All communications between the technical staffs of the two companies had reportedly stopped. Ten years earlier, Bill Gates had rushed into a department store in Boca Raton to buy a new tie because he wanted to look his best when he went before IBM to argue that Microsoft develop the operating system for the first IBM personal computer. Now, the ties that bound the world's biggest computer maker and biggest software maker seemed as threadbare as an old pair of jeans that had gone through too many washes.

Executives at Microsoft and IBM downplayed any differences. Steve Ballmer denied there were conflicts. "You may not understand our marriage," Ballmer told *Business Week*, "but we are not getting divorced."

But events seemed to suggest otherwise.

In September, IBM joined with Metaphor Computer Systems in a venture called Patriot Partners to create software that would allow a program such as desktop publishing to run on a variety of operating systems. Thus, programmers would work with Metaphor technology rather than Microsoft's when creating new software. Stewart Alsop called the deal the "opening salvo" in a seven-year plan by IBM to regain control from Microsoft.

Alsop had recently had an encounter with Gates that convinced him the ten-year marriage with IBM was on the rocks. Gates was supposed to address a software entrepreneurs' forum in Palo Alto, but he was running late after an all-day meeting with IBM's Jim Cannavino in Milwaukee, Wisconsin. Gates arrived about five minutes before he was to speak to about 600 people. Afterwards, Gates and Alsop went to a bar at the Il Fornaio in Palo Alto, next to the hotel Gates was booked in. The speech had gone well, and Gates was really up and having a good time. Alsop, knowing IBM and Microsoft were going through a terrible strain, decided it was the right time to ask about Cannavino.

"Whenever you talk to him," Alsop said of Gates, "if you raise any subject about personal computers he will immediately focus on it, and start rocking back and forth, looking you straight in the eye, asking the fundamental questions. You've got to remember, he really knows everything. He knows the right questions to ask to find out if you are just bullshitting him. So I asked him. 'What do you think of Jim Cannavino?' By luck, I hit a hot button. He started ranting and raving, saying 'You would not believe what this guy was telling me,' how Cannavino was telling him, Bill Gates, how he should be running Microsoft.

"It was clear," Alsop said, "that Gates had to restrain himself from saying more about Jim."

On September 10, *InfoWorld*, the highly regarded trade publication, added fuel to the debate about a Microsoft and IBM split when it reported that Gates had taken a group of executives from Lotus Development Corporation to dinner and after a few too many drinks began trashing IBM and Cannavino, saying IBM wouldn't be around in ten years and that he, Gates, would rule all—sort of a Microsoft Über Alles. One of the Lotus executives went home and wrote a memo about the incident. It eventually found its way to Cannavino's desk, according to *InfoWorld*.

The story, by *InfoWorld* gossip writer Robert Cringely, was picked up by the national press, and Microsoft issued a strong denial that Chairman Bill had ever said such things about their good friends at IBM. Most everyone assumed Microsoft's "thought police," as the company's aggressive public relations people were called by some in the media, were trying to cover Gates' ass.

"If the story is true. . . ," wrote *InfoWorld*, "it shows that Bill Gates is no diplomat. It also shows the depth of the troubles in the relationship between IBM and Microsoft."

When George Gilbert read the story in *InfoWorld* about Gates trashing IBM after one too many drinks, he was shocked and disturbed. Not only was the magazine's account wrong, but he couldn't understand how his private memo about an evening spent with Gates, a memo which he intended *only* for the eyes of his superiors at Lotus, had fallen into the hands of Jim Cannavino at IBM.

The six-page, single-spaced memo had been written the first week in May just after the annual Computer Bowl, where the industry's best and brightest get together to see who knows the most computer trivia. It's a playful version of the old College Bowl that was so popular in the 60's. In 1990, the Computer Bowl was held at the World Trade Center in Boston, not far from Cambridge and the headquarters of Lotus Development Corporation.

Gilbert, a product manager at Lotus, had met Gates the previous year when he spoke at nearby Harvard. Gilbert was a big fan. Gates was his hero, a fellow techie who had made good— a sort of *Revenge of the Nerds*. "He showed all those guys in suits who walk around saying 'We know business and you're just a nerd,' " said Gilbert. "What's appealing about him is that his success has not gone to his head. Through it all, what still counts is making good products."

When they met at Harvard, Gates had put Gilbert in touch with some of his people at Microsoft about a job, but after an interview Gilbert decided he was not ready to leave Lotus or the Boston area. Gilbert next saw Gates at the Computer Bowl, and when it was over he went up to him to say hello. His two young companions from Lotus, Mary Fenstermaker and Jenise Ellis, also wanted to meet *the* Bill Gates. None of the three were close to being "executives," as the *InfoWorld* story would describe them. Gates asked the three if they would like to talk some more back at his hotel, the Boston Harbor. They met in the bar.

Contrary to the report in *InfoWorld,* no one got drunk, according to Gilbert. The bar closed less than an hour after they arrived, and the most anyone had was a couple of drinks. They talked for more than four hours.

"It was like we had gone to the mountaintop and heard the words of God," said Gilbert.

Gates talked openly about himself until the sun came up, as he never does in interviews with journalists, where he tries to keep the focus on Microsoft or the industry. But that night in the bar of the Boston Harbor, Gates talked so much about himself that Gilbert and his friends had to keep steering the conversation back to industry issues—they were interested in insights on the industry from the industry's leading spokesperson. Although Gates thoroughly enjoyed himself, he would come to regret that his candor that night was later used by his bitter enemy, Lotus Chairman Jim Manzi, to further drive a wedge between Microsoft and IBM.

Surprisingly, Gates told the three that developing a 16-bit version of OS/2 was one of the best moves he ever made, despite the widespread perception that it was a mistake. He felt it helped cement Microsoft's relationship with IBM; but now "the forces were shifting so that IBM needed [Gates] more than he needed them," as the memo stated.

Gates admitted that Microsoft had been dragging its feet on the next version of OS/2, which still had a lot of bugs in it. "What incentive does Microsoft have to get it out the door before Windows 3.0?" he asked. He predicted that six months after Windows 3.0 was introduced, Windows would have a greater market share than Presentation Manager ever would. "OS/2 applications won't have a chance," Gates said.

At the time, Lotus had invested heavily in developing applications to run on OS/2, as had others in the industry. These companies would later complain they were hoodwinked by Microsoft into staying with OS/2 long after Microsoft had secretly decided to give up on the new operating system and concentrate on Windows. According to them, this gave Microsoft a huge advantage when Windows 3.0 was released, a charge Gates would strongly deny.

Gates did not, as the *InfoWorld* article stated, mention Jim Cannavino that night, according to Gilbert. Nor did he "trash"

IBM. What he did say was that he believed IBM would "fold" in seven to ten years.

Gilbert and his friends were amazed by how much Gates knew about Apple and IBM at the highest levels. "We got the impression that *nothing* happens within IBM without his knowledge," Gilbert wrote in his memo. "We also got the impression he knows everything going on at Apple."

Gates went on to talk extensively about the culture and organization of Microsoft, and why it worked. The corporate hierarchy was flat, with few layers at the top, according to Gates, who didn't believe in having a lot of vice-presidents. Too many companies, he said, handed out vice-president titles like "water to lambs." At Microsoft, Gates had nine business unit managers—eight men and one woman. Some came out of MBA programs; others rose through the ranks. Each unit was organized the same way, with a product manager, development manager, program manager, and user editor. The program managers, Gates explained, had the most important jobs at Microsoft, because they were responsible for product specifications.

To make sure development groups remained on the cutting edge, the company resorted to Darwinian management methods—survival of the fittest. Every six months, developers were reviewed by their peers and those in the bottom five percent were fired. "There are other jobs out there," Gates told Gilbert. "If they don't have what it takes to work at Microsoft, they can go to Boeing or back East."

Microsoft had managed to keep its development teams small, even as the company had grown, an accomplishment Gates was proud of. He said he had only 18 developers working on the company's entire spreadsheet business, and he wanted to get that number down to no more than 14. Lotus, he pointed out, had about 120 programmers in its spreadsheet business. It takes discipline to stay lean, Gates told them.

Gates went on to talk about Microsoft's "architects," the seven software samurai who advise Gates and explore new technologies. The seven, who included Charles Simonyi and Gordon Letwin, are the heavy thinkers of the company, he said. (Each programmer is rated at one of six levels, from 10 to 15. When a programmer makes it to 15 and becomes an architect, it's a little like being made a partner in a law firm. Huge stock options follow a huge party.)

Microsoft had been successful, Gates felt, because of the caliber of people it hired. Prospective employees must display ambition, intelligence, expertise, and business judgment. But it was intelligence that counted the most.

Gates pushed his people hard because he wanted them to be better. Each day, he said, they should come to work thinking "I want to win." They also must understand the shifting priorities between work and family, which sometimes meant working weekends. The combination of ambition and wanting to win every single day is what Gates referred to as "being hard core."

Shifting the conversation back to himself, Gates also described the new "home" he was building, a $10 million-plus affair with giant high-resolution screens on the walls of all public rooms, displaying images from a computer CD database.

Looking forward into the industry's future, Gates predicted the software race would be over in 20 years. By then, he felt, computers themselves would be writing better software than people.

The day after their evening rap session with Gates, Gilbert and his companions from Lotus met at a beach and decided to write up as much as they could remember of the meeting. "It had been incredibly exciting," said Gilbert, explaining why he wanted to record Gates' thoughts. In addition, Gates had said some things that Gilbert felt was important information to be shared with others at Lotus. Gates, for example, had asked Gilbert why Lotus never sent any of its technical people out to Microsoft to hear about things the company was doing. Gilbert thought senior technical people at Lotus should know Gates had essentially extended them an invitation.

One of the three who had been present that evening, Mary Fenstermaker, didn't agree with the decision to write the memo and refused to put her name to it. "I didn't want to have anything to do with it," she said. "My impression was that Bill Gates had no idea, nor did he expect, a memo to result from our chat."

Nonetheless, Gilbert went ahead, sending the memo to four people at Lotus. One of them, Bruce Johnston, sent it on to Lotus Chairman Jim Manzi, titling it "Notes from a Gates Date."

"The following report is blunt, unedited and liable to piss you off," Johnston wrote of the Gilbert memo.

It was Manzi who told his secretary to send a copy to Jim Cannavino at IBM, according to a well-placed source at Lotus. Manzi had had a long, unhappy history with Gates. They had not spoken in three years as of 1990, nor have they spoken since (although they occasionally trade verbal jabs through the media).

A former journalist who rose through marketing to become the head of Lotus, Manzi took over as chairman in 1986 when Mitch Kapor left to pursue other interests. At the time, Gates and Kapor were negotiating a merger with a 50–50 split. Manzi blocked the deal, and he and Gates had avoided each other ever since. The fact that the merger didn't go through was probably just as well for Microsoft, which overtook Lotus in 1987 as the world's number one software company. On August 16 of that year, when Gates got the numbers from his business office for the previous fiscal year, he sent an electronic message to Microsoft employees telling them how excited he was. The company, he pointed out, was number one in every respect—sales, profits, units, leadership, and people.

Manzi, in sending the Gilbert memo to Cannavino, seemed to be attempting to fuel the fire smoldering between Microsoft and IBM. George Gilbert came to regret his decision to write it. "It was my misfortune and bad judgment to put myself in a situation where something I did could be used against Bill Gates," he said.

Exactly one week after *InfoWorld* reported on the Lotus memo, Microsoft and IBM announced they were reaffirming their relationship by recasting it. In fact, it was double talk. Cannavino told reporters IBM would take over much of the OS/2 development, while Microsoft was free to push Windows. The *New York Times* likened the announcement to "an earthquake that rattles windows and breaks china but leaves the roof intact."

As a result of their decision, Microsoft quickly shifted about 160 of its programmers who had been working on OS/2 over to Windows. The announcement that the two companies were going to follow separate paths left software developers more confused than ever about which direction the industry was headed. Who was going to set the standard? Would there even be a standard? Should they stick with Microsoft and its DOS and Windows or go with IBM's OS/2 and Presentation Manager?

"It's the Balkanization of the desktop," said Jim Manzi in a much-quoted remark.

Executives at IBM and Microsoft continued to insist there was nothing fundamentally wrong in the relationship. They were still partners, Cannavino said. Few in the industry believed it. The general feeling was that Microsoft, not IBM, was now riding the crest of the personal computing wave.

There was certainly a lot more interest in Windows than OS/2 at the fall Comdex in Las Vegas two months later, where it was announced that Microsoft would cosponsor a new trade show called Windows World Exposition Conference in May 1991, to coincide with the spring Comdex. Gates was keynote speaker at the Las Vegas show. He recalled for the audience that when he had last addressed the group in 1983, he spent a total of ten minutes preparing his speech, and his father ran the slide projector. This time, Gates had a polished, Madison Avenue look. He wore an expensive black suit and used a $50,000 movie-quality video called "Twin Points," a takeoff on "Twin Peaks," the popular TV show shot in the Seattle area, to enhance his presentation. For this speech, Gates had rehearsed for about

12 hours with Jerry Weissman, the Silicon Valley speech doctor. Weissman had helped the chief executives of several computer companies get over their phobia of public speaking or, as in the case of Gates, taught them the elements of a more polished and forceful delivery. But Weissman could do little about Gates' squeaky voice, which still cracked occasionally like a teenager's.

One of Gates' themes in his spring Comdex speech was what he called "information at your fingertips," in which the personal computer becomes a high-tech supermarket, with customers able to choose from a range of text, voice, and video information.

A month after Comdex, IBM announced it was joining forces with Microsoft and other computer makers to develop multimedia technology. But IBM and Microsoft continued to square off over what should be the standard of the present—Windows or OS/2. At the end of January 1991, the *Wall Street Journal* reported that Microsoft was abandoning OS/2 entirely. It would be three more months before Microsoft admitted as much. The divorce was final.

"Microsoft is now driving the industry, not IBM," Fred Gibbons of *Software Publishing* told the *Journal* in January. He added that Microsoft "won the game on fundamentals, not on Machiavellian techniques."

Many people who had done business with Microsoft would soon publicly disagree with such a nice-guy assessment when another bombshell was dropped on the industry with the announcement that the Federal Trade Commission was investigating Microsoft for possible antitrust violations. Microsoft, it seemed, was in the same dilemma Big Blue had just gotten out of ten years before when the two climbed into bed together. Microsoft now had to contend with perhaps its most fearsome adversary yet, the might and muscle of the U.S. government.

The first public whiff of trouble regarding the FTC came not from Microsoft, the industry press, or the hordes of reporters from the national media who for years had been flocking to the Silicon Forest outside Seattle to write about the company. Instead, the news came from a Wall Street analyst.

Late on the afternoon of March 11, 1991, Rick Sherlund, an analyst at Goldman Sachs & Company, Microsoft's investment banker and one of the principal underwriters for its public offering five years earlier, issued a report suggesting that a "probe" of Microsoft was underway.

Microsoft issued its own brief statement the next morning. The company admitted it was under investigation by the Federal Trade Commission, and it was cooperating fully. Bill Neukom, Microsoft's vice-president for law and corporate affairs, said Microsoft had been notified by letter the previous June of the FTC probe. The scope of the investigation, Neukom said, was narrowly focused on the joint news release by IBM and Microsoft at the Comdex trade show in Las Vegas in 1989, a statement that was intended to clear up industry confusion between Windows and OS/2, and to squelch rumors of a serious feud between the companies. That five-page, double-spaced statement on IBM letterhead, issued on November 13, said Microsoft would hold back features for Windows in order to help industry acceptance of the OS/2 operating system. Neukom said the FTC was concerned that the statement indicated anticompetitive collusion. Neukom went on to say that Microsoft had quickly changed its mind about the strategy outlined in the news release and included the features in Windows 3.0.

As far as Microsoft was concerned, the FTC concerns now seemed moot. How could the company be accused of crippling the product when Windows was clearly a success? But it was just such a flip-flop that had competitors, especially those who had developed applications for OS/2, grumbling about Microsoft's unfair trade practices.

As usual in such matters, the FTC had nothing to say publicly about what it was after. In an interview with the *New York Times*, Gates said he had talked with the FTC investigators, who assured him they were looking only at potential problems raised by the November press release. "Every question in the case, every document requested, related only to the IBM–Microsoft announcement," Gates said.

But the din from the press was loud and damaging. Microsoft's stock dropped nearly $7 a share to $95.75 in the two days following the disclosure, as nervous shareholders bailed out. "Antitrust" is one of the most feared words in the lexicon of American business. IBM had spent 13 years, created an entire legal department, and filed more than 200,000 pages of court briefs defending itself from antitrust action, all the while seeing profits decline. IBM won, but another company, AT&T, lost and was later dismantled. Of course, the Federal Trade Commission was not the Justice Department—the department that had instigated the IBM antitrust suit—but any government investigation was serious business.

The FTC investigation of Microsoft had not started within the agency; someone in the personal computer industry had complained. Which company or person had done it? There were enough suspects to fill a dozen whodunit mystery novels. The depth of resentment against Gates and Microsoft was so great that Microsoft had actually been booed when it won a prize at a recent software awards dinner.

Chairman Bill's reputation could not have been more formidable. No one in the industry made a move without considering the likely counterresponse from Microsoft. Competitors feared him. Some had publicly admonished him. Others said that Gates misused his power in the industry to stifle innovation and quell challenges to Microsoft's superiority.

A few months before the announcement of the FTC investigation, the cover of the last issue of a failing magazine called *Business Month* featured a picture of Bill Gates' head—there was no mistaking the oversized glasses sandwiched between the mop of sandy hair and supercilious smile—resting on the torso of a beach-going muscleman, half-naked and posed like Charles Atlas. Beneath the armpit of the pumped right bicep was the caption: "The Silicon Bully: How Long Can Bill Gates Kick Sand in the Face of The Computer Industry?"

It was a question that had been asked throughout the industry many times before. As Microsoft's hegemony grew, less influential software publishers and nervous computer manufacturers had asked some variation of that question with increasing frequency in the cocktail lounges of Silicon Valley and over lobster dinners in Boston restaurants. Many had personal tales of woe to relate: how Microsoft had bested them in a business deal, how Gates' subordinates had appropriated a promising new technology, how Gates himself had subjected them to an embarrassing intellectual mugging in a business disagreement.

In the *Business Month* article, author James Henry compiled a damning indictment of Gates through the observations of two dozen of his computer industry peers. As if to underscore how careful competitors had become not to cross Gates, few of those interviewed agreed to be named. One unidentified IBM executive said he would "like to put an icepick in [Gates'] head."

Software luminary Mitch Kapor, founder of Lotus, implied Gates maintained power by suppressing the excellence of smaller rivals, all for the sake of market share. Gates, Kapor intimated, was a software Judas who sold out the industry's shining promise for wealth and control.

"Gates has clearly won," Kapor was quoted as saying, "the revolution is over, and the free-wheeling innovation in the software industry has ground to a halt. For me it's the Kingdom of the Dead."

Gates and Kapor were old friends, and Kapor's comments clearly hurt Gates. "Mitch is obviously down on me," Gates would later tell *Playboy* magazine, which profiled him. "I mean, 'Kingdom of the Dead?' Where do I go from there?"

Stewart Alsop had told the *Seattle Post-Intelligencer* shortly before the *Business Month* piece hit the stands, "It's remarkable how widespread the negative feelings toward Microsoft are. You now have not only software applications but hardware companies worried to one degree or another about Microsoft's control of the business. That's unheralded."

Gates had his supporters, even among those who competed against him. They ascribed the industry attacks to that green-eyed monster—jealousy.

"Bill is not a nasty guy to compete with," said Gordon Eubanks, one of the industry's pioneers and president of Symantec, which makes database software. In the late 1970s, Eubanks developed a BASIC that competed with that of Microsoft's. "I do know of instances where he used his influence, but who wouldn't? This isn't a race where there's a handicap. Bill doesn't go around carrying a 100-pound sack on his back. That's what some people think should happen."

Vern Raburn, Gates' longtime friend and now a competitor with his own software company, said Gates is such an intense competitor that people often mistake his intensity for ill will. "I get angry about the bully stuff being written about Bill," he said. "We all love the little guys and hate the big guys, but we all want to be the big guys. There are some people out there that are basically saying untrue things about Bill Gates, that he's immoral, he lies, he goes over the edge. It's just not true. . . . It's not always fun competing with him, he's a tough competitor. But he's not immoral."

Oft-quoted industry analyst Esther Dyson said Microsoft was hated because it was so successful. "They've gotten where they are by doing a good job," she said. "Doing a good job isn't illegal."

But even friends felt Gates needed to work on his image as the industry's bad boy. Ruthann Quindlen, who helped take Microsoft public and danced the night away with Gates at Annabel's in London during the road show, said she thought Gates should become "less Machiavellian." With every negotiation, she said, Gates and Microsoft have an "I-win" mentality. "They are the IBM of Software, but they are not taking the view that everyone can win with them."

With so much "Bill bashing" going on in the industry, few believed the FTC investigation was as narrowly focused as Microsoft claimed. In the weeks after the announcement, more and more of Microsoft's competitors emptied their spleen to the national press. Some of the bile was obviously starting to get to Gates. In an interview with *USA Today*, Gates fired back at those who claimed the FTC probe was much broader than Microsoft had acknowledged.

"There's no truth to what they [critics] are saying," Gates said. "And whenever someone asks me about this thing I say 'Just get somebody who is willing to put their name in print with these lies, because they are just direct lies.' You can slander people behind the scenes a lot. But this time somebody might be caught red-handed because this is just out and out baloney."

Gates was asked if he felt persecuted by all the anti-Microsoft sentiment: "No, I've developed a new view that being successful is not a fun thing sometimes. There is just a phenomenon where people don't like a company as successful as ours."

Although the price of Microsoft's stock was being hammered by the constant stream of negative publicity, Gates professed not to be concerned. He said Microsoft's stock was probably too high in the first place and needed to come down to a more realistic figure. "Let's say the stock dropped in half or a third. Big deal. I don't have a short-term interest in that issue. Ask any Wall Street analyst which company never over promises what's going to happen, always talks up the risks in their business and takes the long-term approach. It's Microsoft. Besides, I have an infinite amount of money. I would still order the same hamburger. Believe me I'm not thinking about the stock price. I'm thinking about software products."

The initial FTC investigation of Microsoft did indeed focus only on the November 1989 press release at Comdex from Microsoft and IBM, according to government sources. But as the FTC bloodhounds went sniffing around, visiting the industry's major players, they heard over and over again similar complaints about the way Gates and Microsoft did business, about questionable business practices unrelated to the matter of the Comdex press release. The investigation began to grow.

Occasionally, the federal investigators came across dead ends or determined allegations made against Microsoft were unfounded. One such dead end came from a company called Intuit. Several people in the industry had told the FTC to look into what big bad Microsoft had done to Intuit, a Silicon Valley company of 250 employees with annual revenues of $18 million. The company's success was due to a hit software product called Quicken, a money-management program that was outselling its leading competitor by five or six to one.

In October 1990, an FTC investigator approached Scott Cook, chairman of Intuit. Microsoft was poised to bring out its own money-management application for Windows 3.0, in direct competition with a product Intuit was readying. Cook knew he was about to face the fight of his life.

The tale Cook told the FTC investigator was a familiar one. Like others in the industry, Cook had done the slow dance with the Microsoft mongoose. It started in 1989 with some joint promotion efforts at retail software outlets. Then in early 1990, Microsoft's Jeff Raikes approached Cook at a Software Publishers Association meeting. "We don't see a lot of companies we really respect," Raikes said. "You seem to be one that does things right. We might be interested in acquiring you. Do you have any interest in that?"

Cook thought it over and a week or two later told Raikes he was interested. But after some preliminary talks and the exchange of some financial information, Gates squelched the deal as too costly. Several months passed and Microsoft returned with another offer. This time it wanted to work with Intuit to develop a personal finance product for Windows.

"They really liked the Quicken brand name because it's so well known," said Cook. "So the arrangement they were talking about was that they would build the product, and just license our brand name. They also wanted our advice on how to build it."

Finally, a meeting with Microsoft's Mike Maples was scheduled. Maples was head of the vaunted applications division. At the meeting, Maples told Cook that Microsoft planned to enter the business with its own product. There would be no partnership.

"He told us his guys had come to him with all the ways the deal had been proposed, and he couldn't figure out a way to make it work," Cook said of Maples.

In late 1990, Microsoft announced its own personal finance product for Windows, called Microsoft Money. Other software publishers began telling cocktail party stories about how Microsoft appropriated a lot of information from Intuit during the negotiations, information it could use to compete against Intuit later.

"It's a rumor I've confirmed personally," said one software publisher. "Microsoft stole a ton of stuff from the Intuit folks."

Said the CEO of another software company: "Microsoft went down to Intuit and said, "We'd like to buy your financial package because we want to get into the business.' They examined it, found out all their plans, made a totally frivolous offer and then announced that they were producing their own."

Cook, however, told the FTC investigator that Microsoft did nothing wrong.

"Microsoft was naturally trying to learn as much as they could. But we knew that. We weren't born yesterday. Even at the very beginning of our discussions, even before they told us they might enter the market, it was kind of obvious. They are a big company. Very smart. You don't show them your crown jewels. A lot of the guys who are complaining about Microsoft are kids that got took, kids who exposed their private parts to Bill Gates to show off—'Gee, look how good we are.' But they are not thinking that Bill Gates is a smart competitor, so Microsoft naturally tries to learn as much as it can about existing software products."

Cook said he told the FTC it was wasting its time investigating Microsoft. "They are pestering one of the best run companies I've ever seen," he said, "a company that should be the model for American industry. . . . When you lose to Microsoft, it's because you snooze."

But the FTC also heard from other industry executives far less generous in their praise of Microsoft. By mid-April of 1991, Microsoft was forced to acknowledge the investigation of the company had gotten much bigger. The word "monopoly" was used for the first time to describe the scope of the federal probe. Microsoft said it had been officially notified that the FTC was looking into allegations that the company "has monopolized or attempted to monopolize the market for operating systems, operating environments, computer software and consumer peripherals for personal computers." In other words, the probe now covered every aspect of the company, from Windows and DOS to the tiny Microsoft Mouse.

Said Bob Kleiber, an analyst for Piper, Jaffray & Hopwood in Minneapolis, "All of a sudden, the FTC has said 'Where there was just smoke before, now we think there's fire.' You don't dig deeper if you haven't found anything."

Once again, with the announcement that the investigation had been expanded, the national media jumped on the Gates-bashing band wagon.

"Can anyone stop Bill Gates?" the headline of a cover story in *Forbes* asked. *Newsweek* ran a story on Gates entitled "The Whiz They Love to Hate," which devoted more than a page to the Bill-bashing saga. A Sunday *New York Times* article ran beneath the headline "One Day, Junior Got Too Big." "From Computer Whiz to Bullying Billionaire" was the headline of a front-page story on Gates in the *Seattle Post-Intelligencer* newspaper.

Said Philippe Kahn, chairman of Borland and one of Gates' most outspoken critics, "No one wants to work with Microsoft anymore. We sure won't. They don't have any friends left."

Nearly two decades since he cut his first profitable business deals at Lakeside, Gates had emerged as the undisputed leader of the computer software industry. But disputes were raging over what kind of leader he was.

———————

As far as Bill Gates is concerned, business is war. You fight to win. Gates' friend Heidi Roizen, president of T-Maker, an $8 million California software firm that makes the popular WriteNow word processing application for Apple's Macintosh computer, has been one of those who has faced that competitive side of Gates in business. Some years ago, T-Maker came out with a new, faster version of its word processing program at a discounted price. When Gates learned of this, he priced Microsoft Word to undercut Roizen's product. Microsoft had many times the revenue of T-Maker, but no piece of business was too small for Gates.

"He's kind of won the world fair and square, but it sure doesn't leave a lot left over for the rest of us," Roizen said. "It's frustrating to be up against him. While I'd prefer he not be in quite so much control of the world, I think that he's earned it."

When her company first began competing against Microsoft, she and Gates would compare sales figures on how WriteNow was doing against Microsoft Word. During one encounter with Gates, she made the mistake of telling him her company had just shipped a thousand copies of WriteNow to Apple. Gates was furious. He whipped out a note pad and began questioning her like a prosecutor. Who did she sell them too? Who signed the purchasing order? Who authorized the sale? Have you shipped them yet? Later, over dinner, Roizen asked Gates what he was going to do with the information. Gates said he planned to call Apple and demand they not buy those 1,000 units of WriteNow. Gates never made the call. But he did give his friend some free advice about himself.

"Heidi," Gates said, "don't ever tell me anything you don't want me to use against you."

Because he is so competitive, Gates looks to take advantage of any business opportunity that lets Microsoft win. But others wonder if he plays fair.

"It's not *whether* you compete, but *how* you compete," complained John Warnock, chief executive of Adobe Systems. Warnock's Palo Alto company rose rapidly in the late 1980s to dominate the software that controls the size and shape of type on computer printers. This font technology was an outgrowth of work Warnock did at Xerox PARC in the 1970s. Around 1989, Gates asked Adobe for the right to include those programs in Microsoft's operating software, arguing that a linkup might vastly expand Adobe's markets. But Gates did not offer any royalty money, and Warnock refused. Gates then declared war on Adobe. He announced an alliance with Apple, Adobe's largest customer, to produce its own font software. Adobe's stock subsequently collapsed, plunging more than thirty percent.

"Microsoft positioned itself as experts in the field and they never produced a type face in their life," said Warnock, who had an emotional and public falling-out with Gates. "What they were doing was not advancing the industry. Having multiple font standards is craziness. . . . Bill is extraordinarily competitive. Winning is important. But when the industry suffers, yeah, it's too important."

Despite the frontal attack from Microsoft, Adobe hung in, and by 1991 Microsoft had disbanded the team working on its printer software. The developer in charge had resigned, and programmers were shifted to other projects. Apple was once again Adobe's main customer.

Complaints about how Microsoft does business are common, even from those who have entered into business arrangements with Microsoft.

Bob Metcalfe, founder of 3Com Corporation, likened a disastrous joint marketing venture with Gates in the late 1980s to "black widow spiders mating—you'd be lucky to get out alive." Metcalfe said Microsoft double-crossed 3Com and precipitated his company's first multimillion-dollar quarterly loss in 1991.

With $400 million in revenues, 3Com was well established in the flourishing computer networking market. As PCs proliferated, they were being used by more and more businesses as communications devices and for sharing information. PC computer networks allowed many PCs to link up and work together.

The undisputed leader of the networking market, with a seventy percent share, was Novell Corporation, owner of a best-selling network operating system called NetWare. Gates had been eying the market for several years, trying to get a foothold. He believed the market rightfully belonged to him. In the fall of 1988 Gates dispatched Ballmer to 3Com, who arrived bearing a demonstration program to show that Microsoft's own network operating system—OS/2 LAN Manager—was well along in development. Ballmer proposed that the two companies team up to finish off development of the system, which would be based on computers running OS/2, and market it through 3Com's extensive dealer network.

Alan Kessler, 3Com's general manager, was open to the idea. He believed, like most others at the time, that the match of IBM and Microsoft was the irresistible force of the industry. OS/2, rightful heir to DOS, was going to take over the PC world. An operating system based on OS/2 seemed the perfect antidote to Novell's persistent success in that field. If all went well, 3Com and Microsoft would set the new industry standard.

"Microsoft," Metcalfe recalled, "really wanted to take Novell on."

Kessler and Mike Murray, chief of Microsoft's network business unit, negotiated the deal in the weeks leading up to Christmas, faxing draft documents back-and-forth and haggling over the phone. Eventually, just one small obstacle remained; 3Com wanted Microsoft to help pay an up-front cost to a third-party developer whose technology 3Com had incorporated into some of its work. Ballmer stubbornly refused. Kessler called him in desperation just before Christmas, trying to complete the negotiation. "C'mon Steve," Kessler implored, "for God's sake,

Christmas is next week, let's put a little something under the tree for all of us and go home."

Ballmer relented, and the deal was done.

Gates was not involved in the negotiations, but he was familiar to 3Com executives. Metcalfe had known him since 1979, and they were on good terms. Gates and Ballmer attended a 3Com press conference announcing 3Com's first product. Metcalfe, who had once worked at Xerox, steered Charles Simonyi to Microsoft when he was considering leaving Xerox. The two companies had occasionally collaborated in marketing since then, and 3Com was licensed to sell Microsoft's first venture into networking, a product called MS Net.

Tension in the new partnership, however, began to build almost immediately. Their first joint press conference on the development effort was marred by squabbling between the two companies' marketing departments, according to Metcalfe. Gates' presence at the event did not ease the strain. 3Com had been counting on the public relations mileage it could get out of a partnership with Microsoft, but the Redmond company's marketing department seemed determined to shove them out of the limelight.

"They made it clear it was a Microsoft operation," Metcalfe said. "It wasn't a joint press conference, it was a Microsoft press conference. That's how it was positioned and received, and it was extremely disappointing. We had committed a substantial number of dollars and people over a few years to this deal, and the attention we received and the credit we were given were not commensurate."

The friction didn't ease after development got underway. Programmers for 3Com, responsible for writing some of the low-level code, weren't getting along with the Microsoft engineers writing the higher level LAN Manager software. As the project progressed through 1989, both groups fell behind schedule. Code written by Microsoft programmers, who had limited experience in networking, was breeding bugs.

"Our engineers were treated like shit by Microsoft people," Metcalfe said. "They ended up testing all the buggy software, and whenever anything was wrong, Microsoft's general position was it was our fault. Our engineers were forced to suffer daily indignities in the face of these obnoxiously arrogant programmers. One of my friends referred to them as the Hitler Youth."

Bugs and battles between programmers were not unusual. But when LAN Manager was introduced in October 1989, few were happy with the quality of the product. Customers had difficulties with it right from the start. Sales suffered accordingly.

"LAN Manager was fairly immature," said a former Novell executive. "It clearly was not as strong as other network operating systems that were already out in the market, such as NetWare and others. We felt it had quite a ways to go before it was going to be a viable product. And we also felt that this was just phase one of a grander marketing plan."

Gates had personally joined the fray. He was pitching the product to some of the largest companies in the nation. Bearing free software, he would meet with in-house computer technicians, trying to convince them to abandon Novell and NetWare for Microsoft and LAN Manager. "Bill would take the time to talk to them directly and say, 'Gee, can I answer any questions as to why you should be developing for the OS/2 platform?' " said the ex-Novell executive. "We also heard a number of instances where Microsoft and IBM would go into the large corporations, go right up to the manager of information systems level and say, 'This is the future, LAN Manager is where the future is going to be, and Novell is part of the past.' "

Novell marketers countered with their roundhouse punches. When they began selling a new generation of NetWare, they expected Microsoft sales personnel would be out disparaging it. Microsoft, they felt, was nearly certain to attack it for system reliability, because the new operating system was programmed in a way that made it faster than LAN Manager, but—

according to conventional wisdom—less protected against major system failure.

In an attempt to counter that attack Novell engineers thoroughly tested LAN Manager, trying to find a way to make the program "blow up" from a remote work station.

"It didn't take very long," said the ex-Novell executive. "I'm sure it was less than a week. Not only could we blow up the server, we could virtually put it into Never-Never Land, where you had to reboot and reinstall the whole operating system again. Once we found that, we packaged that up and went on a road show and actually went to the industry analysts, and we said, 'You may hear some issues relative to reliability. What we'd like to demonstrate to you is that no system is protected, no matter what you do.' And we would set up the LAN Manager and commence to blow it up. We'd do it right in their offices.

"We heard from the rumor mill that Microsoft did in fact go back in to the analysts three or four weeks afterward. And they did begin to open up the issue of reliability. The analysts, from what we understood, said 'Oh yeah, watch this,' and they blew up LAN Manager. They said, 'Don't talk to us about system reliability.'

"We'd always heard (Gates) was emotionally attached to LAN Manager. We always thought we could turn the tide against them, because we didn't have a rational businessman competing against us, we had a guy who was emotionally attached to a product that couldn't compete."

Microsoft had a tough sell on its hands with LAN Manager for other reasons. OS/2, introduced in December 1987, was not moving well, as noted earlier.

"They made OS/2 and LAN Manager appear to be inseparable," said an industry expert. "That was a mistake. They forgot the most important common denominator, and that was all of the DOS users. The DOS user was a second cousin in this LAN Manager environment. It was expensive to migrate from DOS to OS/2, and they felt they were being abandoned."

3Com, meanwhile, had become by far the largest seller of LAN Manager, selling more than seventy percent of the copies. But the company was getting killed, because of the licensing agreement it had signed to seal the deal with Microsoft. 3Com, gambling that LAN Manager sales would soar, agreed to pay Microsoft a minimum monthly royalty payment, no matter how many of the products were sold. When the market didn't develop, 3Com found itself paying Microsoft for thousands of unsold copies. LAN Manager had been licensed to numerous companies to sell. With the various companies jockeying for position, customers were confused. Frustrated with the slow sales, Microsoft took a drastic step—it decided to sell LAN Manager directly, and did so through 3Com's own well-developed network dealer channels. That meant Microsoft was now competing with its own partner.

Metcalfe felt the move was nothing less than a double-cross, although the contract didn't specifically prevent such a move.

"The response that I got," said Metcalfe, "was, 'You ought to negotiate your contracts more carefully. You were stupid.' "

"We were adults," Kessler said. "We were big boys and girls when we signed the contract. There may be some provocative things you can say about Microsoft, but it's also appropriate to say that this was a legal, binding document, and we signed it. We signed it on the belief that certain things were going to happen to the OS/2 market, they did not happen, and it was not incumbent on Microsoft to give us relief. If I were them I would have, but I'm not them. They chose to enforce the letter of the agreement."

In late 1990, 3Com managed to negotiate its way out from under the crushing minimum royalty agreement and terminate the relationship. Nonetheless, in its fiscal quarter ending in February 1991, 3Com took losses topping $40 million, mostly due to the Microsoft partnership and a reorganization sparked by the ill-fated deal. Metcalfe believed 3Com had been victimized by the falling-out between Microsoft and IBM as OS/2 faltered and Windows sales grew, and by the "rapaciousness" of Microsoft's cadres of young, zealous deal makers.

"The arrogance of Microsoft in this partnership was unbearable, it drove our people crazy," Metcalfe said. "It's just bad business when your customers and your partners emerge damaged from deals with you. Microsoft is a billion-dollar company growing fifty percent a year. That creates a lot of pressure on people, especially young, inexperienced people, to perform and deliver. And sometimes those pressures set aside the niceties."

Despite the disagreement, Metcalfe still likes Gates. "I think the world of him. What's happening is a bit out of his control. He's created a monster. . . ."

In January, 1988, Microsoft set out to capture another segment of the network market with Ashton-Tate, the top database software publisher, and Sybase, a California minicomputer software publisher. Ashton-Tate and Microsoft planned to share development responsibilities creating an OS/2 version of SQL Server, a program that manages network databases. For Ashton-Tate, the partnership represented a chance to co-opt Microsoft, which had not yet come up with a database program to challenge Ashton-Tate's leading product, dBASE. It also represented an offhand endorsement of dBASE, since the product's anticipated upgrade, dBASE IV, was to be used in SQL Server.

The deal took an inordinately long time to work out. The negotiators deadlocked frequently, which required Ed Esber, head of Ashton-Tate, and Jon Shirley to intercede and get talks moving again.

Esber recalled later that it was a complicated agreement.

"In a complex relationship, it's very hard to capture the essence in a contract on a piece of paper," Esber said. "You have to approach it in two styles. The way I approached it was, we'll have a partnership and in the spirit of the partnership we'll resolve issues. The way Microsoft approached it was, we will get on paper every loophole we can get, and the legal document is the relationship.

"That was the difference," he said. "I viewed the relationship as something between two people that, as in any relationship, would require the two parties to work together to resolve issues that weren't anticipated. I think they viewed the relationship as the contract, the exact legal language in the contract, and nothing more."

A few hours before the January announcement of the deal with Ashton-Tate and Sybase, Gates placed a call to his chief competitor in the languages arena, Philippe Kahn of Borland. There had been rumors that Microsoft was going to buy Ashton-Tate—in fact, the firms had talked about merging previously. Gates, evidently not wanting to upset his Borland rival, allayed Kahn's fears of the Microsoft/Ashton-Tate alignment.

"We're making a deal with Ashton-Tate, but you don't have to worry," Gates told Kahn.

"Bill will only do things that give him an advantage, but this was one of the rare times he was boasting about it," said Kahn of the phone call from Gates. "It became a joke for him to see Ashton-Tate give away the store that way."

On that note, the partnership formally began. It was not an auspicious beginning. It ended on an equally bad note. Ashton-Tate thought Microsoft had promised to deliver a server that would work with NetWare, so the product would reach the largest possible customer base. Gates, naturally enough, wanted his own LAN Manager to be boosted, rather than Novell's product. Less than a year into the project, Ashton-Tate engineers discovered that SQL Server wouldn't work well with NetWare. Novell would need to modify its product to make it work.

Esber believed Microsoft had broken the spirit of the agreement. Fearing SQL Server would flop if it were captive to the relatively puny LAN Manager market, Esber went to Novell. The two companies negotiated a joint marketing and sales agreement for a server product that would work with NetWare, since SQL Server did not.

Just days before the Novell and Ashton-Tate partnership was to be announced Esber ran into Gates at a software conference, who had gotten wind of the Novell deal. In a crowded hallway, he tore into Esber, calling his deal with Novell stupid, ranting that it couldn't be done under the contract Ashton-Tate had with Microsoft. Gates threatened to sue.

In deference to Microsoft, Esber called off the Novell deal at the last minute, but the rift between the companies could not be mended. Microsoft had an escape clause in the contract that allowed it to break the deal if dBASE IV were late. The software was late, and Microsoft terminated the contract.

"Both parties walked into the agreement with certain expectations and promises from the other side," Esber said. "Both sides failed to meet the expectations of the other . . . but there certainly was one party trying harder to make it work than the other."

Microsoft has become notorious in the industry not just for capitalizing on the technological advances of others, but, as some claim, for predatory pilfering. They complain that Microsoft repeatedly approaches small companies developing promising new products, ostensibly to talk about a partnership. After Microsoft is given a glimpse of how the software works, it suddenly loses interest in the deal—only to announce later that it has been working on surprisingly similar, but competing, software.

"If I've got an innovative product and I show it to Microsoft," Esber said, "I have to understand they will at some point in time appropriate some of the ideas—in a legal manner—and it will show up in their products."

Micrographx, a Texas company which develops graphics software for PCs, founded by Paul and George Grayson with $5,000 borrowed on a credit card, had just such a problem. Micrographx had a long history with Microsoft. The company was one of the few that hung with Gates and Microsoft during the lengthy delays in bringing the first version of Windows to market. Micrographx was a big Windows booster, and the relationship was symbiotic. Microsoft even loaned the tiny company $100,000 to help it survive the delays and programming changes, which the Graysons paid back 18 months later. Micrographx was the first independent software company to put a product on the market for Microsoft Windows—In-A-Vision, a drawing program released in July 1985, six months before Windows was shipped.

When Microsoft and IBM shifted development efforts from Windows to OS/2 and Presentation Manager, Micrographx had to change its applications software to run under the new operating system. To ease that labor-intensive task, the company came up with special software, called Mirrors, that essentially translated Windows programs into programs for OS/2. Microsoft liked the potential of Mirrors, and a Microsoft executive was sent to Texas with an offer. Microsoft wanted to pay Micrographx for the right to use Mirrors to modify its own Windows applications for OS/2. Micrographx would license Mirrors to other companies, and Microsoft would help promote it through technical seminars.

"It was going to be a real cooperative thing," said a software industry official who was familiar with the deal. A tentative agreement was reached with Mike Maples, Microsoft's vice-president for applications software, and a letter of intent was signed by both companies.

Immediately upon signing the letter of intent, Microsoft demanded to see the source code for Mirrors—in essence, they wanted to look at the very guts of the program. Paul Grayson balked at first, but finally sent it. He became more uneasy when Microsoft assigned an operating systems engineer to evaluate the product. Only the applications side of the Microsoft house was supposed to see the code; operating systems engineers, if they saw it, could write their own program and promote it in competition with Micrographx.

Grayson called Maples to protest. "Don't worry, he's working for me," Maples said of the programmer. "He's going to be the technology guy helping all the applications people use Mirrors."

A few weeks later, a Micrographx developer was talking to the Microsoft engineer. He was summarily informed of some bad news: Microsoft had decided to write its own Mirrors-like software. The engineer who had been evaluating Mirrors was shifted immediately back to report to Ballmer, head of operating systems.

The Graysons were stunned, then angered, convinced Microsoft had deliberately set out to appropriate their product. But after a year of complaining, they got no satisfaction from Microsoft. Maples told them there was nothing he could do, a sentiment Ballmer reiterated. Even Gates refused to acknowledge their complaint.

One Micrographx official, who did not want to be named, said of Microsoft: "Their attitude basically was, 'We'll pay you what we said, other than that go away and leave us alone, and by the way, are you going to sue us?' They didn't believe Micrographx would sue them, and didn't seem to care if we did. Their attitude was basically, 'Screw you.' "

Micrographx was planning to go public, and felt it couldn't afford a blow-up with Microsoft. The Graysons swallowed their pride and let the matter drop. Eventually, Microsoft placated the Graysons with a cross-licensing deal that Gates said was unusually generous. Nonetheless, the Graysons felt used and manipulated by Microsoft.

"I characterized it at the time as date rape," said the industry official familiar with the deal. "Micrographx went out with Microsoft in good faith, and they took advantage of them, and then they wouldn't return their phone calls in the morning."

Paul Grayson was later quoted as saying: "I half-jokingly say there is only one person with fewer friends than Saddam Hussein. And that's Bill Gates."

A company that ran into a similar problem with Microsoft was the Go Corporation, a tiny startup company in Foster City, California, developing software to control small computers that recognize handwritten words. This cutting-edge technology is known as pen-based computing. Hoping to convince software companies to develop applications for its product, Go showed its secret software to several companies in confidential demonstrations, including a team from Microsoft.

In January 1991, just a week before Go was set to announce its innovative product to the press, Microsoft made a preemptive strike with its own announcement. Gates said his company was developing handwriting-recognition software called Pen Windows. Microsoft's design team included an engineer who had been briefed by Go. A few weeks later, Microsoft said 21 computer makers were "considering" building hardware around the Pen Windows software.

Go officials were stunned.

"Anybody who shows Microsoft confidential information is taking a risk," said J. Jerrold Kaplan, Go's founder and chairman.

Keith Toleman, marketing director for a Florida software company, told *PC Week* magazine, "It's gotten to the point where companies won't go in and undress in front of Microsoft" in order to secure a joint development agreement.

In a *Fortune* magazine interview that included Steve Jobs, Gates denied pilfering from Go.

> Gates: I contend technology breakthroughs can happen by extending what we already have. Let's take handwriting computers. . . . The software will come either from Microsoft or from a U.S. competitor named Go Corporation. That's going to be a major breakthrough, and who do you give credit to?
>
> Jobs: I think everybody gives credit to Go, but Go will be crushed.
>
> Gates: That's one of the nastiest comments I've ever heard. I've been working on handwriting since long before there *was* a Go Corp.
>
> Jobs: Really? I didn't know that. Most people would say that Go is the company that first tried to commercialize that technology.

Gates: Well, Go hasn't shipped anything yet, and I'll ship my stuff before they ship theirs.

Microsoft's Ballmer dismissed complaints that Microsoft has taken advantage of software companies. "Number one, we've never stolen anything from anybody," he said in a *PC Week* story. "But do we, like every other smart company, look at the works of others and try to get smarter by understanding what our competitors do? That we do."

Few companies, other than Apple, have dared sue Microsoft (although Go Corporation is reportedly considering legal action).

"If you are a software developer, you would think twice about taking Microsoft on," said Tim Bajarin, executive vice-president of Creative Strategies, a market research and consulting group that works with many of the leading players in the industry on strategic planning. "Microsoft has a massive legal department, and you still need them. You don't bite the hand that feeds you. You need their technical support. And if you are a hardware developer, you better have good relations with Microsoft because you need that operating system."

One competitor that did sue Microsoft was Z-Nix, a Pomona, California, hardware company that makes a mouse device for computers. In November 1990, the same month *Business Month* printed its article on Gates entitled "The Silicon Bully," Z-Nix filed a $4 million lawsuit against Microsoft in federal court in Los Angeles. Tiny Z-Nix, with a mere $6 million in annual sales, dared to accuse giant Microsoft of violating the Sherman Act, which prohibits a company dominating one market from using its position to control another market. A 98-pound weakling had hit the biggest kid on the block with brass knuckles.

The story of Z-Nix's suit hit the papers the next day. Frank Yeh, Z-Nix's vice-president of sales and marketing was quoted as saying, "It's time for us to stand up to Microsoft's unfair trade practices and stop the slow death of innovation in this industry."

The suit claimed Microsoft dominated computer operating environment user interfaces for the PC with its best-selling Windows 3.0 program, and it was using that control to run Z-Nix out of the mouse business. Z-Nix is one of a handful of U.S. firms that manufactures computer input hardware, including a device called the "Super Mouse." It competed with Microsoft for a share of the mouse market. Microsoft had been the dominant mouse maker for the PC since 1983, selling 500,000 of the mouses by mid-1987. But by 1990, its market share of more than fifty percent was eroding, partly because of companies like Z-Nix.

The introduction of Windows 3.0 had fueled a burst of mouse sales, and Z-Nix had wanted to capitalize on that increased demand. In a not atypical alliance, Microsoft and Z-Nix struck an agreement that allowed Z-Nix to bundle its Super Mouse with Windows for resale. In return for the license to sell Windows, Z-Nix agreed to pay Microsoft a royalty of $27.50 for every copy of Windows it sold.

The California company had been marketing the package when Microsoft changed its mind about letting competitors ride along on the wave of Windows popularity. Without warning, Microsoft informed Z-Nix that the royalty had doubled to $55. At that price, Z-Nix officials said, the company would lose money. Having poured the equivalent of a year's profit into the Windows promotion, Z-Nix had its back to the wall. Finding itself cornered, the company bared its teeth. The result was its antitrust suit.

The suit was settled just hours after Microsoft's legal people learned of the suit in the Seattle newspaper. An attorney for Microsoft flew to Pomona to meet with Z-Nix. That same day, Microsoft proclaimed victory, saying Z-Nix agreed to retract allegations that the Redmond company used its marketing muscle to force Z-Nix to redesign its Super Mouse. Terms of the agreement were never publicized, but Z-Nix officials said they got what they wanted—the Super Mouse/Windows bundles stayed on the shelves of software dealers.

Having tangled with Microsoft, Z-Nix attorney Thomas Chan, a Los Angeles lawyer seasoned in computer law, had this to say of Microsoft:

"This is one of the few companies where the businessman wants to drive a harder bargain than the lawyer. They are really the toughest negotiators I've encountered in the industry. Small guys, they don't even talk to you. It's just take it or leave it. With big guys, they push and push and push and push, and at the last minute they up the stakes. That's got to be because of Bill Gates."

One reason Gates pushes so hard is fear—he is always looking over his shoulder. "You always have to be thinking about who is coming to get you," he told the *Wall Street Journal*. It's a message and attitude that filters down through the company. A couple years ago, Gates said his products managers ought to wake up thinking about their main competitor. He even suggested they go so far as to get to know the names of their competitor's children and birth dates.

"It is a competitive edge we try and hone," said Jeff Raikes, then manager of Microsoft's word processing division, of the chairman's remarks about knowing the competition. "Bill expected me to always be thinking about my competitor. If you just say 'We're No. 1, that's good enough,' that kind of comlacency will lead to failure in a business as dynamic as ours." A week after Gates made his remarks about knowing one's competitors, Raikes has a photo of WordPerfect's executive vice-president's children on his desk. And he sends them birthday gifts.

Perhaps as a result of this attitude within Microsoft, Microsoft Word, for years trailing far behind WordPerfect as the industry's best-selling word processing application for personal computers, has steadily closed the gap. Twice a year, Gates personally visits WordPerfect's best customers, demanding to know why they continue to buy WordPerfect when Microsoft Word is so much better.

Pete Peterson, WordPerfect's executive vice president, has said he would love to see Gates mellow out. "I wish he'd get married and have a couple kids so he couldn't work as many hours as he does."

It's a plaintive cry from many in the computer industry today.

A few years ago, Pete Peterson described Microsoft as the "fox that takes you across the river and then eats you." He was making the same complaint others in the industry have made many times since, that Microsoft has a huge advantage over its software rivals because of DOS. The resentment has been festering like an open sore since the deal with IBM more than ten years ago which gave Microsoft control of Big Blue's operating system. The person who controls the operating system, many feel, controls the direction of the industry, and at the moment that is Gates. Microsoft has forced a generation of software developers to write applications that conform to its standard.

WordPerfect may have decided it was time for someone to shoot the fox. When Microsoft announced in April of 1991 that the FTC investigation of the company had been expanded, the *San Jose Mercury News* quoted several industry sources as saying the folks at WordPerfect played a "lead role" in lodging complaints against Microsoft. Officials of the Utah-based company acknowledged they had talked to the FTC, as had a lot of others in the industry.

At the heart of the FTC probe is not Microsoft's aggressive style or the way it does business, but whether or not Microsoft's dominant position has chilled competition and thus hurt consumers. Proving that Microsoft has engaged in anticompetitive practices would be very difficult and could take years of litigation, according to many legal experts. The federal government had a much stronger case against IBM and was unable to beat the computer giant after a bruising and costly ten-year court fight. The FTC would have to walk a fine legal line in trying to make a case against Microsoft. Antitrust laws are intended to keep companies from engaging in conduct that generally tends to hurt competition. But it's difficult to determine the difference between aggressive business practices and anticompetitive behavior. Has Microsoft abused its position or just out-hustled and outfoxed others in the industry? The computer business is so complex that some legal experts don't believe the FTC even understands the issues well enough to contemplate a suit, much less win one. It's also considered unlikely the government could mount much of an attack against Microsoft, since the company does have competition in operating systems. AT&T has a small part of the market, and two years ago Digital Research, long since having given up on CP/M, came out with an operating system called DR-DOS. Although DR-DOS has not yet gained a real industry foothold, it is cutting into Microsoft's market for DOS. More to the point, Apple Computer has its own operating system for the Macintosh. The only applications area where Microsoft clearly dominates is in applications for the Mac, and that's because Gates took a risk in 1981 that Apple's new computer, then only a prototype, would survive in a very competitive industry. The Mac might well have failed had it not been for Microsoft applications like Excel.

In 1991, Microsoft controlled about a quarter of the applications market. Although application products accounted for fifty-one percent of Microsoft's revenues in 1991, the bulk of the company's profits come from the systems side. Microsoft does not come close to dominating the Big Three of applications—word processing, databases, and spreadsheets. Word-Perfect is far ahead of Microsoft Word, Lotus 1-2-3 is still ahead of Excel, and Microsoft has nothing to compete against Ashton-Tate's dBASE.

The reason so many companies have complained about Microsoft, however, is that they feel it crosses the line in the separation of church and state. Competitors like WordPerfect and Lotus, as well as many others, suspect Microsoft gives "sneak previews" of changes in its operating system to its applications people so they can be out the door first with products. Microsoft's application programmers, they fear, get information on a new feature in DOS or Windows far in advance of outside application developers. Still, even if this occurs, there is probably nothing illegal about Microsoft's applications group benefiting from knowledge of the company's systems developments, according to legal experts familiar with antitrust laws. And Microsoft *does* invite its competitors to Redmond to be briefed on any changes in its operation system. The company even hired an ombudsperson to keep watch over the systems and operations people to appease outsiders.

In theory, Microsoft keeps the playing field level by segregating the operating systems division and the applications division. Information is not supposed to flow freely between them. This imaginary partition is called the "Chinese Wall," a term borrowed from the securities industry to describe the separation between investment bankers, who have inside knowledge of stock sales, and stock brokers who could profit from that information. Still, Microsoft's competitors complain that the company's Chinese Wall is full of holes, and Microsoft adds fuel to the fire when it shifts workers between applications and systems.

One senior application programmer at Microsoft, who has been with the company since the early 1980s, said the Chinese Wall is a creation of the media, not Microsoft. It doesn't exist, he said. "I remember Bill Gates saying many times, 'There is no Chinese Wall.' Somebody got this idea there was this wall between systems and applications so we wouldn't talk to each other. There's no such thing. We don't have any separation here, just one big company. . . . We don't have any limits to our corporation across those boundaries. We never did. And there's no reason to. That doesn't make sense. This is the real world, isn't it? If somebody wants to write application for our operating system, they're going to take what they can get, right?"

Stewart Alsop, for one and there are others who agree with him, said the fundamental advantage Microsoft has is not the operating system but Bill Gates. "He never allows Microsoft to goof off. He always deals with the problem. Every other company allows something else to get in the way. But Gates is tenacious. That's what's scary."

He noted that the first versions of Microsoft Word and Windows were market failures because they didn't work well. But Gates kept coming back until he got it right. "Bill always comes back, like Chinese water torture," Alsop said. "People are scared of Microsoft because they are so persistent. They have executed better than any other company. Others don't feel they are capable of competing with Microsoft. It's a lack of self-confidence. Every other company has screwed up. Does Microsoft have an unfair advantage that results in inferior products in the industry? That's the myth. That's what all the competitors want you to believe. . . . Microsoft has made it harder to compete because it's constantly addressing problems. It single handedly forced Lotus to improve its products. Lotus was not doing a good job of upgrading its products. But because of Excel, Lotus clearly felt a competitive threat. . . . That's the irony. The reason Microsoft has such a hold on the industry, a monopoly, is that they make better products."

Nonetheless, many in the industry would like to see the "monopoly" they claim Microsoft has broken up by splitting Microsoft's operating and applications divisions into separate companies. One example of such a separation occurred at Apple. In 1987, Apple Computer spun off its application software group into an independent company known as Claris Corporation.

After the FTC broadened its investigation of Microsoft, there were rumors the company might do just that—divide—and not wait to see what came of the investigation. In fact, the company chose just the opposite tactic when Microsoft reorganized in early 1992, and Mike Maples was placed in charge of both systems and applications. Maples had previously been vice-president of applications and Steve Ballmer vice-president of systems. The move was hardly one that Microsoft would have taken if it were running scared of the FTC.

Microsoft refused to back off in the face of the FTC probe, even as government investigators carried out boxes of documents from Microsoft. Among other things, the FTC ordered Microsoft's legal department to notify all employees they were not to kill any E-Mail dating back prior to mid 1991. If Microsoft was worried about complaints it was monopolizing the industry, it didn't show it. At an applications briefing for reporters well after the announcement of the FTC investigation, Maples said, "If someone thinks we're not after Lotus and after WordPerfect and after Borland, they're confused. My job is to get a fair share of the software applications market, and to me that's 100 percent."

Although Gates professed not to be concerned about what the FTC might find, a Microsoft manager close to Gates said Gates was hurt by the viciousness of the attacks against Microsoft in the wake of the probe.

"The FTC investigation was a lightening rod to bring computer people forward and say that it would be helpful if Microsoft was hobbled in some way," Gates told *Newsweek* in June of 1991. The *Newsweek* article ended with an apt passage from John Steinbeck's novel, *Cannery Row:* "The things we admire in men, kindness and generosity, openness, honesty, understanding and feeling are the concomitants of failure in our system. And those traits we detest, sharpness, greed, acquisitiveness, meanness, egotism and self-interest are the traits of success. And while men admire the quality of the first they love the produce of the second." The same, apparently, was true about Gates.

Shortly after the unveiling of MS-DOS 5.0 in New York in the spring of 1991, a confidential state-of-the-company memo from Bill Gates to key executives, outlining potential "nightmare" scenarios for Microsoft in the year ahead, was leaked to the press. A very different portrait of the "megalomaniac" Gates that some in the industry pictured emerged. The memo revealed a Gates motivated by fear, rather than arrogance. The reaction on Wall Street may have made his memo the most costly in corporate history.

In the six-page memo, Gates said his worst fears for Microsoft were coming true. IBM was "attacking" Microsoft in systems software, Novell was "defeating" Microsoft in networking and "more agile, customer-oriented applications competitors" were releasing applications for Windows. Gates candidly talked about all of the problems facing Microsoft, from differences with IBM to the FTC investigation and the Apple lawsuit.

The Apple lawsuit clearly represented the biggest threat to Microsoft, at least in Gates' mind. "Microsoft is spending millions to defend features contained in every popular window system on the market and to help set the boundaries of where copyrights should and should not be applied," he wrote. "I think it is absurd that the lawsuit is taking so long. . . . Our view that we almost certainly will prevail remains unchanged." But Gates also went on to say that if the judge hearing the Apple case rules against Microsoft, it could be "disastrous." Apple was seeking more than $4 billion in damages from Microsoft. The real concern, however, was not the money, but having to make fundamental changes in the product, which could set Microsoft back several years.

Not surprisingly, IBM received a fair amount of attention in the memo, as well. Gates asked his executives to refrain from publicly criticizing their former partner. "We will not attack IBM as a company and even our public attack on OS/2 will be very professional," Gates said. "Eventually, we will need to have a neutral relationship with IBM. For the next 24 months, it may be fairly cold. . . . We can emerge as a better and stronger company and people won't say we are the standard because IBM chose us." Gates bluntly said that the breakup with IBM meant Microsoft would no longer have to accept IBM's "poor code, poor design and other overhead."

The *San Jose Mercury News* obtained a copy of the memo from a Microsoft source and printed portions of it. Other papers, including the *Wall Street Journal,* ran the story as well. In the end Microsoft, concerned that the national media was only focusing on negative aspects of the memo, eventually released it in its entirety to the industry press.

Rick Sherlund, the analyst with Goldman Sachs & Company who first broke the news about an FTC probe of Microsoft, said of the memo, "There's no arrogance here. Bill Gates is open-minded, intellectually honest and motivated by fear of competitors." Despite the gloomy picture painted by Gates, Sherlund still recommended buying Microsoft's stock. But the reaction on Wall Street was quite different. Microsoft's stock fell dramatically as investors reacted to the bleak message Gates had delivered. Both Gates and Microsoft suddenly looked vulnerable. Word of the memo knocked the company's stock down more than $8 in one day, to $103, in over the counter trading. Gates, who at the time owned 38.8 million shares, lost $315 million on paper.

About the same time Gates was delivering his memo, IBM Chairman John Akers was delivering one of his own. IBM was facing yet another quarter of poor earnings. For the second consecutive year, overall annual sales had declined—the first time that had happened since 1946. Once a stock market leader, IBM's reputation and leadership were being questioned. Akers decided it was time to read the riot act.

"The fact that we are losing market share makes me goddamn mad," Akers complained in his tirade, which also made its way into the press. "The tension level is not high enough in the business—everyone is too damn comfortable at a time when the business is in crisis."

Once *the* name in computers, IBM's overall market share worldwide had slipped to about twenty-three percent, down from nearly forty percent in 1983 when its PC was taking the personal computer market by storm. Tough times require change, Akers told his executives. And IBM was about to make one of its biggest ever, forging an alliance with rival Apple Computer to take on a common enemy—Microsoft.

A few years earlier such an alliance between the archenemies, whose very battles had defined the personal computer industry, would have been unthinkable. But times had changed. Apple and IBM had both slashed prices and squeezed profits, all the while watching their shares of the personal computer market shrink. Apple's share was down to fifteen percent, and IBM's share was down to seventeen percent. Despite their past differences, they now needed each other.

Other companies were forming technology alliances, too. In April of 1991, a group of 21 computer hardware and software companies, led by Microsoft, Compaq Computer, and Digital Equipment Corporation, had made a pact to develop a new standard for advanced desktop computers based on a chip known as RISC (Reduced Instruction Set Computing). Members of the new alliance, called ACE (Advanced Computing Environment), had been meeting secretly for several months. An executive from one company in the alliance described the project as the "second coming of the PC." The RISC chip does just what the name implies—processes information easier and faster than ever before. Neither Apple nor IBM had been asked to join the alliance. Although the new technology was not expected to have much of an effect until well into the decade, Apple and IBM saw the ACE alliance as a real threat.

Both IBM and Apple had things to gain by working together. Apple veteran Michael Spindler, chief operating officer, had convinced Chairman John Sculley he could deal a blow to Microsoft by joining with IBM, and at the same time help get Apple out of its slump. In addition, Apple was looking for a partner to build a RISC chip for its planned line of work stations, a growing area of the computer market. IBM, on the other hand, had been impressed with an advanced new operating system that Apple had been working on for several years, code-named Pink (the project was reported to be behind schedule and over budget, which could have been one reason why Apple wanted IBM's help). If the two companies could work together and finish the system, they could then build computers compatible with each other. Microsoft's power, and threat, would be greatly diminished.

"We want to be a major player in the computer industry, not a niche player," Sculley would say later. "The only way to do that is to work with another major player."

IBM may have had a hidden motive in wanting to team up with Apple. Some industry insiders believed that if Apple won its landmark copyright suit against Microsoft and Hewlett-Packard, it would then go after IBM for Presentation Manager, since it is very similar to Windows. But Apple would be less inclined to go after IBM if it were a partner.

Publicly at least, Gates did not seem worried. Addressing industry consultants in Seattle in mid-June, Gates said an alliance between Apple and IBM might be good for the industry. "There's no way anybody can feel bad about something like that because we need more cooperation in this industry," he said.

On July 3, the day before Independence Day, Apple and IBM put an end to all the speculation. They announced in a brief press release, without elaboration, that Jim Cannavino of IBM and John Sculley of Apple had signed a letter of intent to enter into a wide-ranging accord to share technology. It had been seven years since the infamous Apple commercial for its new Macintosh computer had run, comparing IBM to an Orwellian despot.

"Who would have thought these two companies could possibly have anything in common," said Richard Shaffer, publisher of *Computer Letter*. "It's like a surfer girl marrying a banker."

Wrote Bart Ziegler of the Associated Press: "Can a company with a flagship product named after a fruit kiss and tell with a

global giant that favors zingy product names like PS-2 Model
30 and 286-E21?"

Several analysts called it the "deal of the decade." Said
Charles Wolf of First Boston Corporation, "I don't think anything stranger has happened." The consensus among reporters,
analysts, and industry executives was that the proposed alliance
represented nothing less than a direct attack on Microsoft. "I
don't think you can write the Apple–IBM story without a lot of
credit going to Microsoft," Edward McCracken, president of
Silicon Graphics, a PC vendor, told the *Washington Post.* One
industry analyst called the new partnership an "anti-Microsoft
axis."

At Microsoft, reaction to the official news varied. "We're
flabbergasted," Steve Ballmer told *Time* magazine. "This does
not bode well for future cooperation between IBM and
Microsoft."

Gates told the *Wall Street Journal* the deal did not make
sense. "You've taken everything that's unique to Apple and put
it in this joint venture. What's left . . . Apple has sold its birthright. That's sad." He went on to dismiss the new threat, saying
Microsoft now had one competitor where before it had two.

In the aftermath of the IBM-Apple announcement, Gates
was off to spend the Fourth of July holiday at a party his parents
hosted at the family compound on Hood Canal. The guest list
included Warren Buffett, Katherine Graham, the former Washington Post owner, Meg Greenfield, and several other journalists
and state politicians. It was the first time Gates and Buffett, who
both had personal fortunes of at least $4 billion, had met. The
just-announced deal between Apple and IBM came up only in
passing, and Gates showed little interest in the topic. He was
much more interested in talking mathematics with Buffett and
playing tennis with some of the others.

Microsoft, generally, seemed relatively unconcerned about
the IBM-Apple alliance. Mike Maples, vice president of applications, in a pep talk for several hundred of the troops outside

the applications building, said he didn't expect to see any useful products out of the alliance before he retired. Then he corrected himself. "No, I don't expect to see any products before *you* retire."

Tim Paterson, the programmer who developed DOS, expressed what others at Microsoft felt—that it was good to be rid of IBM, which had become a millstone around Microsoft's neck. Perhaps some of that so-called Blue Magic would now rub off on Apple. "Look at the three biggest bombs Microsoft has had—Windows 1.0, DOS 4.0 and OS/2. And who was our partner on two of those? IBM. Have we ever done anything with IBM that wasn't a bomb? No."

Many Apple employees, particularly software engineers, shared Gates' sentiment that the company had given away its birthright in joining IBM. An early meeting between about 100 IBM people and 50 Apple employees reportedly went badly because of the cultural differences. Jokes were soon making the rounds on both sides of the country. At Apple the grim question was, "What do you get when you cross Apple and IBM?" Answer: "IBM."

It was not until early October that Apple and IBM finally signed the papers officially creating their historic alliance. More than 500 people attended the news conference in San Francisco, where the two companies spelled out details of their technology-sharing agreement. They announced they would work with Motorola in developing RISC chip technology to be used in future Apple and IBM personal computers. But the big news was that IBM and Apple were establishing two joint venture companies, one called Taligent and the other Kaleida. Taligent was to develop an advanced operating system based on the Pink project Apple had been working on. Kaleida was to create multimedia computers that combine sound, text, and video on the screen.

Sculley predicted at the news conference that the joint venture would make the heyday of the personal computer revolution in the 1980s seem tame by comparison. The alliance, he said, "will launch a renaissance in technical innovation."

But several months later, Apple and IBM were still mired down over the makeup of the two jointly owned companies. Corporate boards and CEOs had yet to be picked. "If it's taking them this long to figure out who's president, what's going to happen when they disagree on an interface icon?" asked Nancy McSharry, program director of International Data Corporation, a market research firm.

At the same time the alliance between Apple and IBM was being put together, there were several other alliances in place or in the works that had the potential to reshape the personal computer landscape. Borland International acquired Ashton-Tate, the leading database maker, strengthening Borland's position as the number three software company, behind Lotus and Microsoft. Novell, the leader in office networking, acquired Digital Research, which produced DR-DOS, the only industry clone of Microsoft's operating system. And IBM also agreed to market software under license from Lotus, Microsoft's fiercest rival. Microsoft and Digital Equipment Corporation, too, announced a broad alliance to make Windows available on Digital's vast computer networks.

It will take time, perhaps years, to know how these new alliances will change the balance of power in the personal computer industry. Other battles were far less distant.

At the fall Comdex in Las Vegas, IBM staged a glitzy show to formally introduce its beleaguered version of OS/2. It had earlier promised the operating system would be ready to ship by the end of the year, a boast which prompted Microsoft's Steve Ballmer to say he would eat a floppy disk if IBM met that deadline. IBM announced at Comdex that OS/2, as Ballmer had predicted, was delayed, and would not be out before early spring of 1992. Microsoft planned to release another version of Windows to hit the market about the same time, backed with an $8 million television advertising campaign.

There were many in the industry who believed IBM had made a serious blunder by sticking with OS/2. When IBM Chair-

man John Akers announced in late 1991 a top-to-bottom reorganization of the monolithic computer giant into independent
business units, the move was seen by many as an attempt to
catch up with mistakes like OS/2. IBM had poured more than
a billion dollars into its development, even though the industry
seemed to support Microsoft's Windows. OS/2's future was further clouded by the IBM/Apple joint announcement that they
would eventually develop a new operation system.

"This has to be the greatest disaster in IBM's history,"
George Colony, president of the consulting firm Forrester Research, told the *Wall Street Journal* in a front page story on the
OS/2 debacle. "The reverberations will be felt throughout the
decade."

At the end of 1991, IBM reported a loss of $2.8 billion, its
first annual deficit ever. Revenues fell 6.1 percent from 1990
to $64.8 billion.

Microsoft, on the other hand, reported profits were up fifty-
five percent and its revenues were up forty-eight percent during
the last three months of 1991. While almost every other major
software company, including Lotus, was laying people off in
1991, Microsoft had been adding as many as 70 new workers a
week. By the end of the year, employment had reached 10,000.
Shuttle buses now carried employees around the sprawling 260
acre campus, where several more buildings were under construction. Microsoft had overtaken the Boeing Company as the
largest Northwestern business in terms of market value. Microsoft, worth an estimated $21.9 billion at year's end, had even
surpassed General Motors in market value. The company's stock
had risen a staggering 1,200 percent since it went public in
1986. Figuring in several stock splits, someone who invested
$1,000 in Microsoft when the company went public would have
made about $30,000 by 1992.

As Microsoft's stock shot up to record highs, so did the
stupendous wealth of the company's top executives. Microsoft
had the unique distinction of having produced three billion-

aires—Bill Gates, Paul Allen, and Steve Ballmer. Filings with the Securities and Exchange Commission showed at least 16 Microsoft executives were multimillionaires. Former president Jon Shirley led the pack with $112 million; Scott Oki, who had started the International Division, and retired in January of 1992 at age 43, had $28 million; Jeff Raikes, who came over from Apple was worth $23 million; Bill Neukom, the former partner in the law firm of Gates' father, $21 million; Frank Gaudette, who took Microsoft public, $7 million; and Mike Maples $3.5 million. There are believed to be over 2000 Microsoft employees who had reached the magical status of "millionaire" by 1992. Chris Larson, Gates' schoolmate from Lakeside and Microsoft's first programmer, had enough money in 1992 to come forward with a group of investors, including the owners of Nintendo, with a $100 million offer to buy the Seattle Mariners baseball team.

Bill Gates, the man who made it all happen, had steadily closed in on the top spot of the *Forbes* Four Hundred list of richest people in America. In the magazine's October 1991 issue, Gates was ranked second behind entertainment mogul John Werner Kluge. *Forbes* estimated Gates' worth at $4.8 billion, and Kluge's at $5.9 billion. On the first day of trading on Wall Street in 1992, Microsoft's stock closed at $114. The stock had split 3 for 2 several months earlier, and it was higher than before the split. Gates was now worth an estimated $7 billion. On paper, at least, the former Lakeside hacker who had a dream of a computer in every house was now the richest person in America.

Bill Gates sometimes has to be reminded that he is one of the world's richest men.

"He clearly has no pretenses about being rich, anymore than he did when he was young," said Dan Bricklin, who has known and competed against Gates for many years. "I know people an awful lot poorer than him who flaunt it. He doesn't."

Vern Raburn recalled meeting Gates not that long ago at the airport in Phoenix, Arizona. Gates was dressed in slacks and a casual shirt open at the neck. Raburn was struck by how little his friend has changed. "Here's like the fifth richest man in the world, " said Raburn. "There's no entourage, and he's just loping along, saying 'Hey how are you? Let's go get a hot dog.' "

Gates, who still flies coach rather than first class, explained to *Playboy* magazine in 1991 why he does not indulge himself in perks such as limousines and chauffeurs and private jets enjoyed by other Fortune 500 executives. "It sets a bad example. I think eventually you get used to those things, then you're just abnormal. I'm afraid I'd get used to it."

Much has been made recently about American CEOs helping themselves to huge salaries and hefty bonuses at a time when the revenue and profits of their companies are declining. Eyebrows and voices were raised, for example, by the salaries of the group of U.S. auto company executives who accompanied President Bush to Japan in early 1992 on a trade mission. Lee Iacocca, CEO of Chrysler, had made $4.5 million in salary and bonuses in 1990, the last year such information was made public. Harold Poling, CEO of Ford, was paid $1.8 million in salary and bonuses. And Robert Stempel, CEO of General Motors, received $5.2 million in salary and bonuses.

Based on Microsoft's performance, Bill Gates should be one of the highest-paid CEOs in the country. But Gates receives a very modest salary. In 1991, he earned $274,966 in salary and bonuses, according to Microsoft's latest proxy statement, making Gates only the fifth highest paid executive in his company. (Michael Hallman, Microsoft's former president who was fired in early 1992, was the company's highest-paid executive in 1991 with a salary and bonus totalling $604,290.)

Gates has said any number of times that he doesn't care about the money, nor does he bother to follow the stock market.

Money, he has said, is not a distraction from work, nor will it become one.

Examples abound that show just how conservative Gates is when it comes to spending money. Friend Heidi Roizen recalled driving into Seattle with Gates for a meeting at the downtown Sheraton Hotel, looking for a place to park. They were running late, and Roizen suggested the hotel's valet parking.

"Yeah, but it's $12 and that's not good value," Gates told her.

"I'll pay the $12," Roizen said.

"That's not the point," Gates replied. "They overcharge for parking."

Said Roizen of the incident, "That's really indicative of Bill." But he is not cheap, she added. "I've never known him to be cheap about picking up the dinner tab or something."

Despite his disdain for a flashy lifestyle, Gates hardly lives a Spartan existence. He does indulge himself with a few luxuries. He has a taste for expensive champagne and keeps his refrigerator at home stocked with a half-dozen or more bottles of Dom Perignon. And he has never outgrown his love of fast cars. Although Gates drives a Lexus to work and still owns the Mustang he had in high school, he recently bought a $100,000 Ferrari 348. Two years ago, Gates and Paul Allen each bought one of the fastest production cars in the world—a 1988 Porsche 959, with an estimated top speed of more than 200 miles per hour. (The cars sit side by side, gathering dust in a U.S. Customs warehouse in San Francisco. Porsche built only 29 for the American market. The cars, which do not meet U.S. safety and pollution standards, were to have been imported under a legal loophole, but the EPA closed the loophole. To pass crash safety tests, at least four would have to be destroyed. At $320,000 a vehicle, it would be a pretty expensive demolition derby. Each car now would probably fetch about $1 million. Gates proposed a crash test by computer simulation, but the Department of Transportation has recommended the cars be shipped out of the country.)

Most of Gate's wealth, of course, remains in Microsoft stock and thus is susceptible to the vagaries of Wall Street. This helps to explain Gates' attitude toward his fortune—he is leery of counting paper assets as wealth. At the end of 1991, Gates owned about 57 million shares of Microsoft stock, representing about thirty-three percent of the company's total shares. While he has not diversified much of his wealth, he has cashed in a lot of stock over the years. According to The Invest/Net Group, a company in Fort Lauderdale, Florida that tracks insider trading, Gates has sold nearly $300 million worth of stock since Microsoft went public in 1986. In October of 1991, for example, he sold about one percent of his holdings for $67.5 million. Earlier in the year, he collected about $50 million in cash when he sold 500,000 shares on the open market. No one knows what Gates is doing with all this cash. But some of it is going to finance his new home, which the local media jokingly refer to as San Simeon North, a reference to the William Randolph Hearst castle in San Simeon, California. The most oft-quoted price tag for this high-tech Xanadu is $10 million, but that's only a guess. No one really knows but Chairman Bill, and he isn't talking.

As far back as 1984, Gates told a reporter about the kind of home he envisioned, with advanced displays in rooms that could be commanded to call up images and music by remote control. Gates said back then that his home of the future would be overseen by a computer a little like HAL—the run-amok computer in *2001: A Space Odyssey.*

Thanks to his wealth, Gates' vision is fast becoming a reality. Under construction for more than a year, the house is located on the other side of Lake Washington from where Gates lives now, in the community known as Medina, which has the highest per capita income in the state. In 1988, Gates began buying up seven lots on nearly four acres for $4 million. The property includes 415 feet of waterfront. Trying to be sensitive to his neighbors, and because the property is situated on a steep hill-side, Gates designed about eighty percent of his home below

413

ground. From the water, the house will resemble a small neighborhood, with five different structures, or pavilions, above ground. None is higher than two stories. All the major structures will be connected under ground. With enough living space to cover a football field, it is supposed to be finished by 1993. There will be three kitchens, a 60-foot-long swimming pool, a 20-seat movie theater, two elevators, a manmade stream, a dock, a beach and lagoon, a meeting hall big enough to accommodate 100 people, offices, a computer center, an underground garage for as many as 28 cars, a 14,000-book library, an exercise room with a trampoline, and a game room.

In addition, the public rooms will have high-definition television screens mounted on the walls. Guests will be able to call up images from a vast electronic library, a computer databank containing great works of art and photography. The digitized images will be stored on computer disks similar to CDs. In one room, these TV screens will show the view from the top of Mount Everest at any time of day and in any weather condition. The system will incorporate music, sound, and video into computer programs that can be manipulated by the guest with the wave of a "magic wand." Gates has made a point of saying he's not just building a home, but a computer conference center exploring the limits of today's—and tomorrow's—home computer technology.

Gates founded his own company, Interactive Home Systems, to buy up the electronic rights to the world's greatest works of art. In early 1991, the company bought electronic rights to about 1,000 art works owned by the Seattle Art Museum. The company is still negotiating with the Smithsonian Institute, the National Gallery in London, and the Art Institute of Chicago. Gates is well aware of the commercial potential of this new computer technology, known as multimedia. And he is not the only player in the field. In late 1991, Eastman Kodak Company purchased Image Bank, the nation's largest supplier of stock photos. Microsoft was also trying to buy the photo company. But Gates does have a jump on the competition. In 1991, Microsoft bought a sizeable interest in Dorling Kindersley Ltd., the London book publisher known for its popular "The Way Things Work" series. Gates has said he believes electronic publishing could be a $1 billion business by the end of the decade. Competitors are already worried that Gates will dominate this field, too.

The home Gates is building will have three childrens bedrooms, as well as one room for a live-in nanny. Gates is always thinking ahead. But for now he remains one of the nation's most eligible bachelors. Gates is sometimes besieged by women who want to date him. One woman who was a member of Mensa, the society for people with high IQs, wrote to Gates asking him about software for her Macintosh. Gates not only delivered the software, but met her in Atlanta for an evening on the town. Another woman at Microsoft sent Gates an E-mail invitation to lunch. A low-level employee in Microsoft's information center, she didn't expect a reply.

Gates did reply, however, informing her he was very busy at the time but would be in touch. Several months later, she heard back from Gates by E-Mail: "What about tomorrow?"

The employee took Gates to lunch at a nearby restaurant on the back of her motorcycle, and over the next few months the two went out dancing several times at some of Seattle's trendy nightclubs, usually hitting several clubs in an evening.

"I thought he was the most fascinating man I'd ever met," the employee remembered.

Dan Graves, former export manager for Microsoft who left the company in 1991, recalled an evening with Gates at a chalet in the French Alps at one of Microsoft's international sales meeting . Gates flew in by helicopter. "We partied all night, everybody," Graves said. "When I walked out at 5 o'clock in the morning I almost stepped on Gates on top of a woman out on the lawn."

"Bill likes to have women in his life," said a Microsoft executive who has known Gates for ten years.

For the last few years, Gates has had an on-again, off-again romance with a product manager in Microsoft's marketing division. Neither will comment about the relationship.

Because he comes from a close-knit family with traditional values, close friends expect Gates eventually to marry and have children. "His family is an important part of him," said Paul Allen. "I don't want to put words in his mouth, but I expect him to have a family one day."

Gates himself has said he expects to be married before 1995. And he expects to have children eventually. But Gates has also made some rather unfatherly remarks over the years. After a personal computer forum in Tucson, Arizona, two years ago, Gates was having a beer with half a dozen industry acquaintances when the conversation turned to the number of people in the computer industry who were starting families. Gates, who had been quiet for some time, suddenly blurted, "Kids are a problem." Later, he elaborated with the curt pronouncement, "Babies are a subset."

"As much as Bill wants children, he may never be able to take that step," said his friend Vern Raburn, who recalled a conversation he had with Gates in 1990, when Gates came down to Phoenix to help Raburn celebrate his 40th birthday.

"He was flabbergasted that his parents were in their 60s," said Raburn. "He can't figure this out, and that's because Bill consciously tries to protect and maintain this 9 year old in him. . . . That's the fun part in him. That's a part you can't find in most people. That's why he doesn't want to get married, because you can't be 9 years old and be married. When you are married, you become your parents."

If Gates carries with him occasionally the attitude and spirit of a child, it is a spirit seen most clearly through his love of games. Each July he throws a huge bash known as the Microgames at the family compound on Hood Canal, a kind of recreation of the games he played as a child at Cheerio. About a hundred industry friends and guests vie for prizes. Gates and his family are the judges. Each year, the games have a different theme. A couple years ago, the theme was African Safari. There were prizes for everything from African Jeopardy to shooting blow darts. Gates once had six tons of sand trucked in to see who could build the best sand castle. The Microgames end with contestants composing and performing a rap song. It is the ultimate kid's birthday party for adults—with Chairman Bill the ringmaster.

Gates gives another, much larger annual party for his employees. In August of 1991, nearly 10,000 employees turned out for Microsoft's annual picnic at a sprawling private park in the foothills of the Cascade Mountains east of the Redmond campus. More extravagant yet is the annual Christmas party. In 1990, it was held in the new, 170,000-square-foot Washington State Convention Center. The trade room floors were turned into familiar New York City landmarks, such as Greenwich Village, the Hard Rock Cafe, and Little Italy, each with its own distinctive menu and decor. Yellow taxi cabs were parked inside, on the floor. Actors were paid to come dressed as New York City street people.

While morale at Microsoft is high for the most part, employees do complain about the demanding pace, especially those who work on the development side. The work ethic has not changed much at Microsoft over the years. One well known businessman on the Eastside, where Microsoft is located, said he runs into a lot of "Microsoft widows."

"The joke among them is, 'We hope Bill will get married. Then we will finally get to see our husbands,'" he said. "The sense from these wives is that Bill is a nerdy guy who has no appreciation of people's real lives. Microsoft does crazy things, like telling an employee they have to be in Hawaii tomorrow. In this day and age of two parents raising kids, that's hard. People see Microsoft as being hostile to families. It's a great place for the young, unmarried devoted types. But as Microsoft employees age, there's more and more tension between the company's standard practices and people starting to raise families. But they are locked in because of the stock options. They can make so much money."

Ida Cole, Microsoft's first female executive, recalled that Gates scheduled the 1990 retreat for company executives on Mother's Day.

"You know, most of those guys are married, most of them are fathers. There were lots of complaints," said Cole. "But Bill still had it. What he did, though, was compromise. He let them all go at noon on Sunday so they could have the afternoon at home with their families. . . . Bill loves his mother. That's not the issue. But the company has always taken this incredible priority with him. I'm sure he never thought [holding the retreat on Mother's Day] would be a consideration for people."

Gates continues to keep his finger on the pulse of the company, and all critical decisions pass through him. In early 1992, Gates fired Michael Hallman, Microsoft's president of less than two years, in a major reorganization of the company. Hallman, a former executive with IBM and later with Boeing, wasn't getting the job done, Gates bluntly told reporters. Hallman had replaced Jon Shirley, who retired in 1990. As part of the shakeup, Gates announced that a triumvirate would now share the presidency. He said Microsoft had become so large that no one person could handle the duties of the number two job. Rather than going outside the company, Gates chose three close friends and Microsoft executives—Steve Ballmer, Mike Maples, and Frank Gaudette—as the ruling troika to replace Hallman.

Although analysts were surprised by the move, it showed that Gates is still very much in control. And that's what investors like to hear. Microsoft's stock surged nearly $5 a share the day the shakeup was announced.

It's impossible to imagine a Microsoft without Gates at the controls. Those who know him best say he is as driven as ever, and as long as he's in charge Microsoft will not be threatened as the world's leading software company.

"We have this vision of where we are trying to go, and we're a long ways away from it," Gates said during a recent interview in his modest office. A large picture window looks out over part of Microsoft's huge campus. But Bill Gates is not the kind of CEO who spends valuable time admiring the view.

"You gotta watch out for the anticlimax," he went on in response to a question about what it felt like to be the chairman of the world's largest software company. "I mean, we are not on top of the networking heap, or the spreadsheet heap, or the word processing heap. Computers are not very easy to use. We don't have information at our fingertips. There is one thing that is fun—I look out there and see fun people to work with, who are learning a lot. That's cool, and that feels good, but we're not on top. Yes, our revenues are bigger than anybody else's, but if we don't run fast and do good things. . . ."

His voice trailed off, leaving the sentence unfinished. Gates got up and walked over to his desk to return to work. "Believe me," he said as the interview ended, "staring out the window and saying 'Isn't this great,' is not the solution to pushing things forward. . . . You've got to keep driving hard."

Index

Ada, Augusta, 68
Adams, Brock, 9, 17, 46
ADDS (Applied Digital Data Systems), 112–13
Adobe Systems, 382
Advanced Computing Enviroment (ACE), 404
Adventure, 205
Aiken, Howard, 68–69
Akers, John, 403, 408–9
Aldrin, Buzz, 22
Alex. Brown & Sons, 322, 324
Alger, Horatio, 218
Allen, Paul
  at Honeywell, 59–60
  at MITS, 83
  at TRW, 48–51
  and Bill Gates, 33–34, 62, 66–67, 119, 129–30, 131
  character of, 159, 162
  class-scheduling program of, 44–47
  and Computer Center Corporation, 30, 32–33
  and DISK BASIC, 98–99
  finances of, 409–10
  on Gates family, 15
  and Harvard University, 82–83
  and IBM, 170, 186–87
  and Lakeside prep school, 21, 24–26, 336
  and Lakeside Programmers Group, 41
  lifestyle of, 412
  and Microsoft, 2, 88–91, 93–99, 107–10, 132–33, 135, 137–38, 235–38
  and Microsoft BASIC, 74–81, 91–94, 99–107
  as Microsoft stockholder, 330
  and MITS, 85–88
  and MS DOS, 186, 194–96, 202–4, 340–42
  ownership of stock by, 325
  and Pertec, 115
  post-Microsoft activities of, 326, 361–62
  responsibilities of, 226
  and Seattle Computer Products, 185
  social life of, 235
  and SoftCard, 157–59
  as space enthusiast, 198
  and Traf-O-Data, 44–45, 59
Allen, Woody, 272
All I Really Need to Know I Learned in Kindergarten (Robert Fulghum), 18–19
Alsop, Stewart, 248, 313, 345–46, 349, 352, 358, 364–65, 375–76, 400
Altair 8080
  designing BASIC for, 74–81
  introduction of, 67, 72–74, 85–88
  marketing of, 91–92
Apple
  collaboration of with IBM, 404–9
  computers, 111–12, 251
  and development of Excel, 281–87
  formation of Claris Corporation by, 400
  and IBM, 214
  Macintosh, 267–70, 398

and Microsoft, 120, 134, 157–59, 220–21, 314–18, 351–56, 402
  sale of public stock by, 320
  and Windows, 363
Armstrong, Neil, 22
ASCII, 123
Ashton-Tate, 320, 326, 388–90, 398, 408
Asimov, Isaac, 6
Astro, 112
Asymetrix, 326, 361
AT&T, 155, 398
Atari, 164
Atkinson, Bill, 317–18
Atlas, Charles, 374–75
Atwood, Colby, 39
Augustine, Brad, 37, 44
Autobiographical Notes (Albert Einstein), 22

Babbage, Charles, 67–68
Bajarin, Tim, 362, 394
Ballmer, Steve
  at Harvard, 62–64
  before joining Microsoft, 163–65
  and Bill Gates, 237, 273
  and Blair Newman, 156–57
  character of, 228, 249, 324
  and Charles Simonyi, 220
  and Digital Research, 212
  finances of, 325, 326, 356, 409–10
  and Go Corporation, 394
  and IBM, 4, 139–41, 169, 170, 186, 188–89, 190–92, 206, 364, 406, 408
  and Micrographx, 392
  and Microsoft, 207, 210, 292
  recruiting style of, 258–61
  responsibilities of, 1, 226–27, 246, 291, 401, 418
  and Seattle Computer Products, 203
  and 3Com Corporation, 383–84
  and Windows, 250, 308–13, 348–49
BASIC, 23, 28, 73–74
Bauer, Eddie, 288
Bennett, Jill, 272–74
Bily, Raymond, 225, 234–35, 246, 249, 277, 278
Black Comedy (Peter Shaffer), 47
Blue Magic (James Chposky and Ted Leonsis), 167, 186
Bogle & Gates, 341–43
Bonaparte, Napoleon, 35
Borland International, 277–78, 408
Bradley, Dave, 190, 192, 198
Braiterman, Andy, 55, 56, 60, 61, 63, 110
Bricklin, Dan, 145–46, 353, 410–11
Brock, Rod, 143, 183, 185, 194–97, 199, 202–4, 215, 340–44
Brodie, Richard, 242
Brubeck, Dave, 1
Bryan, William Jennings, 8
Buffett, Warren, 406
Bunnell, David, 72, 92, 95, 96, 101, 103–4, 116, 125–26, 131, 236, 242
Burroughs, Edgar Rice, 6
Bush, George, 411
Bushnell, Nolan, 57
Business Week, 201–2
Byron, Lord, 68

421

Cannavino, Jim, 364–65, 367, 370–71
Cannery Row (John Steinbeck), 401
Carlson, Paul, 39, 41
Carter, Jimmy, 9
Cary, Frank, 170
Catcher in the Rye (J. D. Salinger), 35
Caulfield, Holden, 35
C-Cubed
   See Computer Center Corporation
CDC
   See Control Data Corporation
Chan, Thomas, 396
Chaplin, Charlie, 215
Cheatham, Tom, 66, 82–83
Chposky, James
   Blue Magic, 167
Chu, Albert, 108, 109
Churchill, Winston, 115
Claris Corporation, 400
COBOL, 73–74
Cole, Ida, 290–94, 418
Colony, George, 409
Commodore, 111, 134
Commoner, Fred, 64
Compaq Computer Corporation, 233–34,
   347, 404
Computer Center Corporation, 26–33
Computer Notes, 92, 102, 126
Computer Power and Human Reason (Joseph
   Weizenbaum), 34–35
Computer Technology Development, 67–74
Control Data Corporation, 41–42, 112
Cook, Scott, 378–80
Corporate Culture, 125–29, 159–61, 221,
   263–66, 275–77, 290–94, 417–19
Corr, Kelly, 341
Courier, 112
Creative Strategies, 394
Cringely, Robert, 365
Crippen, Robert, 198
Crunch, Captain, 205–6
Curry, Eddie, 86, 94, 96, 98–99, 102, 106,
   115–17, 130, 202–3, 211–12, 213
Cybernet, 41–42

Davidoff, Monte, 77–78, 94, 97, 102, 126
Davis, Jim, 363
DEC
   See Digital Equipment Corporation
Delta Data, 112, 113
Denman, Donn, 317
Diamond, Joe, 275
Digital Communications Associates, 354
Digital Equipment Corporation, 404, 408
   and Bill Gates, 20
   computers of, 31–32, 70
   and Microsoft, 137
   and MS-DOS, 212–13
   software of, 29, 33
Digital Research, 354, 408
   foundation of, 175
   and IBM, 179–82
   and Microsoft, 174–79, 211–13
   operating system of, 183–84, 398
Discrete Mathematics, 66
DISK BASIC, 98–99, 109
Dorling Kindersley Ltd., 415

Dougal, William, 38
Drill, Scott, 61–62
Dvorak, John, 313
Dyson, Esther, 376

Eagleton, Thomas, 46
Eastman Kodak Company, 414
Edison, Thomas Alva, 270–71
Edmark, Carl, 12, 38, 39–41, 235
Eggebrecht, Lewis, 170
Einstein, Albert, 272
   Autobiographical Notes, 22
Eisner, Mark, 266
Ellis, Jenise, 366
E-Mail, 275–77
ENIAC (Electronic Numerical Integrator and
   Calculator), 69
Esber, Ed, 388–90
Estridge, Don, 168, 172–73, 189, 214, 216,
   345–46
Eubanks, Gordon, 177, 223, 376
Evans, Dan, 14, 89
Evans, Kent, 20, 21, 24, 26, 30, 33–34, 38,
   39, 42–43, 45, 46
Evans, Marvin, 24, 44
Excel, 278–87

Falcon Technology, 341–42
Federal Trade Commission, 3–4, 372–81,
   397–401
Fenstermaker, Mary, 366, 370
Feynman, Richard, 271
Fire in the Valley, 42, 78, 186
Florence, Philip, 282–83, 293
Flynn, Errol, 100
Forbidden Planet, 72
FORTRAN, 73–74, 109
Fortune, 137, 271, 322–23
Frankston, Bob, 146
Friedman, Neal, 261–64, 350
Friedrich, Otto, 230
FTC
   See Federal Trade Commission
Fulghum, Robert
   *All I Really Need to Know I Learned in
      Kindergarten*, 18–19
Fylstra, Dan, 145–46, 217

Gates, Kristi, 10, 17, 48
Gates, Libby, 12, 93–94
Gates, Mary Maxwell
   connections of, 136, 189
   early life of, 9–10
   as Microsoft stockholder, 325
   relationship with Bill Gates, 10–17, 34–
      35, 89, 133, 274–75, 359
Gates, Trey
   See Gates, William, III
Gates, William, III (Bill)
   appearance of, 3
   and Apple, 314–18, 352
   at Honeywell, 59–60
   at Lakeside prep school, 18–20, 35–41
   at TRW, 48–50
   and Borland International, 277–78
   business tactics of, 381–97

character of, 125–32, 159, 270–74, 274–77, 287–90, 336–40
childhood of, 6–8, 10–17
class-scheduling program of, 44–47
and Computer Center Corporation, 26–33
and creation of DISK BASIC, 98–99
and Cybernet, 41–42
driving of, 240–41
early computer experience of, 20–26
and Excel, 278–87
family background of, 8–10
on future of computer industry, 365–72
and Gary Kildall, 174–79
and Harvard University, 53–67, 81–83, 110–11
and IBM, 139–41, 168–74, 183–87, 188–90, 190–93, 194–202, 344–51, 363–65
and Information Sciences, Inc., 42–44
and James Towne, 245–48
and Jon Shirley, 247–50
and Kay Nishi, 330–33
lifestyle of, 223–24, 235, 410–19
and Macintosh, 268–70
management style of, 161–63
and Microsoft, 88–91, 93–99, 107–10, 117–25, 132–38, 146–49, 207–210, 215–16, 225–26, 238–45, 264–66, 290–94, 304–6, 319–30, 333–36, 352, 372–74, 377–81, 397–401, 401–10
and Microsoft 8086 BASIC, 142–45
and Microsoft BASIC, 74–81, 91–94, 99–107
on Microsoft's competitors, 211–13, 216–17
and MITS, 111–17
and MS-DOS, 1–3, 340–44
negotiating style of, 149–53
opinions of, 374–76
programming hiatus of, 34–35
and Scott MacGregor, 253–55
and Seattle Computer Products, 202–4
and SoftCard, 157–59
success of, 2
and Traf-O-Data, 44–45
and Windows, 250–53, 255–58, 294–304, 306–14, 356–59, 359–63
work habits of, 235–38
and XENIX, 155–57
Gates, William, Jr., 9–10, 11, 12, 14–17, 34–35, 133, 325
Gaudette, Frank, 321–22, 326, 327, 329, 410, 418
General Electric, 20, 109, 134, 157
Gibbons, Fred, 322
Gilbert, George, 365–70
Gloyd, Karen, 57–58
Go Corporation, 392–94
Goddard, Robert, 116
Gold, Tony, 177
Goldman Sachs, 321–22, 324, 328–29
Graham, Katherine, 406
Graves, Dan, 415
Grayson, George, 390–92
Grayson, Paul, 360, 390–92
Greeley, Horace, 8
Greenberg, Bob, 126, 137
Greenfield, Meg, 406

Gruen, Dick, 33

Hackers (Steven Levy), 87
Hallman, Michael, 411, 418
Hanson, Rowland, 242–44, 245, 291
Hardy, Andy, 270
Harvard University, 53–67, 81–83, 110–11
Hearst, William Randolph, 413
Heath-kit, 137
Henry, James, 375
Hertzfeld, Andy, 268, 283–85, 316–17, 353
Hewlett-Packard, 353–54
Hitachi, 224
Hollerith, Herman, 68
Homebrew Computer Club, 100–101, 103
Honeywell, 59–60
Hopper, Grace, 29
Hucks, Bill, 50–51
Hummer, John, 337
Hussein, Saddam, 392

Iacocca, Lee, 411
IBM
    and Apple, 267–68
    computers of, 165–68, 204–6, 214–16
    and development of initial computer technology, 68–69
    and Digital Research, 179–82
    and Microsoft, 4, 139–41, 164–65, 168–70, 170–74, 186–87, 188–90, 190–93, 194–202, 344–51, 356–59, 363–65, 371–72, 402–9
    and MS-DOS, 2–3
    and Windows, 253, 257, 308, 314
Ichbiah, Daniel
    The Making of Microsoft, 11
Image Bank, 414
IMSAI Manufacturing, 175
Inamori, Kazuo, 224
Information Sciences, Inc., 42–44
Info World, 200–201, 257, 365–66
Intel
    and Gary Kildall, 175
    microprocessors of, 71–72, 142, 345
    and Microsoft, 113, 134, 152
Intelligent Systems Corporation, 112
Interactive Home Systems, 414
International Business Machines
    See IBM
Intuit, 378–80
Isaacson, Portia, 123, 168, 323, 326
ISI
    See Information Sciences, Inc.
Isyx, 112

Jackson, Henry "Scoop," 14
Jenkins, Jim, 54
Jobs, Steve
    and Apple, 100, 316, 317, 320
    and Bill Gates, 251, 267–70, 283
    and Excel, 285–86
    on Go Corporation, 393
    and Macintosh, 219, 220
    and Windows, 315, 355
    and Xerox Corporation, 253
Johnston, Bruce, 370
Jones, Jim, 265

Jordan, Michael, 11
Julius Caesar (William Shakespeare), 67

Kahn, Philippe, 277–78, 380, 389
Kaplan, J. Jerrold, 393
Kapor, Mitch, 278–79, 282, 285, 310, 322,
    370, 375
Kassar, Ray, 164–65
Kay, Alan, 231
Kessler, Alan, 383–84, 387
Kidder, Tracy
    The Soul of a New Machine, 193
Kildall, Gary
    at Computer Center Corporation, 30–31
    background of, 174–75
    character of, 213
    and IBM, 179–82, 206, 240
    and Microsoft, 175–79
    operating system of, 154, 158, 173, 184,
       223
King, Frank, 360–61
Kleiber, Bob, 380
Kluge, John Werner, 410
Klunder, Doug, 278, 282
Knepper, Susan
    The Making of Microsoft, 11
Konzen, Neil, 306
Kyocera Corporation, 224

Lakeside Prep School, 18–26, 35–41, 44–47
Lakeside Programmers Group, 26
Lammers, Susan, 218
    Programmers at Work, 23
LAN Manager, 382–88
Laptop Computers, 224–25
Larson, Chris, and Lakeside Programmers,
    44, 93–94, 97, 107, 126, 131–32, 144,
    333, 410
Lawrence Livermore, 112
Leeds, Richard, 199–200, 211
Leithauser, Brad, 61–62
Leitner, Henry, 64, 66
Leonsis, Ted
    Blue Magic, 167
Letwin, Gordon, 137, 297, 299–300, 325,
    356, 369
Levy, Steven
    Hackers, 87
Lewis, Andrea, 126
Lexar, 112
LifeBoat Associates, 177
Lipkie, Dan, 255, 306
Little, Gary, 39
Lotus
    agreement with IBM, 408
    and Microsoft, 230–33, 278–87, 365, 400
    profits of, 326
    sale of public stock by, 320
    spreadsheet, 211, 229–30, 258, 295–96,
       398
    and Windows, 310, 360–61
Lowe, Bill, 167–68, 170, 171, 205, 346–48,
    358
Lubow, Miriam, 126–27, 136, 192–93, 209,
    231

McCarthy, John, 31

McCracken, Edward, 406
McDonald, David, 341
McDonald, Marc, 24, 107–9, 118, 121–22,
    134, 137–38, 154, 198, 326
McEwen, Dorothy, 175, 179
McGovern, George, 46
MacGregor, Scott, 253–55, 257–58, 261–62,
    277, 294–304, 306, 309–11, 348
Macintosh, 267–70
    See also Apple
McLain, Tom, 42
McSharry, Nancy, 360, 408
Maestretti, Gary, 38
Magid, Lawrence, 353
Magnovox, 112
Magnuson, Warren, 14
The Making of Microsoft (Daniel Ichbiah and
    Susan Knepper), 11, 42, 186
Manzi, Jim, 358, 367, 370
Maples, Mike, 379, 391–92, 400–401, 406–
    7, 410, 418
Mark 1, 68–69
Markhula, Mike, 269
Marquardt, David, 209, 321, 326
Marsh, Bob, 105
Martin, Eff, 322
Maxwell, Adelle Thompson, 8–9, 15
Maxwell, James Willard, 8–9
Mellencamp, John Cougar, 272
Metaphor Computer Systems, 364
Metcalfe, Bob, 156–57, 219–20, 382–85,
    387–88
Micrographx, 390–92
Micro Instrumentation and Telemetry
    Systems
    See MITS
MicroPro, 146, 211, 217, 239–40
Microsoft
    and 8086 BASIC, 142–44
    antitrust investigation of, 372–81
    and Apple, 220–21, 314–18, 351–56
    business tactics of, 381–97
    consumer products of, 146–49, 238–45
    corporate culture of, 11, 125–29, 159–61,
       221, 263–66, 275–77, 290–94, 417–19
    and Digital Research, 174–79, 211–13
    early years of, 107–10
    effect of IBM clones on, 233–35
    and Excel, 278–87
    and Federal Trade Commission, 3–4
    financial position of, 207–210
    foundation of, 88–91
    growth of, 333–36
    hiring practices of, 258–63
    and IBM, 4, 139–41, 164–65, 168–70,
       170–74, 186–87, 188–90, 190–93,
       194–202, 204–6, 344–51, 356–59,
       363–65, 371–72
    and Macintosh, 268–69
    major stockholders of, 325
    management structure of, 304–6
    marketing of, 117–25, 149–53
    and MITS, 93–99, 111–17
    move to Seattle of, 132–38
    and MS-DOS, 1–3, 215–16
    operating practices of, 397–401
    overseas expansion of, 225–26

and Pertec, 115–16
prospects for future of, 401–10
sale of public stock by, 319–30
and Seattle Computer Products, 183–85, 194–97, 202–4, 340–44
and SoftCard, 157–59
success of, 2
Windows, 250–53, 269, 294–304, 306–14, 359–63
and XENIX, 155–57
Microsoft BASIC
development of, 74–81
marketing of, 91–94
pirating of, 99–107
Microsoft Word, 238–45
Microtype, 156–57
MITS (Micro Instrumentation and Telemetry Systems)
and Altair 8080, 79–80
history of, 71–73
and Microsoft, 93–99, 111–17
and Microsoft BASIC, 91–94
and Paul Allen, 83, 85–88
Money, 137, 231
Motorola, 113
MS-DOS, 202–4, 340–44
Multiplan, 221–22, 229–33

National Cash Register (NCR), 109, 134
NEC, 135
Nelson, Greg, 61–62, 75
Neukom, William, 323, 373, 410
Newell, Gabe, 312
Newman, Blair, 156–57, 209
Newsweek, 137
New Yorker, 1, 338
The Night the Bed Fell (James Thurber), 47
Nikora, Leo, 255–56, 296–97, 301, 303–4, 306–9, 334
Nishi, Kay
background of, 122–23
and Bill Gates, 330–33
and IBM, and Digital Research, 140, 170, 186
and laptop computers, 224–25
and Microsoft, 135, 144, 145, 154
Norton, John, 50
Novell Corporation, 383, 385–86, 389–90, 402, 408

Odyssey (Jon Sculley), 355
Oki, Scott, 225–26, 227, 236, 326, 410
Opel, John, 189
O'Rear, Bob, 133–34, 136, 139–41, 142–44, 185–89, 194–96, 199, 206
Orr, Michael, 160
Orwell, George, 267
OS/2, 344–51, 356–59
Osborne, Adam, 75, 148, 168, 223–24

Palmer, Arnold, 11
Papadimitriou, Christos, 65–66
Pascal, Blaine, 148
Paterson, Tim, 143–44, 158, 182–85, 194–96, 199, 203, 204, 215, 341–42, 407
Patton, George S., 245
Pauley, Jane, 262

PDP-10, 20–21, 28–29, 82
PDP-8, 70
People, 137, 270
Pershing, John J., 8
Personal Computing, 96
Personal Software, 145–46
Pertec
and Microsoft, 115–16, 126
and MITS, 113–14
Peterson, Pete, 351, 397
Poling, Harold, 411
Popular Electronics, 26, 67, 72–73, 75, 85, 87
Presentation Manager, 344–51
Processor Technology, 104–5
Programmers at Work (Susan Lammers), 23, 121
Prusky, Jonathan, 231, 241, 242
Public Stock, 319–30

Quarterdeck, 256–57, 307–8
Quindlen, Ruthann, 303–4, 324, 328, 376

Raburn, Vern146–47, 158, 217, 228–29, 245, 303, 376, 411, 416
Radio Shack, 134, 224–25
See also Tandy
Raikes, Jeff, 208, 222, 227, 232, 234, 278, 287, 291, 378, 396, 410
Rand, 112
Randlett, Peter, 39
Rasch, Ingrid, 259, 265, 276, 335
Raskin, Jeff, 269–70
Reed, Sandra, 357
Richardson, Jean, 290–91
Roach, John, 120
Roberts, Ed
and Altair, 72–73, 86–87, 91–92
and Bill Gates, 101–2
and Microsoft BASIC, 74–75, 78, 79–80
and Microsoft
and MITS, 71–72, 104–6
Roizen, Heidi, 381, 412
Rona, Monique, 26
Roosevelt, Franklin, 35, 115
Rubinstein, Seymour, 175, 239–41
Russell, Steve, 29, 31–32, 33, 56
Ruttenbur, Jerry, 279–81
Rydacom, 112

Sams, Jack, 164–65, 168–74, 179–82, 187–90
Santa Cruz Corporation, 155
Sarubbi, Joe, 216
Sculley, John
and IBM, 214–15, 404–5, 407
on Lotus, 285
and Microsoft, 316–17, 352
Odyssey, 355
and Steve Jobs, 316
Seattle Computer Products
finances of, 215
and Microsoft, 183–85, 194–97, 202–4, 340–44
A Separate Peace, 35
Shaffer, Peter
Black Comedy, 47

Shaffer, Richard, 405
Shakespeare, William
  Julius Caesar, 67
Sherlund, Rick, 373, 403
Shirley, Jon, 225, 247–50, 279, 280, 286,
  294, 300, 305, 321, 322, 325, 326,
  329, 341, 351, 388, 410, 418
Shockley, William, 69–70
Simonyi, Charles
  background of, 217–20
  and Excel, 278
  hiring of, 99, 227, 384
  and Macintosh, 268
  as Microsoft stockholder, 325
  and Microsoft Word, 238, 242, 244
  and Multiplan, 221–22, 230
  and Paul Allen, 198
  responsibilities of, 297, 369
  and Scott MacGregor, 253–54
  and "Simonyi Revenue Bomb," 208, 292,
    333
Smith, Harry, 201
Smith, Steve, 147–49, 149–52, 178, 210,
  255
SoftCard, 157–59
Softklone Corporation, 354
Software Arts, 146
Software Review, 222
Solomon, Les, 72–73, 87
The Soul of a New Machine (Tracy Kidder),
  193
Spindler, Michael, 404
Stalin, Joseph, 115
"Star Trek," 72
Steinbeck, John
  Cannery Row, 401
Stempel, Robert, 411
Stephens, Anne, 47
Stocklin, Paul, 21
Stratton, Dorothy, 235
Stroum, Samuel, 89–90
Sun Microsystems, 328–29
Sybase, 388–90
Syndes, Bill, 167, 168, 170, 171–72, 180,
  193, 201

Tandy
  computers, 111
  and Microsoft, 119–20
  See also Radio Shack
Tarter, Jeffrey, 356
Tate, Ashton, 310
Technology Venture Investors, 109–10, 325
Tektronix, 148, 227, 262
Texas Instruments, 114, 134
3Com Corporation, 155–57, 382–85, 387–
  88
Thurber, James
  The Night the Bed Fell, 47
Time, 78, 137, 230, 272
T-Maker, 381

Toleman, Keith, 393
Torode, John, 175, 181–82
Towne, James, 227–28, 236, 245–48, 249,
  262
Traf-O-Data, 44–45, 58
TRW, 48–50
Turbo Pascal, 277–78
Turner, Dale, 6–8, 111
2001: a Space Odyssey, 413

Uttal, Bro, 323, 324

Van Wieringen, Dan, 12
VisiCalc, 145–46, 221–22, 231
VisiCorp, 217, 239, 251, 256–57, 307–8

Wallace, Bob, 133, 138, 208, 220, 221
Wall Street Journal, 135, 271, 288–90
Warnock, John, 382
Watanabe, Kazuya, 135
Watson, Thomas J., Sr., 165
Weiland, Richard, 24, 26, 30, 33, 42–43, 98,
  107, 125–26
Weissman, Jerry, 371–72
Weizenbaum, Joseph
  Computer Power and Human Reason, 34–
    35
Whitten, Greg, 277
Wilkinson, Dick, 27–28, 42
Winblad, Ann, 274, 337–40
Windows
  development of, 250–53, 255–58, 269,
    294–304, 306–14
  emphasis on, 356–59
  reintroduction of, 359–63
Winkless, Nelson, 96, 124
Wolf, Charles, 406
Wolf, Tom, 61–62
Wood, Marla, 136–37, 144, 161–63
Wood, Steve, 108–9, 114, 118, 119, 120,
  125–26, 128–29, 131, 132, 134, 135–
  36, 137, 144–45, 148, 159, 162–63,
  176, 177–78, 326
WordPerfect, 396–97, 398
WordStar, 146
Wozniak, Steve, 100
Wright, Fred, 23–24, 27

XENIX, 155–57
Xerox Corporation
  computers of, 218–19
  and Microsoft, 150–51
  and Windows, 269

Yeh, Frank, 394
Young, John, 198

Ziegler, Bart, 405–6
Zilog, 112
Znaimer, Sam, 54, 55, 56, 57, 61, 110
Z-Nix, 394–96